Teachings of His Holiness

Shantanand Saraswati

TEACHINGS OF
HIS HOLINESS SHANTANAND SARASWATI

A Selection

The Society for the Study of Human Being
New York

Copyright ©2010 by The Society for the Study of
Human Being, Inc.

This publication copies source material with kind permission
of the copyright holder The Society for the Study of Normal
Psychology, London, England.

All rights reserved. No part of this book may be reproduced,
stored in a retrieval system or transmitted in any form or by
any means, electronic, mechanical, photocopying, recording
or otherwise, without the prior permission in writing
of the copyright owners.

This publication is for study purposes only.

For information, address The Society for the Study of
Human Being, Inc., Box 20281, New York, NY 10025.

Reprinted by The Study Society in 2018 with grateful
thanks to Bill Hager.

www.studysociety.org

ISBN 978-0-9561442-9-4

A catalogue record for this book is available from the
British Library.

Dedication

*This book is dedicated with continuing gratitude and love to
His Holiness, Shantanand Saraswati*

P. D. Ouspensky

Dr. Francis C. Roles

and

Nicolai Rabeneck

Contents

Introduction	ix
Absolute	1
Activities	12
Ahankar	20
Antahkaran	29
Attachment	38
Attention	46
Bliss	54
Buddhi	63
Chitta	71
Consciousness	80
Consistency	88
Discipline	106
Drama	114
Emotion	122
Energy	132
Faith	142
Good Company	150
Grace	160
Gratitude	169
Gunas	173

Gunas II	182
Happiness	202
Heart	209
Householder	220
Knowledge	229
Knowledge in Action	250
Ladder	256
Laws	264
Love	280
Manas	288
Observer	297
Obstacles	307
Obstacles to Meditation	315
Param Atman	321
Prakriti	338
Rest	349
Samskara	357
Sanitan Dharma	368
Self	377
Sheaths	387
Stillness	395
Truth	403
Unity	411
Glossary	420

Introduction

The content of this book is the result of an instruction given by Dr. Roles to the New York group on May 28th, 1976.

"When I came over, I came over from my point of view, to see if the True Knowledge—the very precious Knowledge—was being scattered or lost in any way. Because this Knowledge the Shankaracharya has entrusted to us and we have to keep it absolutely pure. I think the chief danger which may come to this group is that people take little bits of the Knowledge that they like—and forget all others... so the Knowledge is being broken up into little pieces. But that's no good for Self-realization. For Self-realization —for the group as a whole, or for any individual—you must have the truth, the whole truth, and nothing but the truth."

The material in this volume has been organized into chapters by topic. Thus some of the passages and stories from audiences with His Holiness will be repeated as they refer to more than one subject.

This book has been created to be read according to topic of interest.

The Society would like to express our deepest appreciation and gratitude for all those who made these audiences with His Holiness possible, and who transmitted his teaching in a most transparent and unadulterated manner. Particular enduring gratitude and thanks is extended to Dr. Roles and His Holiness, Shantanand Saraswati, our teacher.

Absolute

H.H. Once a king announced that he would give his kingdom to any person who would come to him at 4 o'clock. But what the king did was this: In his capital city he put up splendid stores containing everything that can be had—jewelry, gold, silks, toys, books, works of art—anything anybody could want. And at every gate and in every quarter there were people giving away all those things free! Thousands thought it was a good idea and started out to get the promised kingdom, but they let themselves be persuaded to go to the shops and satisfy their desires and enjoy themselves. So they forgot what they had set out to do, and lost themselves among all those ornaments and jewels and clothes.

But one man didn't listen to any of these people; he just went straight through without letting anyone dissuade him, and met the king at the appointed time; and when he had been given the keys of the kingdom, he took over the government, while the king, following his abdication, went to the forest for peace and quiet. The first act of the new king was to put in prison all those people who were making free with somebody else's property under false pretenses.

The same can be related to our work. If somebody wants the kingdom, he has to go straight inward for it, and (if he asks at the right moment and in the right way) he will get it. That is the kingdom about which Sanatan Dharma tells.

* * *

Dr.R. Hundreds of people have been indebted for what H.H. gave them, including the story of the "King and Seven Gates" which made a great impact.

H.H. The story of the king and the gates was in fact a story of the Absolute and Atman. The Absolute being the king invited all individuals to come to get the kingdom. The one, who had clear vision and determination to stop for nothing in the way, got to him and inherited the kingdom. The story was only a fabrication with Atman as the subject, the gates which offer the miraculous hidden forces are different steps of the Ladder, and the king is the Absolute.

* * *

Dr.R. In the course of years and after hearing quite a number of variations of this story, we are now seeing its application on the subtle (psychological) level. The quotation "one man who met the king at the appointed time" is always the Atman whose voice and presence must be distinguished by any individual from the multitude of "I's" who forget what they set out for.

H.H. The subtle body recalls all this, but the unified state is the causal state of the Atman and one should reach that. Then, when one comes out of meditation, one would see that during all the activities of the world one does not identify oneself with thought or feeling, hand or foot, etc. One remains the Atman and gets all these servants to recognize his sovereignty and work for Him.

* * *

H.H. One can see Sanatan Dharma as laws given by the Absolute. When the creation starts it runs on certain laws and exists on laws given by the Absolute. Certain people see these laws as they are. This may be seen here or anywhere else according to other religions—Mohammed who realized Allah, or Christ who realized God, or anywhere. They are the people whose level is so high that they can see the natural laws direct from the Absolute working through creation. There would be no difference as to these laws seen by an Indian or anybody else. They are the basic principles. But there are numerous secondary laws which are enacted according to the land and time—man-made on the basis of those original laws. They differ because you see them through traditions and different types of culture all over the world. But, in a sense, the Sanatan Dharma is the Knowledge of the Absolute. It comes into existence with the creation and is seen by different people, and after the cessation of this creation it dissolves again into the Absolute.

* * *

Q. Are there any specially privileged places or people?

H.H. No. Anywhere, anytime, anybody who is looking for this knowledge must get it, because the Absolute is not for a single race, color, creed or nation; it is for everybody who desires this kind of knowledge.

Q. How can a man put himself more fully under the subtle influence of a teacher?

H.H. The physical world, the universe, the whole of creation is the will of the Absolute. Everything is contained within Him. He is not contained within creation, but creation is contained within Him. He rules over everything. We are not contained in our body, although the individual lives in the body. Body is under the individual, the "I," the Atman. When a disciple can expand his being to the level of the subtle world, then he can have relations with the realized man in the subtle state. Unless he expands like this, he cannot have that relationship.

In the physical world the water is said to be ten times more than the earth; heat is still ten times more than water; air is ten times more than heat; space, ether, is ten times more than the air; space itself is covered by an element called Ahamkar which is again ten times greater than ether. Further, Maya covers the whole of the universe and is again ten times greater than Ahamkar. Reflected Consciousness or mirror (Chitta) is ten times greater still. Atman covers all this and is the Ultimate. The same applies to individuals: We all have the same five elements out of which our body—the body of dust—is made. Another element is the mind—the intellect—and then our individual self, then the Atman. Unless one realizes that everything in the outside world and within oneself is just the same; unless one gets that expansion seeing that whatever happens in the universe happens in oneself, one cannot realize that nothing makes any difference. You do not become concerned or annoyed with what happens within yourself. Until this stage is reached, this subtle relation of disciple to realized man is not possible. Everything you perceive and see must become as your own Self. Then it is possible that this subtle relationship can be established.

* * *

H.H. The natural state of the Atman is peace and bliss. From this grew desire and so creation began with action and expansion. Action and desire form the two poles between which creation rises and falls, so that the eternal peace can be manifest in different ways. There is a new drama every time one is completed. Those actors who are detached play their parts in peace; those who are identified experience suffering. The spiritual exercises which have been given and which we now discuss are for those who take the drama for real. They offer a way of escape from the bondage of the parts through detachment. With the first act of creation the Absolute provided for those who would become identified and who went against the natural way. He provided this system so that they could recover detachment. This system is therefore not man-made.

The appeal of freedom is universal to those in bondage, but there are two kinds of freedom—transitory and absolute. The servant is naturally pleased at the end of his working day and is in a better state than when at work. Children are jubilant when they rush from school. A particular school had to close for a week because the teacher had malaria. After a week he was still not fit, so the children were given another three days off. On hearing this news one child remarked, "How wonderful it would be if the teacher died and we could have a holiday forever." This indicates the two types of freedom. Everyone wants some freedom from bondage. The freedom given by the Shastras (traditional codes of laws) is one which lets a man work yet be free. This is available to those who have fallen from the natural path of freedom.

* * *

Q. Is it useful to have this feeling of expansion during the day when we are not meditating?

H.H. Yes, it is useful provided it does not conflict with the work of the day. There are two types of work: work which involves attention. When you have to pay attention to your work then you shouldn't do this; when your attention is not required for some habitual work, then you can spare yourself for expansion, because inducement of such a feeling of expansion unites us again with the whole cosmos; and through this unity our heart is charged and we can always tap some extra energy through it.

A type begets the same type—a mango tree will always produce the same type of mango and can't give rise to any other fruit on its branches. Man begets man, animals beget their own kind within the species and the family. So every species begets its own type. If that is the law, the creation which is begotten by the Absolute, must also be of the same substance and type. Thus the creation itself is of the same substance of which the Absolute is made. It is only because of ignorance that we can't see this creation as Bliss, Consciousness and Truth, and thus we forget the eternal laws (dharma). Truth, Consciousness and Bliss must beget His creation of the same type of Truth, Consciousness and Bliss. Once this ignorance is removed, it is easy to see that the whole creation is imbued with Truth, Consciousness and Bliss.

* * *

Q. How to bring about expansion?

H.H. By feelings and thoughts. The microcosm is made of the same substance which made macrocosm. The body is made of elements of earth, water, air, fire, ether, mind, intellect and Atman. The Universe is also made of the same. In Consciousness the elements are united and the body expands to embrace the Universe. This is possible only when full knowledge of microcosm and macrocosm is given to the aspirant, and then there is the element of all-flowing love. Once we create the feeling of love we are connected to everything we love. Feeling and thought processes can bring about expansion; in doing so one doesn't have to run around the universe, but just gradually to expand oneself to embrace all that is in the universe. Running around is only done by the mind, which is not needed. Keep hold of the center which is the Self, and expand it to embrace all that is the Absolute.

H.H. One should feel the self being the Universal Self. The universe can be represented on a piece of paper indicating all boundaries of lands and mountains, oceans, nations, rivers, population and so on. This small piece of paper becomes a microform of the universe though that is so very extensive. This body is also a replica of the macrocosm. One who knows how to follow and understand the map can understand the Universe. One who knows the Self knows the Absolute. The Self is the Absolute in microcosm.

The macrocosm is the biggest form of Universe, composed of five elements, mind, intelligence, consciousness and Atman. Senses are the Indra, mind is Moon, Buddhi is Brahman, Atman is the Absolute. The microcosm is made of the same elements. The clay employed to make a big house or a small cup is the same in both the forms. The water of river Ganges in full glory is the same as in a small pot, though they differ in weight and volume. The difference in macrocosm and microcosm is in weight, size and form but not in consciousness. In consciousness they are one and the same. The separateness is the result of ignorance.

Dr.R. There seems a lot of difference in effect between a small quantity of fire and a large quantity. The nature may be the same but effect is different?

H.H. Every matter has two types of properties, general and special. The general property of both fires are the heat and they both burn whatever is put into them. The special property is subject to their shape, size, weight and so on. Once the small fire merges in the big fire, it assumes all the special properties of the large fire. It virtually becomes the large fire. So does Atman when relieved of its bondage become one with the Absolute.

* * *

Dr.R. This feeling of expansion here comes through an idea—the idea of drama, or the same substance of Creator in creation. Can the feeling of expansion be created by exercise or other means?

H.H. No, this is the activity which is beyond physical activity and is in the sphere of ideas. Through the idea, the mental activity can be brought about. One should understand this thing—that all our physical and bodily functions are governed by that substance which pervades the realm of the ideas. From the realm of thoughts all activities take origin. When we talk of expansion, we give an impulse to the heart, and expansion starts taking place, and in that light a unity is achieved with the substance which prevails everywhere. The creation begotten by Absolute is itself Truth, Consciousness and Bliss. In expansion a connection with this is established and you feel the whole cosmos as your own Self.

* * *

Dr.R. This is going to make for clarity in London where there is this discussion going on, and this has made everything clear.

H.H. All these discussions show that nobody has fully experienced either way. The effort should be made to go on *one* Way earnestly; and once you have reached the end of that Way, immediately you are on the second Way and you don't have to work too much and start from the beginning again, because by the time you have reached and fulfilled the Way of Knowledge, you would be quite a long way on the Way of Love as well. The desire and thirst for the other Way will be so intense, and your being will be so high that everything will happen very quickly. If you take the Way of Knowledge, don't think that you would be satisfied with these words—not at all. Once you have really understood things love will spring up. You cannot do without it.

So it applies the other way round too. The people who have really loved something, they will see that knowledge is not far away, and it will always be available to them whenever they need it. The best thing is to keep on one track sincerely.

The Absolute which exists, and wishes to expand itself, starts with the Prakriti. The Absolute is called Purush. This Absolute is consciousness and knowledge; and the emanation which follows from this desire, which is termed as Prakriti—Nature—is the aspect of love. So the moment creation starts, this knowledge and love just keep on expanding and they exist as long as creation is there. The same applies to us.

Take a man and a woman. The dharma of a woman is to serve the husband, and the dharma of the man is to keep the woman safe and care for her, protecting her in all aspects. This protecting is the quality of knowledge. This sense of protection is arrived at through the knowledge, whereas the service to the man comes from love. These are the two streams which are brought together in a marriage. If both work properly and both play their part in life harmoniously, they enjoy life; and then they depart to whatever place they belong after their life is complete. This is the ideal man-woman relationship.

In India for all those who are celibate and love no wife, as H.H. himself, Buddhi is supposed to be their wife. They look after Buddhi and protect it; and Buddhi serves them and keeps them going. They are the husband of the Buddhi.

* * *

Q. Why is the meditation here for us now, and how can it be traced back in history?

H.H. God is always present, and in the same way the meditation is always present and has been present since the beginning of history. The Absolute is Eternal, the Knowledge is Eternal. Our creation has existed so very long and everything happens in the same old way. Human beings have been eating since they were created; they eat even today, but their way of eating may differ in time and space. Meditation has existed all through the creation, but given differently in different ages. Just now, realized men have made it available to many more people because of the needs of the time; that is how you heard of it. As a child one eats food and as adult also one eats, but the taste differs; and again everybody has different taste for form, color, sound and so on, and everything is available all the time. One gets what one needs.

Meditation is available because people need it and in the form in which they can take it.

Q. Does this meditation give only contentment and bliss or can truth be obtained through it?

H.H. The Absolute is complete Peace, Bliss, Consciousness and Truth. When one establishes the connection with the Absolute through meditation one gets to the Source of all Bliss, Consciousness and Truth. Then one realizes one's wholeness. Meditation is to disperse that feeling of incompleteness, which we experience, and which is due to ignorance and impurities, and to lead us to completeness. Completeness includes everything. All these abstract expressions which men make are just facets of completeness.

* * *

Dr.R. One doesn't seem to want *longer* meditation. Half-an-hour is quite enough, but in addition one does want to go straight to this place of no activity for one minute or two minutes when one job is over before beginning another job, so one doesn't get further and further away from the Truth of the Atman.

H.H. The measure of time in relation to meditation has been told, and this should suffice for a happy management of our affairs inside and outside. If in certain situations one finds oneself tired, one can easily turn inside for a minute or two and find a balance. Whenever one starts a new work one can easily turn inside for a minute or two, and also when the job is completed. There is this tradition in India to start work with prayer and finish with thanks to the all-powerful Absolute. The same can be done by turning inside at start and finish of the work in hand.

* * *

Q. How would the mantra be appreciated, would it be sound or substance?

H.H. The whole Universe is divided in two—I and the rest! This is the world of division and we live in this world of duality. The method of meditation is to lead us from duality to unity. This method is not the end. It is like a rope through which we can go into the well or come out. Once the necessary job is accomplished it is left behind. The mantra is not unity, it only leads to unity where the world of division has no validity. This unity is the Absolute, known as Truth, Consciousness and Bliss. Once we reach there, a miraculous alchemy takes place, and the being is charged with energy just as one gets a motor battery charged for further use. If in meditation, after sounding the mantra, we start looking for anything, maybe a sound or substance, we in fact undo the meditation. When we talk of appreciation, we presuppose the duality. In deep meditation we don't even appreciate the peace, truth, bliss or consciousness; we in fact *become* peaceful, truthful, blissful and conscious of the Self. One must give up all such ideas of appreciating anything about mantra. This is exactly opposite to what meditation stands for. Start the mantra and do nothing and follow the mantra. The mantra will naturally settle down into that unity where there is no activity and no division.

* * *

H.H. In the practical field of world when a destination has got to be reached, when a particular work has got to be done, rules are necessary and the rules must be obeyed and carried through, because if they are not obeyed, the work will not be done. This is the outward working. The other work which is in the inner field, where the unity of the Atman and the Absolute is concerned or where the meditation is concerned, that field must be very liberal. It must be open to everybody to find his own time and place and his own desire to work on it, because any application of force in this matter would be detrimental to the object of meditation itself. So as far as the meditation is concerned, full freedom must be given because unity of peace and bliss will arise only in freedom and not in bondage.

* * *

H.H. The first Shankaracharya said that pursuit of happiness or eradication of suffering cannot be the ultimate end. The ultimate aim can only be that which is ultimate; aim can only be that which is ultimate, never changing and peaceful. Thus he showed the line of Consciousness, Bliss and Knowledge. Leave the changing, suffering, or pleasure, and work on Consciousness, Bliss and Knowledge, because that is the Absolute.

* * *

Dr.R. The Shankaracharya stressed that the chief point of all the teaching is that one should think all the time about what is real, what is great, what one really is—eternal and unchanging—and not analyze what is keeping one away from it; not analyze, not go into one's weaknesses and pettiness, but always keep your sights on the great and in any moment to shed anything else and go for that, to look up rather than down.

Activities

H.H. All activities of the human race are governed by sattva, rajas and tamas, these three gunas. Whatever the activity may be, these interplay in that, with our nature, our essence, whatever essence we have; with our natural self we are governed by the atmosphere around us. If we have sattva in us, and if we are in a place where sattva is dominant, where the atmosphere is governed by sattva, then there is free play between our sattva, and development prospers. But if we are placed in a situation where tamas is dominant and everything is governed by tamas, then our sattva is subjected to tamas and there is no rise of sattva in those surroundings. It's quite possible that the common man would just add more tamas and lose sattva there. When there is no dominance of sattva or no dominance of tamas we can see ourselves as we are; we act as we are made, according to our natural assets. So the outward effect, the atmosphere which contains sattva in itself, is partly responsible for the development of sattva in human beings.

All the gunas are everywhere in the world: sattva is everywhere, tamas is everywhere, rajas is everywhere. But when particular situations arouse dominance of one, then we feel it. Even in the West, where good people assemble, one can see the rising of sattva and experience it. For example, whenever we go to a temple or holy place in the jungle or along the bank of a river, whatever we are in our natural state with as much sattva as may be, the particles of sattva, which form the atmosphere around these places, around the realized man, along the banks of the sacred river, around the temple in the jungle, they unite with the sattva in us, and with this unity, happiness and bliss are created, and this subscribes to the development of sattva. This is the sympathetic situation; in unsympathetic situations we are starved of sattva.

Activities 13

Dr.R. So, little progress is possible in unsympathetic situations. One wants to try to collect in a situation as much of this sympathy as possible.

H.H. Of course it's one of the important matters for the human race. But common men, ordinary men cannot do this; they are just controlled by the atmosphere, by the external situations. But men who are on the Ladder, who have realized the possibilities to some extent, who can outweigh the situation with their own sattva, they can influence the situation and improve the atmosphere with the sattva that is in them. But common men just follow the stream.

Dr.R. But supposing we have a house with a fine Tradition behind it; a house where we perform Initiations and guide the meditation; where we listen to high ideas, listen to His Holiness's words; where perhaps we have special music; would all this not imbue that house with more sattva and make it especially sympathetic to development?

H.H. All this *does* help to create a better situation; they form the sattva particles in the atmosphere and these particles in turn have that effect on everybody who comes within that circle. If somebody is receptive and sympathetic in feeling, he will take them home and make them his own. He will gain something of development just by coming again and again to such a place, on being initiated there. He says it is decidedly so; that such things do affect the essence of people as well as the atmosphere of the place.

Dr.R. There's one thing our people will want to be clear about and that is the nature of rajas, how you recognize it. We understand tamas by which everything goes completely inert. But rajas can be good in a way because it produces movement in a given direction. Could His Holiness explain to us how we should understand rajas in ordinary life and recognize it?

H.H. Activity is everywhere, not only in rajas but in sattva as well. But the activity of rajas is the activity of confusion, indecision; you don't know what you are doing, but you are just doing things. The activity of sattva is clear, decided, leads to happiness and good. It is the Way, it is the Ladder; activity on the Ladder toward sattva is right activity. Activity with confusion is not right activity leading up the Ladder.

Dr.R. Isn't rajas shown by a kind of feverish exaggeration and excitement which enters in?

H.H. (laughing) The expression is marvelous. Most worldly activities are in that category—people don't know what they are doing. They think they are doing right and they just go on doing things. He quotes from the *Bhagavad Gita* where the Lord Shri Krishna says to Arjuna that the good deeds, the good ventures, the right activity, look quite opposite to the people with rajas and tamas dominant. They think the good activity is bad and bad activity is good. That's because of their ignorance and domination by rajas and tamas.

He says Buddhi is like your machine [tape recorder]: If you tune it toward sattva it will take sattva, give sattva. If you tune it the other way—toward rajas and tamas, you can't get sattva. In the life of a disciple the chief problem is to make his Buddhi clean and precise, so that he shall be able to distinguish what *is*, from what *is not*.

Dr.R. Is an example of Buddhi being tuned in the wrong direction, the strife between religious sects and the persecution of heretics, all that?

H.H. The wars in the name of religion and the sectarian differences are the product of confusion in Buddhi. When Buddhi is not related to Atman, these things manifest in the activities of these people. They are not, after all, supposed to be high on the Ladder at all; they are inferior people, and their inferior minds create all these difficulties for themselves and others.

Dr.R. Would you tell us the chief ways to make our own Buddhi pure?

H.H. Love the truth, and leave the untruth. That is the cure.

Dr.R. Is it true that unless he achieves pure Buddhi as described by Lord Sri Krishna later in the *Gita*, man cannot see the full truth and nothing but truth?

H.H. Pursuit of truth cures and clears the Buddhi; just in this single activity both are achieved, the truth comes and Buddhi is cleared and cleaned. But if the direction is the other way, with the pursuit of the untruth, then the Buddhi becomes muddled and the result is pain and suffering.

Dr.R. Does the muddle arise from bad emotion—jealousy, anxiety, worry, anger? How does it begin to get control?

H.H. They are not bad in themselves. If you use them for selfish and worldly ends they are bad; but if you use them for attainment of Self-realization or for spiritual development, they can help it on the way up the Ladder.

Dr.R. That seems to apply to pride. There is a good kind of pride that takes you toward realization and high standards of behavior; and then there are other bad kinds of pride. Is that true about all these feelings?

H.H. Explains the *six qualities* which result in happiness or in suffering. The first is the *desire*. If desire is for the happiness of Atman, then all resulting activities are good; if it is only for the body, then all activities resulting will be wrong and lead to suffering. The second one is *anger*. While you are educating someone in certain behavior or in certain principles, then it is helpful to you and to the student as well; but if anger is simply to punish someone or lower his position or revenge yourself on him, then it is not. The third is *regard* for something; if you have good regard for a saintly person, it would create love, but if you have regard for undesirable types, then it will lead to tension and trouble. The fourth is the *desire to accumulate things*; if this desire is toward your own property, it is right; you must defend your property otherwise you can't live in the world. But if you are doing anything to grab the property of others, it is surely wrong. The fifth is *pride*. If you have pride that Atman is great and you are looking forward to meeting with Atman and you feel great, this pride is not wrong; it helps you on your way. But if you think only that your body is great, then everything collapses and you go down. The sixth is *relating things, telling things to people, giving information*. If you give good information that helps others and they benefit by what you say, it is good. But if you give some information that leads to distrust, that brings trouble.

The difference between the good man, rather clever in the good sense, and a fool, is this: If you give something to the good man he makes good out of it. If you give something good to the fool, he will destroy it. Here is an example: Take a good piece of wood and give it to a carpenter or a wood-carver; he would make a useful piece of furniture and present it in a beautiful way. Whereas a good piece of wood if given to a fool would perhaps be burnt or thrown here and there. So your cleverness lies in using these six qualities to good purpose. Nothing is bad for a good man.

Dr.R. The difficulty is to see beforehand what's going to come out of some situation. Perhaps by understanding thoroughly the three gunas one may be able to see beforehand what will be the result of one's words or actions?

H.H. The acts of a good man are bound to be good whatever they may seem outwardly; but the acts of confused men whose minds are not clear, whatever their intentions may be, are bound to be wrong. He says the importance of training is so great that unless anything is learned by somebody, unless he is taught by some better person, he won't know what is right and what is wrong. Efficiency comes only after being trained; once you have learned from a better person, you will not do wrong. So in deciding these things one requires training. Any questions?

Dr.R. One part of our teaching is about the three components—three gunas—in each activity. And it says that it's not only the proportion of the three gunas that matters but their order of action which gives either this result or that result. In His Holiness's system is there anything equivalent to that?

H.H. There are two things, the outer and the inner; the inner is the feeling or motive, and then there is the outward action, and the interplay of these two can determine the result of the action. The interplay can be quite different; even if the motive is good and the action is wrong, it might lead to wrong results. Or if the action is good and the motive is wrong, it will lead to different wrong results. We can see the relation of these two and understand to some extent how our actions take shape. As an example, if you are angry with a student and you give him some punishment, you know that the result is going to be good. Another instance: You know that a certain person is your enemy, you talk sweetly with him just to get the information, and you know the result is going to be a fight between the two. So, in all these situations, these types of actions have different types of effect.

A man of understanding knows everything, and he is most attentive, so he can see everything, can decide the mode of action and know the result as well. The common man who does not know all these things, acts like a machine. To him the inner and the outer are just one thing. For a realized person, he knows the result he wants and adjusts the genesis of the action in his thought to the performance of the action, so as to give the desired results. And there lies his efficiency in diagnosing the action and getting the results.

Dr.R. As a man who loads his gun, adjusts his sights and gives the right pressure to the trigger hits the bull's-eye, then does it follow that the same action performed by a man with consciousness can produce quite different results from exactly the same word or action by someone with less consciousness?

H.H. Although outwardly the actions look the same, yet if you observe carefully and minutely, you will see the subtle difference between the two. The actions of a realized man are efficient and free, whereas the actions of an unrealized person are comparatively crude or excited.

Dr.R. Also one has noted the tone of voice! One can say something very direct to a man, and if the tone of voice is right he will not take offense. I've been noticing very much how different the tones of voice and the quality of the actions of the realized man are from other people's.

H.H. As an example the word RAM. A man who does not know what "Ram" is, or who has not accustomed himself to speak the word—this word is very light on his tongue. But in a realized person or one who has pronounced such a word again and again and has realized its essence, the word acquires weight in him, it gets a *different* tone, and the tone becomes rich (with overtones and undertones). That gives the difference between two kinds of people saying the same word.

* * *

H.H. When you go to sleep you go into tamas and come out fresh in the morning. This is because you haven't spent your energy during sleep and you have been simply recharged. Although fresh, you haven't had any extra energy. You remain where you are but you are fresh to face your activities of the day. For example, a king looks after his subjects through his servants to keep them in order and peace, and confers with his ministers to manage the state properly for prosperity. In his private chambers he amuses himself with wife, children, dance and music, etc. and retires for his own consultations with the Buddhi, and lastly goes to sleep. A common man has also to go through three types of activities: the coarse, the subtle and the causal. In the coarse set-up we go about after our daily bread; in the second we consult Buddhi for development, and in the causal we dive deep into the Self and get extra energy for further progress. Even [a] good ten minutes of proper meditation will give us enough energy to cope with 20 to 30 hours of work.

Q. Does the possibility contained in any moment depend upon remembering the Atman?

H.H. Remembering Atman is certainly essential, but if at the beginning, at the end, and somewhere in the middle one remembers the Atman, then the activity will be supported by sattva or the Truth. It is not necessary to keep on remembering the Atman all through the activity related to any moment. What one needs is to start the activity by remembering the Atman, and thus the initial sattva will be available with which one would be able to perform the activity to its full and true effect. One may again remember Atman in the middle of the activity and at the close. If the activity is performed without remembering the Atman, then it is quite possible that rajas or tamas would take over, and one would not face the occasion with enough sattva and miss realizing all the possibilities of that moment.

* * *

Our mind has the property of thinking of something or other all the time; it cannot remain idle. Thinking of the Param Atman leads to happiness, but thinking of worldly things leads only to unhappiness in the end.

Ahankar

H.H. Wisdom lives in the heart of all of us, but instead of flowing as a constant stream, it flows and ebbs intermittently. This is why we act sometimes rightly and sometimes wrongly; sometimes we are virtuous, sometimes sinful. Every year you assemble here for the mela and no doubt you benefit from the contact and preachings of the holy men you find here. But this effect does not last, and by the time of the next mela many of you lose what you gain and become as you were before. Then you attend another mela, gain something only to lose it again. So this alternate gain and loss goes on indefinitely, each neutralizing the other and your remaining days of life becoming fewer and fewer. Even during your ordinary life wisdom shines and fades intermittently. We are very holy at times, and very unholy at times; sometimes we dream of having become a king, sometimes of being reduced to beggary. The reason for all this is that we have pushed Param Atman into the background and kept Ahankara in the foreground.

The word "Ahankara" is frequently treated as a synonym for pride in ordinary language, and we consider it as an undesirable quality. If you have any Ahankara at all, better raise it sky-high, otherwise let it go down, down, down.

A mahatma used to say, "There is no mahatma like me." People said, "It is the limit of Ahankara to say so. How does it behoove you, who are a mahatma?" He replied, "Everyone else is either better than me, or worse. But none is exactly the same as I, so I am right."

This has a deeper meaning. Indeed every one of us is unique, having no equal anywhere in the world. Still, it has become fashionable nowadays to talk of equality. But how can you find equality *anywhere* in the vast field of creation? The world exhibits nothing but variety, and variety means nothing but the existence of differences. If these differences—the differences between one thing and another disappear—then the whole world would disappear, as it does in a state of dreamless sleep.

* * *

Dr.R. We really must devote our spare time and energy more to escaping from the mental prison which confines us within narrow limits of happiness and usefulness. I think many of us have felt frustrated because while there are times when we feel our full potentiality, the rest of the time we don't come up to it. Now we've been encouraged by the growing conviction that this prison is really an artifact that is self-produced. In the real inner world there are no walls or barred windows. Our minds have wonderful potentiality: When fresh and quiet they immediately give us all we want. There is no need to do things to our minds or to put artificial restraints on them. Our bodies also are not machines only and by no means to be despised. In fifty years of medical practice, I found increasingly how marvelous they are if treated fairly. The things they put up with! The way we misuse them! Yet, the compensatory mechanisms they produce when circumstances, or bad habits, make them go a little wrong are quite incredible. In fact, the human heritage of mind and body is capable of producing anything you want exactly when you want it, if you only learn how to use it rightly.

The prison is something different. *The prison is the fake feeling of I.* There is a real and necessary feeling of "I," which we always have and which we can't do without; for the loss of this genuine feeling results in nervous breakdowns. We don't, and can't afford, to do away with the feeling "I am, I exist," but it is of different kinds. It can be small and narrow if applied only to oneself as an individual. It can be rating one's attainments at higher value than they merit; or it can be under-rating oneself. I think that we have had such clear teaching about this (which has taken a very long time to understand) that if we don't act on it now, and really understand what is necessary to do, we'll miss out and just stay in prison, studying the prison walls and the bars and the habits of the wardens and the disadvantages of being where we are!

This "feeling of I," which in Sanskrit is Ahankar, can be confined to that of one tiny individual, an infinitesimal atom, in which case it is known as Vyashti—like one tree in a forest. Or it can be enlarged, enlarged until it can include the great forest itself and even the universe and see them differently. So the prison consists in escaping from the limitations, which the individual has built up for himself, and until he is out of prison for a moment or two he doesn't realize what a restrictive and unnecessarily small and tedious life he has been living.

* * *

Dr.R. When one feels the Ahankar, one always feels a limitation, a small circle, due to this feeling (which changes with the gunas); and *through allowing this* one comes to limit one's "I" to one's own body or good character or brilliance of performance or one's intellect or knowledge or whatever one seems to have. These are small circles created by the ego when governed by rajas or tamas, and are therefore extremely limiting. The other ego, which is sattvic, is related to the Samashti or Universal Being instead. . . . So when the feeling of "me and mine" arises in relation to anything in the outer or inner world, this Ahankar will be governed by aggression and excitement (rajas) or by inertia and depression (tamas). On the contrary, if the feeling is derived from "Thee and Thine," then all activities or all vantage grounds to which Ahankar rises in any individual will be of service to him and to the community.

* * *

Q. It seems that the absence of the dualism of regarding oneself as subject or object relates very much to being *still* in spite of the noisy market?

H.H. A man may steal and be punished as a thief, or perform good deeds and be commended; but the power of Consciousness, which remains only a *witness*, is neither thief nor good man.

Thus all claims of being the "doer of actions" or "enjoyer of objects" relate only to ego (Ahankar). When True Knowledge dawns, then the distinction between witness and doer actually takes place and one understands that one is really the witness and not the "doer" or "enjoyer." This witness is the stillness, while "doing and enjoying" make the din of the market the realm of movement and of commerce. As Lord Krishna says in the *Gita*: "Only the fool whose mind is deluded by egoism considers himself to be the doer."

As long as one is claiming to be doing and achieving, one becomes the movement instead of the stillness.

If one has a coat and hangs it in the wardrobe, the inanimate coat can't go to anyone's body; it must remain where it is. But when you put it on it will go with you everywhere. The same with *the ego when it claims to be the owner* of mind, body and consciousness, and then it goes with one everywhere like one's coat. No sooner is it disclaimed, however, than it goes back to the place where it belongs, namely the Prakriti, one's innermost nature. Then the Atman, having no tie or attachment, becomes the witness discarding all claims of doer and enjoyer like the coat.

Conclusion: So what makes the difficulty in an attempt to be conscious even for two minutes in meditation and in everything we do? It's not the body or the mind itself but the *feeling of ego* one carries with one all the time. Discard this and leave it in the wardrobe; then in due course we shall receive from above what we want.

* * *

R. L. Dixit While looking through some old papers a few days ago, I came across a Hindi verse by a contemporary saint on false Ahankara, which has been the subject of our correspondence. I do not know whether he is still alive. He is so pointed and direct about it that I enjoyed reading it. I am giving below some of the ideas from his poem, thinking that you would also enjoy them.

He begins by saying that this false Ahankara, the "I," is the very fundamental sin which mankind has committed. It is the *father* of all other sins, and all other sins are its offspring. It is wrong identification, wrong knowledge. It is the root cause of this world and all its sorrows. On account of this the whole joy of living is lost, truth becomes untruth, the all powerful becomes powerless, the whole universe is cut down to a few feet (the body), the king becomes beggar.

The unattached becomes attached. The stayable becomes unstayable. The bodiless gets a body. The clean becomes unclean. The clever becomes a fool. The solid becomes hollow. The hollow becomes solid.

By thinking "I" to be a body, the eternity gets a beginning and an end. A thing which can neither be born nor die seems to be born. It makes one thing look two, then two become many and start fighting among themselves.

A dog entering a room with mirrored walls, sees so many dogs. It barks and barks until it is completely exhausted.

Its remedy is to practice "giving up"—detachment. If this detachment is constantly practiced, these wrong ideas and the false Ahankara will gradually decrease. As it goes on decreasing, your sufferings will also decrease. Finally, the head of the false "I" will be cut off, and you will settle down to your true Self—the Atman.

* * *

H.H. After all, what is Ahankar? It is one's attachment to a thing, and attachment has to start with the Self. Either you can attach the Self to the body, or to the *mind*, or to the Self itself. You can do whatever you like, but in each case it is this relationship of the Self —either to a limited thing, or to a large thing, or to the unlimited.

If someone dives deep into water and finds something important at the bottom, then if he wants to exhibit or claim the thing, he will have to come out with it—bring it above the surface—only then can he claim that this is what he has found. As long as he is below the water there is no possibility of establishing the claim; it is there, but he cannot claim it.

In fact, the body, the mind, the universe—whatever we have here—is all one, but we can come out in some way and make a claim on some particular thing. If we know that the whole thing belongs to the same deeper level, or to the Absolute, then even if we are making a claim to our body, we are not really establishing a deep relationship, or bondage, between our Self and things because the claim has to be made. The world is there for action and enjoyment, but without any attachment. This one has to learn: Unless this comes it is very difficult to find any sort of relationship, and Ahankar always seems to trouble one. Otherwise, Ahankar will be there, but without any trouble to the individual.

* * *

H.H. The last barrier to the Atman is Ahankar, the feeling of "I"— I, the one who is meditating, or I am the one who is about to go over the barrier into the unity. As long as one sticks to this, the unity is impossible. We have to learn this and make sure in oneself that when one reaches a spot of this nature, one should drop even the idea of the feeling of "I." Everything is to be given up, even the sense of I. Once the sense or feeling of I is given up, only then is unity possible.

A certain man went to a holy man to be initiated in meditation. He was asked as to what things he saw on the way. He said, "Among all those things I saw I remember a donkey very well." He was then asked to remove him from his memory. The poor man tried hard, but failed and expressed his inability to do so. The holy man said that the art is to drop the memory. This memory or the feeling of "I" is the greatest and the last barrier to meditation. The man who meditates or the man who observes must be dropped so that he is able to merge into one.

When one knows that one is still, one is not still, and when one knows one is at peace, one is still away from it, because the great barrier is still there to recognize "I" and its relation with peace and stillness. In complete peace or stillness there is no "I."

* * *

Q. Can one watch as one grows spiritually? Can you see your growth?

Dr.R. No. Really, the more you think you're doing absolutely nothing, that you're a useless bit of clay, probably the quicker you're growing—not depressed about it, but just not doing anything; and you realize that you aren't [doing anything] and that it's the Param Atman doing everything. We're just receivers and transmitters, taking no credit at all to ourselves.

* * *

Q. It appears that one's individuality is only part of the "delegated adaptability" of Param Atman, so are we to be good receiving stations and transmitters according to our level of understanding?

H.H. In answer to the question, one's concept of "I" is of two types: the real "I" is the Atman, but the Atman by itself does not receive anything. It is there, and it is everywhere, just like the Absolute, so it does form something more, and that "something more" is a part of this universe, and we call that Ahankar, the ego. This ego is part of the Antahkarana, which includes several things—the Chitta, the Manas, the Buddhi, the body and everything. Atman uses this machinery to experience the Knowledge, the Being, and the Bliss. So this "I" is now made into two—the inner one which is the Atman, and the outer one which is the Ahankar.

To appreciate oneself as just "the receiving station and transmitter" is the best understanding one could have, because it is only the Absolute which has manifested itself as the creation, which is passing through and being manifested or expressed by Himself, which is the Atman.

When people understand and think that this Ahankar *alone* is themselves—that Ahankar alone is the "I" and there is nothing beyond it—then they start creating boundaries and these boundaries are made of the understanding, or the Knowledge, or the ideas which they have. It is not just the single body which creates the boundary, but everything to which the individual relates himself—the concept of family, etc.

This act immediately puts obstacles to the natural and full flow of energy from the Atman, and man lives by the little flow, which he naturally cannot stop. Some boundaries are small, some are large but, in fact, all this which is within the boundary, or which creates a boundary, is not the real Self. The real Self is the Atman; it has nothing to do with this universe, and yet the whole design of this universe is there for its enjoyment. So, when you separate these two, it is only then you come into difficulties.

But, if you keep both together, and feel that you are the receiving station, and transmitting it as a necessary part of the universe, then you would be able to enjoy the universe —you would be able to do what you are designed to do. If one wanted to find out the definition of Real "I," then *whatever you cannot give up is Real "I," and whatever can be given up is the other "I," which is the universe.*

* * *

H.H. If you begin to be what you are, you will realize everything, but to begin to be what you are, you must come out of what you are not. You are not those thoughts, which are turning, turning in your mind; you are not those changing feelings; you are not the different decisions you make and the different wills you have; you are not that separate ego. Well then, what are you? You will find when you have come out of what you are not, that the ripple on the water is whispering to you "I am That," the birds in the trees are singing to you "I am That," the moon and the stars are shining beacons to you "I am That." You are in everything in the world and everything in the world is reflected in you, and at the same time you are That—everything.

H.H. In refusing to give up Maya, we invite all sorts of troubles. As the Jiva, or individual, is a part of the Absolute, it is fundamentally eternal. It is fundamentally all knowledge. It is fundamentally all joy. But look at eternity fearing death; look at knowledge missing the most important knowledge; look at joy missing all joy and looking for it elsewhere.

It is the business of Maya to make things look just the opposite of what they are and to deceive the individual so that he can be kept in prison as long as possible. [This is the game we have to play, a sort of Blind Man's Buff.] But surrendering one's individual to the Universal Self or Param Atman removes the illusion of Maya.

Then there is a dawn of True Knowledge and we realize that no real death lies in wait for us; that no knowledge is hidden from us; and that the fullest joy is always with us, whatever the conditions. Someone asked: What happens when True Knowledge dawns? I replied, that there would be nothing to happen then. All the happenings happened before that birth and none thereafter.

Antahkaran

Q. Two things people find very valuable which H.H. has said, are that it is the Chitta which climbs the ladder, and that it is necessary to keep the door of Chitta open to the Absolute. In the early Records we find H.H. did not give us the word "Antahkarana" but seemed to use the word "Chitta" for the causal body. Later he described Chitta as one of the four functions of the Antahkarana. Could he say whether in the above two examples (the ladder and the door of Chitta) this is the Antahkarana as a whole, or as one function of it?

H.H. The Antahkarana is one, and the four factors, which have been described to you, are the four functions which the Antahkarana performs. They are not four individuals doing the work of Buddhi, Manas, Chitta and Ahankar—not four separate elements. It is ONE inside the individual and sometimes it thinks, or remembers, and that we call Chitta. Sometimes it gives a decision, and that function we call Buddhi. Sometimes you have some perception or a unified perception of anything, or a desire, or you have some alternative idea, which comes out of mind, then you call it Manas; and when you make any claim in relation to your property, or your body, or your own idea, then that function is called Ahankar. Consciousness of Atman reflects in Antahkarana —that is the philosophical background—and these four functions take place, if the Antahkarana is sattvic, then the Consciousness will reflect more; there will not be impediments, and then your Chitta, or Buddhi or Manas or Ahankar will work much better.

For example, you cannot use two gears at the same time, although there are four of them! The same applies here. While using your Chitta, there is no possibility of your Buddhi being active at all. When Buddhi is active, there is no question of the others working—only one works at a time. Antahkarana is one;

but these are four functions which have been recognized so that we can understand ourselves better.

Q. So it is the Antahkarana as a whole, which climbs the ladder?

Sri J. Yes.

* * *

Q. I was very interested to hear yesterday about the causal body and Bhawana. Could H.H. say more to explain this, which was new to me?

H.H. The causal body is known as the inner instrument (Antahkaran), which you have heard about. In Antahkaran, all these four components are joined together—synchromeshed; it is a single unit and there is no division in Antahkaran as such. These four parts are for the subtle body where they have to take certain types of action.

This unit of the Antahkaran is the source of Bhawana, out of which come the attitudes underlying different types of desire. These desires first arise in Manas; it is the Manas, which arouses the desire. But any desire is always supported by a certain emotional attitude—attitudes of liking or disliking, good or bad. So whenever a given person has a given desire, he takes his attitude to it from the Antahkaran, which gives it a particular color, the color that is in the Antahkaran. Manas has no particular color of its own, but it picks it up from the causal body where everything is united. If it is rajas or tamas or sattva, whatever the color may be, that will be followed by Manas. Between an activity and its consideration by Buddhi leading to a judgment as to right or wrong, there is a state which is known as Bhawana, this emanation from the causal body.

Manas resorts to activity, whereas Buddhi considers whether right or wrong; and besides there is a judge as in court cases brought by a barrister or solicitor. All that which is stored is certainly stored in Chitta. There you have these four.

Dr.R. A practical point is that when we are trying to be One, it is marvelous to think of a single inner organ like the Antahkaran, whereby all the other functions get programmed, rather than analyzing one's psychology into different parts. This would be a very refreshing idea in the West—the idea of an inner organ with four gears or aspects depending on the concentration of three forces, and, on a higher level synchromeshed or "integrated." Can we take this as correct?

H.H. agrees that this simile is quite suitable.

* * *

Q. We have previously understood these four functions of the mind as organs in a hierarchy, in the order Ahankar, Chitta, Buddhi and Manas. But now it seems that His Holiness says they are not so much organs and not in a hierarchy, but functions, each having a different place, so we have to change our thinking.

H.H. Atman is only a viewer, and what it views is knowledge. It is with this power that the Manas does its work of Sankalpa and Vikalpa, Chitta does its chintan and Buddhi gives its decisions. What the hand of our body, the eyes of our body, the nose and ears of our body are doing are actions; when our eyes see we think that "I am seeing" but the body is seeing; similarly with Chit power —Absolute power. When it descends into the body it divides itself into four channels and without that power nothing can be done. It appears as Manas, Chitta, Buddhi and Ahankara.

All these functions of thinking, taking decisions, etc., take place in the Antahkarana only, not in the Atman. Atman provides the power with which these four work; the power coming from the Atman into the Antahkarana divides itself into four streams which ultimately do manan, chintan, taking decisions, and identifying ourselves with the physical body. Until we get the power of Chit neither Buddhi can give decisions nor Manas do its work, nor Chitta etc. Thus we are getting three entities—one is absolutely pure Atman, second is taking the form of Chit—we may call it universal Buddhi or Samashti, and third is that portion which is providing light [power] to the Antahkarana.

One part is pure and unmixed—unpolluted—call it Chit. When

it comes into the Antahkarana it divides itself into four parts. The portion of that light which decides, we call by the name of knowledge. That portion of the light, which thinks of doing this and that, we call Manas; that portion of the light, which does chintan, [thinking] is called Chitta and that portion which makes us say "I am this, I am that; I am black, I am white," is called Ahankar.

Here is an example of a car: When the car is in perfect working order, its various parts are all working well. The car won't run until the driver actually activates the battery, and then it starts. Similarly, the current exists there, but until the switch is pressed it won't work. In this case the power is Chit power coming from the Absolute. Now when that power activates this machine of the body in that case it is Vyashti. The whole universe—that is Samashti. Atman is the driver. What is Atman? I will explain. Atman is that thing which we cannot separate from ourselves; it is defined in various ways; and in this context I give another way of finding out what Atman is. Atman is that thing which we cannot separate from ourselves. Other things we can separate, but Atman we cannot.

Q. Could His Holiness explain the relation between Atman, Param Atman and Chit?

H.H. Param Atman is Samashti (universal) and Atman, Vyashti (individual). Vyashti descending into the Antahkarana manifests itself according to the sanskaras stored. When raindrops contact the ground, they become contaminated by the dust. While the water is uncontaminated we can drink it and it will keep us in good health, but when we use it without purifying it, it becomes the root of illness. Similarly, when the Chit power descends into our Antahkarana and combines with good sanskara it uplifts and benefits us. But by intermixing with dirty sanskara it causes our downfall.

Q. Is Chitta what we ordinarily think of as the heart?

H.H. Yes, we think of it as power. *Karan* means "instrument," *antah* means "inner"; *Antahkaran* means "inner instrument."

Q. We think that it is important that that which is received from Chit should be passed on, should not only be received but should be transmitted to anywhere and everywhere. It is important not to block it but to allow it to flow.

H.H. We cannot prevent its flow. It is automatic. We should rather think whether it is spreading rightly or wrongly when it gets mixed up with the sanskaras stored in the Antahkarana. It flows out taking the color of the sanskara. If these three things are clear to you, then all your doubts will be removed.

* * *

Q. We were told that the Atman, which is unlimited, descends into the Antahkarana, which is limited. How can that which is unlimited enter into that which is limited?

H.H. When the light of the sun descends, the sun does not descend, yet we cannot separate the two, the sun and the light of the sun! In the same way the Atman descends into the Antahkaran,

Q. It seems with the sattvic state the four components all work for the Self in their own way. As we are we are working most of the time in ignorance. Is there a precise procedure in the Holy Tradition from which to start, and what plan of action is necessary to clean the Antahkaran so that it seeks Truth?

H.H. We have to cleanse the Antahkarana. There is dirt in the Antahkarana due to the gunas—sattva, rajas and tamas. We remove this dirt by providing light. What is this light? Is it the light of the sun, the moon, electric light, or something like that? No, none of those. The light is the light of Atman.

We can see the image of the sun in the water, but when there are ripples in the water, then, in this case the images appear to be quivering. The quivering is in the water, not in the sun! If the water is dirty to a certain extent the image is not clear, but the dirt exists in the water not in the sun.

Q. What are the methods of purifying and clearing the Antahkaran?

H.H. I will explain in detail, though some are already well known, good action, holy action, holy thought and service; considering everybody to be part of the same Param Atman; treating other people as our own selves; remembering that the same pure Param Atman permeates all the living beings which we come across, as a universal brotherhood. These are the things, which purify the Antahkarana and provide light with which the Antahkarana is purified.

Sun, moon, fire, electricity, stand for four of the sources of light. A fifth source is knowledge, which activates everything. It is not a physical light—vibrations in ether—like the light emitted by the sun, moon, etc., but it is a thing which enables us to know. We can call the light of knowledge a light but it is unlike the light we get from the sun. It is simply that which enables us to know.

Knowledge has two faces—one is yes, the other is no. Acceptance/rejection. Whether it is so or whether it is not so. If we sit in a dark—completely dark—room where we can see nothing, we shall still see one thing and that is our own Selves, the Atman. So sitting in a dark room that which knows something like "I am here," that is knowledge. That knowledge is to be joined up with this physical light by which we are seeing all things. The joining of these two results in our worldly progress. Unless that sort of knowledge we possess sitting in a dark room, "that we also exist," joins up with external knowledge then action cannot take place.

All other lights become powerless in the absence of the light of knowledge.

The eye by itself cannot see anything. There must be light, [and] the brain—just the intention of seeing the thing we are looking at. We may be looking at a thing and not seeing it. We can also see a thing but not understand it; that is also no good. Seeing and understanding both become possible with the power of Chit.

Knowledge is the giver of light to light. It provides light to worldly light but even if the worldly light does not exist, the light of knowledge does.

Q. The words of a realized man seem to bring this light of knowledge to the darkened Antahkarana.

H.H. The realized man is not putting anything into the mind of the unrealized man. There is no transfer of anything; the words of a realized man only awaken a thing which already existed in the mind of the other person. Here is an example: In the darkness a piece of rope looks like a serpent. Is the serpent in the Antahkaran or in the rope? It was in the Antahkaran, so the removal of wrong ideas, that is the imparting of knowledge, that is all the words of a realized man do.

* * *

Q. From a flash of "insight" this observer sees the dance of the gunas with detachment and the drama of creation without identifying with it. Is this the starting point of art? My experiences of bliss are pointers to a joy beyond description—is this joy beyond the limits of sense-dependent art, or is the source of real art even beyond this joy?

H.H. The Absolute knows and experiences all the names and all the forms; and all the possibilities are also known to the Absolute. The creation with all its diversities flows out from Him because it is already in existence. The same applies to the individual. In each individual and within each Antahkaran the knowledge of all names and forms with their possibilities are present in a seed form. Unlike the Absolute, the individual is not aware of these so he doesn't know that he knows. When he grows in his being or is able to clear off his cloud of ignorance, then he sees what he has. The need also accounts for such situations as when an individual becomes a medium of inspiration and expression—both. It is only a sort of loss of memory that makes one think that a new knowledge has come about, but in fact it is always there with him and in the cosmic Chitta [Consciousness] together. Once he tunes in, then he takes out of his own wealth of names and forms.

* * *

Dr.R. In 1965 Your Holiness said: "In each individual and within each Antahkaran the knowledge of all 'names and forms' with their possibilities is present in seed form. The individual doesn't know that he knows."

My question: When an individual becomes a medium for "inspiration" and expression of creativity, what is happening in his Antahkaran? Are these seeds maturing into plants via the subtle level? Has one somehow to tune in or draw near to Atman with abundance of sattva, in order to get those results?

H.H. It is true to say that of all the knowledge, and all the love, and all expressions that one can think and do to express the happening within the Antahkarana (the latter means artistic activity); all these are present in seed form. But as far as any given individual is concerned, those expressions are governed by time, space and matter. The possibility of complete realization of this abundance of all knowledge, or all love, or all activities, is not possible. What does really happen is that a particular person with a supply of just enough knowledge and love, feels satisfied and complete within himself. Through this he might be in tune with the Absolute. But it would not be right to say that any single person can make use of all the knowledge, or all the love, which the Brahman Himself controls.

He then gave an example of the river Ganges: The river is flowing with curative and auspicious waters. All the time people are going there and taking part of the Ganges to their home, or dipping in the Ganges; and even if millions and millions of people have baths there and take away some water with them [a pint or two], the Ganges will remain the Ganges. It will not dry up.

And so all this eternal Knowledge, and love, and creativity is available to individuals according to the laws of time and space and matter.

Even Brahma, Vishnu, Shankara and all these great figures who have happened to be the proceeding deities of creation, they also have their Antahkarana. But their Antahkarana does not contain the whole of everything that the Brahman holds.

H.H. The system is always the same—that one must dive deep into Self—into this great ocean of Bliss. When one reaches that level and comes out having soaked or bathed in it, then one finds that this Antahkarana, which is the medium of all expression for the individual, by itself *regenerates everything as new*, new for meeting each situation as it arises. So this gives you a creative faculty to meet the situations and provide new solutions every time there is a problem.

There may be a hundred questions, but all these questions will be easily met by this *Antahkarana* ["inner organ" or soul] when it has come out of this ocean. All knowledge hasn't been exhausted by the Vedas and the Upanishads, for very much more is still held in by the Self and keeps on emerging as new creations. The trouble is not in the expression as to how one deals with the problem; the trouble is that all that anyone can experience is in the realm of diving deep, and going inside.

If one has learnt to dive deep without any load and to go to the base—the bottom of this ocean—then there is nothing which a man really needs; everything will be provided, everything will be ready made for him, And he will make it ready for everyone.

H.H. The process of giving takes place only when one has acquired. So, the system of meditation has been prescribed to all of us for this deep dive into the Self. The Self is like the great ocean full of Bliss, and it has a very sweet taste—one who dives deep comes out with radiance and a sweet smile on his face, and with enough light to guide himself and others around him

So, it is only a question of acquiring the ability to dive deep into this great ocean; and if one comes out with even one drop of this Bliss of the Self, then one would be good enough to guide the destiny of oneself and one's fellow men.

Attachment

Q. Can the Shankaracharya give guidance about the present state of the world?

H.H. From the beginning of creation all are after happiness, which is in man's nature. But when mankind becomes "attached" to happiness, then a wrong type of happiness is created and a distinction has to be drawn between this happiness and pure, detached happiness. Unnatural pursuit of happiness multiplies our miseries, our distractions, our sorrow and everything we don't want. Throughout creation there have been civilized and good people who have taken up the task of mending these ways and of correcting people so that there will be a return to natural happiness. God the Absolute in His Majesty, although creating everything, never attaches Himself to anything. He is aloof. It is His desire that everyone should do his duty also but should remain aloof. When bad things creep into the world and misery reigns over creation, certain impulses are given. Then either a single man or a school crops up somewhere and ultimately succeeds in mending things and bringing the world back to a stable state. This is only possible through mankind. It cannot be done by God directly.

* * *

H.H. The path to Param Atman via knowledge is beset with many obstacles, which are such that only a few can get through. Even when a major progress has been made, the greatest risk comes toward the end where Maya tries to beguile us. If we begin to falter at that stage, then a downfall takes place, which undoes everything. Pleasant impediments, being of a tempting nature, are actually far more dangerous than the unpleasant ones, because the former possess more appeal than the latter. It is attachment to worldly things, which is the root of all troubles.

Either you accept the Param Atman first and then proceed to know Him, or you try to know something first and then accept. The important thing is confidence and not effort. If you go on living in the present, then the past and the future would take care of themselves.

For raising the thought level, thinking of Param Atman is the right thing. If you think that everything is Param Atman, then love deepens. But if love decreases, we fall. Actually, it is love which is our greatest asset.

* * *

H.H. The variety and diversity in creation is necessary because it is the will of the Absolute. All this is simply for the entertainment of the Self, but during the entertainment, when someone becomes attached to one or the other aspect, then, and then only is hate introduced by the individual. Hate is not part of the original design. This hate creates strife and conflict, which the Absolute did not create. The conflict is the outcome of these attachments (Raga and Vasana—attachment and desire). Therefore, one should try to refrain from them. If one is unable to eradicate attachments from the minds of others, at least one should eradicate them from one's own Antahkaran. If someone has a strong desire to get rid of attachments and hate, then some help can be given with love and affection. If anyone is set on strife and separation at all costs due to hate, the scriptures and wisdom cannot help. Shri Krishna says in the *Bhagavadgita*:

> This knowledge may not be explained to those who lack self-discipline and devotion and have no desire to serve, nor to those who speak ill of me. (18.67)
> He who teaches this supreme secret to my devotees, showing the highest devotion to me, shall doubtless come to me. (18.68)

The simple message is that, unless one is ready to inquire, listen and act with love, one cannot be helped or have one's unhelpful samskars transformed. God has not created a quarrelsome universe, but a loving one. In this loving universe some take it very rigidly and get attached to only one aspect of the drama as the only reality. They cannot tolerate another view; they create strife and conflict and do not hesitate to destroy others. The fact is that the Absolute did not initiate attachment and hate—this is a superimposition created through the Antahkaran by strong preference for one or the other aspect. One should not cultivate this attitude and should always be ready to help those who seek help.

Help can be offered anywhere, even under a tree—there is no need for a palace! My teacher was a loving and disciplined sage. He used to teach under a tree laden with fruit. He saw that the falling fruit disturbed the meditation of his disciples. The teacher simply looked up at the tree, and it immediately stopped producing fruit although it continued to flower.

Transformation depends upon an overriding desire to transform. Although the Self is perfect, superimpositions seem to abound. One must have some deep desire to look for possibilities of purifying unhelpful samskars. Creation is tri-formal; some people are sattvic, others are rajasic or tamasic. Tamasics are very rigid. Whatever view they hold they presume it to be the only one. The Absolute provides for everyone, but only seekers make the effort to enlighten themselves through inquiry, reason, devotion and meditation. Valmiki did listen to the sages, followed their advice and developed his latent creative power of poetry. When more individuals change, society becomes more unified. Beauty lies in variety and wisdom dwells in unity. There is no real conflict, hatred or strife.

Creation is governed by the laws of nature, which are the expression of love. Nature assists those who seek transformation and punishes those who are attached to rigidity and do not want to change. This is the lesson.

* * *

Q. How does one get rid of attachment?

H.H. Attachment is a disease either material or spiritual. The remedy is good company: The company of learned men on the way, or a school where the real knowledge is discussed and given. Go to them and listen peacefully. These may influence and eliminate the disease.

* * *

Q. How could one make oneself free from attachment to wealth, power, position, art, sport and so on?

H.H. This calls for knowledge: The knowledge of the ever-changing world. Wealth, power, art, sport, etc. are changing facets of the world. One must work as much as one wishes for them, but one must remember this: that either these subjects will change or one will have used all his powers and can't hold them any more. That will be the point of disappointment. The fact that a stream of true knowledge runs beneath all worldly things should never be forgotten. This stream of real knowledge is never changing and promises to keep one alive when every other forceful thing of the world has passed by.

* * *

Q. Is there any way of increasing growth and scope of selfless love?

H.H. Only through complete lack of desire and attachment. If there is no attachment, all actions are guided by selfless love.

* * *

Dr.R. In my group we felt recently that we had been making a mistake about the three gunas. We began to dislike rajas and tamas and to long for sattva. There was much talk about sattva, and we became very attached to it. Then I came across Lord Krishna's words again: "He who shuns not the guna which is present nor longs for that which is absent, and he who rises above the gunas, shall become one with the eternal." This helped several people. Yesterday your Holiness seemed to be saying the same thing. The simile of the car driver not concerned with his gears but with his destination is very enlightening. Does the rise above gunas mean first not to be attached to our actions and their results?

H.H. The creation is full of these three gunas. Everything is evolved out of these three gunas and nobody can escape them. What we can escape is the clamoring for them and once we have escaped clamoring for any of the gunas things should be easy, but it would be impossible either to collect one of them and leave the other, or use one of them or leave them. This will be impossible because every man, every action and every thing is full of the three gunas. No one can escape and we have to work in conformity according to the need.

Attachment in any form with anything is bound to bring misery and bondage, so keep off the attachment, even to sattva.

To meditate is to be in sattva, but after meditation when you walk away from the place or in any activity you take to, you come into rajas; when you go to sleep you have to come under tamas. To be in the world, to live in this creation, one has to use sattva for a certain period, rajas and tamas for certain periods. One should not think that because sattva is better one should have it all the time. It would be against nature and it will not be possible. So if one sees that sattva is good, one should attempt meditation with more feeling and attention compared with other activities.

The creation is full of this trinity of sattva, rajas and tamas. This is the primal factor. The same three forces are repeated all through the creation to its grossest form. For example, knowledge, change and ignorance; evolution (creation), existence and dissolution; in Sanskrit grammar: first, second and third person, or masculine, feminine and neuter gender, and so on. The pattern of three created right through the first impulse in creation to the end product. A discriminating [man] should be able to see more of it, in every form of creation. But one thing must be kept in mind that, although these three forces are working through the creation, there is another factor which only observes the coming and going of three forces reacting on each other.

There was a certain man who kept a placard with a reminder before him that "Even this will pass." All experiences and impres-

Attachment

sions were followed by this reminder, and he ultimately became only the observer of events, without any reaction of pain or pleasure.

Although we like to have sattva which is pleasant and better than others, let us not hanker after it and be greedy about it. When sattva comes we see it; and when others [gunas] come we again just see them work and move on. Conclusion is that we must not be "attached" to any of them, and keep observing.

* * *

Q. Yesterday, the Shankaracharya told us that the Absolute was available everywhere, His love was available everywhere, and all one had to do was to surrender. I was going to ask why is it so difficult to surrender when one wants to so much. At the very end I saw that one had to surrender even the desire to surrender.

H.H. The reason is our attachment to the world. Take the example of the sun and clouds: The sun is always there, but the clouds come and cover the sun and we are unable to see it, although the sun is still in existence. The world and our attachment to it—these are the reasons [surrender is difficult]. This is the chief hindrance to realizing the Absolute. The method to overcome this hindrance is prayer, meditation and things like that. When we are able to reduce this hindrance by work on it, then we get some sort of a union with the Absolute and there is joy, bliss.

We cannot have two priorities at the same time, either give priority to the Param Atman or to the world. As soon as the priority given to the world is given up, Param Atman is there. Take the example of the balance: When the two pans of the balance are empty, then the level is perfectly horizontal. As soon as something is put in one side it comes down and the other side rises. Similarly when the mind is not relieved of these worldly desires and things like that, then that side of the balance weighs down.

So, to experience utter bliss it is necessary to free the mind, to free the balance of the weight we are putting on the worldly side. Worldly matters are due to rajas and tamas but thoughts of Param

Atman belong to sattva; the more we have them, the more joy and bliss we experience.

* * *

Q. What is it that surrenders the Buddhi?

H.H. It is the Self itself, and the Self needs no indication or information about to whom to surrender, because he surrenders to himself. So the little Absolute surrenders Buddhi to the big Absolute!

Q. So to achieve that, all Ahankar has first to be removed?

H.H. After all, what is Ahankar? It is one's attachment to a thing, and attachment has to start with the Self. Either you can attach the Self to the body, or to the mind, or to the Self itself. You can do whatever you like, but in each case it is this relationship of the Self —either to a limited thing, or to a large thing, or to the unlimited. If someone dives deep into water and finds something important at the bottom, then if he wants to exhibit or claim the thing he will have to come out with it—bring it above the surface—only then can he claim that this is what he has found. As long as he is below the water there is no possibility of establishing the claim; it is there, but he cannot claim it.

In fact, the body, the mind, the universe—whatever we have here is all *one*, but we can come out in some way and make a claim on some particular thing. If we know that the whole thing belongs to the same deeper level, or to the Absolute, then even if we are making a claim to our body, we are not really establishing a deep relationship, or bondage, between our Self and things because the claim has to be made—the world is there for action and enjoyment, but without any attachment. This one has to learn—unless this comes it is very difficult to find any sort of relationship and Ahankar always seems to trouble one. Otherwise Ahankar will be there, but without any trouble to the individual.

* * *

Q. Can you say more about detachment?

H.H. When hermits are in the forest they surround themselves with fire. This keeps even the most violent beasts at bay.

Q. What is the fire with which we should surround ourselves?

H.H. Love. Love keeps attachment at bay. Attachment comes when you do things for motives of profit and self-interest. Detachment has nothing to do with profit or with loss for that matter. If you love either one person or everybody and it is not reciprocated it makes no difference to your love. Self-assertion does not exist in Love. Love brings equilibrium. If your love embraces the cosmos, then Cosmic Consciousness looks after you. True Love is only experienced when attachment has gone from the coarser forms.

Attention

H.H. Our eyes receive impressions, but they don't see without the sensory part of the brain. So sensory mechanism observes eye and is itself observed by Buddhi. Buddhi observes intellect but is itself observed by the changing ego. But the ego is being observed by "Real I" (Atman), which alone is not observed by anything else but itself. So Atman alone is the True Observer, and the more you try to observe, the nearer you get to "Real I."

Dr.R. Our first Teacher was always saying, "Observe, observe, observe," but without special methods we never managed to get very far.

H.H. Nevertheless he was absolutely right, you had the right training.

Once there was a king who felt the need of a saint, but there wasn't one around, so he sent a minister and servants to search everywhere. They combed all the forests and found various hairy men, supposed to be holy, but they couldn't find a real saint. So, in desperation, after the first month of the three allotted to them, the minister said to one of the servants, "There's nothing for it. *You'll* have to do it. You'll have to sit meditating and perhaps in two months you'll look the part, and anyway some hair will grow on your head and chin!"

He duly did this and the king came and recognized him as holy and bowed down to him. The situation thus having been saved, the minister said to the servant, "All right, now have a haircut and get on with your job, serving me." But the servant said, "No, I don't serve you any more; for while I was meditating I discovered what I was really wanting, and now I'm going for that alone."

Dr.R. (comments) This story was told to illustrate the relation of ordinary "ego" to the Atman. It was told with great gusto and laughter.

H.H. "State of attention" can only be reached by detachment. And you have to begin with the body. Make the body attentive and then you will be able to make the mind attentive also.

* * *

Q. How does one use attention gained during meditation in worldly actions after meditation?

H.H. In the beginning stage the gain is small, so one doesn't really have much attention to use. By practice and sincere meditation one grows the power of attention, which can be used after meditation. In six months of *sincere* meditation one can easily store enough to last ten times the time of meditation. But people sometimes meditate for the sake of meditation or feel duty-pressed or maybe they do it for show. Such meditation is no meditation. It is waste of time. Sincere meditation even for ten minutes is helpful. In deep meditation one meets the void first, but as our nature is, we like to cling to something, and if there is nothing there most people get frightened and come out to dwell in their fanciful imaginings. To be sincere is to stay there, in that void which contains the Atman. This is the simplest method to reach the Source of all and everything. Other systems are hard. It was found that very many disciples gave up such systems because of the [rigid] discipline. Their impurities surface and [the disciples] rebel against the discipline. Those who survive get along the Way. The method of meditation is comparatively very easy. Easy for anyone, but one has to be *sincere* to do this.

* * *

Dr.R. Today we would be grateful for clarification of the subject of "attention," which is considered in our system as the chief practical weapon and an essential part of Self-remembering. I've heard it said too that, "Attention is the only path the Buddhas have trod."

H.H. Attention is the source of success; success depends upon attention; and [then] he gives efficiency as the other side of attention. We can combine both those words in one and then see [that] attention and efficiency are the same thing. Then he describes that only men high on the Ladder have this; the realized man having the greatest attention, he can do anything in the world, but will have complete attention. Even if he is in turiya or in samadhi he will have complete attention at his disposal. The ordinary man has no attention—floating attention—one moment here, next moment there. Neither here nor there. Their attention is always diverted from one moment to another, which gives them no result! Without attention, he says, nothing can be done. This is a very, very important factor in the life of any aspirant or disciple.

Dr.R. May we hear something more about the relation between sattva guna and attention? [Unless] emotion is there [and] one's heart is in it, attention is just scattered and ineffective.

H.H. [He explains the relation of sattva to attention.] There is no attention in rajas and tamas. Rajas is the state of movement when everything is moving, and tamas is the state of inertia—nothing moves, but nothing exists, rather dead. So attention can only be with sattva and attention can only be helped by sattva. But although sattva and the attention are so close, they are different. Sattva creates bliss, whereas attention does not create bliss. But whereas people with sattva experience bliss, if they have no attention they can't retain it. So with attention prolonged experience of the bliss of sattva is achieved; otherwise it will come but will be lost.

* * *

Dr.R. In Allahabad H.H. spoke about attention and sattva. Could he say more about their relation?

H.H. Attention and sattva are very much related. There are two stages of sattva. One is rare and the other is mixed with rajas. A celebration like yesterday was an example of sattva mixed with rajas. People were attentive and there was a lot of activity going on, while there was a sprinkling of sattva all around and people seemed to float in the stream of good emotion. This attention is through action toward sattva. The other is an attention which one feels in deep meditation, which comes with pure sattva. In pure sattva there is complete attention, which also brings in peace and bliss.

* * *

Dr.R. Attention directed by will is one thing; but cannot attention be aroused by emotion, yet [be] caught and held by the object, so a man becomes a prisoner?

H.H. The two kinds of attention—the attention given and the attention caught—can be related to the difference between attention of realized man and of disciple. The disciple has to attend to the words of the realized man, but the realized man catches the attention of the disciple; however forceful the words of the realized man may be, if the disciple is not attending, they will have no effect. So the important thing is for the attention to be given; that is the prime factor in understanding anything. Anybody who wants to learn anything must attend. The other force may be there, but it is powerless if the student or disciple does not give attention.

* * *

H.H. To meditate is to "Be." To be One. One without a second. Here is an example: In very ancient times when Dattatreya was walking along a street a marriage procession came by. He stopped at the door of a shop where arrows were being made. The shopkeeper was busy doing his work and did not care to look at the procession. After the procession was gone, Dattatreya wanted to know why this man did not enjoy this merry procession. He called him and asked if he had seen a marriage procession. The shopkeeper said no. He also said that he did not even hear any noise because he was busy shaping the point of the arrow. In shaping the point he became one with it, and the world of the senses did not exist for him at that time. The same applies to meditation. In meditation one is just One. One becomes the Self. The method of meditation is only a process by which this is made possible. Absolute meditates and becomes the Creation; we meditate and become the Absolute.

* * *

Dr.R. The story of the arrow-maker last year has made a great impression on many people in London. One writes: "I would like to repeat the question: 'How could we acquire the attention of the arrow-maker?' Until I have learnt to dive deep through attention more often, and get real rest, how can I be of real use?" We have thought that this kind of attention when you wouldn't hear a wedding is only to be had during real meditation.

H.H. The attention employed by the arrow-maker would differ from stage to stage in completion of his work. The arrow was made in different stages. First the rough form was created and gradually the shape was refined until it came to the most delicate stage to shape and sharpen the point. According to the coarseness or fineness of the work involved, one would see that the fullness of attention also changes. If the work is coarse, one doesn't need to use the finest energy by giving pointed attention because coarse energy would be good enough to accomplish the job. As the work progresses and comes to finer stages, it would demand more and more attention and when it comes to the last stage or the finest work, only then would one need to use one's finest energy available and put in greatest attention. When one reaches the stage of full attention as experienced by the arrow-maker, one would see that the outer world is practically cut off and a love of Self takes over and this keeps one busy with full attention on the work in hand. All this is known as Dharana. This means "to hold on," which is described by Patanjali in his Yogasutras in the words: "To hold on one's attention at a point is known as Dharana." This does not actually relate to meditation; meditation is something different.

* * *

Dr.R. It seems to me that the ordinary man is like this machine [the tape recorder]. It takes everything equally, loud noises, children shouting, everything without discrimination. When we play it back to translate His Holiness' words we listen with all our attention only to his voice.

H.H. Yes, the simile is right. In the life of a disciple, his attention keeps growing and the complete Attention comes only at the highest stage. But as he treads the steps of the Ladder one by one, he increases the degree of his attention. In the ordinary men there is no increase as such; they get whatever they happen to want this moment or the other moment. That is quite a good description of the difference between an aspirant and a mechanical man.

* * *

Q. I would like to ask if the attention, which His Holiness has talked about, should be brought into ordinary affairs as much as possible? Could His Holiness say something on this?

H.H. The practice of meditation as it has been given is an exercise in attention and then its transformation into pure consciousness. Pure consciousness (samadhi or turiya) is the center of energy. Once one reaches that state and then comes out, this energy can be channeled in the way the individual prefers. When used in ordinary affairs, the result is efficient, beautiful, loving, peaceful and evolutionary. On the other hand it can be used for the Way, the Ladder or yoga. It can also be used to help those who want to join the Way or the Ladder of Knowledge.

The regular practice of meditation increases this store of energy like one's capital in the bank, which can be invested according to the choice of the individual himself. The abundance and purity of this energy refines one's attention and all work carried out under that attention.

* * *

Q. Is it right to think that effort, the third step on the Ladder, is the effort needed to practice attention, and that this is no longer necessary when one feels "the Pull of the Way?" Is this in line with what His Holiness has told us that Dharana [concentration] goes into Dhyana [meditation] and Dhyana goes into samadhi? Is true will, or the will of the Atman needed in order to practice attention?

H.H. The difference between true will and ordinary will is that true will concerns the Truth, whereas ordinary will concerns itself with worldly matters. Truth in its purest form is that the individual and Brahman are the same.

Attention is necessary for every type of action, worldly or spiritual. People attend naturally to what pleases them, but the pleasant is not necessarily the same thing as the good. The good is that which leads to realization that you are the Absolute. To move toward the good one needs discipline. The Ladder of Knowledge and the system of yoga are two ways, which prepare and provide the way to Self-realization.

The yoga system is eightfold. The first four steps are to regulate the physical body and its conduct. Therefore, yama, niyama, asana and pranamaya bring about a healthy body free from unnecessary rajas and tamas to attend to the discipline of the subtle body.

Pratyahara initiates bringing the mind to attend to one point again and again. Dharana applies this attention to stay still in time. When this capacity of attention to stay at one point is mastered, then Dhyana begins which, in its subtlest form of total stillness, is called samadhi. Samadhi with an object brings about efficiency, and samadhi without object is being [or experiencing?] the Self as the center of all energy. Artists, musicians, poets, writers etc. also reach that point of unity and see all aspects of their creative work in one single point, and then their skills manifest in creative work. Likewise, this yoga system is similar to the Ladder of Knowledge. Here, the good impulse which initiates the move on the Ladder begins with a will for Self-realization and is followed by decision regarding the truth about Self and nonself, who am I, what is this world, what is my relation to the world and its creator etc.? Only when a decision is accomplished can the aspirant move with attention and some devotion to make systematic efforts [Tanumansa]. Through these efforts impediments fall away and Pull of the Way [sattvapatti] is established. This happens due to the increase of sattva in one's being and knowledge. This then clears the intellect so much that Insight and Abundance follow, leading to Turiya.

* * *

Q. How can I learn to attend to the present moment?

H.H. We should take recourse to our own sacred natures. A natural solution has a sweetness of its own while a forced solution does not.

Bliss

H.H. The Absolute creates the creation when He looks outward. When He is looking within no creation takes place. So the creation is outward-bound and, due to the nature of creation, body, mind and Buddhi become outward-bound too. Discipline turns them toward the "within." In Self it is all Bliss, Consciousness and Truth.

* * *

Dr.R. People are happy and unhappy during the day according to the circumstances. When H.H. speaks of being happy, does he mean to make an effort to come out of unhappiness, or be happy in spite of circumstances?

H.H. This creation is a movement. In this movement whatever is favorable to mind is pleasant and whatever is unfavorable is pain. The creation of pleasure and of pain is of the mind. The Atman feels and feeds on bliss, and is not at all moved by or desirous of pleasure or pain.

* * *

H.H. The knowledge of anything is the source of pleasure or pain. With knowledge we associate ourselves with things or events and then derive pain and pleasure. This is the nature of worldly knowledge. In ignorance there is no pain and no pleasure, no bliss. But behind the structure of knowledge flows the true knowledge, which does not bind us. This is spiritual knowledge. With this we rise above the results of pain and pleasure and enjoy bliss even in the midst of actions.

* * *

H.H. This kingdom within or the heaven within is the reservoir of peace and bliss. No violence can reach there. Devotion is the gentle art of unity.

In our worldly life we look for pleasure, and we strive hard to snatch those moments of pleasure. Once you get an atom of bliss as a sample, you long for more. The craving for pleasure becomes less because of the depth and strength of pleasure in bliss. For example, you don't care about the well when you get to a river or an ocean. The bigger and better thing reduces the importance of small and inferior things. Dive in with devotion and swim around gently in that blissful heaven which is within you.

* * *

H.H. Meeting people and coming together is very good. But meeting the Atman is far better. One must prepare oneself inwardly and outwardly and be perfectly clean, fully dressed, fit and alert. When one goes to meet the Atman, the King, the Emperor, one must leave the relatives and attendants and have audience in peace and quiet. When the audience is over one comes out to meet the attendants and relatives according to their rank. While going in, leave body, senses, mind and Buddhi, one by one; and while coming out meet Buddhi, mind, senses, body, and the world one after the other. The purpose is to meet in bliss; preparation to get still, comfortable and ready is necessary. One should allow some time to still the body and also for the inner machinery to stop.

* * *

H.H. The meditation is also a new way for people and one meets all hazards of senses, Manas and Buddhi. By persistent effort one will get over them and be used to them and ignore them while making our passage from body to Atman. Beyond Buddhi and in Atman all these experiences of pleasure, pain, striving of the material world don't exist. Atman knows only Bliss and Consciousness. When one gets True Knowledge, then Buddhi becomes clear and takes commands from Atman and gets them carried out by Manas and senses. Only then does it know what is real pleasure—Bliss—and what is not.

* * *

H.H. Meditation has three qualities; its use can be described in three ways: first, nourishment; second, cleansing; third, healing. We need food every six hours to keep the body going, a bath every twenty-four hours to keep it clean, medicine every so often if ill—if homeopathic every seven days! As body needs these things, so whole system needs this service, except Atman which in fact does not need anything, being complete in itself. But activities of rajas and tamas collect impurities. Meditation cleans them out. If no impurities, no need for meditation. Meditation is not an end in itself. Bliss is the ultimate end. It is the nature of the Atman to be blissful, but rajas and tamas deprive it of bliss. Meditation cleans out everything so that Atman reaches its natural state of bliss.

* * *

H.H. There is no attention in rajas and tamas. Rajas is the state of movement when everything is moving, and tamas is the state of inertia, nothing moves, but nothing exists—rather dead. So, attention can only be with sattva, and attention only be helped by sattva. But although sattva and the attention are so close, they are different. Sattva creates bliss, whereas attention does not create bliss. But whereas people with sattva experience bliss, if they have no attention they can't retain it. So with attention, prolonged experience of the bliss of sattva is achieved; otherwise it will come but will be lost.

* * *

Q. If we think of impressions as a food, could you say that good impressions feed the essence?

H.H. There are three kinds of food—physical, subtle, and causal. Our body takes physical material for the maintenance and growth and sustenance of this physical body, so we eat, drink and perform various acts; this is for the material physical body. For the subtle body, we use all these five senses to acquire knowledge from this world. The third level is the food of bliss, which is food for the Atman itself, but this food is not collected from outside; it is collected from within, but only if these instruments—the physical and mental—are kept clean and pure. The bliss is inside the individual. People think that when they have experiences from the world that are pleasing to them, that the bliss is coming from the world to them, [but] that is not the real situation. It is only the interaction of the senses with the material world, but the creation of the bliss is from within, and it will create the bliss only to the extent you have cleaned and purified your two instruments—the physical and subtle bodies.

Q. We were always taught, by Mr. Ouspensky, that there were three types of food—the food we eat, the air, and impressions—and they each set up a process in the body. The impressions did not get very far because there was no inner bliss to meet them, so that they just remained static. That's why I asked the question.

H.H. The elements responsible for the creation of an impression are certainly outside the individual, and it arises from the interaction of the individual and the world. The brilliance and the goodness, which are substantially part of the impression, are also created by the Absolute Himself. All that we get and see or touch is made with the subtle elements: the elements of earth, water, fire, air and space. All these five elements create all material things, and these five elements are five measures of qualities. So the earth element gives smell, the water part holds all the taste, and the fire element holds all the form, beauty and color, seen through the eyes, and air gives movement and touch and speed, and space gives sound and space itself. With all these things are created the beautiful objects of the world, which create impressions. Behind all these qualities are other subtle factors which have been previously described, ultimately pointing to the Absolute. It is the bliss of the Absolute, which in the course of certain movement creates all these beautiful things, which create impressions. If the individual has good, pure, healthy body, healthy mind and good essence (sanskar), then the bliss within will respond equally to this golden brilliant form. If by chance anything is wrong with him physically, mentally, or emotionally, the interaction will not be nice inside, though outside it will seem to be nice. Or, if the picture outside is not so beautiful, but the inner man is blissful, then he will be able to take good impressions from the very raw materials of the world.

To describe how the food works within us, all that we have described in connection with food has all these qualities within it—good or bad—when we take it as food in our being, then there is a sort of liquid or elixir which is secreted within our body, which is not of the food, and this is supplied by our own constitution. The origin of this elixir of life, Amrta, is added to whatever we take in and then it goes on into our stomach, and then within thirty-three days the whole food is transformed into all sorts of finer elements of our body—blood, bones, marrow, and even into mind. When good food is taken and digested properly in a good body, then you can see the effect in the good health of the individual; his face is bright and brilliant and alert and attentive. If the food is not good and he cannot digest it, then the effect it causes will be sloth and misery and all muddy impressions. This is the way the whole cycle is maintained.

Q. Could you say that the elixir of the non-physical impressions is the present moment?

H.H. In the present moment this elixir and the knowledge and the authority of the existence, they are all mixed together. In the present moment everything is put before you together.

H.H. Pure consciousness is the power emanating knowledge and bliss, and gives existence to the whole creation. And this creation, which we see is also the manifestation of pure consciousness, embodying everything all together. The whole creation is full of knowledge, total in existence, and full of bliss. There is nothing wrong in this creation. There is nothing wrong in pure consciousness. And yet, we do experience rights and wrongs. These rights and wrongs arise because of the intermediary realm of our being, which is the subtle body composed of Manas, Chitta, Buddhi and Ahankara. If these are not pure and healthy, then anything can happen. Whatever does happen will be according to the measure of impurity of these four elements of our Antahkharana. Brain is a part of this Antahkharana. So whatever impressions, conscious or not so very conscious, which we gather through these agencies —the instruments of the brain—depend on the level of functioning and the structure of the brain. The satsang is created only for cleansing this subtle body. If the subtle body is kept pure and the interpretation through the subtle body is pure, you will never experience misery or bad impressions. In deep sleep [shushupti] there is no impression of any sort although the brain is there, our body is there, our senses are there, the breath is there, but there is no impression of any sort. Nevertheless the prana is in action; otherwise our sense of continuity would be lost. So something is in action. Consciousness is also there knowing itself to be there, although we cannot respond to praise or abuse inflicted by anyone. During sleep we cannot register any of these, but nevertheless the existence of the consciousness is there and the working of prana is also there to maintain our being. If there is anything that is missing, it is the experience of the world we live in.

An example is the sun. When the sun is shining it can be reflected from anything that is reflective or shiny, like water or glass. Even leaves can reflect the brilliance of the sun at certain times. Now, whether the image of the sun is going to be dirty or clean depends on the water. If the water has a lot of mud in it, you will not be able to find a good reflection of the sun in the water. If the mirror is not clean, the sun will appear to be dirty, as the mirror is dirty. It would be wrong to say that the sun is dirty, or the image in the mirror is dirty. The image is perfect, the sun is perfect, but it is the intermediate part, the mirror, which has certain blemishes, which create the distortion in the reflection. So that's where the difficulty lies, in this instrument, the brain, which creates all these different images. If it is dirty, it will create dirty impressions; if it is not functioning properly, it will not give the proper and true impressions. If one wants to keep it clean, one has to keep with the satsang and keep on trying to cleanse it.

* * *

Q. I understand H.H. to have said that pure consciousness is always present. Could he say more about the relationship of conscious experience to the brain?

H.H. Sat is that which exists no one can question that. Chit is of a different nature. It is consciousness and in conjunction with Antahkaran some are more conscious than others according to their knowledge, just as electricity is one and the same but differences in voltage make it more or less powerful. This is because there is confusion over consciousness in the body or the body in consciousness and one has to analyze through reason to experience the difference. Bliss pervades everywhere but reason shows that though conditions for bliss are in the physical world, bliss is appreciated only by the consciousness in the body. The body is only the instrument.

Another example is sound through a microphone. No doubt the sound comes through it, but the sound does not belong to it. The microphone is only instrumental in magnifying the sound. Moreover the man who speaks cannot claim that the loud sound is caused totally by him, for the microphone is instrumental in magnifying his sound. Thus, through rational analysis, the understanding acquired is that the mixture is a sort of superimposition or illusion. When understanding of the truth emerges then one realizes that the physical is merely an expression of consciousness. Then one begins to appreciate the importance of consciousness in comparison to the inanimate physical world. A child is born, he grows to youth, and then manhood and old age, deterioration and death. Consciousness is always with the body, and exists even after its death. Consciousness is not subject to birth, growth, decay or death, but because of association it seems to be so, but this is untrue and of no value. A man who meditates properly begins to love the universal, and the individual body looks insignificant; he knows that all these appearances are the product of the mixture of consciousness and the inanimate in the Antahkaran. In consciousness there is nothing like small and large, or any other qualification. The body together with the Antahkaran is the means of reasoning because it can't be done otherwise, but the same can become an impediment. Having accepted it as the means of reasoning, one can develop detachment. If one does not do so, then it becomes a hindrance and ultimately the body will come to its end. So this situation feels like a mixture of consciousness and the inanimate, although it is not so in reality. In reality it is all full of consciousness. The body does not hold consciousness, but it appears in it. It is one consciousness, and in this limitless sphere bodies seem to appear although they do not have real existence in their own right.

Light in a room does not exist by itself, but comes in through the window. The light is everywhere but limited objects exist in that light. Similarly the body is like a room and one presumes that consciousness exists inside the body, but in fact it is everywhere and pervading every part in and out of the body. The bodies may disappear, but consciousness will still exist. The individual through his senses and Antahkaran tries to enjoy this creation but, due to ignorance, he has some adhyasa [mistaking something else for reality] and develops moha [deluded attachment] not prema [true love]. Through delusion he enjoys, but does not appreciate bliss or anand. He knows and experiences pleasure and pain. If and when his adhyasa is removed, delusion is dispelled and then, in true knowledge, he acquires love [prem] and enjoys bliss. Therefore bliss or anand is beyond pleasure and pain [sukha and dukha].

* * *

H.H. The Absolute has manifested Himself in the office, in the family, in the close quiet of the bedroom, and even in deep sleep when not even the senses interfere with the individual.

Now, somehow we have forgotten that the Absolute is immanent everywhere and is ready to meet us with its full force—not only that one meets the Absolute in Samadhi with full force, but this Absolute is ready to meet you as a table, as a chair, as food and everything. It is the ignorance, which has covered our vision, and we have to come out of this ignorance—we cannot do it unless we go into meditation. When we have learnt to come very close to this undifferentiated unity of the Self, then we will see that the Absolute, which appears to be outside and seemingly separated, becomes united with yourself and there may be a time when there is no beginning, there is no end, there is no inner, and there is no outer: It is the same Absolute available everywhere, and there is never any separation. Whenever any unity is experienced it immediately brings bliss into actions, and this can only happen when there is consciousness active. All unity takes place in consciousness and in every conscious act there is this bliss supporting itself. So when one takes food, picks up a piece of fruit, which is juicy and one tastes and experiences the freshness of the juice, a little bliss bursts out in the enjoyment of eating, and the sweetness of the taste. Vedas declare the Absolute as "Rasa Vai Sah," "He is the juice or essence." Now this bursting out of the enjoyment, even if in eating an ordinary thing like fruit, is in essence an experience of the consciousness of the Absolute Himself, because the Absolute has manifested Himself as the juice, and the fruit and the eater.

Buddhi. The physical effort is the primary, for from here one can affect the working on senses and mind. First the body is naturalized to discipline the mind, and when mind is obedient, then the Buddhi. When Buddhi is pure then it opens the gate for the individual [Ahamkar] to see one's own real Self. Here all efforts and disciplines become useless. This is the domain of Bliss, Consciousness, Truth. The efforts on body, Manas and Buddhi are simultaneous through knowledge and discipline. Essential effort is only that which removes the present barrier of body, Manas or Buddhi.

* * *

Dr.R. I wonder what is it that makes me meditate.

H.H. It is Buddhi in pure state. It works like a mother. She cares and works for the betterment of the child and protects from dangers and difficulties, warns of the impending dangers and keeps him away from bad influences. Buddhi in pure state reminds one and chases one to work for betterment. Good company enhances the chances of development and bad company would dim it out.

Dr.R. Is it through the pure Buddhi that one could communicate with the Master at a distance?

H.H. When the stream of pure Buddhi reaches a high level of sattva, then the communication becomes possible and thoughts can be relayed and satisfactory message received. Just as one can communicate through the wireless system in the physical world, there is a similar system of communication provided in human beings. It is latent. It works only when one reaches a high level of consciousness. One would then be able to read the thoughts of others and communicate.

Dr.R. Is it that in pure Buddhi intellect and emotion are *one* and one can know the Truth by intuition?

H.H. Buddhi, the pure intellect, is the active principle. It earns for the Self and passes the valuables to heart, which holds the treasury. Every one of these valuables comes only through Buddhi. It is the only instrument we have through which the values of everything

Buddhi

H.H. In the life of a disciple the chief problem is to make his Buddhi clean and precise, so that he shall be able to distinguish what *is*, from what *is not*.

Dr.R. Is an example of Buddhi being tuned in the wrong direction, the strife between religious sects and the persecution of heretics, all that?

H.H. The wars in the name of religion and the sectarian differences are the product of confusion in Buddhi. When Buddhi is not related to Atman, these things manifest in the activities of these people. They are not, after all, supposed to be high on the Ladder [of Self Realization] at all; they are inferior people, and their inferior minds create all these difficulties for themselves and others.

Dr.R. Would you tell us the chief ways to make our own Buddhi pure?

H.H. Love the Truth, and leave the untruth. That is the cure.

Dr.R. Is it true that unless he achieves pure Buddhi as described by Lord Sri Krishna later in the *Gita*, man cannot see the full Truth and nothing but Truth?

H.H. Pursuit of Truth cures and clears the Buddhi; just in this single activity both are achieved, the Truth comes and Buddhi is cleared and cleaned. But if the direction is the other way, with the pursuit of the untruth, then the Buddhi becomes muddled and the result is pain and suffering.

* * *

Q. We have been told that effort is a necessary step on the Ladder of Self-Realization. We have found through our own effort that physical effort in this work is no use. Essential effort seems necessary. What is essential effort? How can we come to it?

H.H. The efforts are necessary unless Buddhi is fully cleansed of impurities, and mind, senses and body are made subject to pure seen or unseen are derived and also given away as well. The heart, which is the seat of emotion, keeps the treasure. At the moments when one finds unity with outer world, Buddhi allows heart to respond directly. When one is saturated with sattva and Buddhi is pure and heart is responding, then Truth is flashed by intuition or one gets inspiration under (?) state of Being. One can't command such situations.

* * *

Q. In trying to keep intentions (i.e. thoughts) and deeds consistent, one often seems to run up against a state of inertia in the body. For example, one knows one should practice some useful exercise, such as calligraphy or music, and something in one even seems to desire that, but one finds oneself watching television instead— seldom an enlightening occupation! The key seems to lie in feeding and strengthening the heart, i.e., the emotional center. What help can the Shankaracharya give on this problem, please?

H.H. This is because of untrained Manas, which is always ready to fall for coarser subjects which are mostly related to physical and sensual enjoyments. Manas considers them more important, and so likes to dwell in such activities. The worldly physical things have a certain importance in life, which need to be attended to; but work on Self-realization also has certain important factors which need one's attention. This way the pull of the world and the pull of the school create conflicts. One wonders about what one must do first.

This is the domain of reason [Buddhi]. Reason is there to decide what is more useful to the Atman, and this can only come about through personal experience. If one observes one's activities, one will soon find which will give more and lasting goodness. Having found the importance of good work, one should stand by it. When one has to see an important person, then one gives more time and care to meeting him. The schoolwork is for meeting the most important of all, so one must logically do just that. If one fails to do that, one hasn't known the importance; for with that knowledge, no one really can afford to indulge in inferior things.

Manas [desiring mind] goes for pleasure; Buddhi stands for good; and good is important in comparison with pleasure. Follow the Buddhi and just practice good work again and again. Make sure what is important; having done that you would not need anyone to tell you what you must do.

A mother helps a child to learn to walk, and then she lets go of his hand. The child may fall and if he does, the mother gives support again and tries again until the child walks by himself. The child trusts the mother. The school is the spiritual mother; follow her, she asks you to do work for your own help. The more you spend your time in good activity, the more good will be available, and in due course you will develop a taste for good activity which, one day, will become natural; the Manas will have been trained to do more important work rather than less important.

Children have to give more attention to learn. The new teacher also has to study to teach, but not like the children. An experienced teacher simply walks in, and without any exertion he conducts his teaching; and all this only because one practices one's work again and again until it becomes natural and easy.

* * *

Q. I would like His Holiness to confirm that it is the purpose of purifying Buddhi to transform impressions and choose only those impressions, which are of service to the Atman. Does this remain the most crucial work in Self-realization? Is this the way to purify the Antahkaran?

H.H. Buddhi is one aspect of Antahkaran, which has four aspects or four functions of the subtle body: Manas, Buddhi, Chitta and Ahankar. These aspects have been explained in detail some time ago.

Manas is the instrument which collects all the sensory impressions from the outside and projects desire, concepts, etc., from inside. If Manas is at peace and is under one's control, then it takes impressions as they are; that is true impressions and necessary desires. If it is sensually passionate and agitated, then impressions are faulty and desires are unnecessary ones.

Buddhi works on the data received by Manas. A steady and trained Buddhi can analyze the right and wrong of any topic in a way that its choices or decisions are useful to the Atman. Otherwise an impure Buddhi will plead for wrong choices and wreck one's life.

Chitta is the store of memory and attitude. A pure Chitta can preserve truth in the memory and provide a positive or useful universal attitude; whereas impure Chitta will have selfish, greedy or unjust attitudes; the memory would become unreliable and complexities would develop to create constant worries.

Ahankar is called ego. Here there is a direct relationship with the state of affairs contributed by Manas, Buddhi and Chitta, together with the samskar of the individual. Through the Ahankar the individual exposes the state of his being and understanding at that moment, with his desires, ambitions and worries. Love, hate, and indifference manifest from here. The purified state would manifest desires of a universal nature.

The Self being limitless becomes known through these various limitations. Without some limitation of the universal to the individual, there would be no Ahankar. True knowledge, a rational approach, justice and mercy, fellowship etc. are its better manifestations. Ego always makes claims, and all claims are limited. When pure ego aspires to reach the limitless, it can only do so by disclaiming limitations. This is the essence of all wisdom. When all claims are dismissed then the individual is free, he does everything right, and for him there is no difference between the individual and the universal. Therefore purification of Buddhi really involves purification of all four factors of the Antahkaran. Then it becomes transparent, and inner and outer are not separated by any impediments.

One of the simplest ways to appreciate viveka is the concept of me and mine. The body, house, wealth, family, car, etc. are all "mine," but not "me." "Me" is the owner, the knower, and "mine" is that which is owned and known or knowable. "Me" is pre-eminent and exists by its own virtue, whereas "mine" is subject to "me" and exists for the service and pleasure of "me." Whether things "mine" exist or not, "me" does exist. The car is "mine" and I can use it or sell it, therefore it is disposable, but "me" is not disposable. Everything "mine" is limited, but no one can limit the spirit that is "me."

The way to liberation is to see the difference clearly. Even Antahkaran is "mine," Buddhi is "mine." Once this wisdom dawns, then one can begin to live in freedom with or without possessions and claims within the world. "Me" and "mine" creates duality only because what is called "mine" is presumed to exist independently. With this idea people begin to possess them, claim them, and get attached to them in case they lose them. In freedom they are not lost, but one is free to use them or not. [Here "me" represents the Spirit, and is not to be confused with pride].

* * *

Q. All knowledge is always there and always available, but it does not belong to us. A flash of understanding! Yet to make it mine will limit, if not destroy, it. Truth [when] given in a simple phrase [is] so divinely illuminated that it contains the wisdom of many books. How, then, are we to communicate with each other on the physical level?

H.H. Knowledge is the material of consciousness, and it is available all the time and at every place. This is experienced in two ways as Aham [I am] or Idam [this is or that is]. All knowledge, which is composed of these two types of experiences, can be had only through machinery supplied to all beings. The machinery consists of the senses, Manas, Buddhi, Chitta and Ahankara. These are all one has, for there is no other instrument of knowledge. So one can get all knowledge through this machinery. This machinery is also created by the Self who uses it, and so it has all possible functions to perform for knowledge. Only with these can you experience, know, record the knowledge, and make use of it in communication. It may seem that by claiming it or making it "mine," the knowledge is limited; but if one knew that it was everywhere and available to all who care to use their machinery, then it would be an unnecessary burden to claim it or make it "mine." But whatever you do, claim it or not, you must experience to get it.

Eyes see everything; but the eye does not see itself, and yet we all know that seeing is done only by the eye. One can see all "Idam," the world around; but one can't see one's Manas or Buddhi, Chitta or Ahankara. By inference from their work, we all know them to be there—but only by our own experience—and know them as "my" Manas or "my" Buddhi. If this machinery is used properly, then all knowledge and inferences would be right.

The question of communication pre-supposes experience. If one has experience, then one only needs to learn the language and communicate fully to those who have—or could have—similar experience and know your language. Since all men have the same machinery, there is no obstacle in knowledge and communication.

Aham [I am] experiences everything through the subtle body and senses, but Aham can't be experienced by subtle body and senses. Idam alone is experienced through subtle body of Manas, Buddhi, Chitta and senses. Idam is composed of Pratyaksha [immanent or present to the senses] and Paroksha [beyond or away from senses but comprehended by mind]. Aham is neither Pratyaksha nor Paroksha so it is called Aparoksha, that is, "not beyond." One cannot know the Knower by any means, for the Knower alone is the cause and experiencer of knowables. The Aham or the Self is Truth, Consciousness and Bliss. No one can ever show Truth, Consciousness or Bliss for they are always experienced through something, and things are always physical. At most one can define Truth as that which remains the same in all three times, i.e., remains the same in past, present, and future. In physical world there is nothing which could remain the same in past, present, and future; only Consciousness or Bliss or Truth remain the same, and that is the Self who experiences all things and can communicate through the common medium of language. Those who have experience, they alone can communicate.

For example, take grains of salt in a salt-bed, which have been extracted from seawater. If they wish to fathom and measure the depth of the sea or ocean, they might get back into it again. The only thing that could happen to them and their curiosity is that very soon they will be dissolved into the sea, and that curiosity will also be dissolved, for they themselves have turned it into sea and they are sea. How could they know it by being themselves? As long as one is divorced from the experience, there will always be curiosity.

Absolute is like an ocean and individuals are like grains of salt. Curiosity makes them jump into the ocean. Some use mechanical devices, some use logic, Manas, Buddhi and Chitta, etc. The best way is through the reason; when reason is awakened and its gate open, then all divisions vanish and there is only one ocean. Those in search of knowledge have experience; become one with the Absolute, and then curiosity vanishes. Aham and Idam become one, and then there is never any problem of communication. Curiosity is a sincere act from the side of non-realization, but only a comic act from the side of Realization! Realize and communicate.

Chitta

H.H. Two kinds of forces live in all of us—good and evil. Their coexistence leads to conflict, and conflict leads to unhappiness. Had there been no such conflict, there would have been a perpetual state of happiness. Forces of evil like desire, anger, etc., exist in saints also, but the difference is that they [saints] do good to others instead of harming them. Liberation implies freeing the Chitta from this duality of good and evil.

The universe also unfolds itself in two ways: One way is the way of "Avidya," ignorance, in which we imagine ourselves to be the "doers" of actions, and are, therefore, subject to the law of "karma," i.e., "As you sow, so you reap." The other way is like the performance of a drama, in which the actor, acting as a thief or a saint, knows he is not a thief or a saint. For him, therefore, the law of karma does not hold.

For example: In cases where Param Atman took the part of a man according to Hindu scriptures, he was not really a man. Thus, he was not bound by the "karmas" he did as such [a man].

This cannot be the case with a person who identifies himself with his actions. If anyone thinks that *he* has won a victory today, the law of karma lays down that he would suffer a defeat tomorrow.

* * *

H.H. No worldly action, however good, can be entirely free from evil. No worldly pleasure can be obtained without causing pain to someone. Every sinner has a virtue. Should we, then, abstain from action in order to get away from evil?

The way to rid oneself from evil is to cultivate the attitude that it is nature that is acting through the body, and not the Self. The body is the machine of nature to produce action. Your Self is only the witness, and not the doer. It is through nature that Param

Atman is making the whole universe dance, but He does not dance Himself. He makes our Manas, Buddhi, etc., dance; but none can make Him dance. He is the Reality and the Truth, and there is no place where He is lacking. The states of Chitta are not the states of Atman. Meditation, practice, samadhi, etc., are all states of Chitta. Even digging the ground for the service of Param Atman is heavenly, while even worship of Param Atman for worldly ends is hellish. For practicing remembrance of Param Atman, do not wait for a suitable opportunity. Do not think of today or tomorrow. You can do it whenever a feeling of devotion arises in your heart, paying no heed to the hindrances present.

* * *

H.H. Nature is not free to act independently. The power puts up various shows to please its Master. Nature, owing to its subordinate relationship with Param Atman, wants to win His favor. This can only be done by producing things, which He can like and only the well-produced things would be liked.

Our hands, feet, eyes, ears, etc., are intended by nature to act correctly, so that Param Atman may be pleased. But owing to ignorance, we believe that they are meant to please the world!

Though Param Atman is limitless, yet we have to see Him in the limited things first. Seeing Him in the limited things would eventually lead us to the unlimited Param Atman. The inertness of the Chitta stands in the way of realizing Him. Love has the power to remove this inertness and give us a glimpse of Param Atman.

* * *

H.H. Chit is power. Chit is a synonym of Buddhi, Chit—the power—indicates Samashti. And Chitta is a part of the Antahkarana, which does the function of chintan. Chit is not power but that power in which all powers are concentrated. Chitta can only think of what Buddhi tells it, nothing else, like a storeroom which goes on storing the facts.

Atman is only a viewer, and what it views is knowledge. It is with this power that the Manas does its work of Sankalpa and Vikalpa, Chitta does its chintan, and Buddhi gives its decisions. What the hand of our body, the eyes of our body, the nose and ears of our body are doing are actions; when our eyes see we think that "I am seeing" but the body is seeing. Similarly, with Chit power—absolute power. When it descends into the body it divides itself into four channels and without that power nothing can be done. It appears as Manas, Chitta, Buddhi and Ahankara.

All these functions of thinking, taking decisions, etc., take place in the Antahkarana only, not in the Atman. Atman provides the power with which these four work; the power coming from the Atman into the Antahkarana divides itself into four streams which ultimately do manan, chintan, taking decisions, and identifying ourselves with the physical body. Until we get the power of chit, neither Buddhi can give decisions nor Manas do its work, nor Chitta, etc. Thus we are getting three entities: One is absolutely pure Atman, second is taking the form of Chit—we may call it universal Buddhi or Samashti—and third is that portion which is providing light [power] to the Antahkarana.

One part is pure and unmixed—unpolluted—call it Chit. When it comes into the Antahkarana it divides itself into four parts. The portion of that light which decides, we call by the name of knowledge. That portion of the light which thinks of doing this and that, we call Manas; that portion of the light which does chintan [thinking] is called Chitta, and that portion which makes us say "I am this, I am that; I am black, I am white," is called Ahankar.

* * *

Q. When Self-realization takes place, is it a state which one knows and has no doubts about?

H.H. State is an object of time and place. It isn't a state which one realizes, it is an experience. Once this experience is achieved then it stays there. It is always there, because the Self knows what is there and what is not. He lives in eternity and will go on doing so even if the forms take different shape. Once realized or experienced there is no doubt; the doubts are at the level of Manas and Buddhi.

Stillness of Chitta is essential for Self-realization. In India there are hundreds of people who are very well educated and know practically everything, but their Chitta [Consciousness] is not still and so they don't have self-realization at all. They just talk for the pleasure of ear and tongue. Then there are people whose Chitta is still but they don't have the knowledge; but once they are given a little direction they catch the way and carry on easily. The other ones, with profound knowledge and unstable Chitta, can't proceed for Self-realization. Meditation is the system which stabilizes the Chitta [Consciousness], and in circumstances like this, meditation is prescribed so that the people who are removed from real understanding and overloaded with knowledge should be able to realize the Self.

Self-realization is not experienced gradually; it is the Chitta that rises step-by-step on the ladder. Self-realization happens in a moment and then it stays always there.

* * *

Dr.R. One asks all this because one wants to create an ever-present image of oneSelf, the Atman, or of his appointed fully-realized man. Is this done in Buddhi if it is stilled and purified?

H.H. Yes, this is the point of it, and it is done if Buddhi is still and pure, but where there is tamas one cannot keep the image one wants. He says Buddhi is the element which discriminates, but the actual store of all the knowledge is Chitta. For instance, a man goes to the market and earns his livelihood, and when he comes home he either gives the money to his wife or puts it in the safe. Buddhi also gets knowledge by discrimination and stores it in Chitta. But Chitta, which is a sort of filing system, can file things wrongly; or things may get mixed up in the filing cabinet. So Buddhi cannot get the right thing at the right moment when wanted. It is very important to improve the filing and store our references systematically and keep them separate and classified so that Buddhi can make the best use of knowledge stored. Of course Buddhi also absorbs unwanted and even dangerous things when it is not still, when moving about with Manas.

* * *

Dr.R. We still do not understand just where Bhawana fits into the scheme of things. Is it on the causal level alongside Antahkaran, or with Chitta felt in the heart [part of the subtle level]? My need is really to understand the relation of Bhawana to Antahkarana.

H.H. Yesterday we were told about the two centers, the heart and the head; in the heart appear the Chitta and the Manas, and Bhawana springs from these two. All the desires or the doubts are raised by the Manas. The first glimpse of the desire is first glimpsed by the Manas. It comes in collaboration with the Chitta, Chitta being the store [memory] of all the knowledge and everything a man can call his capital. But this relation of Bhawana is not a constant and smooth process. Sometimes it is abundant and all in one direction, and sometimes it is very scanty; just as one sees the ocean, there are waves small and big. But this is how the nature of Chitta works.

[*Dr.R.* The most important part of our long-term memory mechanism is the power to recall previous experiences of Consciousness —the special province of Chitta.]

Q. I just feel very lucky to be here with Dr. Roles, and I remember what His Holiness said at the beginning of our last visit, when he spoke about "catching the spiritual influences which are available here." I feel I would like to make best use of the time to do this. Could His Holiness say more about this, although I realize he has partly answered it this morning?

H.H. The questions and answers must certainly be carried through before the mind can come to rest; so the individual's questions must be exhausted far enough, at least for him to be free from the load of them. That must be done, and be done carefully.

But apart from this, there is the Chitta ["reflected Consciousness"] of the individual which could give him Bhawana—a state of pure emotion, one aspect of which is "faith." So, if one is full of faith, i.e., connected with this Bhawana or pure emotion, then one's state is charged with certain magnetic qualities and this is common to everyone. [Faith, that is, not in men but in the benevolent and omnipresent Self.]

In certain individuals this influence is more powerful than others; but, having come into contact with it, one simply needs to allow this magnetic force to work without impediment. Then it will attract these charged particles from the atmosphere.

When this happens one will be impelled to seek more of this influence and store it, so that one experiences a deeper relationship with the unity around, and this is what His Holiness prescribes. One should just let the influence come into one's experience [through penetrating this "cloud of unknowing"].

* * *

H.H. This human body is very closely related to the atmosphere—the entire cosmos. The positions of the various stars in the heavens, in orbit, are actually reflected in the human body also; all of these satellites, their corresponding element is to be found in man also.

Q. So man is a miniature universe. When he said the sun was in the right eye and the moon in the left, can we think of it as the right being active and the left passive?

H.H. That is correct; but it has also a connection with the Manas. It is very difficult to find the equivalent to "Manas" in the English language. The word "mind" is actually the *activity* of the mind and is divided into four different categories according to our philosophy; for the word "mind" there is no different word for each different category of work, which, according to us, is the function of the mind. Manas, Chitta, Ahankara, Buddhi—these are the four elements which construe the mind. The functions of all these four are different. Manas and Chitta, they sort of do all the thinking, and are connected with the heart; while Ahankara and Buddhi are the functions of the brain and take decisions. Manas and Chitta do the Sankalpa [fantasy]; Vikalpa, and Ahankar and Buddhi take decisions and are connected with the brain part.

* * *

Q. We are told that asking questions helps our progress toward Self-realization. Where does a good question come from?

H.H. Chitta is the store. Here many products can be stored. Some store good knowledge, and some people store rubbish which is not appreciated by Atman or Buddhi and there is no ready refusal to accept what is not true or good. Then one has to dispose of it, and a question arises from the Atman as to the disposal of whatever rubbish is collected. Just as a trader, when by mistake he gets hold of a faulty product, he goes on to sell it quickly. So when the Atman or Buddhi gives a call that there is something untrue or impure about certain ideas or habits one has stored, then it produces a good question. Those who question, alone purify.

There are two types of trader. A good trader, if by chance he has somehow got a faulty product, then he would not put it on the market for he does not like to trade bad products and deceive his clients. He will destroy it and replace it by a good product even if he has to do so at his own loss. The other, wicked, traders would get cheap and useless products and sell them under any pretext and deceive their clients. Even on spiritual level these are seen. People take to rubbishy ideas and keep on trading in them, while very few stay firm to get only true Knowledge and then give that to others.

* * *

Q. Being in H.H.'s physical presence again emphasizes the fact that during the months of absence His Grace has never left me. Thanks to this and the meditation, the three hindrances, which H.H. mentioned at our last visit seem to be slowly clearing, and I am in receipt of universal grace more frequently. I am deeply grateful and hope that with H.H.'s continuing help, the hindrances may be removed completely so that I can be open all the time to those graces, which I now know to be always available.

H.H. To be able to acquire universal grace constantly all one needs to do is to keep one's door open, open in the direction of the Absolute. One's door is not in fact a physical door, but the door of the Chitta, so one's Chitta should be open to the Absolute, and the universal grace of this Absolute is always being charged through the universe, so it is available all the time. But even with these three hindrances, which do impose upon us and compel us to forget, they need not affect us very much.

For example, on the road one usually finds that there are lampposts about half a furlong apart, and one sees that the light from lampposts at this distance converges, so that the darkness between them is lost, and the same happens in the life of the individual.

If the memory of this universal grace is kept alive all the time, then it acts as the connection, and [it] means one would be able to get universal grace all the time. Even if it is not constant in the individual, and he remembers and his memory is enlivened after a little interval, whatever has been done during this interval according to these hindrances will be washed out, cleared, burned out so one would always be within the realm and the effect of the universal grace. So keeping one's Chitta open toward the Absolute, and keeping the memory that one is receiving the universal grace is just good enough. Whether it can be done for short intervals or constantly would decide how much one gets of this universal grace.

Here is a linguistic example—the word for grace is *kripa* or *daya*. If you turn the word, then *daya* becomes *yada* because they are made of the same sound. So on one side it is memory which is *yada* and from the other side it is the grace which is there, so in fact it is one single connection, but from an individual point of view it is memory of the Absolute, and from Absolute's point of view it is His glory and grace being given to the individual.

* * *

Q. H.H. said that to receive universal grace constantly, the door of one's Chitta should always be open to the Absolute. What is it that will hold Chitta open to the Absolute even during a busy working day?

H.H. When one is busy during the day one can do one thing: Before you begin any particular action one should remember the Absolute, and when this action has been completed then one should remember the Absolute again. If it is possible some time during the action also to remember, that is well and good; otherwise if one could remember the Absolute at the start of a job and at the end of a job He would presume that the Chitta of the individual is open to the influence of the Absolute during his busy day or busy job.

Consciousness

Q. The idea of survival after death, whether in the form of rebirth or in other forms, remains an enigma. Is it true that the invisible threads that bind human beings to creation—the Creator—are eternal for everyone, or does their eternity depend on the achievements of the soul during cycles of existences? To put it differently, does the soul that moves upwards become eternally integrated or united to the Creator, whereas vegetating souls are inevitably separated from Him, and that would be their kind of eternity, unless or until they come to find a way out to escape?

H.H. The idea of survival after death in any form would not remain an enigma if one understood the true meaning. According to the Sanskrit system this is known as Purarjanma, and by *janma* or birth is meant "appearance of a form in time." It can be easily verified in the phenomenal world of manifest forms that nothing disappears. One always finds that a form either transforms into finer substance or disintegrates into coarser substances. This is governed by the law which was discussed some time ago that every manifest form is running to meet its cause and during this chase, it reflects many forms.

The whole creation has two predominant factors which are called matter and consciousness. The material world owes its existence to consciousness, and consciousness can only be and always is manifested by matter. Each supports the other. On the basis of these, the whole of creation is taking its measured manifestations and after fulfilling its destiny it goes back to its cause. This is what one calls the Law of Cause and Effect. Every cause produces the inherent effect and every effect conceals its cause within it. Behind the Law of Cause and Effect there are two stages. One is the real stage where only the consciousness is experienced which results in happiness, and the other is the Laya stage where the forms are still and without any experience. These are also known as Turiya and Laya. The substance of the creation passes between this Turiya to Laya, and all the manifest forms arise in between. This "in between" is the movement in eternity. This eternity is one and on this underlying thread of eternity the consciousness takes manifold forms through changes. Thus a point of appearance of a form which in substance exists in eternity is called birth, and the point of change appreciated by consciousness is called death. Once this idea of birth and death is understood, then it becomes easy to appreciate the idea of rebirth which is based on this continuous movement.

The other two points raised were about the integration and separation related to eternity. There is in fact no integration or separation, because everything is consciousness. The beings are all held by consciousness which is Atman, and which is perfect and single and knows no integration or separation. This Atman is eternally blissful. The terms integration and separation are used owing to the ignorance at the level of mind. Even so, the integration which is more of a refining process [cutting down the cloud or dust] is possible only through a good company. Unless one comes within the circle of good company, it is very difficult to escape from the flux of movement which runs through the creation. In common life people get involved with the movement and thus can't see the substance as it is. In good company one is sometimes blessed with moments of stillness and sees things as they are. If one increases these moments of stillness, one will see the unity which is always there. The True Knowledge and the disciplined work help one to be still. Regarding separation one can refer to what Arjuna asked Shri Krishna, "What is it that forcibly takes one away from the reality and compels one to do what one really doesn't want to do?" To this he was told that the ultimate reason is the desire. Although there is nothing good or bad in the desire itself, yet depending on what company one keeps, one learns to desire good or bad.

To sum up, if one finds that the idea of rebirth is a reality, then integration or separation are no more than a thin or thick cloud of ignorance. Knowledge and discipline both are needed for so-called integration, and denial of these is separation. Good company is the only way to escape.

* * *

Dr.R. The Creator has provided everything that one needs. Why is it that when it comes to remember there is a barrier?

H.H. Atman is a part of the Absolute. The Absolute is the creative force (Maya), and Atman is surrounded by ignorance which is a shadow of Maya. The Absolute is limitless, creative, the giver; He never claims anything for Himself, for "He is." Atman is separated from Him only in ignorance. That's why we have limits, boundaries; we possess and we claim. This is all ignorance. The Absolute created the Universe and we create boundaries: "This is my land, this is my country." In fact land belongs to none. You can claim for some time, but in the end you have to leave everything. He creates men; we create the Indian and the English. The creation is Consciousness, but we think it very coarse because of illusion in ignorance.

Once a holy man was traveling. In the evening he wanted to stay for the night in a palace. He asked the door-keeper. The door-keeper inquired of the owner who refused and said, that this is not a hotel nor an inn, where people come for a time and move on.

The holy man asked the owner, "Who built this palace?"

"My father," came the answer.

"Now you own the palace?"

"Yes, I am the owner."

"Who will own it after you?"

"My sons," said the owner.

"Who after your sons?"

"My grandsons."

"This looks like an inn. People seem to come and stay for some time and go. Wouldn't you call it an inn? Had it belonged to your father, he could have certainly taken this with him."

The owner realized what was wrong with him. As long as Atman is covered with this ignorance, as long as it claims it will not remember, it will not unite. When one knows the Truth, one breaks down the barrier and unites with the Absolute.

* * *

Q. I have been asked by the BBC to join a panel of people discussing *happiness*. It sounds promising, doesn't it?

H.H. One should keep in mind that people have forgotten the real meaning of happiness. People take pleasure for happiness. Pleasure and pain are derived from material things and their association with one's state of mind (ego). Pleasure and pain chase each other like day and night. Man's relation to pleasure and pain is always temporary and always changing, and everyone gets his share of these two like a daily ration from the ration shop. Happiness [anand] is one of the natural manifestations of the Atman [Self]. There are three states: Bliss [happiness], Consciousness, and Truth. The real self can never exist without these three aspects. This is a higher state of Consciousness. When one reduces the real self to a mere petty desire or associations, then one gets pleasure when desire is fulfilled and pain when it is not fulfilled. This may also contain happiness but only to the extent of the truth involved in that desire or association. Some happily subject themselves to pain for a purpose. This purpose would in that case have a grain of truth. This happiness is always just above pleasure and pain. You go to a theater and see actors in laughter and tears and because you are only watching and observing the play without being involved in it, you come out happy. So happiness is that which is derived from truth and consciousness. In the case of the play, from the true characterization and conscious plan, you enjoy truth and consciousness. One should be very careful not to confuse happiness with pain and pleasure

* * *

Q. We are told that to realize the Atman and the absolute nature of Atman it is necessary to rise above the gunas. Does the attention in sattva help in this way?

H.H. The nature of the Atman or the Absolute is Truth, Bliss and Consciousness. The manifestation starts with Prakriti and with sattva as the finest of the gunas. To reach the state of Bliss and

Consciousness we start from where we are. A man of tamas must rise above to rajas, and the man of rajas must also rise above to sattva. With abundance of sattva one rises to the state which is without any activity. The light of the sun is not the sun, but sun is only qualified with the light. The Atman is like a sun and sattva is the manifestation like light. Attention is "applied consciousness." When the consciousness is applied to some thing, then we call it attention, and this attention is possible only if enough of sattva is available to direct us toward the Atman. So-called "attention" with tamas is going in the opposite direction toward inertia or death.

* * *

H.H. The Absolute creates the creation when He looks outward. When He is looking within no creation takes place. So the creation is outward bound and, due to the nature of creation, body, mind and Buddhi become outward bound too. Discipline turns them toward the "within." In Self it is all Bliss, Consciousness and Truth

* * *

Q. His Holiness has said that sincere meditation is necessary, and sincere meditation is staying in the void. But in the void Universal Mind seems full of shapes and names. In the void how does attention work and does Chitta hold the mind to Truth?

H.H. Chit [Consciousness] is like a seed-form in which all the names and forms have their existence. In time they manifest, and also in due time they are withdrawn in it. Whatever there is, is within Chit. Everything in the universe is within it, and it is the cause of all things in form and name. The Manas, Buddhi, Chitta and Ahankar are all subtle manifestations of Chit. In our practical life the Buddhi lights up the forms and names and they are stored up in Chitta.

Q. How in meditation, in the void, does attention work, and how is one held to Truth? Is this the work of Chitta?

H.H. The moment one enters into the void, or the so-called nothingness, as he has said, first all the manifested and phenomenal world is primarily and basically based on Chit, which is Consciousness. This consciousness is also known as Atman. When one sees "nothing," or one feels void, actually the attention is there, otherwise there couldn't have been any cognition of "nothing." So this "nothing" is a proof that there is something awake and attentive to observe. Although the name and form is not recognized, the void that we know as "nothing" is being recognized, and that is Consciousness or Chit.

The impressions of names and forms which we gather are collected in Chitta. This is again the same consciousness, but it is manifested and has taken name and form; and because it is manifested, it has its limit. The forms and names are natural manifestations of the consciousness, and the Chitta can hold to truth only in such measure as it has the true forms and names in its store.

* * *

H.H. There are people who, with the use of their Buddhi, can achieve higher levels of consciousness. Their information is correct and their calculations are precise, so with the right use of Buddhi they can see events in great depth. They can see the past and also visualize the future. This is the art of Buddhi, but there are some occasions when the wave of sattva lifts up the consciousness to a great height. This could happen by chance or by some necessity. The result is usually extraordinary. It enlightens the person far beyond the reach of common levels. This type is rare. Here is a story which illustrates the subject. This was given some time ago, but it seems necessary to restate it.

Two persons went to a king and wished to display their art. One of them was a painter who said that he would paint a mural. The other claimed that although he will not touch the brush and paint, yet he will show the true copy of what the other man paints. They were given a room with a partition in the middle. One was painting and the other cleaned the wall thoroughly, plastered and kept on polishing. After the completion of the painting the partition was dismantled and one could see the same mural being reflected on the other wall. Here are two types: One is like the man with information, skill and art, and the other is like the man of sattva whose wall is clear and reflective and reflects whatever there is. The abundance of sattva is more like the polished wall which does the job without any art, skill or information.

* * *

Dr.R. Could H.H. say something about "insight"?

H.H. Eyes are our means of sight for the outer world. One develops an inner eye with True Knowledge. This is the highest state of Buddhi. In purest form of Buddhi, the Atman gets flashes of the True Knowledge which is not available by other [physical] senses. It depends upon the level of consciousness. At the top consciousness comprehends everything, at lower levels according to its level.

Dr.R. Does the "Insight" begin to appear at the fifth step?

H.H. At the fifth step of the ladder the attachment to the material world and desires becomes loosened. One realizes, due to the True Knowledge and sattva, that the attachments and attractions of the world are not good for the Self and drops them completely away, and thus all the sheaths, bondages, walls and clouds are caused to vanish and the sight becomes clear within and without. This is how one gets "Insight." This state of being practically rolls through the lifetime. Turiya is usually experienced at the last lap of life. Twenty-one days of continuous Turiya would stop the material function of the body, and the Atman will merge into the Absolute. Turiya is a rare state to experience.

* * *

Q. When Self-realization takes place, is it a state which one knows and has no doubts about?

H.H. State is an object of time and place. It isn't a state which one realizes, it is an experience. Once this experience is achieved then it stays there. It is always there, because the Self knows what is there and what is not. He lives in eternity and will go on doing so even if the forms take different shape. Once realized or experienced there is no doubt, the doubts are at the level of Manas and Buddhi.

Stillness of Chitta is essential for Self-realization. In India there are hundreds of people who are very well educated and know practically everything, but their Chitta [Consciousness] is not still and so they don't have Self-realization at all. They just talk for the pleasure of ear and tongue. Then there are people whose Chitta is still but they don't have the knowledge, but once they are given a little direction they catch the way and carry on easily. The other ones, with profound knowledge and unstable Chitta, can't proceed for Self-realization. Meditation is the system which stabilizes the Chitta [Consciousness] and in circumstances like this meditation is prescribed so that the people who are removed from real understanding and over-loaded with knowledge should be able to realize the Self.

Self-realization is not experienced gradually; it is the Chitta that rises step-by-step on the ladder. Self-realization happens in a moment and then it stays always there.

* * *

Dr.R. The material given by H.H. has been marvelous. But it seems one is now going to deprive oneself of the pleasure of sitting before his presence.

H.H. The feeling of separateness is only in the physical, material world. The world of Consciousness knows no separateness; there everything is united. Although it is good to get together, many individuals are separated (according to the line of actions which they take). One must rise above these things [separate feelings] and be united in the conscious world.

* * *

Q. Is one presented with opportunities during one's life when a conscious effort can alter one's future? Or does every conscious action determine future moments?

H.H. The first part of the observation is right and acceptable, but the second is preferable. The whole creation is designed in such a way that whatever work you perform has its effect, and we have been given this concept of Prarabdha, Sançita, and Kriyaman[†] in the Sanskar system, through which everyone gets the result of what he has done previously. In ordinary life it is sometimes seen that someone does not seem to be working hard for anything, and yet all the wealth and glory of the world is showered on him. There are occasions when one comes across very brilliant and hardworking young people with very little good fortune from their efforts. These are the two extreme situations. When the Prarabdha is very strong and compulsive, then it either forces good fortune or prevents it, but the general law is "cause and effect"—if you do conscious work there will be good results; if you do conscious work today or tomorrow or the day after tomorrow, it is going to bear fruit. H.H. prefers those who take the challenge in their own hands, apply their consciousness and keep on working as hard as they can. Even if their sanskar does not bear immediately a great result, it is going to create [circumstances] for the next order of life which is to follow; so in any case if you work hard and if you are presented with good opportunities, well and good. Even if it doesn't give good results now, do not be disheartened because you are preparing for a better order of life next time.

* * *

H.H. In the *Gita* it says that from consciousness and its contact with the world comes the desire. If the desire is not fulfilled, then anger arises. If anger does not fulfill the desire which was originally there, and there are more hindrances, then a bond is created between this man [who had the desire] and his desire; he persists by hook or by crook in fulfilling his desire. Because of this, his mind gets agitated. The agitation of mind dislocates reason in his Buddhi, and when this happens the man is almost destroyed. From this you will see that if you can create more sattva by ex-

---

[†]*Prarabdha*: the portion of Sançita Karma that determines one's present life. *Sançita*: the sum of all actions by the Jiva in past lives. *Kriyamana*: the effect of the deeds of the present life to be experienced in the future.

tension of your emotions, by study, by whatever means, then the sattva will be there, there will be less rajas—all these creative works will follow.

There was a holy man to whom two people went for advice to become disciples. Before accepting them he asked one of them to fill the water pot outside with water. This boy went and saw that it was more than half-full of water. He returned to the holy man and said there was plenty of water in it, so he would certainly get fresh water when it was used up. The holy man asked the second one to go and fill the pot—he also saw that there was enough water, but he immediately got ready and took a bucket to the well, drew and filled it completely and then returned and reported to the holy man and asked if they could begin work. The holy man refused to accept the first boy but accepted the second as a disciple.

If one can keep one's mind really open—open to good influences without any attachment to success or failure, without any agitation in the mind, or laziness in handling anything which comes before us in the course of our daily life—then in spite of all the difficulties arising, one will keep on improving one's inner being and the world in which one lives. That is the way to live.

* * *

Q. I am rather confused by your answer about samadhi being available between decisions. I had always understood that samadhi was an exceptional and definite state to which one aspires and which is only available after much work.

H.H. What we have so far taken is two desires between which samadhi does appear—there are three factors in the desires. The first factor is the desire, which in Sanskrit is called Ichcha—and from this comes the Sankalpa, conceptual form of the desires. Here desires are a spark of the consciousness for something. Sankalpa names that something; it forms a sentence, even if it is not a manifest sentence, it is in the mind. Then it is referred to the Buddhi, which has to approve whether the desire is reasonable or not. If it is reasonable, then a decision is taken and the individual goes ahead with the action. If it is not reasonable, it is withdrawn and goes back to the consciousness and remains there. The manifest goes back to the un-manifest. There are the three factors. Decision here does not really mean logical decision about any particular problem where many factors are involved. This is a private, personal decision, whether one's desire is desirable or not.

* * *

Q. I understand H.H. to have said that pure consciousness is always present. Could he say more about the relationship of conscious experience to the physical brain?

H.H. Pure consciousness is the power emanating knowledge and bliss, and gives existence to the whole creation. And this creation which we see is also the manifestation of pure consciousness, embodying everything all together. The whole creation is full of knowledge, total in existence, and full of bliss. There is nothing wrong in this creation. There is nothing wrong in pure consciousness. And yet, we do experience rights and wrongs. These rights and wrongs arise because of the intermediary realm of our being, which is the subtle body composed of Manas, Chitta, Buddhi and Ahankara. If these are not pure and healthy, then anything can happen. Whatever does happen will be according to the measure of impurity of these four elements of our Antahkarana. Brain is a part of this Antahkarana. So whatever impressions, conscious or not so very conscious, which we gather through these agencies —the instruments of the brain—depend on the level of functioning and the structure of the brain. The satsang is created only for cleansing this subtle body. If the subtle body is kept pure and the interpretation through the subtle body is pure, you will never experience misery or bad impressions. In deep sleep there is no impression of any sort although the brain is there, our body is there, our senses are there, the breath is there, but there is no impression of any sort. Nevertheless the prana is in action, otherwise our sense of continuity would be lost. So something is in action. Consciousness is also there, knowing itself to be there, although we cannot respond to praise or abuse inflicted by anyone. During sleep we cannot register any of these, but nevertheless the existence of the consciousness is there, and the working of prana is also there to maintain our being. If there is anything that is missing, it is the experience of the world we live in.

An example is the sun. When the sun is shining it can be reflected from anything that is reflective or shiny, like water or glass. Even leaves can reflect the brilliance of the sun at certain times. Now whether the image of the sun is going to be dirty or clean depends on the water. If the water has a lot of mud in it, you will not be able to find a good reflection of the sun in the water. If the mirror is not clean, the sun will appear to be dirty, as the mirror is dirty. It would be wrong to say that the sun is dirty, or the image in the mirror is dirty. The image is perfect, the sun is perfect, but it is the intermediate part, the mirror, which has certain blemishes which create the distortion in the reflection. So that's where the difficulty lies, in this instrument, the brain, which creates all these different images. If it is dirty, it will create dirty impressions; if it is not functioning properly, it will not give the proper and true impressions. If one wants to keep it clean, one has to keep with the satsang and keep on trying to cleanse it.

* * *

H.H. If this question of birth and death is taken in the light of the three levels of existence, one would see there is no difficulty in understanding it, just as in our common life there is unconsciousness occasionally, sleeping, dreaming, waking and samadhi. All these states can be experienced right here in this body. So in the same way in the greater plan, birth and death are just one level which remains behind when one has left one level and gone into another level; the initial connection is always kept through the Atman, but most of the experiences are left behind, just as we leave the experience of our dream, yet something is carried on.

Q. Consciousness is an elusive term—here one moment and gone from the body at the last breath. What is its substance?

H.H. The *Sat* ("I AM") is the substance of consciousness. Sat or Consciousness or Knowledge was never made; they appear of themselves by the will of the Absolute.

Just as one can make a table out of wood, though you cannot make the wood itself. The wood appears from a seed in the form of a tree. You cut down the tree and then from the wood you can make anything you like. The *differences* between these two, the ones which appear by themselves and the ones which are made from those things which have appeared, are great.

The five elements have appeared out of the *will* of the Absolute. Within these five elements [of ether, air, fire, water and earth] all the forms in creation would arise, and then fall back into those five elements. They keep on changing their forms in this way.

The same would apply to the fact that men, by their volition and the use of all that is available in Nature, may transform natural things [clay, wood etc.] into different forms. These forms will in the end be dissolved into the five different elements. So within five elements all forms will come into play and be dissolved back into all these five; and the three bodies [physical, subtle, causal] make their appearance out of the interplay between these five elements. But consciousness just appears by the *will* of the Absolute and works through all these forms which are made available in creation.

Men too. Men appear in this world through the laws of nature; they will keep on appearing. But man cannot make men as nature makes them. At most, man can make replicas of men in clay or in stone, wax, or metal or any other material they choose, and create an exact copy. But under no circumstances by the use of any extra agency except the natural laws [laws of sex and reproduction] can men be created as they are.

A natural flower appears out of the natural laws. If men wish to recreate flowers they will have to use some other materials to make copies of the flowers. They will never be able to reproduce the original flower. If the original or real flower has to come, it will only come through nature. In the same way, for example, it can be shown that anything which comes into play or is created, will have to die. But the original cause, Consciousness, is not something which can be related to substance: For all substances take form through Consciousness.

* * *

Q. It has been said that we begin to get a flavor of Truth, Consciousness and Bliss as aspects of the universal. They are also aspects of the physical universe. For instance Truth is seen in such things as the laws of physics which are consistent, i.e. true on all scales and at all times and places. Consciousness and the observer are beginning to be seen as the ground of the manifested universe, but Bliss is more illusive. He asks, Can H.H. give us more guidance on how to see bliss on the scale of the universe?

During these audiences H.H. has said to us that variety and diversity are beauty—is this a way to see the manifestation of Ananda on the scale of the universe?

H.H. Sat, Chit, and Ananda can be experienced through the physical world as well. It is not the case that in searching for them one has to get away from the physical world to see them. But it is certainly true that people equate it with pleasure of the physical objects. They believe that the experience is arising through the physical body, not from the spirit which dwells within. This is a basic misunderstanding. For example, take a ball of iron: It is black, hard, cool and heavy. When it is subjected to the intense heat of fire it remains round but changes color, becomes less hard, turns hot and less heavy. The fire permeates every part of it. If it is removed from the fire it slowly comes back to its natural black, hard, cool and heavy state. Only the fire is missing. Similarly the spirit in the body, like fire in a ball of iron, is the cause of change or transformation. The body is inert, the spirit is the cause of animation. This is why experience is through consciousness which permeates the body like fire in a ball of iron. If they are separated, no one can experience anything let alone Ananda.

Sat is that which exists—no one can question that. Chit is of a different nature. It is consciousness and in conjunction with Antahkaran some are more conscious than others according to their knowledge, just as electricity is one and the same but differences in voltage make it more or less powerful. This is because there is confusion over consciousness in the body or the body in consciousness and one has to analyze through reason to experience the difference. Bliss pervades everywhere but reason shows that though conditions for bliss are in the physical world, bliss is appreciated only by the consciousness in the body. The body is only the instrument.

Another example is sound through a microphone. No doubt the sound comes through it, but the sound does not belong to it. The microphone is only instrumental in magnifying the sound. Moreover the man who speaks cannot claim that the loud sound is caused totally by him, for the microphone is instrumental in magnifying his sound. Thus, through rational analysis, the understanding acquired is that the mixture is a sort of superimposition or illusion. When understanding of the truth emerges, then one realizes that the physical is merely an expression of consciousness. Then one begins to appreciate the importance of consciousness in comparison to the inanimate physical world.

A child is born, he grows to youth, and then manhood and old age, deterioration and death. Consciousness is always with the body, and exists even after its death. Consciousness is not subject to birth, growth, decay or death, but because of association it seems to be so. But this is untrue and of no value. A man who meditates properly begins to love the universal, and the individual body looks insignificant; he knows that all these appearances are the product of the mixture of consciousness and the inanimate in the Antahkaran.

In consciousness there is nothing like small and large, or any other qualification. The body together with the Antahkaran is the means of reasoning because it can't be done otherwise, but the same can become an impediment. Having accepted it as the means of reasoning, one can develop detachment. If one does not do so, then it becomes a hindrance and ultimately the body will come to its end. So this situation feels like a mixture of consciousness and the inanimate, although it is not so in reality. In reality it is all full of consciousness. The body does not hold consciousness, but it appears in it. It is one consciousness, and in this limitless sphere bodies seem to appear although they do not have real existence in their own right.

Light in a room does not exist by itself but comes in through the window. The light is everywhere but limited objects exist in that light. Similarly the body is like a room and one presumes that consciousness exists inside the body, but in fact it is everywhere and pervading every part in and out of the body. The bodies may disappear, but consciousness will still exist. The individual, through his senses and Antahkaran tries to enjoy this creation but, due to ignorance, he mistakes something else for reality and develops deluded attachment, not true love. Through delusion he enjoys, but does not appreciate bliss or Ananda. He knows and experiences pleasure and pain. If and when his delusion is dispelled and then, in true knowledge, he acquires love and enjoys bliss. Therefore bliss or Ananda is beyond pleasure and pain.

* * *

Dr.R. Is there any further advice His Holiness can give on the subject that the Atman alone is real and looks on all the changing events and situations as a passing show, without getting involved?

H.H. In order to appreciate the Self described in the *Upanishads* one needs simple methods. Many such descriptions have been given in the past, but more light can now be thrown on the subject. The states of Consciousness experienced in deep sleep, dreams, the daytime state, spiritual awakening, samadhi, etc., are governed by the influx of sattva, rajas and tamas from people, situations, and events. These all undergo change, but the Observer who sees them all as a "passing show" always remains the same. This Observer never registers any change in itself; if any modification appears, then this must happen to the individual [Ahankar] since change is its very nature.

For example, pure gold always remains gold while its uses and shapes and forms are liable to many modifications [variations]. The sky remains the same, while storms, clouds, rain and snow keep on changing our view of it, and yet do not affect the sky in any way. [One experiences this vividly every time a plane takes us up above the cloud ceiling]. The waves of the sea cause no loss or gain to it, the waves are only on the surface; at the bottom of the deep blue sea there is complete stillness. In the same way all these passing shows of the gunas, do not change the Atman, but only provide variety in its appearance.

* * *

H.H. There are five states of one's being: the awake state, just as we are experiencing here. Then when we go into deep sleep and know nothing; then the dream state where everything is created spontaneously, which is not of this creation directly. Then the fourth state is the unconscious state when for some reason someone becomes unconscious and completely detached from all outer or inner connections. The fifth state is samadhi. Samadhi is also very much like deep sleep where there is no action being performed and yet consciousness is there—either savikalpa consciousness or nirvakalpa consciousness.

Turiya is something beyond this—it is unqualified and since it is unqualified it cannot be called a state of the individual, so it is not enumerated as one of the states. In Turiya there is no notion of any sort: It is the Absolute by himself; that is Turiya, and Turiya simply means singularity—oneness. It is also known as Brahmi, as described in the *Gita* by Sri Krishna. Turiya is acquired when sattva is predominant, and it is only through the predominance of sattva that the stillness is achieved. This stillness can be experienced in action, in samadhi, in meditation, in knowledge, in devotion—everywhere.

* * *

Q. His Holiness has spoken of meditation itself as yoga, practice of meditation as dharana, and the repetition of mantra as japa. Could he say more about it?

H.H. This is a journey of the individual consciousness [Vyashti] inward to the Universal Consciousness [Samashti, the Absolute]. One starts the mantra, and repeats the mantra, one initiates this at the level of the personality [the Vyashti], and then this repetition of the mantra is leading on to the bare thread of meditation which is the dharana. This movement is aimed at only one thing, and that is to cut out or diminish the activity—the rajas-involvement in life. Although it is known as the "practice of meditation" yet this "practice" is leading toward the end of all activity. Slowly and gradually this march toward non-activity takes place until one reaches the realm of union, which is stillness or unity of both outer and inner worlds. This is the experience of Self as universal; here there is no duality and there remains no *place* to move on to, and there is no *time* to change to, for He is the place, the time and also the substance. In that profound silence, stillness or yoga, all movements stop, and there is only "One without a second" and that is Atman Himself, the Observer.

This does not mean that all relationships and agitations would have disappeared from our inner universe, for it only indicates that there is no initiation of any agitation from the personality. We know that there are five levels of consciousness known as unconscious, sleep, dream, awake and samadhi. This particular state [Turiya], which we are considering, is unique and does not come under any one of the five "states of consciousness."

When one comes away from that state then one feels joyful, just as when one goes to see some great man one returns with indescribable joy and enthusiasm feeling that everything seems good, beautiful and pleasant. That state of yoga is devoid of all vikshepa, agitation, desire, need, ignorance, and is profoundly still, without any hankering, fully satisfied and complete in all respects.

Consistency

Dr.R. I am asking not for myself alone but because in Western cities, like London and New York, the cry from among our more experienced people is always for more sattva. They know very well by now that if they had abundant sattva, things would become right. How to answer this cry? Does it involve a way of living, reading Scriptures, helping each other, thinking of the realized man?

H.H. The sattva is described mostly as light—a light, which is a steady light. So one of the major manifestations of the presence of sattva, is this illumination in any type of work one takes on. If one finds one is afraid to tackle a new situation or one has doubts on certain types of subject, they instantly mean lack of sattva.

What can one do to change the situation so that there is abundance of sattva in one's being? The collection of certain good qualities is very essential. The good qualities are these:

1) One should always love to speak the Truth; so there is no disparity between what one thinks and what one says; or between what one says and what one does. There should be complete correspondence of ideas with activities.

2) Cultivate the love of people, encouraging them in turn to express their love through certain types of activity.

3) Be magnanimous in dealing with those around you, and the other things which come within the influence of a realized man.

With increase of those good qualities one would see that the sattva is increased.

One of the major factors is that Manas, Buddhi and Chitta must all come together and stand simultaneously. There should be no division between these three: that one should run on one line of action and the other should run on another line of action. So there must be complete unity of heart and mind and activity. It is only through these means that it is possible to increase sattva. And then one could see that whatever the situation[s], howsoever new they might seem to be, one would handle them with great patience and love, without putting a foot on any wrong lines at all.

* * *

Q. How can I have His Holiness's help to dive deeper?

H.H. There are three ways in which this help can be taken: The *first* one is within the field of activity, and quite a number of disciplines and of meditation practice have been given us for the physical body.

The *second* is in the realm of the subtle body or mind, through which one communicates whatever one has within. Whatever one feels, whatever one thinks, one communicates and tries to get further guidance which is, of course, being done here and now.

The *third* realm is of the Bhawana or the emotion. This is by far the most potent of the fields. In this field the aspirant gets inspiration—inspiration to move on the spiritual line. This is what usually takes one to the deeper levels.

To be on the deeper levels is to be in the purified states of these three types of function. So when the activity which one undertakes is entirely tuned into the Truth (that True Knowledge which has been given to one), then the physical activity will take one to the deeper levels. When the ideas, the True Knowledge, which is being imparted to the aspirant are held in their true and pure form without being adulterated with any other ideas or doubts, these then purify the mind and take it through to the deeper level.

This third way to the deeper level is the realm of emotion, and for that the meditation has been prescribed, and the more one does it properly, the deeper one goes. One comes to a state where there is no division in the act of meditation; then one will find oneself at the deeper level. It is only through these three ways that one can go deeper. Whatever one says, one should do; whatever one thinks, one should say; and whatever one feels, one should express.

* * *

Q. Yesterday His Holiness spoke of consistency at the end of the answer to a question. Is it this that can provide the thread of remembrance through the day and keep a little light in the darkness?

H.H. There is a Shloka in one of the Scriptures (*The Manusmriti* [*The Laws of Manu*]). The gist is that a good man who wants to go on the spiritual path speaks what he feels, and does what he speaks. That is, he speaks from pure feeling. When he has impure feelings, he tries not to speak or rush into action or express them. A bad man does the reverse: He *feels* something and *says* something else; he *says* something but *does* something else.

If one really did speak what one feels, and do exactly what one says, then this would build up the inner strength of the man and, because of this clarity and unity of his mind and sincerity of his heart, the way will be fairly clear for him.

There is an example from the life of Rama when he went to Janak-Puri. He was taking a stroll in the royal gardens and he happened to see Sita there. He had only Lakshman with him, so he said to Lakshman: "Why is it that I had a glimpse of this girl in the garden? The tradition of our great family (of Raghu—Raghu was the first king of this solar dynasty called Raghurvansha) is such that the men of this family should never have a glimpse of any woman unless he was destined to marry that woman. So it seems that this girl will be married to me."

This is the sort of purity one gets only if one follows pure feelings and expresses them in true words, and does exactly as one says. If one learnt this system, kept this consistency, then one would grow—one would become more serious and have more strength of character. This brings unity into a man and creates a sort of depth. To this unity and depth of the individual the glory of the Absolute descends and then manifests all around all that one knows of the glories of the Absolute.

Q. What you have said, does that signify a certain order of action? You mentioned twice: "beginning with feeling, and then speak what you feel and do what you say." Is this order important in this connection?

H.H. It is not only important, but necessary, for this is the ulti-

Consistency

mate thing that happens—it belongs to the pattern of nature. This is how things do happen, but by ignorance we do not follow this sequence, and complicate ourselves. Ordinary man—common man—does not go by this sequence. Men who want to go on the way should follow this sequence.

* * *

Q. When the Chitta is pure and is open to the Absolute, can it then be said that the causal body operates and controls the subtle and physical bodies?

H.H. When the Chitta is open to the Absolute it also happens that the Buddhi works according to the promptings of the Atman, and if this is the situation, then everything in the physical body, in the subtle body and the causal body works in response to one order, which means that whatever is done, whatever is said, whatever is thought conforms to one single idea—one order—and in that case, everything is right. Everything is controlled at causal level.

If it is only Manas and Ahankar giving the order to the individual, then it is probable that all the bodies will not fall in line, there will be disparity between what is thought, what is resolved, and what is said and what is done. When one sees that somebody is thinking about one thing, saying something else and doing something else, then this is the act of a man whose Chitta is not open to the Absolute, whose Buddhi is not working in conformity with reason, whose Manas is not following the dictates of Buddhi, nor does the body and the intellect. Here is a Sanskrit saying:

When the thoughts and utterings, whatever one says and does, follow the same thing, then these are the marks of a good man. If they do not correspond to each other, they are the marks of a bad man.

There is a good way to check if the Chitta is pure or not: When the Chitta is pure and the promptings come from the Atman, then the effect of the causal body on the subtle body, and the effect of the subtle body on the physical body is felt, and seen to be felt. But if it is the work of Ahankar and Manas, then there will be no effect on the physical body or the subtle body, rather the other way round: The physical body will affect the subtle body and so on. This is the way one can see if one is following the Atman or the Ahankar, whether the internal organs are pure or impure.

* * *

Q. Is greater consistency of behavior and action, on the three levels, something which can be learnt or is it a matter of being? Does the consistency take place when Buddhi is free from worldly entanglements?

H.H. Greater consistency of behavior and action is possible only by greater consistency and purity in Buddhi. Buddhi is the instrument by which we take decisions. But decisions can be followed by counter decisions. This is still done by Buddhi. It is powerful enough, or weak enough, to take a decision and discount it later on. This can be seen when we talk about worldly entanglements, which engage Buddhi constantly, and leave no opportunity for its purification through spiritual means. But if we have purified and cleaned our Buddhi, then all these decisions can be taken in worldly affairs without inconsistency and entanglement. It will be free and it will give you much more opportunity for consistency in your behavior and actions, with much more refinement.

Ultimately it will seem that we need to clean our Buddhi; because of its extensive use in everyday affairs, we seem to fall into grooves of decisions and these grooves are from Buddhi, but it is not activated. It can, however, be activated. It should be given enough data to consider what is necessary for a good and consistent decision on all levels of one's being. If you have not supplied your Buddhi with proper data and spiritual food, you cannot take a proper decision. If you see someone a long way off you may think that he is a friend. But as he comes closer you may find that he is not your friend. But a man who has learnt to see things properly waits a little, weighs up the information properly, decides once and for all what is right and reasonable, and then consistency follows.

Consistency

* * *

H.H. Every individual or society knows the truth within because it was discovered long ago and has been made available to everyone ever since then. Though the truth has always been proclaimed, it can hardly be said that this known truth has been put into practice properly. The proper way to act is to keep total unity and consistency between thought, word and deed (Manas, Vani, Karma). Thoughts, concepts, ideas, desires, aims, resolutions and ambitions must be spoken out exactly as they arise without any distortions or concealment. Thus one must speak out one's mind truthfully. If the mind is exposed truthfully, it does not matter what is there— others can take true positions in relation to the natural law, i.e., the truth. It should be understood that sanskars differ, and everyone can't always think of truth as it really is. But this is no hindrance. If the truth is spoken then others will either come to help and save the situation or take a proper stand. If injustice is involved, one will be taken to task and the injustice removed. If the desires and concepts are just, they will be met justly.

There is a further complication. When it comes to action most of what has been said is not what is enacted. The result is total confusion. People say A and do B. In this way there is no proper communication or contact with the individual or even with the voice of a society or religion. This is the cause of confusion from all sides. There is no meeting point, so there are obviously confrontation points. No one can reason because there is no reasonable man with whom to reason. All religions are victims of their own making. They want one thing, they say another, and to get their way they behave entirely against the natural law.

Everything about individuals, societies, nations, and religions these days is ambiguous; their thoughts are secret, their speech is secret, and their deeds are secret or deceptive. How can peace and happiness prevail when everything is deception? It is more so now than ever.

If people take to right thinking, right speaking and right action they will become mahatmas [saints], that is what every soul naturally is. Deception is possible by bypassing the Self and taking to secret ways, ignoring the Self. When the Self within is ignored, the man becomes duratma. (Mahatma is a great soul, duratma is a wicked creature!) Those who do not listen to the Self, which always knows the truth, create wars in the name of religion, nations, societies, cultures or civilizations. The Self is glorious by itself, it needs no transformation or improvement. All that is needed is to express it truly. If conformity and consistency can be brought between thought, speech and action, then the Self and its glory will be seen and enjoyed.

One may ask what is the reason for this situation? The first cause is greed. Things are limited but plentiful and sufficient for everyone to be shared on equal terms. But some people want to have more than others. This causes imbalance of desires and thoughts. Every greed is concealed by beautiful speech and deception. Those who lead societies, nations or religions want to secure their positions for eternity. So they try to create suitable machinery to support their position of power. If one has become Prime Minister, then he wants to remain there all his life, so many aspirants for the position are deprived. The third aspect is the Ahankar or ego. He thinks he is the best man available for the job, the wisest, cleverest and most efficient, and so no one else has the right or capacity for the best job. These three factors induce people to do away with consistency in thought, speech and action. This causes war. The use of deliberate misinterpretation together with hypocritical language creates confusion, and people are lured to kill each other.

Apart from what is happening in the Middle East, in India too the same situation is prevailing. People seeking political power use the term "secular" in a very deceptive manner from greed, power and pride. Secular implies equal respect for all religions, but in order to secure and preserve political powers they misuse it against the majority, which could be liberal or tolerant. But injustice by deception cannot last for long. There is a proverb which says that untruth cannot be hidden for too long, like cow dung in water cannot be hidden—it will float to the surface. When untruth is seen, then ordinary men who do not seek either profit or power will seek honest men. If they appear things will improve.

As long as consistency between thought, speech and action has not become part of human life, wars will keep on visiting humanity on a global scale, or on a national, social, family or personal scale. It is ultimately independence, freedom or Swatantra, which is the victim of greed, power and pride through inconsistency between thought, speech and action.

* * *

Q. When, for a while, ego is quiet and one's role is being naturally fulfilled, Love seems to be the unifying force, and discriminating mind seems to work within it. Is this the right relationship?

H.H. This is exactly what is meant by the "unity of thought and word and deed, when you think and say what you feel, and do what you say." This, again, is very much connected with the opening of the heart itself, and one penetrates into the stream of the Rasa, the Bliss, through which everything can be properly and nicely regulated, and one ceases to feel any difficulty in one's activities or one's relationship with people.

Discipline

Dr.R. Always before it was *we* who had to start the talks by putting our own questions. This time we asked if His Holiness had anything *he* wanted to say on this last morning. Is he satisfied with the progress during the month?

H.H. To bring about any development in the human race, discipline is necessary. Discipline cannot be given without a fully realized man. Connection with one who has himself realized the full possibilities is essential. Once a school gets this connection, then the possibilities are there for them also.

There are two kinds of possibility in such relations. The first is special *knowledge*, and the second is *doing*—putting that knowledge into practice. It takes very little time to know something; you can learn things in no time! But to acquire the capacity to put that knowledge into practice, needs a long time. It requires consciousness, patience, and of course numerous checks in confirmation as you go. Because if you hear something and continue acting on it, perhaps, you might not have fully understood the thing and have gone off line.

* * *

Dr.R. At Ram Negar some people were packing their bags and saying "Good-bye, forever," but I said I certainly have one more life to lead because of all the muddle and things left undone, and things to be put right. Which is right?

H.H. Told a story of Brahma, the teacher, who had two disciples Indra and Virochana. At first Brahma said to them that this body is Brahma, and Virochana thought, "Of course that is so." So he nourished the body and established a system based on body. But Indra had a doubt. He said, "Well, the body will die after some time, how could it be Brahma?" So he went back and put his question. The teacher said, "All right, I can give you the answer but you should stay here 30 years and follow the discipline." After 30 years he said that "Mind is Brahma," but when Indra had tried that, again he had doubt and went back, saying, "Well, it doesn't seem that mind can be Brahma, because when we sleep, we don't know the mind." "All right," said the teacher, "Thirty years more of discipline." At the end of that he said, "The Life Principle is Brahma." But this didn't satisfy Indra, so he had to do another 30 years. This time he was told, "Intelligence is Brahma," but he was again dissatisfied. After which Brahma said to him, "You should stay just 11 years more, making 101 years all told." So then because of this discipline which he underwent for 101 years, his mind, his Buddhi, his intelligence, had become very sharp, and his whole body so pure that he was able to get full realization of the final answer given by Brahma, who told him, "Brahma is what everybody knows and what nobody knows." And by repeating this Indra realized himself and Brahma also.

The discipline purifies the disciple; if somebody comes to a hasty conclusion, if he thinks that by a few words he has got realization, he is a fool and will get nowhere. But if another person gets things slowly, and by discipline then he is on the right path. The worthwhile realization is a slow way [digesting everything with deliberation], but the right way.

* * *

H.H. Experience of freedom is possible after proper understanding of the concept of freedom. Freedom in Sanskrit is Swatantra, which is a compound of "swa" and "tantra." *Swa* means self and *tantra* means discipline. Thus a free man is one who is self-disciplined. Self-discipline means that all those factors of one's physical, intellectual and emotional activities, which are not useful for the Atman, must be controlled by oneself and not by anyone else. Whatever is useful and good for the Self should be accepted and put into practice. Even if something is pleasant, if it is not useful for the Atman it must be rejected and controlled. There may be objects or actions, which are pleasant to the senses, profitable to the mind and conducive to a feeling of happiness for the present, but the result on a long-term basis is harmful to the Self, so they must be curtailed. Discrimination between useful and harmful to Atman arises from viveka and satsang. With the growth of self-discipline the latent powers of the Self manifest. This provides confidence and clarity, and one begins to act freely with natural measure. The opposite of Swatantra is Paratantra, dependence, when one does not have control of actions or discipline in oneself. When sensory pleasures, temporary gains, sense of power and devotion for the sake of future inheritance motivates one's actions, then one is not free but dependent. Such a person has no sense of measure. Therefore one who has developed the capacity to refrain from useless actions in ignorance, and naturally goes for measured and just actions in the light of the Self, is a free man. His actions do not leave a mark behind to be cleaned later.

* * *

H.H. One has to be always on the alert and not allow everything to happen as they want. This is down the stream. The way of development needs watching and discipline. If one has lost his opportunity of the company of good men or discipline, one may as well let oneself loose to suffer for long. The human form is the platform where discipline is available; miss your chance and you go on repeating the same miserable life in eternity. The mind [Manas] thinks that the world is true and likes to live with it in ignorance. This is illusion, and to cure this illusion the discipline is prescribed. Now even *this discipline shouldn't be taken to be true!* The Truth is that one really is Atman and the Absolute, but one doesn't know this secret because of ignorance. Once you realize your real Self, the discipline also becomes useless. If you have a thorn in the foot, you take it out with the help of another thorn and throw both thorns away after use! So in some way even the discipline is illusion, but this illusion only will undo the fundamental illusion of ignorance.

There was a dhobi [washerman]. He used many donkeys to carry his load. One day he fell ill and asked his son to load the donkeys and take them with the washing. He loaded them and tried to move them toward the river but they didn't budge an inch. Seeing they weren't tied up at all, he was surprised at what happened and went to ask his father. The father said, "Oh, I should have told you this also. In the evening I touch their feet as if I am trying to bind them with a rope; and in the morning, I touch them again as if I have undone them." The boy also did the same, and then each donkey started to move. The fact is that the donkeys all thought that they were not freed and therefore they couldn't walk! So is the condition of all human beings. The ignorance is illusory, and to remove this one must undergo another illusion in order to realize one's real state; but this is very essential and one has no choice to evade it.

The Absolute creates the creation when He looks outward. When He is looking within no creation takes place. So the creation is outward bound and, due to the nature of creation, body, mind and Buddhi become outward bound too. Discipline turns them toward the "within." In Self it is all Bliss, Consciousness and Truth.

* * *

Dr.R. Now it is a question of not resting anywhere unless one reaches the goal. His Holiness has given us wonderful material. How best could we present it in the West to let them profit from it?

H.H. This work should be done in moderation. The people who take the responsibility to further this knowledge and the discipline must be sincere with themselves and others and also completely honest with themselves and all around them. Tell only as much as you know and what you have experienced. Never try to say anything more than that. If help would be sincerely needed, the Inner Circle is always there to give help. In an organization, the greatest trouble arises when to support the truth they resort to subjective glorification of truth, they make it look glittering to fulfill their ambition to spread the Truth. Such organizations don't do much good and crumble down in time according to the glitter they apply. No show business, no glitter and no quick work is required. Take the work patiently, practice what you are told, then tell to those who earnestly want it. Keep your relations with them completely honest. This is the sure way to success.

* * *

H.H. In the Eighteenth Chapter of *Bhagavad Gita* Shri Krishna tells Arjuna about the sattvic, rajasic and tamasic activities and their result. The sattvic activities are painful in the beginning because of discipline—unless the discipline becomes natural. The pain is only felt by body, senses, mind and Buddhi. The result of these activities is eternal pleasure to all and Bliss to Atman.

For example, infants find it difficult to learn the alphabet and they look around at the walls and sky, or scratch the ground because they find it difficult. Once they have learned the language, reading and writing is an unending source of pleasure. A disciple has to train his body, senses, mind and Buddhi to conform to the discipline and it is painful indeed, but leading toward pleasure and bliss!

* * *

Dr.R. How may one become free of the effects of the three gunas?

H.H. One can never be free of the three gunas, but one can acquire a situation where gunas don't matter. Our life exists because of these three gunas, and absence of any will disrupt our existence. The creation has two partners, Atman and matter. They are all mixed. Common men can't see the difference, as one can't see butter in milk. When you churn and process the milk then the butter comes out, and you can leave that butter in the buttermilk and will see that it floats.

Discipline is the churning process in [the] life of a disciple. Once he is thoroughly processed his Atman comes out clean, and then it never gets mixed again. One has to live in the world of gunas, but one can learn to float over it and not be affected. A doctor never gets sick because he sees a sick person. He diagnoses the disease and prescribes a medicine and leaves it happily. So [does] a realized man: [He does] everything with the gunas and still keeps aloof.

Q. We consider our thoughts as our own, but are they really part of the passing show into which we tap, picking up the influences. I feel they are not our own.

H.H. It is true that much of what one presumes to be one's own thoughts is derived externally from the Samashti, the passing show of the universe, and it is influenced by the samskars, which make a cover over the Antahkarana. But as well as this there is much that is the Self. The universe is not outside the Self, for it has come to exist through the Self. Therefore, it is equally possible to have one's own thoughts.

External and internal influences do shape one's thoughts, but only if Buddhi is weak and immature. In order to get rid of their unwanted influence one needs discipline. If the discipline is followed properly by discussing material provided to the groups, and through meditating regularly and properly, one's Buddhi ought to become mature: [It ought to] be able to judge the usefulness of every floating thought, concept or principle, and to accept whatever is useful to spiritual development, leaving the rest. When Buddhi has become pure then all external and internal influences are properly analyzed and made use of, or new thoughts can be created to overcome difficulties or to make further progress.

Agriculture is a good example. In farming, the field is prepared by clearing and preparing the soil. Fertilizers are applied to make the soil more productive and then the seed is sown. When germination takes place new shoots spring up, but not all of them are the seed sown. Many weeds also grow and they grow faster than the crop. The farmer goes into action to pull out the weeds so that his crop can grow properly. Later on a few more little weeds will come up, but they are stifled by the strength of the crop. This weeding out, which in us is either internal or external, is necessary. Similarly in spiritual life there are internal thoughts from samskars and external thoughts from society, family, religion or bad company. They must be rooted out while disciplined and spiritual thoughts must be nourished. For this Buddhi must be mature, through viveka or reason, to eliminate all attachments and hatred. The light of Atman is always available for creative purposes apart from gathering true knowledge from outside.

* * *

Dr.R. We have to tighten up the aim and the practice and effort each person puts into it during the day, rather than from a superimposed tightening up of externally imposed discipline. We want to remain liberated people and not be bound by a rigid system of rules and regulations.

From now on there's no such word as *can't* in relation to Self-realization. People say they can't meditate. It's absolute bosh! If they stood to get a thousand pounds for meditating twice a day, they would do it quite easily!

People say they can't stop turning thoughts during a meditation—bosh! Stop them. Come away from them. There's nothing we can't do in that respect.

We can't change the world; we can't change history or anything, but we can carry out the simple things that go toward Self-realization.

We can do something useful in line with the Param Atman. There's never a moment when we cannot do something; but this discipline must come from inside, it cannot be imposed by an external organization, and it comes through love. When realizing that we have nothing of our own, all doors open to us.

* * *

Dr.R. We want to try to carry with us on return to London the lovely inner peace and clarity of mind, which we enjoy in H.H.'s presence. Is there any special *self-applied* discipline that he would recommend—for instance, control of restless and involuntary movements at times when rajas comes instead of sattva?

H.H. At such times there is only one thing to be recommended and that is love of Atman, love of the Self within. Having achieved love for the Atman, all that which is non-Atman, which is apart from Atman, will be set aside because it will not be so attractive, and if the worldly things, which are non-Atman, non-Self, have lost their attraction, then one will find inner peace and clarity of mind and restfulness. Sattva is certainly for the light through which all the energy is made possible, and having acquired some light and energy one must use it in some activity. Having used energy in activity one must also go into tamas to get oneself charged so that one can begin the next day.

* * *

Dr.R. I felt a wave of confidence at the end of this meditation. After all, what are we worrying for? In truth we are not separate from one another, not separate from the realized man and therefore from Atman. The clouds seem to melt away when one remembers that.

H.H. He is blessed who has that confidence. It is a grace. It is the outcome of all our efforts on the way and the mercy of God. Here in India, having all this available tradition, much of it in its natural surroundings, only one out of millions awakes to be attentive and walk on the path. If in the West where distractions are multifarious [and] life is full of material attractions, a group of people have risen to avail themselves of this confidence, it must be wonderful. This is very valuable. Those who come out for discipline, and with their effort awake, and find this confidence, eventually exercise their proper influence in uplifting the masses. They are the blessed.

* * *

H.H. Dr. Roles was a very liberal and universal man with an open mind. His devotion toward the discipline and meditation was great. He was constantly working toward realization of the fullness of the Self, always trying to find the way to the ocean of bliss. This same spirit of enquiry and the constant practice of this discipline are needed by every member of the Society.

Drama

H.H. The basic nature is pervading everything, and once we start experiencing it in all things, then you will be able to enjoy it whatever your circumstance. So the main use of the intellect [Buddhi] is that it should be used in seeing, observing, and feeling the all-pervasiveness of that perfect nature just as when you see a tree, then your Buddhi should be able to convey to you that the basic nature which is in me is also in the tree.

It is another matter that this basic nature is making its appearance in different forms. In a creeper it is tender, in a stone it is hard, in the leaves of the tree it is green, in the translator it is in another form. The form may be different but the basic nature is the same. So when your Buddhi sees or appreciates this fact of the all-pervasiveness of nature, then in your everyday life, your normal duties, you will be able to enjoy the circumstances in which you are placed. Here is a story from the scriptures.

At one time there was a demon known as Rakshu, who was fighting with Indra. At one stage of the fight when he was distracted, Indra's sword slipped out of his hand. Being disarmed, he was afraid that Rakshu would kill him. At this point Rakshu stopped, and said: "Don't worry! It is all a theatrical affair that we are fighting, and you have been given this job to fight me, so pick up your own sword again and then we will go on fighting. You needn't be afraid."

So it is with the sort of feeling that, when it develops, one will find that in whatever circumstances one is placed, one will realize that this is all a play, and if one realizes it is all theater—a drama— then whether an enemy comes before you or a beloved one comes before you, you will be able to behave as you should behave in that particular occasion, and your Buddhi will not misguide you. You will be guided correctly.

H.H. To be "natural" is to be straight and pure and, if one achieves this, then one is certainly "natural"; but being natural should not be taken to mean that one should be crude or naked.

The whole creation, after all, is a drama, a play; and the whole play has to be performed in a particular style and manner. There is a role for each actor, a costume for each actor, positions and actions for each actor, and lines for him to speak. Unless an actor wears the costume designed for his role; [and] if he doesn't use the lines written for the part, then he will not affect the audience in the way the producer intends. So, if the play is to be performed it must be done in the right way to produce the required effect on the audience and give them the pleasure which the play is designed to produce. To respond to the appropriate dress, the proper language, and the proper distance between the audience and the players, is also a part of the "natural" presentation of the play.

When one says, that "one has to be natural," therefore, one must keep this in mind, and keep the right distance from anyone with whom one has to establish a relation. What one has to watch is that one's performance should not get crooked or artificial; *one should not elaborate*, but do only what is necessary. If we learn to keep to this, then our role will be well-played and the whole play will be recognized by us as "true to nature."

* * *

Q. In the Producer's directions for the drama of life, how much scope is left for individual improvisation?

H.H. Every actor is created as free and independent to do whatever he likes—to act the way he wants. There is no bondage or compulsion of any sort, because all individuals are given basically all the power and authority and glory of the Absolute, to use in whatever act they are designed to perform.

What the Absolute has reserved for Himself, as the producer of the play, is the right to reward the actor, to offer him extra remuneration, to praise the actor or to reprimand him and even punish him if he has not acted properly. So, although freedom is there for the individual either for improvisation or depredation, nevertheless the result is not in the hands of the actor. That follows from the Producer, in this case the Absolute.

* * *

H.H. Attachment means to consider as ours what really belongs to Param Atman: our body, our house, our wealth, our son, etc. Give up this feeling and get rid of all troubles. Do not think that the world around you, i.e., your house, your money, your body, etc., are unsubstantial. Rather it is your feeling of attachment to them that is unsubstantial. Whatever is happening around you is right. But what is wrong about it is the view you are taking of it. If you could correct your viewpoint, you would be happy. The world is a great show, which God is staging around you in the shape of the universe; but it is a mere show. Your birth is a show, your death is a show. Actually there is neither birth nor death. Know that and you would be happy. The common outlook is that the world is everything and that Param Atman is nothing. It is a crime to hold this view and the punishment for it is to be imprisoned in this physical body. You cannot be happy while undergoing a term of imprisonment. Our mind has the property of thinking of something or other all the time. It cannot remain idle. If it doesn't remember the Param Atman, it thinks of the world. Remembering the Param Atman leads to happiness, and thinking of the world leads to unhappiness. It is true that people do not find it easy to hold the Param Atman in mind and the reason for that is lack of practice. As long as the ability has not been acquired there will be difficulty. But the ability can certainly be acquired. You have a mind. You have a body. And you have intelligence. Let the mind be trained to remember the Param Atman; let the body do service to Him; and let the intelligence discriminate.

* * *

H.H. The Creator created the universe in all its different aspects and forms. He observes the drama which He has created. All who take part in this play and know its mystery and essence are detached. They play their part and enjoy it. Those who do not know its mystery become identified with their parts and are bound by them. When they lose their identification they too can enjoy playing their part in the grand drama without being bound.

There was a man from the country who visited his city relatives. To entertain him, the relatives took him to the cinema. They bought expensive tickets for the back row, but their country cousin was insulted at being put at the back. He insisted that they sit in the very front. All went well until suddenly a lion appeared on the screen and looked as if it would jump at the audience. Our friend took his stick and struck at the lion to defend himself. The screen was broken, the film stopped, and the place was thrown into darkness and confusion. At first no one could understand what had happened; then they realized that in the audience was a man who had never been to a cinema before and took the film to be real.

The same applies to those ignorant people who regard what goes on in the world as real and become identified and involved leading to foolish actions; when the real significance of the grand drama is known these people can play their part with detachment from themselves and enjoyment.

* * *

Q. May I return to the great drama of the Creator. Are there any roles which are particularly difficult to play, and if they are played with detachment do the actors get a special reward?

H.H. This play is a pleasant play—there are no difficult parts. Difficulties are when actors take the play to be real through ignorance. Then even ordinary acts become big and terrifying and cause fright and pain. If the act is pleasurable, then these ignorant actors become infatuated by the pleasure.

* * *

H.H. The natural state of the Atman is peace and bliss. From this grew desire, and so creation began with action and expansion. Action and desire form the two poles between which creation rises and falls, so that the eternal peace can be manifest in different ways. There is a new drama every time one is completed. Those actors who are detached play their parts in peace; those who are identified experience suffering. The spiritual exercises which have been given and which we now discuss are for those who take the drama for real. They offer a way of escape from the bondage of the parts through detachment. With the first act of creation the Absolute provided for those who would become identified and who went against the natural way. He provided this system so that they could recover detachment. This system is therefore not man-made.

Dr.R. Would you tell us some more about the idea of the drama of creation as a means of developing non-attachment?

H.H. The Creator starts the creation as a play with the help of Maya. The relationship of the Creator and Maya is the same as the relation of an individual [Atman] to ignorance. The ignorance is a shadow of Maya, just as the individual is a reflection of the Absolute. The Absolute plays with Maya and knows it to be play and thus amuses Himself; the individual doesn't know that because of ignorance. So he has to take recourse to knowledge [True Knowledge]. With this True Knowledge—which is again all about Maya —he gets to know Maya. Then he understands that all that play in the universe is only a drama. The knowledge of this is True Knowledge. In the moving aspect of our Chitta [Consciousness] and because of the impurities around it, Chitta is deprived of that Knowledge. Lakshman saw the impurity and speed of Chitta in his dip.

* * *

Q. What kind of physical action could engage the attention and imagination of all good men toward harmony and instruction from above in the same way as war does when it is necessary to fight evil for survival? Can any peaceful venture unite society toward harmony when material prosperity keeps it spiritually idle and blind?

Drama

H.H. The Creation is complete all the time in peace and in war too. Even war is a play, a drama of the Absolute organized by divine forces and un-divine forces, and the Absolute enjoys the drama without being attached to either of them. War comes because evil forces become dominant, and to keep up the balance the good and just forces also get united to stop evil. War is a lesson for the ignorant not to do such and such or to take the consequences; but for a wise man it is nothing more than a drama and he takes his place as the situation requires. To try to bring about a situation or organize good men toward harmony as in war is a mere fantasy. The wise man always looks toward the Self. Improve your own being and the rest will be done.

* * *

Q. The remembrance of Param Atman during the day is an increasing comfort, and nowadays everything is more pleasant. Even unpleasant things seem less important than before. However, one feels on a dreamy plateau where, because of the pleasant life, the *need* to keep moving on the path is less sharp. One is not complaining about the increased happiness, but though one feels the greater presence during the day, one's meditation does not seem deep enough and one seems more caught in a dreamy phase. Can His Holiness advise?

H.H. One of the fundamental characteristics of life on this earth is the worldly illusion of being the independent doer—of having free will. It is very difficult to maintain that individuals are the doers of anything, for the whole creation is a manifestation of the Absolute who is the real Doer. He has made His whole show in such a beautiful pattern that it keeps changing from one moment to another, and must keep on multiplying also. The whole thing is going on by virtue of the creative impulse given by the Absolute; He is the independent one, He is the free one, and He is the real Doer.

* * *

H.H. The reason people get involved and try to get away from religion and spiritual activity is that they consider this misery to be real and ultimate. They find that it has no place in creativity. But the tradition we have been given derives its origin from Narayan [Vishnu] himself and teaches that all creation is a play, a drama. Whenever we go into a theater and see drama with actors performing, some may be wailing or crying, some may be beaten, some may be laughing, but in reality they do not cry, none of them really feel the pain of being beaten, and they are not necessarily unhappy or happy. It is all a scene being played efficiently, or inefficiently, by these actors. Once we get the concept that this whole creation is an act or a drama, then we enjoy it; we get detached and everything falls into proper perspective.

Some people like to eat sweets. In order to be able to take more sweets, it is a very curious fact of life that they take the opportunity to eat bitter and sour things so that their sweet taste is once again enlivened to allow them to eat more sweets. They want sweets, but in order to have more sweets, they resort to bitter and sour tastes. Now, this bitterness and sourness are considered to be misery by some people. In fact, they are just one of the various tastes.

Once you know that this is a drama and that everybody has to enjoy this, then you do not call it misery. If you call it misery, then you will find that even Indra, who is the Lord of this Universe, the Brahma, the creator of this universe, also has certain miseries and worries at his own level. Even so, from that point of view there is nowhere in the whole of creation where this doesn't occur. Either you can accept it as blissful or miserable; it depends on how you place yourself in relation to this drama. If you are attached to the drama, if you think it is real, then the general picture is of misery. If you are detached, if you think it is a drama, and there is a part to be played by you, then it is all blissful. Everyone in this creation is destined to die, to disintegrate one day, and this is the biggest fear in the lives of all beings, even Indra, because he will have to leave the place for another Indra. But once you accept it as drama, then it is only changing the part and there is no misery involved. There is a story, the inside story of the creative world.

Brahma is supposed to be the creator or our universe, or perhaps all different universes. Once it occurred to him that he is a very busy man and he works very hard and he needs a holiday and a rest. He went to Brahman[†] and put his application to be released for a little while. Brahman accepted it and released him. When he [Brahma] came out of the creative realm he saw thousands of people standing at the gate. He wanted to find out who they were, particularly as they all looked like Brahma himself. He went to ask them, and one of them said, "We are not allowed to disclose our identity." But he persisted, wanting to know what the crowd was there for. One of them relented and said, "We are all applicants for the position of the Brahma. When a Brahma retires one of us will be elected and promoted, and all the others will have to keep standing in the waiting area." Seeing this he got frightened and immediately turned back and went to Brahman again and requested him to cancel his leave as he was now ready to work. One of the attendants of Brahman said, "Do not consider yourself too big; this creation is multiple, there are myriads of creations and myriads of Brahma waiting to take over each creation. There is no end to it, you are just one little speck out of all these clouds of drama."

Seeing this picture, one can understand that the whole creation is too big and that the whole thing is nothing but a drama. We ought to accept it as a drama so that we don't get involved too much with the miseries or denounce religion or spiritual world.

[†]Brahman-Prajapati (?) [teacher of the Gods].

Emotion

Q. When a doctor is dealing with serious or difficult diseases, he becomes very concerned with the result he is trying to achieve. How to get over this dilemma?

H.H. Atman is, in fact, surrounded by three bodies, physical, subtle and causal; and all the three bodies are inter-related. On the *physical level* there is a healthy state and a state of many diseases. On the *subtle level* of the mind, there are also diseases caused by wrong points of view as well as those resulting from physical disease. In fact, ultimately, all the physical diseases owe their origin to something wrong on the level of the mind.

Bad emotions further can come through the "emotional center" (Bhawana) in the *causal body* [something very like what we have called the Higher Emotional Center]. The ailments of the subtle and causal level must be treated according to their own levels. The "emotional center" is not only "feeling" but also is close to the seat of pure cognition of Truth (viveka—which seems to be the Higher Intellectual Center). Physical illness must be treated by the appropriate physical means; mental illnesses by good ideas and improved attitudes and ways of thinking; and the causal by fine emotions and emotional truths.

[He then gives a simile which can be applied to all three levels]. There are two kinds of patient, the one with a physical illness who takes the prescription or recommendation with a smile and in good faith; and there is the other kind of patient who puts up a resistance to the treatment, and this negativeness hinders the process of healing. These people must be treated mentally as well as being given physical treatment.

There was a millionairess from Delhi who suffered from diabetes. She was very fond of sweets. These she used to obtain secretly from her servants. This was unknown to her doctor and her family, who became very concerned, because the more her doctor treated her, the worse she became because of the secret eating of sweets. A new doctor was called who visited her before breakfast and examined her and suspected that something was in her stomach, though she denied having eaten anything. Her relative also said she had no food for three days. But in fact she arose early and obtained more sweets from the servants and ate them.

The new doctor still suspected she had something in her stomach. By persistent questioning of the servants, he found the true state of affairs and so was able to put the matter right.

As for the dilemma, there is none! If one attends to one's work, the result takes care of itself; for the result is bound only to attention while at work.

* * *

Q. I was very interested to hear yesterday about the causal body and Bhawana. Could H.H. say more to explain this which was new to me?

H.H. The causal body is known as the inner instrument [Antahkaran] which you have heard about. In Antahkaran, all these four components are jointed together—synchromeshed; it is a single unit, and there is no division in Antahkaran as such. These four parts are for the subtle body where they have to take certain types of action.

This unit of the Antahkaran is the source of Bhawana, out of which come the attitudes underlying different types of desire. These desires first arise in Manas [the body-mind mechanism]; it is the Manas which arouses the desire. But any desire is always supported by a certain emotional attitude—attitudes of liking or disliking, good or bad. So whenever a given person has a given desire, he takes his attitude to it from the Antahkaran which gives it a particular color, the color that is in his Antahkaran. Manas has no particular color of its own, but it picks it up from the causal body where everything is united. If it is governed by rajas or tamas or sattva, whatever the color may be, that will be followed by Manas.

Between an activity and its consideration by Buddhi [intellectual discrimination] leading to a judgment as to right or wrong, there is an emotional state which is known as Bhawana—this emanation from the causal body. Manas resorts to activity, whereas Buddhi considers whether [it is] right or wrong; and besides these the heart stands as an impartial judge, as in court cases brought by a solicitor and argued by counsel. All that which is stored is certainly stored in Chitta [the memory store]. There you have these four.

* * *

H.H. How to alter the situation that we suffer from? Only the *strong desire for purity* can change things. If the desire is strong, then some movement toward sattva is possible. If the desire is weak, our efforts will be weak. So the key to transformation of muddy substance into pure, is the intensity of the desire for purity and simplicity.

The colors which he mentioned that are added to the bottle are related to the desires of the mundane world. The more you entertain those desires of the mundane world, the more muddy and cloudy the water [mind] will become. The mud, the turbulence, and the colors which come into play are one's desires, but are subject to movement. It means they come and go. To get them out can be done only through this sattva, pure reason (viveka) and the study of truth.

All the turbulence can go. [It] can easily be removed to restore the light of Atman shining through the purity and tonality of Buddhi, purity of Manas, and Chitta and Ahankar; so to clear these things one needs to have strong desire.

Dr.R. Would not this require a change of the emotional attitude that lies behind the desires—which he spoke of in connection with Bhawana?

H.H. The emotional attitude or push is very essential to make the desires strong. All these will come within the compass of the activity of Manas. So this emotional attitude will also be essential.

[*Translator* asks for clarity as to the relation between Bhawana and the other four contained in Antahkaran.]

H.H. These four divisions of Antahkarana manifest in the subtle body in two places. One center is felt in the heart, the other center in the head. Two of these four are felt to be stationed in the heart—the Bhawana and the Chitta. The thinking processes and Buddhi, and the sense of "I" are stationed in the head. The Consciousness reflected in Chitta and the emotional part are centered in the heart. The strength of the heart is greater than the strength of the head. If someone has held something very deadly to his heart—the reason can do little to dislodge this; merely thinking it is right or wrong changes nothing.

Say you like [a particular] food, but you know it is not useful for your body and yet you refuse to accept the dictates of reason and take the food which you love. This always emanates from the heart —which Chitta pervades. If something is held by Chitta dearly, it will not leave quickly.

It will leave if the Buddhi matures with sattva. If sattva prevails, the mind and heart work together hand-in-hand. If they do not work hand-in-hand, there must be a scarcity of sattva, and rajas and tamas have in some way taken over.

So the decision of any person who is full of sattva will always be clear and without any doubt today or tomorrow.

He again mentioned the story of the Delhi millionairess. Though she knew that it wasn't going to help her, she succumbed to her desires because of the Chitta.

* * *

Q. Is it the melting of the heart, that he spoke of to Dr. Roles, that clears out the rubbish to make room for the important ideas?

H.H. Yes, certainly your observation is right. Whenever by good company and good discourse and reason we allow the heart to melt, by the melting of the heart this rubbish is cleared, for melting of the heart simply means the disintegration of impurities. Thus the good influences will crystallize in the heart and stay with the individual.

Q. One feels to enable this to happen one needs a certain humility which some pride in one prevents one. Although the mind tells you this is what is necessary, you can't do it for yourself.

H.H. Yes, humility is very essential for this melting of the heart. As has been previously told there are two types [of people], one predominantly intellectual and one predominantly emotional. With predominantly emotional types it is fairly easy to melt the heart.

Melting the heart is in fact bringing the heart to its natural state. Nothing in fact really happens because impure Ahankar has no reality. It's only the idea of it which exists. Once the good ideas from satsang take their place whatever we think of as impure Ahankar is lost automatically and illusion is gone—the illusion of the Ahankar. Melting of the heart clears the heart and brings it to its natural state, so it should be fairly easy for those who are emotional. For the intellectuals it is a bit difficult because you have got to answer their questions to the end. Only when they are satisfied can their heart melt, because the activity of the mind and the heart are two different things. Heart can take the Bhawana, that is emotion, but the head can take only the idea which is not emotional. So to bring the intellectual to the emotional state where his heart can melt, you have got to answer his questions and tackle them thoroughly and well so that he has no further questions. As long as questions remain, the heart may not melt.

The difference between the pure Ahankar and the impure Ahankar can be described in this way:

We have a body and this body usually has a shadow. In fact this shadow has no independent existence. It is produced because there is some physical source of light which by the laws of nature create a shadow. Whatever movement you make your body will be reflected in the shadow also. But this shadow has no existence of its own, it is not independent. It is dependent on your body and the source of light outside your body, which is in this case the sun or a lamp.

In the light of the Self there is no shadow of anything. If you derive knowledge of your own experience that will be light of the Self.

* * *

H.H. Practice and discipline always lead toward Truth and purification [refinement].To Dr. Roles: You are predominantly emotional. But this has to go hand-in-hand with discourses and knowledge of Truth, by which emotional center [Bhawana] and intellectual center [viveka] are brought together. Only then is it possible that a person would move on the Way easily and with precision. That is why it is essential that discourses must take place to clear out any errors in the mind or anything not fully understood. True Knowledge is the only means to free one from any doubt, or whatever could arise, as a setback on the way of Liberation.

* * *

Dr.R. You said to me yesterday: "But emotion has to go hand-in-hand with discourses and Knowledge of Truth, when Bhawana (Pure Emotion) and viveka (Pure Intellect) are brought together."

Do you mean that the discourses with realized man will correct the mistaken ideas which have taken root in our Buddhi?

H.H. The end of the Way is the same—Self-realization. As we have been told there are two lights, the emotional light or Bhawana and intellectual light or viveka. It is possible that people might traverse to the end by either Way. But it is very possible that there will be certain desires for further inquiry left hidden in the being, about the other Way. To satisfy such inquiries it is essential that the disciple must work on both of these lines, the line of viveka, and the line of Bhawana. Particularly for a person who is destined to be the leader of a group, it is very essential; because there will be a hundred-and-one cases of different types which he will have to tackle in order to give them a lead. So for a leader it is very essential that he should have both ways running together.

Dr.R. We still do not understand just where Bhawana fits into the scheme of things. Is it on the causal level alongside of Antahkaran, or with Chitta felt in the heart [part of subtle level]? My need is really to understand the relation of Bhawana to Antahkarana.

H.H. Yesterday we were told about the two centers, the heart and the head; in the heart appear the Chitta and the Manas, and Bhawana springs from these two. All the desires or the doubts are raised by the Manas. The first glimpse of the desire is first glimpsed by the Manas. It comes in collaboration with the Chitta, Chitta being the store [Memory] of all the knowledge and everything a man can call his capital. But this relation of Bhawana is not a constant and smooth process. Sometimes it is abundant and all in one direction, and sometimes it is very scanty; just as one sees the ocean, there are waves small and big. But this is how the nature of Chitta works.

* * *

Dr.R. What I seem to need in order to transform both the meditation half-hours and my daily life is the prema and shradda which stem from Bhawana. Last year you quoted the prayer of the great poet Tulsidas: "Please by your Grace let my nature be sattvic and with complete balance. Only then will I be able to worship you!" This is my own prayer as well.

H.H. This is by no means a unique situation. Many people who get to know something about Truth or goodness are drawn toward it and try to improve. The majority of them come to attend bhajan, kirtan, recitations and other types of worship. Some are more sincere than others, but propelled by this forceful nature and habit they do the same wrong again and again. Some of them find their way into ashrams also; take to discipline [system] and practice austerities; perform rituals and meditate; but when the real time to stand by the truth or "discipline" comes, they give way to their nature and fall. They repent, pray for forgiveness, even shed tears, take penance and again do the same. Such is their nature.

In Dehradun, in an ashram, an old woman of 80 used to go for satsanga. She would merge herself in bhajan and kirtan, do all other work of the ashram; she seemed a good devotee and was treated as such. But she had a habit of stealing from childhood. One day she stole the alarm clock and then pretended to search, acclaimed horror for satsangi who stole it and made such a show that no one could ever think of her being the thief. Anyway, the satsanga started and very soon the alarm went off. She was right in the front row, and the clock was recovered from her handbag!

Such people are plentiful for they are everywhere. However much practice and "discipline" they do, things turn back to the same point unless this Prakriti is changed. Change is possible only when there is a real desire for change; there must arise one paramount desire for Truth which will permeate this Prakriti and transform it. A real desire is that for which one would not stop anywhere short of fulfillment.

Prakriti, being the basis of the individual, is the most subtle of all causes of motivation. The coarse and subtle aspects of our life can be erased by "disciplines" of physical or intellectual type, but to remove the most subtle nature hidden very deep in one's being is, of course, very hard. This is that most refined sort of sweet longing which lies very low and springs up only at odd moments when one may not be too vigilant. This alone is the cause for all those disciples who don't get real bliss in their devotional work. Here reason fails, but a strong desire can succeed.

A patient may be attended by a good doctor, and good medicine may be prescribed with a regulated diet and all the rest; but if the patient secretly manages to fall for a taste which he can't resist, then all this work will be useless. Here only the patient will have to help himself and by a strong desire to stay with the medicine [that] will help him. Unless he conquers himself, no other outer agency can be of such use—like our story of the millionairess who used to eat sweets and never got cured.

Q. Having come to this conclusion that there is a strong love for a certain thing which keeps one away from purification of Prakriti; if the individual can't do it himself, although he desires to and works for it, and yet he *can't*; then can any other agency be helpful in this matter?

H.H. All possible help can be given up to the limit of Buddhi, but this is beyond Buddhi; and is next to the Atman. All impulses and emanations of Atman start from that point and are affected by it.

Outer help stops after Buddhi. There the individual is alone; he must drop it himself. No other agency can do anything there, not even Grace. Only the Self can grace it.

Dr.R. One is greatly helped if one's faith [shradda] is pure and complete. I have perfect faith in the Shankaracharya, Guru Deva, my own teacher and the great men, but what I lack is faith in my own Buddhi or Prakriti. Above those is the Atman in whom again I have faith. But this lack of faith in my nature hampers me all the time. If I get some access to self-confidence, it is taken by the wrong thing, the Ahankara, and I fall. I believe if I could somehow get more faith in the heart, everything will be transformed.

H.H. The cause of the lack of faith is also the same. This is the last post of transformation. After having felled all other posts, when the aspirant comes to the last and can't cut it down, then he gets into a frenzy. He can't be blamed, for he acts only from deep habit. He even becomes angry with his helpers. He criticizes even the Absolute "for being All-powerful, merciful Absolute, why can't He help transform his Prakriti?" Even Tulsidas [the great poet] when forced by his habits would break "discipline," then in great anger he would complain that "his Lord being All in All, and on whom he entirely depends, does not come to help him." The principle is this: That *only by long practice alone*, could this last post be burned by the fire of matured "discipline." This does not go away by any outside force, just as if you pluck out weeds they grow again until you take out all of the root hidden deep down in the ground. By long persistent practice of "disciplined" work the deep roots of Prakriti are burned slowly, and when they are burned completely, then one easily understands the uselessness of habit. But frustration and anger with helpers and friends exists only as long as the Prakriti is still there. The ultimate work is only up to the individual, to decide once for all that he is going to love only the Truth and leave the rest, and he must stand by it. Only then is the transformation possible.

* * *

Q. I just feel very lucky to be here with Dr. Roles, and I remember what His Holiness said at the beginning of our last visit, when He spoke about "catching the spiritual influences which are available here." I feel I would like to make best use of the time to do this. Could His Holiness say more about this, although I realize he has partly answered it this morning?

H.H. The questions and answers must certainly be carried through before the mind can come to rest; so the individual's questions must be exhausted far enough, at least for him to be free from the load of them. That must be done, and be done carefully.

But apart from this, there is the Chitta ["reflected Consciousness"] of the individual which could give him Bhawana—a state of pure emotion, one aspect of which is "faith." So, if one is full of faith, i.e. connected with this Bhawana or pure emotion, then one's state is charged with certain magnetic qualities and this is common to everyone. (Faith, that is, not in men but in the benevolent and omnipresent Self.)

In certain individuals this influence is more powerful than others; but, having come into contact with it, one simply needs to allow this magnetic force to work without impediment. Then it will attract these charged particles from the atmosphere.

When this happens one will be impelled to seek more of this influence and store it, so that one experiences a deeper relationship with the Unity around, and this is what His Holiness prescribes. One should just let the influence come into one's experience [through penetrating this "cloud of unknowing"].

* * *

H.H. Chitta, when purified and stilled as a reflection of pure Consciousness of the Atman, behaves in such a way that all its behaviors, feelings, thoughts, etc., are at once well settled, organized and deep—so that they are invariably convincing, beautiful and beneficial. The best way to attain this condition is to give up desires and intentions, and to adopt pure and natural ways.

Energy

H.H. The process of our creation is such that, in the pattern of this universe, both physical activity and physical rest are available: During the day you have the activity, and then you retire to get the rest in the night. The same applies to the subtle level and the causal level—the pranas [neuro-chemical apparatus], the mind, the senses, the Buddhi and the Chitta—all these assets are provided by nature, and it is necessary for us all to make use of them. We cannot and we should not put all these things to rest all the time. *We must use them and use them fully* so that we can go back to the rest and get all the energy recharged from the center, and come back again to make use of all these glorious aspects of our Nature.

For example: One goes to the river which is flowing all the time full of water, and puts an earthen pot into it. When you submerge the earthen pot into the river, then the water within and without this earthen pot is the same, there is no difference of any sort. The only barrier is the earthen pot itself, but the earthen pot holds the water which can be used outside the river.

So the stream of energy going through the universe all the time, (Samashti) is held by the individual organism (which is called Vyashti) like the earthen pot. You take the energy from this stream, use it in your daily affairs, and it must be exhausted. When it is finished you go back to the stream, fill it, and exhaust it again.

The same energy system is available to all of us. The ordinary man uses up his energy every day but only knows how to replenish his physical energy; from the rest at the physical level he also gets some rest on the subtle level and causal level, but very little—only what he can pick up by resting physically.

And so he keeps on going, but he does not really get the best out of his life because he does not get any adequate rest either on the subtle level or the causal level. Fortunately we, having seen something of the way, have been given all the conditions and disciplines necessary for finding rest on the subtle and the causal levels.

Another example: Eyes are designed to see everything visible in this universe, but they cannot see if the sun is not there. If one thinks that it is only through the eyes that one sees, then one can try as hard as one can to see in the dark when there is no sun, and one will find that there is no possibility of seeing anything.

But the power of vision requires all the faculties made available to the human being—the design of the body, the design of the senses, and of Manas, Buddhi and Chitta. They are all there to be made use of.

When we prescribe the rest on the subtle or the causal level, we are not meant to keep at rest all these faculties and the subtle body itself. We only need from time to time, as has been prescribed to us during two half hours, to go into the treasury, to go into this stream where the energy is available and make ourselves fresh. So all we need to remember is to go into this stream of the Param Atman twice a day and then let it happen as we have been told, so that the energies are recharged, and then come out in the world and act as the situation demands.

* * *

Q. The questioner asked about coarse and subtle energies.

H.H. There is only one store of energy. The energy is always stored in subtle form and in use it is used as both, like a power house which supplies energy for all sorts of coarse and subtle types of uses. If one supply is exhausted then there must come a gap of rest when extra is supplied. You run a lot and then take a little rest and can run again. The switchover of energy only follows a rest, a break. Even in a motorcar, if you stop the car abruptly then you must change gear and give a fresh supply of energy for further push. In Indian villages we have wells to draw water. The farmers draw much water sometimes to water their fields and the well goes dry, but in the night it fills up again and there is plenty for further use.

* * *

Dr.R. Most people's minds in the West keep on running and that advice is just what they need.

H.H. Mind doesn't naturally run; it is encouraged to run. When Buddhi allows it to run, then it runs. A weak Buddhi is overruled by it. Don't allow the Buddhi to be weak or impure. Few desires and no imaginings are good for disciples. This keeps them in good form.

A running engine uses up the battery, which then needs recharging. A running mind uses all our energy, which must be recharged. In meditation we recharge the energy, but why misuse it? Use it for better purpose. Use it for Atman and then even body and senses will get their share of real happiness. If energy is used too much or too little then there is always the danger of the engine wearing out or getting rusted. So one must have a measure to use proper energy in a balanced way.

Dr.R. I would like to find which are the people who do recharge the energy but leave their engines running too!

H.H. It is only a matter of habit. Some people while away their time in playing cards. These habits are neither useful in the material world nor spiritual world. If one has to have habit, one should have good habit. Although habits are no good for Atman, yet a good habit will at least put one on the better side of the fence. One should never allow the mind to establish his kingdom of pleasure.

There was a disciple attending a holy man. He used to go to the town to collect alms to prepare meal for both. Once he saw a marriage procession. On enquiring about it he was told that a girl and a boy are getting married and they will live in love and live together in peace and happiness. On the way he stopped by a well and to get over his tiredness he tried to take a nap. In his dream he saw himself being married and took his bride home and was sleeping with her. The wife asked him to move over a little and he did, and fell into the well! The people in the town brought him out and asked what happened. How did he fall into the well in the daylight? He told of his dream to the great pleasure of the people and went back to hermitage with the resolution not to allow the mind to create his own kingdom. People fall in the well just for nothing.

H.H. There is a kingdom of Manas to which people resort to get everything they can't get in reality. There they burn up their energy in fruitless activity, in deluding themselves and bringing about their own ruin. This happens when Manas rules over the domain of Atman—the servant imagining himself master.

* * *

Dr.R. The energy accumulated during morning meditation dissipates too easily with the tasks of the day. How can it be more surely stored?

H.H. If one feels necessity one can increase half hour of meditation and decrease activity. This is folly, however. Meditation unites one with eternal resources. If you earn 100 rupees and only spend 75 you save 25 rupees. If you possess unlimited treasure where do you stand? You own everything there is. Strength of Atman is greatest of all, for everything rests on it. In proper meditation one should get enough to keep one going 20 or 30 hours. If one is exhausted after 8 hours, one should check that meditation is right. Two half hours of good meditation provide quite enough energy for all our needs.

Dr.R. Doing one's duty is no problem, but one gets up to a lot of mischief and uses energy on useless work and useless pleasure.

H.H. All work that is useful to Atman is all right—go ahead with it. Some work, which is useless to the Atman, may be dictated by attachment, other by time, place and situation or circumstances. Provided you know that this is useless work you are safe. You are observing, not doing it intentionally, not identified. You may be forced by circumstances to do these things, so provided you know what is happening you need not worry. For example, no one likes to be sick, but sometimes we do get sick for reasons outside our control. Medicine cures the sickness but one does not dwell on it, one enjoys the freedom of good health.

As long as one keeps coming back to useful work, one is all right. In fact one is fortunate, for common people do not know what they are doing, whether it is useful or not.

* * *

Q. It seems to me that His Holiness is trying to get us to understand that, by dwelling on our shortcomings and deficiencies, we are preventing the power of Param Atman from reaching us.

H.H. Your observation is right. All activities which are initiated by an individual are aimed at some sort of gain, gain not in the bad sense, but personal advancement; and whenever one takes to any thinking about one's previous actions, then one gets involved with that deed, and creates a sort of identity between something that happened previously with the person who ponders about it. Since a mistake has been made, you are tying yourself to the mistake. All mistakes are taking away precious energy, which could equally be used for better actions, so if you keep on thinking about your mistakes or shortcomings in the past, then you are wasting energy.

If you can get rid of that waste, then it would be possible for you to engage your attention on the *next moment*, a process which promises to bring you extra energy by merging with the Absolute or Param Atman, or any action related to the Param Atman.

* * *

H.H. Meditation is as much for practical use as for spiritual use. By meditation one's mind is stilled, more energy supplied by which one acts, moves positively, efficiently and can add to his well-being. For practical minded people of today even this is a great incentive. The spiritual use is of course there. Once your tensions [impurities and sheaths] are removed, the way is clear. You become natural and healthy. In healthy state only one enjoys the physical world; in sickness one needs medicine to come to natural state. The world today is spiritually sick and it does need to be healthy. Meditation should relieve that unnatural state to make men free and healthy to enjoy this creation.

* * *

Q. There is the sort, having taken the dive, they refuse to admit it and say, "I am too small ignorant and weak."

H.H. This is a sort of inferiority complex, but the reality is not like that. All of us are the children of Param Atman and have the same rights. Everybody has the full right to experience joy. In doing our worldly activities we go on using up our energy but this utilized or spent energy has got to be recouped. If you go on spending and you don't earn then very soon you will become poor. This yoga of dhyana has a double function: It recoups energy and it takes us toward the Param Atman.

Q. Will His Holiness say more on the recouping of energy?

H.H. I will take two examples: The first one is of a man who does not meditate and attends his worldly duties in the ordinary way. His energy goes on being utilized without being recouped.

Another man also attends to all his worldly duties but he also does the meditation. With meditation he is provided with sattvic rest. Sattvic rest is more powerful than the rest due to tamas, which also recoups energy to a small extent but not to the extent that the sattvic rest gained in meditation does.

For example: In the case of tamasic rest even when he has had his fullest sleep—seven, eight or even ten hours—even after that he is yawning and his eyes don't open properly as if he still needs more rest, as if he hadn't rested fully. This is not the case with the one who has enjoyed the sattvic rest; even a little of it is more powerful than the tamasic rest.

Q. Is the energy that is gained in meditation—need that be expended immediately or is this finer energy stored?

H.H. By adopting a daily sattvic attitude the utilization of energy cannot be too much and that which you obtain—and that which is being obtained—fully compensates for the energy which is being used in our daily activities and there is even more left over for subsequent utilization. A lot of our vitality is spent in rajasic activities, yet even more is spent in tamasic activities. For a man under the influence of tamas, even when he is resting you will find that he is breathing heavy. Then where is the rest he is gaining? He is not getting any rest. The person may even be sleeping but his breath is that of a restless man, so he is under the influence of tamas. Such a person is getting hardly any rest.

Q. Meditation gives us a practical discipline as well as working on other levels. During the rest of the day it seems that we need help from a higher level to achieve stillness. His Holiness said to Dr. Roles that during a pause in our activity we might "reflect the mantra." Could he give any further guidance on what this means?

H.H. Life is a journey. Just as during the night when one travels from one place to another, one comes across lampposts on the road. When light from one lamp ends, the other shows at a distance. There does remain a patch of darkness between. So one moves from light to darkness and darkness to light to complete the journey. When the darkness prevails, then further light helps to cross from darkness slowly to light. Similarly, on the journey of life one needs energy, light and knowledge. When, with the help of inner forces, one proceeds further it is possible that due to many engagements and activities, one forgets the source of energy and feels tired. But when you remember, the energy becomes available again. In the stormy involvement of rajas, it is necessary to keep the memory of that source of all energies which powers the universe. Help is readily available from that universal source to meet all occasions. That same energy is acquired and stored through the act of being still. The energy for events governed by rajas and tamas also comes from the same source. Whenever one feels vikshepa [distraction] all one needs is to pause for a minute and remind oneself of that life-giving source of energy. The act of reminding oneself of the mantra should help relieve tension and tiredness and make one fresh.

Energy

* * *

Q. Some of us now have more time to give to spiritual matters. Could His Holiness please give some guidance as to how best to use the time immediately after meditation? Dr. Roles suggested using this for contemplation of big ideas or something we valued on the spiritual side.

H.H. Having completed meditation properly it is natural that one will have extra and finer energy for the work in hand. The discipline and the knowledge, which has been made available, will inspire the individual to use the energy and spare time for dealing with the situation before one. One should examine the situation and resolve to make best use of the time. Efficiency, precision and reasoning power will improve anyway. Whatever spiritual activity suits one's inclination could be carried on alone or with others.

When one has reached the Atman one is in the unlimited. The unlimited contains Samasti. Thus the field is open to everyone. Before starting any activity with great enthusiasm one must be quite sure that it won't become a source of regret in the end. This can only be decided by the individual.

* * *

Q. I have, at times, felt completely at one with the Shankaracharya. A friend in London who meditates and works in Dr. Roles' group told me that she, in meditation, had also felt totally at one with and as it were, part of the Shankaracharya, even though she had never seen him in person.

It seemed to me, at the time, and from what the Shankaracharya has said this morning that this is quite possible; but I would just like him to confirm it.

H.H. Both the experiences are good and valid. This is how it should be.

One can see from the ordinary experiences of the supply of electricity, that there is a place where the electricity is being generated. It has to be used by different people in different forms; but it can not be directly given by the generating board. It will have to come through some other medium. So, in each house, in each factory, a meter is installed so that the electricity from the generating powerhouse can be made available for the individual to use for different purposes.

The teacher is very much like this meter. If one gets connected to the teacher, "the electric supply" will be available; then it can be used in lighting systems, or in fans or coolers or heaters—or whatever one wants.

One should remember that, in fact, the power supply that one gets from the teacher is not the monopoly of the teacher himself; he is only the bridge—the connecting link between the Absolute and the individual. In his own way he is there to connect himself to the Absolute. When the disciple is connected with the teacher, he is connected with the Absolute, and the force of the Absolute passes through the medium of the teacher to the disciple.

The disciple, in turn, should also think that all this creative capacity (or the energy which is being made available) is not for his own enjoyment, but for the use of everybody around him. Whoever wants it should be able to avail himself of this energy, and this is how this flow of real inspiration (which takes its origin from the Absolute) should be kept going, manifesting and developing through all the forms of this creation.

* * *

H.H. One should never be nervous about being asked to tackle anything. One has all the power necessary to achieve everything within oneself. It is only necessary to remember the power. If people are nervous it is because they forget their potentialities and remember only their limitations. These people get inferiority complex, anxiety and illness. Guide should always remind them of their potentialities.

If a man wants to learn, he needs a teacher, for an expert is always required. Once he has been taught, the teaching remains with him and he can go on by himself. But no single man can do the work for the whole universe so a timetable must be made. Example of factory: It opens at a certain time and shuts at a certain time whether the work is completed or not. We must do the same both materially and spiritually, but we must never become lazy. We should never carry the burden with us once work is over.

Q. Does this mean a literal timetable of stopping ordinary work for meditation?

H.H. Yes, we must regulate times, so as to save and restore energy. If we go on and on thinking thoughts our energy goes and our minds become dull. We should not burn up energy unnecessarily. Example of car: You get in, start up, get into gear and reach destination. On arrival you put gear into neutral, but if you leave engine running, you are wasting energy unnecessarily.

* * *

H.H. The practice of meditation as it has been given is an exercise in attention and then its transformation into pure consciousness. Pure consciousness [samadhi or turiya] is the center of energy. Once one reaches that state and then comes out this energy can be channeled in the way the individual prefers. When used in ordinary affairs, the result is efficient, beautiful, loving, peaceful and evolutionary. On the other hand it can be used for the Way, the Ladder or yoga. It can also be used to help those who want to join the Way or the Ladder of Knowledge.

Faith

H.H. The Param Atman alone is unchanging; it always remains the same. But Param Atman is also manifesting through all the different forms which we encounter and through which we derive knowledge. It is quite possible, therefore, that our concept of Param Atman would keep changing. One may wonder since one's concept is changing, what really is happening. In fact, there is nothing wrong in all this; one's concept must keep on evolving, and one's knowledge and concept of Param Atman will continue to become subtler and subtler. However, within this ever-changing concept of the unchanging Absolute, there is one thing, which never needs to be changed and that is faith in the Param Atman. If one has faith—complete unchanging faith—then one should not worry about changing concepts.

* * *

H.H. If once during our lifetime an unshakeable faith in Param Atman is established—that is, that we belong to the Param Atman and Param Atman belongs to us—then we are out of reach of all harm. At that stage things change their properties for us; a harmful drug becomes harmless. This is how a cup of deadly poison given to Mira, a perfect devotee, lost all its poisonous properties in her hands. We know that substances change their properties during a chemical reaction. Why, then, can this not happen on a more subtle level where much more powerful forces come into play? Faith can change all that. It cleanses you, purifies you, decorates you, and presents you before the Param Atman at your best.

* * *

H.H. In India it is quite possible to get for a few pence a copy of the *Bhagavad Gita*, which holds the philosophy of liberation, but the essence and the truth and the knowledge, which is enclosed in the *Bhagavad Gita* cannot be bought even for a million rupees.

Faith

That truth or the knowledge of the *Bhagavad Gita* is available only if one practices threefold work. The threefold work is as follows: The first is trust, faith. With faith one should prepare oneself and take to the work, in the service of the Absolute. The second is the sincerity with which one attends to the work or the knowledge which is being given, and one tries to understand and put the whole thing into practice again and again. The third is discipline to gain control over the senses and the mind. Control over the senses and the mind is essential, otherwise the disciplines are lost in due course.

* * *

Q. He [H.H.] spoke about *faith* — the faith on the part of the disciple in relation to the teachings of the Master. This has a strong appeal to those back in London, but our difficulty is that the word "faith" is understood in several different ways. Does faith imply acting upon your belief? Could he explain his views on this?

H.H. Faith has two levels. The first level is that after hearing the discourse of a teacher or a wise man, somebody may feel interested and attracted. This would be the first level of faith. But if this is not pursued and knowledge is not gathered, this will die down sooner or later. The second level comes if the advice is taken firmly and put into action, then slowly and slowly this will deepen and a stage may arrive when it would become deep and full. Then there would be no doubt as to what is coming through the Guru.

The word "guru" is made up of two components: the first being G and U, the latter being R and U. The first part symbolizes the disciple who is engulfed in ignorance and is passing toward the Teacher. The other component symbolizes the light and the Teacher who is ready to bring him into the light and liberty and freedom. This certainly is possible. The concept of the Guru is one who takes the disciple from ignorance and brings him into the open light of Knowledge. This is possible only if the disciple's faith is established in the Guru. So establishing the faith in the Guru is absolutely essential.

* * *

Dr.R. At our second meeting on this visit you said: "It is only through faith that the Buddhi is clarified, or it is made possible for the influence of the realized man to pass into the disciple." This kind of faith seems to rise up as remembrance or special memory of the realized man, which comes when the whole being is absolutely still. Is that so?

H.H. Your observation is right. But this is just one of the ways, because there exist many systems by which the influence of the realized man can be passed to the disciple. All these systems could relate to any type of situation, which one has to deal with. If faith (shradda) is necessary, then certainly faith could be applied or created. There may be other things necessary for different individuals —so these should be applied. Just as in the case of disease, if one medicine does not bring a response, then another type of medicine must be administered. Characteristically on this way, because of faith, the mind of the disciple is stilled, and also his capacity to hold the words of the realized man or his leader increases. Since he can hold the words, the practice is likely to be easy, the flow of grace would work, and the level of the disciple would be raised.

* * *

Q. When I came in here this morning, I felt complete re-assurance of the absolute unity that exists in all things, and I was again completely certain that there is no need for any anxiety, and that all things are cared for. How can one hold that?

H.H. When one comes to certain places, which hold a particular type of influence just as a previous questioner has described, there are two ways of holding this experience. One is by the mind— by the thought or Buddhi. If it is held by the mind constantly and one reminds oneself about the experience and the taste of the experience, or the content of the experience, then in the course of time it becomes one's own.

The second way of holding is to hold by faith—shradda—and that is held in the emotional body of the individual. It holds it

Faith

very tight; this is where it is held totally. Having held this from these two standpoints—from faith and from mind, or thought—then it becomes one's own; and then wherever, or under whatever circumstances, or under whatever influences one may move about, one will never lose this experience which has become one's own. And over and above that, one would be able to transmit these influences wherever one goes, provided this influence is held by mind and by the emotion through faith.

There is an example from the life of a Mahatma. A particular Mahatma used to say that all movement is poisonous—not useful to the Self—and yet there is movement all over the creation. So it has to be held somewhere, otherwise the bliss of the ocean will not be experienced and the Self will not manifest; so this movement must be held somewhere.

In the mythology of India, Shiva is depicted as holding that poison in his throat. He does not allow it to go to either the outside or the inside body, or it would kill the truth about both the outer and the inner world. So he simply holds it at the threshold of the outer and inner body. He can do this because he is always in samadhi.

Anyone who has acquired the taste of this great unity of peace in which everybody's soul is cared for, feels that if he could hold this he would, like Shiva or Shankara, be able to keep the peace himself and provide it for others who need it. Thus, Shankara is one who has the peace and can bring peace to everyone.

Q. I remember that His Holiness, at the beginning of our last visit spoke about "catching the spiritual influences which are available here." I feel I would like to make the best use of our time to do this, so could His Holiness say more about it?

H.H. The questions and answers must certainly be carried through before the mind can come to rest; so the individual's questions must be exhausted far enough, at least, for him to be free from the load of them. That must be done, and be done carefully.

But apart from this, there is the Chitta ["reflected Consciousness"] of the individual, which could give him Bhawana—a state of pure emotion, one aspect of which is faith. So, if one is full of faith, i.e., connected with this Bhawana or pure emotion, then one's state is charged with certain magnetic qualities and one is in contact with everyone.

In certain individuals this influence is more powerful than others; but, having come into contact with it, one simply needs to allow this magnetic force to work without impediment. Then it will attract those charged particles from the atmosphere.

When this happens one will be impelled to seek more of this influence and store it, so that one experiences a deeper relationship with the unity around, and this is what His Holiness prescribes. One should just let the influence come into one's experience [through penetrating this "cloud of unknowing"].

* * *

Q. So the habit of too much thinking still goes on and some sharper tool of practice is needed?

H.H. To sharpen the tool, which you ask about, faith is the method and by faith we develop knowledge—knowledge of the supreme and of the fact that you are one with it. Thus His Holiness illustrates the point:

While the child of a rich person [is young], the servants play with him and even at times slap him. But when the child grows up and begins to feel that he is the heir to the estate and he will succeed to the household, then the servants start to fear him and they do not dare to slap him at that stage.

Similarly when a person remembers that he is one with God, is conscious of the relationship with the Lord then the servants— namely the senses, the ego—they automatically come into control and less often lead the person astray.

* * *

Q. I have come to understand clearly during this visit the importance of faith in the life of the householder, and that a man's life is governed, by that in which he puts his faith! Just as, when speak-

Faith

ing of the Vijnanamaya Kosha, His Holiness said that there are levels of relative knowledge, are there also levels of faith? If so, could he please explain these levels?

H.H. Yes, there are three levels—sattvic, rajasic, and tamasic faith. Tamasic faith is very transitory; it comes and goes. Rajasic faith is not able to make a final decision; it is sort of wavering. Sattvic faith is immovable like a mountain.

Q. So, if in the rajasic one, where you said it was not quite able to take a decision, it has the quality of Buddhi there. Is faith related to Buddhi?

H.H. Buddhi is also of three types—sattvic, rajasic, and tamasic. Tamasic Buddhi considers this world to be real and God to be unreal. Rajasic Buddhi is in doubt whether this world is real or not —whether God is there or not. Sattvic Buddhi catches the reality. So the relationship between Buddhi and your shradda is in accordance with the quality of sattva, rajas, or tamas. Sattvic Buddhi will be related to sattvic shradda, rajasic Buddhi will be related to rajasic shradda, tamasic Buddhi will be related to tamasic shradda.

* * *

Dr.R. H.H. continued the conversation by describing the *two sets of laws*—those relating to the Vyashti, the individual (like the story of the unbelieving judge in Varanasi), and the laws of Samashti. It is the first one [Vyashti] which I now want more understanding. One seems to jump sometimes from disbelief and despair to a sort of blind belief. So it is hard to see the laws—even the law of cause and effect on this level.

H.H. The situation where one jumps from despair and disbelief to blind belief comes from a particular type who relies half on his own judgment. He goes according to what he thinks to be right or wrong, and when he has tried every way he knows and has not been able to succeed in the work which he has undertaken, then he finds no solution and surrenders himself to the Absolute, to the will of the Absolute. Whether he really surrenders or not, is very difficult to say, but if one could learn to surrender fully to the Absolute, even after surrender one will have to use one's Buddhi. Surrender does not mean that everything will be done for you—you still have to do the work, and it can only be done through the Buddhi. The effect of Buddhi is that, if it is motivated by the individual's ego, it can perform only limited action. But if the Buddhi is surrendered to the Absolute, and if Buddhi gets its power through the Absolute, then whatever situation arises, the individual who has truly surrendered himself will find that the answers to those questions, those problems, and those incidents will be available, although he may never have given them a thought. This is the way it works.

* * *

Dr.R. One is greatly helped if one's faith is pure and complete. I have perfect faith in the Shankaracharya, Guru Deva, in my teacher, and the great men, but what I lack is faith in my discernment and my own nature. Above these is the Atman in whom I have faith, but this lack of faith in my nature hampers me all the time. If I get some access to self-confidence, it is taken by the wrong thing, and I fall. I believe if one could somehow get more faith in the heart everything would be transformed.

H.H. This lack of faith is the last post of transformation. After having felled all other posts, when the aspirant comes to the last and can't cut it down, then he gets into a frenzy. He can't be blamed, for he acts only from deep habit. He even becomes angry with the helpers. He criticizes even the Absolute for being all-powerful and merciful. Why can't He help transform him?

The principle is that only by long *practice* can this last post be burnt by the fire of matured discipline. It does not go away by any outside force. Just as, if you pluck out weeds, they grow again until you take out all the roots hidden deep down in the ground, by long persistent practice of disciplined work the deep roots are burned slowly and when they are burned completely, then one can understand the uselessness of habit.

In the end it is up to the individual to decide once and for all that he is going to love only the truth and leave the rest. And he must stand by it. Only then is transformation possible.

* * *

H.H. As much as one draws inner strength from meditation, so inner impulses will reach one in time of need. One should have no worry, just faith, that in need help will be available according to the need. In deep meditation all are connected by love and affection. This love and affection demands nothing and has neither reason nor motive, it just is. Have trust and your need will be fulfilled. As you progress, your influence will become more positive. Keep working.

Good Company

H.H. In this creation there is a cycle of lives, which repeats itself 8,400,000 times. Atman is supposed to move through these lives and the human form is achieved at a crossroads, for only in this form may the journey be reshaped for good or worse. Man falls in the middle of creation. On higher level are the gods, and on lower level are the animals, etc. The lower beings and also the higher beings don't have the power to discriminate and act freely according to their will. Both these levels either enjoy or suffer due to their actions during human form. After completing the major reward or punishments they both come back to human form. The gods descend to human form with more sattva, men who are reborn as human beings have more rajas, and animals etc. who come up to human form usually have much tamas. By the time one comes back to human form one has gathered essential effects from different lives but with the new element of discrimination each one is provided with all possibilities leading up to Liberation.

The essential nature of sanskar makes up our attitude. With the power of discrimination is also made available the True Knowledge to discriminate from the untrue. It is only because of such facilities provided to human form that man is made responsible for his actions. The discrimination is the work of the subtle body and this body works on a different scale of time and space; only due to this is it possible to redeem the faults of previous lives or to accumulate enough sin to suffer punishment through 8,400,000 lives.

Subtle body takes most effect from the company one lives with. With good company one may redeem and with bad company one may work one's way to hell. Even in animal forms when the subtle body of pet animals gets closely related to human beings through emotion, then it could equally be possible for a pet to move up to the human form quickly. In the *Bhagavad Gita* has been said that whatever one longs for at the moment of death, one will get in the next life. It is only the most cherished idea that would cross your mind at such a moment so one has to work hard to cherish a good idea. This also is done by the subtle body. In a way anything is possible by the subtle body.

* * *

H.H. The other two points raised by the lady were about the integration and separation related to eternity. There is in fact no integration or separation, because everything is consciousness. The beings are all held by consciousness which is Atman, and which is perfect and single and knows no integration or separation. This Atman is eternally blissful. The terms integration and separation are used owing to the ignorance at the level of mind. Even so the integration, which is more of a refining process [cutting down the cloud or dust] is possible only through good company. Unless one comes within the circle of good company, it is very difficult to escape from the flux of movement which runs through the creation. In common life people get involved with the movement and thus can't see the substance as it is. In good company one is sometimes blessed with moments of stillness and sees things as they are. If one increases these moments of stillness, one will see the unity, which is always there. The True Knowledge and the disciplined work help one to be still. Regarding separation one can refer to what Arjuna asked Shri Krishna, "What is it that forcibly takes one away from the Reality and compels one to do what one really doesn't want to do?" To this he was told that the ultimate reason is the desire. Although there is nothing good or bad in the desire itself, yet depending on what company one keeps, one learns to desire good or bad.

Bad company is the real cause of separation. There is a very learned man in Benares Sanskrit University who knows all the six systems of philosophy. When he was asked to express his faith, he honestly told [H.H.] that although he is noted to be a great scholar and can speak on all the systems of philosophy with great ease and command, he himself is in great confusion and is neither satisfied nor sure of himself. This simply shows that one can store the knowledge and yet be separated. The ultimate thing to ask is one's own Self. If you have money you are confident to buy what you need, and if you don't have money you can't be confident and can't buy what you need. This confidence is one's own, for no one can substitute confidence. If one has cultivated good company and acquired enough divine wealth one can do what one thinks needful, and if not, then there is nothing to have and one feels separated. You may, if you are a successful imposter, present a good face but within yourself you are never sure.

To sum up, if one finds that the idea of rebirth is a reality, then integration or separation are no more than a thin or thick cloud of ignorance. Knowledge and discipline both are needed for so-called integration, and denial of these is separation. Good company is the only way to escape.

* * *

Dr.R. I wish to saturate my Buddhi with sattva so that it would be stronger How to get nearer to this? I find worry eats up the sattva and faith improves it.

H.H. The natural state of the Self is sattvic. When there comes any modification, then it takes the rajas, and the opposite of natural state is the tamasic state. So one can be sure of one thing, that the natural state of the Self is sattvic. We are not going to make it sattvic but we have to simply undo the cloud and the impurities which surround it, and these impurities and cloud together are due to bad company, the company which we have had. The knowledge which we have had—if we have the right knowledge, the True Knowledge, and company of good men—certainly [clears our way] and our destination is near. If one finds that the sattva seems to be decreasing, then one can do this thing: if good company is not available, then at least don't go into bad company, keep away. Because a day in bad company is more harmful than a day in good company is useful, one has got to be very careful about bad company. But if something has been gathered out of bad company, the knowledge of the Self washes it out. It's just as if

Good Company

you are walking on the street and you landed in something dirty, you don't have to cut your feet away but just wash them with pure water. So the knowledge of the Self is the pure water with which you can cleanse all the impurities and one should take care to avoid the company of bad influences.

The bad influences: He gave an example that the sandalwood tree is mostly surrounded by snakes and they keep on biting and biting it, but nothing penetrates; the sandalwood does not take any of the impurities which are concentrated in the snakes. So the Atman, the Atman within, would never take anything because its nature is sattva. It is only the cloud which creates [the illusion] and then one feels that one is quite different [than the Self] but in fact one isn't. Keep this idea central in your mind: that nothing can affect your *Self*. Keep good company, avoid bad company.

Dr.R. Since one is very much alone, what His Holiness means by company is influences from inside one, thoughts and memories?

H.H. When one is alone, in fact one is not alone. One is surrounded by many, and the closest of all those many are Buddhi and Manas. He says Buddhi is more like the wife, and Manas is like a son, so even when one is alone one has the company. One likes a good wife, and nobody hurts her, so one should see that the wife is really pure, and the son is obedient. To do all this there are two types of foods: food, which we put into our body and food which, coming into the mind is transformed into subtle forms. If we get wrong food—bad food—which is not suitable to the Self, then certainly it will create some tensions in the body and that tension will be taken up to the mind as well. So one should be careful in the selection of food. When one takes food one should think that he is simply taking it to keep up the machinery, and he takes in the name of God. I am just putting this to the fire which is within, which is the Atman, and to keep up this body, this place where the Atman lives—fit, radiant, I take the food. One should take pure food. By this, purest thoughts and desires will arise.

As far as desires and thoughts are concerned, one can look at the beacon lights of the life of great men, one can read about their lives and their ways; how they have lived their lives, how they have worked their ways. One can always get inspiration and keep them before oneself in mind and in thought. With these two ways one can certainly have the good company, the essential good company.

Dr.R. Which are the three kinds of food, the food that we eat and the other two kinds? The need seems to be with me to stop wife quarrelling with son.

H.H. When one is alone in the company of oneself, one can mostly take to the life of realized man, the great men. Study their ways and their life because they are the people who give most if one is alone. They are realized, they are under no bond; they are liberated, so everything which we get through them, even by reading or thinking about their life, increases the supply inside. And he gives one illustration that there are hundreds of wagons lying in the shunting yard; they are not mobile and if somebody has to move one, it takes nearly ten or fifteen minutes to push them a little way. But once they are attached to the engine, their speed becomes the speed of the engine. In themselves they have no speed. So the moment we attach ourselves to the realized man, like an engine, he takes us with him and we get the speed. So when one is alone, one should always look towards this end.

* * *

Q. What introduces the imbalance which allows one guna to predominate?

H.H. There are two reasons. One is the common and the other is special. The first reason is the essence, which is responsible for our direction in life. The other is the company. One could get into good company or a bad one and that will play its part toward imbalance, which allows predominance of one guna. A man of good essence may fall into bad company and become a lowly creature devoid of all sattva and come to live in tamas. Likewise a most violent being with worst essence in good company would change the composition.

***

H.H. describes what he means by *Our Own Nature*.
The lower type of people who are under accident or chance have two possibilities. These accidents sometimes lead a man into good company, sometimes into bad company. Even if a boy is placed in a completely foreign environment, his essence could change the place and time and the culture and the environment in which he is to live. Sometimes even a good man may be led into bad ways because of the environment and circumstances. That is the level of ordinary men. If they get good company there is chance of improvement; if they get bad company there is no chance. The other type, are the people who are not governed by any environment at all. They have a germ, which is individual. They *will have their own way*. They may not affect others, but surely they themselves will not be affected by others. That is their quality and those are the people who come to the System; they become the aspirants or the disciples, here, there or anywhere the Ladder is for those people.

Dr.R. You mean it is the inner growth of something inside them, which makes them independent of public trends or opinion?

H.H. Yes. These people have such a strong quality of their essence. Take for example the great runner: Many people run but some few run faster and beat all of them. The people who go for discipleship or go on the Way have something in their essence very strong which is quite different from the ordinary material of which essences are made; and that will shine and that will lead them to some Way—whatever comes within range.

***

Dr.R. I wonder what is it that makes me meditate?

H.H. It is Buddhi in pure state. It works like a mother. She cares and works for the betterment of the child and she protects [him] from dangers and difficulties, warns of the impending dangers and keeps him away from bad influences. Buddhi in pure state reminds one and chases one to work for betterment. Good company enhances the chances of development and bad company would dim it out.

* * *

Dr.R. Does good company mean a group of people, aspirants for Self-realization, and going the same way? Among these some seem to be more useful to the leader than others. One type says, "Oh! How well you talk and I believe everything you say," and another kind, whom I value more and who ask such questions as, "Do you really understand what you talk so 'well' about? Are you speaking from your experience or is it borrowed?" Could such kinds of good company be inside one and as well as outside one?

H.H. The good company is also of three kinds. There are some people who have little sattva within and they naturally respond enough at least to appreciate the good words they hear. Due to lack of enough sattva they fall short and neither raise questions nor practice the teaching. This is the coarsest part of the good company. The second kind raises questions because they think about keeping the teaching pure and making it more practical, and also make efforts to practice the teaching.

But the question you have quoted may be answered thus: The True Knowledge belongs to everyone and in fact everyone knows the Truth, but in this phase of creation it has been forgotten. So the Knowledge has always to be passed from one to the other. Accordingly even this Tradition has acquired it because it was passed from the Creator and continued to this day. One has to inherit, be instructed and then pass it on. Thus although it is always borrowed, yet it is, in truth, one's own. There is of course a danger in knowing that it is one's own knowledge, that some may become proud and claim. This would make them incapable of appreciating further and finer subjects.

The third kind of good company inherits in full and brings True Knowledge into full practice [of creative thinking]. There was a certain man who deposited his treasure of four drums full of gold coins underground in a spot where the highest point of the temple's shadow fell on a particular time and day of the year. He wrote a note in his Will that on such and such a date and time he has deposited his treasure under the zenith of the temple. After his death, the sons tried to acquire the wealth. They even dismantled the top of the temple but all was in vain. They also consulted others, but for a long time nothing came out. One day a holy man came to their house, to whom they told their worry. He asked to look at the note and then advised them to call him a day before the date mentioned in the note, meanwhile to restore the temple in full and exactly as it was. On the appointed day and time he took them to the spot where the shadow fell and told them to dig and unearth the treasure.

All this shows that there are three kinds of good company. First is the physical which only hears and appreciates, the other is of knowledge which analyses and tries to practice and the third is the truth or company of the Self which knows and practices and can show the way, for they hold the keys to all problems. This is mostly received directly through the Tradition.

* * *

Q. How does one get rid of attachment?

H.H. Attachment is a disease either material or spiritual. The remedy is good company. The company of learned men on the Way, or a school where the Real Knowledge is discussed and given. Go to them and listen peacefully. These may influence and eliminate the disease.

* * *

Q. With subtle body's different timescale does it cover many lives of the physical body? If so, does a right action in this life redeem the faults in past lives?

H.H. There are three lines to work on: One is the meditation which should be done with faithfulness and sincerity. It should be done regularly and continuously, twice a day, every day. And then we can take to satsang [good company]. Meditation is also one part of satsang, the company of the Self or Truth. Second comes the company of those beings who have decided to go on the way of development or Self-realization or liberation. In this group falls the realized man—his company or the company of people who are very similar to oneself, and who would like to bring in their personal experiences and discuss them, and who would like to apply discrimination in all their actions.

To help all these we can take the help of the Scriptures. Those Scriptures which discuss the question of the Self and the non-Self, and all those books, which throw some light on these subjects can be picked up from any source.

Working on these three lines—the True Knowledge, the company of Truth-seeking persons, and the company of the Self, these are the three types of satsang which would lead one to the pure Self and do away with all the colors and minimize all our desires except the one desire of the Absolute. Appreciate the desire of the Absolute and then let the Self act.

The real Satsang is the company of the Absolute, the company of Truth, Consciousness and Bliss. On the subtle level where the company is based on True Knowledge one can see some difference. If there are people who are looking for the Truth and try to conduct the affair themselves, it would be much like a class where there is no teacher and progress would be very hard and slow. So it is necessary to put somebody of heavier weight with a group to lead them, and these chains of heavier grades should also be associated with the purest knowledge available. Now this purest knowledge is available everywhere but in certain cases it is caught up with the color and one sees difference, but within the differences the Truth is always present. One has to discover the color and then one would be able to see the pure Self everywhere.

If there were 100 bottles of Ganges water and they were brought together, it will be the same Ganges water, one would not be able to say that there are 100 types of Ganges water, but only that there are 100 types of color of Ganges water. The design of the bottles may differ and the shape. Wherever difference is being experienced it is only in the realm of ignorance; in Truth there is no difference anywhere.

The True Knowledge has been transmitted right from the Creator-Narayan to Brahma and to this date has been kept clear, and one has to find out the clarity and purity where one lives, and with the help of a teacher one should try to find one's way based on all these three maxims:

> The company of the Self—Meditation
>
> The Company of Knowledge—a Group
>
> The company of literature—knowledge outside and through discussions, question and answer.

Grace

Dr.R. At stage three [of the Ladder] H.H. mentions crystals forming in the man—surely these come from above?

H.H. It is explained that there are four types of graces, graces which come from above. The first is the grace of the Atman, the second is the grace of God; third is the grace of knowledge; and the fourth, the grace of teacher. All these forces combine to crystallize a person by the time he reaches the third stage, and the crystals at that time are formed which gives him enough power or enough sattva to prepare for the fourth, and that establishes that he will not come down later on.

* * *

Q. Is one guided toward a teacher or is it luck?

H.H. The establishment of relation between teacher and disciple is not directed by luck or fates but is a process of cause and effect. Actions bear some fruit, and with that one gets also luck or fate. These are always subject to time, action, and place. By luck one gets something, which must vanish within a certain limit of time or place. These laws do not apply to the relation with a teacher, which is twofold. It is based on the grace of the teacher and the receptive faith of the disciple, which bring about this situation [and once the relation is established, it stays till liberation of both, or unity.] When the rains come, the pots which have their mouths toward the sky get filled with water. If they face the earth they would not get even a drop of water. In the same way the grace is raining from the Absolute, True Knowledge, and the teacher. From Absolute the rain of grace is eternal and also from the knowledge, but a teacher appears in a certain age and all those who keep alive with faith get that grace of the teacher.

H.H. All doctrines and Scriptures say that Param Atman can be reached by going through some established system of discipline. But we see people who have tried them all and yet achieved nothing. The reason is that, for union with the Pure Consciousness of Param Atman, we cannot lay down any laws as Newton did for the physical universe, and then feel sure that everything will go accordingly. The union with Param Atman is achieved solely by His grace, when His heart melts on seeing the rock-like determination of the devotee.

An Aryan Samajist [a sect which, among other things, condemns idolatry] and an idol-worshipping devotee used to live side by side. Day in and day out the former pestered the latter to give up idol-worship and to start praying to the all-pervading and omnipotent God. Eventually this pestering became unbearable to the devotee and he made a sincere prayer to his deity, Krishna, to deliver him from his troublesome neighbor.

Then Krishna showed himself to the Aryan Samajist in a dream, but he denounced him in the dream and told him that he recognized no Krishna at all. When he woke up, he saw a vision of Krishna before his eyes. He turned his head away from it, but in whichever direction he looked he saw the same vision. This sent him out of his wits. Telling all this to the devotee he apologized to him for his previous conduct.

The devotee wept before the deity and complained that the Master did not show himself to him despite all his years of devotion, and instead appeared before the other man who denounced him. Then Krishna also appeared in his dream and consoled him that what he did was at his own request.

* * *

Q. Can the aspirant himself bring about the expansion of the Self from the center so that it embraces all things, or does this only come as an act of grace?

H.H. The act of reaching the center and experiencing the expansion, which embraces everything is not, in fact, enacted completely, either by the aspirant himself nor completely by any grace: It is a mixture of the two. There are three types of grace which are in a way constant—always available, always present.

The first grace is from the Absolute, which is in the creation of this universe, and everything is made available to everyone. This is the grace of the Absolute—always available, always present.

The second grace comes through the Shastras, the Knowledge [the Scriptures]. This also is made manifest and declared to the whole universe and is always available; nowadays through books as well, and through teachers all around the world. Anybody, whatever they want, can take to it and will benefit from the grace, which is within the Shastras.

The third grace comes through the teacher, the guru. This grace is a little different from the other two graces. The other two graces are very passive, but the grace of the guru and the effort made by the aspirant are active. The guru cannot directly transform everything in the aspirant unless he makes the effort himself.

Take the example of the sun. The sun when it comes out can be seen by anyone who has the instrument of the eyes to see, but there may be circumstances where the eye is faulty. If the eye is faulty, then one cannot see the physical sun. If the eye is not faulty, there may be other circumstances preventing one seeing it. There may be clouds, which make a screen preventing one from seeing the sun. One may ask the question as to how clouds will be dissolved—whether the cloud will be dissolved first, and then the sun will be seen, or is there some other way of seeing the sun first, and then dissolving the clouds? Might one have access to the Divinity first and then get the blemishes out, or get the blemishes out first and then have access to Divinity? The third situation is that perhaps there is no sun to be seen because it is behind the earth, or there may be an eclipse. These are several ways where one might find oneself not seeing the sun.

The availability of the teacher is to help one to relieve the tensions and gratify the eagerness with which the individual is making his effort, but the individual must also follow the teacher and practice all the guidance given him. If he does so, in the course of time when the cloud is dissolved or it moves away, then he would be able to see the sun.

You can take the simile of lime and coriander. The lime is white and coriander powder is yellow. You mix them and both turn into red. Red here symbolizes love and affection. The efforts of the aspirant and the grace and guidance of the teacher mix together to something which is different and is like love. When both help, then the transformation or diving deep takes place. This would be the unity or realization of the Self.

So, it requires the two passive graces of the Absolute and the Shastras, and the active grace of the teacher with efforts of the aspirant according to the teacher's guidance, to materialize the journey to the center and to experience the complete expansion.

* * *

Q. On our last visit H.H. talked about the three graces; one knows from experience that the guru's grace and guidance is always available, yet one does not seek it enough. Can we be told more about asking for help?

H.H. There are three graces, which are always available; they are constant and ever active, and they emanate from the Param Atman, the guru and the Shastras [the Scriptures]. There is no hindrance within these three sources as far as the availability of the graces is concerned. Although all these three graces are available yet they do not reach the individual, and that is the difficulty. There is this fourth aspect of grace, which is the aspect of the Self—oneSelf—the Atman.

The reason for the hindrance in making use of the graces is because there are three coverings, mala [thick dirt], vikshepa [disturbance], and kashaya [attachment] all due to avarana [ignorance]. These are the three layers, which prevent the availability of these ever-present graces of the Absolute, the guru, the Scriptures, and the Atman.

These work as follows: Mala is that which always takes one in the opposite direction to whatever is available. So even if the scripture is available, even if the guidance of the guru is available, one will turn one's face in the opposite direction and will not heed at all. This is the layer of mala, that's how it acts on the individual. Vikshepa is that which creates temporary hindrances, so instead of attending to one thing, one attends to another—not necessarily opposite. It may be analogous but it will never be on the point one should act on or attend to. This is because of movement in the Manas. This vikshepa comes, the mind gets agitated and impedes the flow of these graces. The third one is avarana: It is caused by ignorance, universal ignorance. Although there may be a little light of knowledge available, the thickness of the universal ignorance will prevent the availability of all these graces to the individual.

To undo these three hindrances, the only course is viveka, discrimination, True Knowledge. It is only through discrimination that all these three hindrances could be removed. This is a gradual process, which will work in time; there cannot be instantaneous removal of all these three hindrances. It will be gradual. The more they are removed, the more you will find that you appreciate and respond to these three graces. If these hindrances are completely removed, then you will see that you have no need to ask for any help, because you will reach the central point, and all universal graces—which are always available—will be yours; and you will act through them without any need for questions or asking for help —the grace will be everywhere, and all the time available without any break.

* * *

Q. Being in H.H.'s physical presence again emphasizes the fact that during the months of absence his grace has never left me. Thanks to this and the meditation, the three hindrances, which H.H. mentioned at our last visit seem to be slowly clearing, and I am in receipt of universal grace more frequently. I am deeply grateful and hope that with H.H.'s continuing help the hindrances may be removed completely so that I can be open all the time to those graces, which I now know to be always available.

H.H. To be able to acquire universal grace constantly all one needs to do is to keep one's door open, open in the direction of the Absolute. One's door is not in fact a physical door, but the door of the Chitta, so one's Chitta should be open to the Absolute, and the universal grace of this Absolute is always being charged through the universe, so it is available all the time. But even with these three hindrances, which do impose upon us and compel us to forget, they need not affect us very much.

If the memory of this universal grace is kept alive all the time, then it acts as the connection, and means one would be able to get universal grace all the time. Even if it is not constant in the individual, and he remembers, and his memory is enlivened after a little interval, whatever has been done during this interval according to these hindrances will be washed out, cleared, burned out so one would always be within the realm and the effect of the universal grace. So keeping one's Chitta open toward the Absolute, and keeping the memory that one is receiving the universal grace is just good enough. Whether it can be done for short intervals or constantly would decide how much one gets of this universal grace.

Here is a linguistic example: The word for grace is *kripa* or *daya*. If you turn the word, then *daya* becomes *yada* because they are made of the same sound. So on one side it is memory which is *yada* and from the other side it is the grace which is there, so in fact it is one single connection; but from an individual point of view it is memory of the Absolute, and from Absolute's point of view it is His glory and grace being given to the individual.

* * *

Q. The fullest bliss seems to come as a grace rather than as the result of special or prolonged efforts. Is there anything one can think of, or pray for, or do which will attract this grace?

H.H. Grace or effort, they do not work just single-handedly. There is nothing like grace without effort; there can't be fulfillment of the effort without grace coming into play. When sincere efforts are being made and there is no self-pride involved in the effort—or achievements resulting from the effort—then automatically the grace starts flowing. With this flow of grace there is the establishment of the effort and its workings, which immediately uplifts the effort of the individual. If, just by making one's own effort and *not* creating the situation where grace could come, then the rajas or tamas usually take over and then many other happenings come into play [which has previously been explained], and the individual has lost the line.

Another situation: If one sat without making any effort and did not bring oneself under discipline or the activities concerned with the disciplines, and simply waited for the grace to flow in one, this would mean that the tamas has completely taken over. You can be sure that, in such circumstances, grace never appears to anyone.

* * *

Q. Is it right to conclude, from all H.H. has taught us, that ordinary man as a replica of the universe is composed of different levels of energy, ranging from fine to coarse, but that through ignorance his consciousness becomes attached to the coarse levels, preferring them to the fine? On death is he liberated from the coarse level and finding himself in the fine levels for which he is unprepared, does he long to go back to the coarse levels to which he is accustomed? If eventually he does so, he forgets all he has experienced. Is this how the individual is bound to the wheel of birth and death? Does the light of sattva, which appears during meditation, prepare the individual for the liberating experiences after death?

H.H. The motive energy is love and it works through physical, subtle, and causal bodies in various levels of coarse or fine energy. It is true that the individual, in ignorance, is attached to coarser levels in place of finer, and this is why he keeps on coming back to the physical form birth after birth. This is part of the laws of nature. The sort of company one keeps is the sort of company to which nature will return you. When a person dies in ignorance he goes to the finer, or subtle, level but very soon comes back to the coarse level he was used to. The laws of nature will compel him to turn back to the coarse level and pay the price for his comfortable attachments. This is the cycle, which is being repeated all the time. But this vicious circle of birth, death, and birth can be broken.

There are three sources of help. They are Satpurusa [a realized man], Sadgrantha [the Scriptures], and the Self. They can be seen as teachers or graces. The company of a realized man is a living force and a grace. His wisdom and example free one from attachments. The Sadgrantha, or Scriptures, are passive sources of grace. They explain the process of release and when put into practice by the aspirant, the bonds of ignorance and attachments can be broken. The third and the most hidden source is the Self or Atman who is always present, but remains unknown. If one can contemplate, meditate, and reflect the inner and deeper levels of oneself, the true promptings will help one to break that vicious circle through enlightenment.

This urge for liberation from the cycle of births is expressed through this threefold prayer: "Lead me from the unreal [untrue] to the real [true]. Lead me from darkness to light and lead me from death to immortality." The Self is the real, the true, the light and the immortal. Those who persist do reach that state of illumination from where there is no need to return or fall into the coarser levels through birth. Even these prayers imply a spirit of inquiry and the knowledge that there is some truth, some light and immortality, which has to be realized through the grace of the teacher, the Scriptures or the Atman. One who seeks will find. But there are those who are so proud, arrogant, and hypocritical that they will not turn toward the truth. They are fully satisfied with whatever they have and, due to their attachment to their possessions, they are punished by nature to keep returning again and again, life after life. The escape route is through the company of the realized man, the Scriptures or the Self.

Here is an example of grace. There was a handicapped man who could not move and had to depend upon the charity of others. People were annoyed by him and ridiculed him for begging. Once a holy man came by and this poor man sought his advice. The holy man made sure that his advice would be fully and truthfully followed. He took the man under a tree and placed him as comfortably as possible and instructed him not to accept any charity for three consecutive days.

The villagers saw this holy man settling him under a tree. They became curious and asked the handicapped man if they could help. But he refused all help. Even when they insisted he refused, obeying the holy man from Self-respect. This reliance on the Self made him strong and his face lit. Within these three days the villagers became aware of his inner force because all his worries and frustrations had totally disappeared. This made the ultimate change and they looked after the man, and the man looked into the grace of the Self. He was provided with all that a holy man would need, and he provided all that the villagers needed to turn inward. The company of a realized man is good enough to change the course of a wretched life into a holy life. The advice that "I need nothing" transformed the situation.

Gratitude

Q. We were told, that the key to opening the heart is gratitude, "How can one give without reservation?" Can we remain open to every human being, and not just those we hold nearest and dearest? Is there any exercise that will tune up our awareness of the divinity in all of us so that we may care, give, administer to the needs of the spirit in man.

H.H. We can show this readily to those who are near to us. How can we show it to those who are away from us? For those who are distant from us we ordinarily express our gratitude through feelings and those who are near to us we express our gratitude through action. The preparation for this is the purification of Chitta. When that is done we discover we are already joined up with Param Atman. It is a delusion that we are separate from him. The preparation for this is a purification. When the purification is done we realize at once that Param Atman is already with us.

* * *

Q. In one place His Holiness spoke of ways to help increase the devotion. I wondered if he could outline just one way?

H.H. When we remember the many mercies or kindnesses which one has got from God, then a sense of devotion develops and this is known as Bhakti. It was so kind of God that he made us a human being where we can use the various elements he has created. Had He not been so kind, had he made us an insect instead of a man, we couldn't use that art. It's only because of the advantage, because of His kindness, for which we have to be grateful and this feeling of gratitude, for all we have freely received, the more humble we are the greater will be our devotion.

* * *

H.H. The basic meaning of the initiation is to establish connection of the Jiva with the Param Atman. The guru who is initiating is only a medium. Through the mantra which he gives, he enables the disciple to establish a connection directly with the Lord. Thereafter he is expected to remember and repeat the mantra given to him and do the dhyana, so that the connection which has been established strengthens and catches root. Whatever he eats after being initiated he should think that it is a gift. Just as when you visit here you offer some fruit, and afterward His Holiness gives you some "prasad"—gift—this is not an offering. After we have received the initiation, whatever we do, we do it with complete surrender to the Almighty, whatever we receive after we have been initiated, for our own use, we should understand it as prasad—a return from the Almighty. We must carry the idea that we own nothing, everything has become God's; we are using everything with His permission and not as owner of it. This helps in the destruction of the ego of the Vyashti—the destruction of the individuals' ego, Ahankar. When Vyashti Ahankar is destroyed, then the pure Aham, the realization of Self, develops.

* * *

Q. Could H.H. explain the concept of Prasad? Could he explain its cosmic and individual aspect?

H.H. Whatever we have is part and parcel of the cosmos. This body represents the earth of the cosmos; mind represents moon; the power of seeing represents the sun; the intellect represents Brahma; Chitta represents Vishnu; and the ego [Ahankar] is the particle of Shiva. Shiva is known to be the God for Ahankar. So that whatever we have, the individual is the particle of the cosmos.

Shiva experiences two states of mind. When He is completely absorbed in His own Self, He feels "I am He." In that union, neither body nor mind functions. But when Shiva realizes His own Self, He dances about in joy, exclaiming, "What am I," "What am I."

Now, coming to the prasad—normally it is associated with what we offer, and then we get back from the Lord, that is the prasad. The gift from the Lord is known as the prasad; but before we get the gift, we make our offering. So when we make an offering the Lord gives it back.

If I may use an illustration of my own [Translator:] You bring the basket of fruits to H.H. and then what he gives you back that is prasad. The best way of prasad—this is connected with Bhakti—is whatever we have got, it is the present of the Lord. In whatever circumstances we have been placed, that is the prasad of the Lord. And that is the best aspect of the word prasad.

Q. What is it that mankind as a whole offers back to the Creator? Does the whole of man have some sort of function in reflecting back to the Creator?

H.H. He doesn't give anything back, he accepts it for himself. According to us, it is a sin to accept anything without its being given by the Lord and being made prasad. We should accept only as prasad and nothing else. And if we accept anything else without offering it to Him first, then that is according to us, sin.

H.H. gives an illustration:

We cook our meals. Now having cooked the meal, if we offer it first to the Lord and then take it as prasad, that will be very healthy. But if, after cooking it, we start eating it without offering it, that would come under the category of sin. It will be very helpful for spiritual progress if we accept everything only after first offering it.

It is so even in doing our work—in performing our duties. Supposing we are in the profession of law, when we start our day's work—we first offer it to Him, "With your help, God, with your prasad, I'm going to argue this case." So whatever we do, we should first offer it even apart from our own consumption, in our work and duty, we can make it a prasad.

Translator H.H. puts a question on your behalf: What is the advantage of prasad? What is the utility of prasad? I said, "Let's hear that, Sir."

H.H. The biggest effect of accepting prasad is that your individual Ahankar is removed. Your personal ego is killed—that is the biggest advantage.

And it purifies your intellect if you accept by taking prasad, you purify your mind and your body. And you become more suitable —eligible—for God's spiritual roles.

* * *

Q. When, for a while, ego is quiet and one's role is being naturally fulfilled, Love seems to be the unifying force, and discriminating mind seems to work within it. Is this the right relationship?

H.H. When one brings to one's knowledge the different aspects of the glory of the Absolute, then one feels grateful for the bounty which is being provided for the individual, and immediately the hard heart melts. If one feels, however, how *little* one is, compared with the glory of the Absolute which is being manifested all around; then that will open the heart. So, *being grateful alone* is the key to opening the heart.

Gunas

Dr.R. Since you have said that the first action of the meditation is to bind together the inner and the outer divisions of the mind [the reasoning part and the feeling part], does it mean that a man who has good days and bad nights is not meditating happily or fully?

H.H. In ordinary man, actions, feelings and thoughts are produced from without. Meditation brings about a situation where these functions arise and are governed from within.

* * *

Dr.R. Mantra can affect in different ways; everybody couldn't have the same experiences: Is it not true that, beside the inherent power of the mantras, a mantra acquires added powers by use? Isn't it like a traveler who, staying in different houses, gains experience and knowledge and the warmth of making new friends; so mantra going to different places in the mind gains new properties? But because men's minds, though made the same, have different contents, so, effects of mantra will be different?

H.H. The real cause of the different effects of the meditation in different people is the distribution and proportion of the three gunas in their own nature; in no two men are they alike. It depends on the former life.

* * *

H.H. In relation to Self-realization, here is the Law of Three as it relates to the three gunas. Of the three, two of them in this case are the poles [sattva and tamas], and rajas is the interaction of sattva with tamas. This simply goes on like the three times, of which there is past and there is future; what we call present is the interaction of these two. The future being passed on into the past is called present. Such is the position of rajas or present—though it is always there, it is not dominant. Man either lives in tamas or lives in sattva, but rajas is always there, which signifies all activity of the present moment.

Sattva is the natural state of man, while tamas is the outcome of inertia. Rajas is needed to give them a push, to give them impulse to go ahead, to move toward sattva. But fortunately or unfortunately many people once again come back to inertia; very few go on to the natural state of sattva.

As an example, in the process of eating the action is rajas. The effect of the eating can be of two kinds: If it is a moderate and well-regulated diet, it gives a good effect and leads to happiness and good health, which we could say is sattva. But if it is not a regular and moderate diet, it can lead to indigestion and some other diseases which could be compared with tamas. So, action is very little, but the effect is prolonged either as tamas or sattva; rajas is the intermediate period of action.

Dr.R. In our teaching, actions are said to be different in their genesis and result according to the nature and proportion of the gunas contained in the action. Do you agree?

H.H. On a lower level actions can be classified according to gunas. But in the higher stages of consciousness all action emanates from consciousness for goodness.

* * *

Dr.R. So to come back to where one is now, I have fairly strong energy, more and more of it, which feels to me like sattva; but sometimes it circulates and feels good, but sometimes it seems to be difficult to fix and hold in any way. Should one be passive about it, or has something got to be done?

H.H. These experiences which you have are the result of time and place. If you have some sympathetic environment these things happen; but in an atmosphere which is unsympathetic perhaps these feelings will be lowered. It's very usual, and what you feel as sattva is very true, and everybody would feel the energy to act more, do more. But one shouldn't be impatient; it is necessary to hold it, hold it; because in holding lies the power.

* * *

H.H. All activities of the human race are governed by sattva, rajas, and tamas—these three gunas. Whatever the activity may be, these interplay with our nature, our essence, whatever essence we have; with our natural self we are governed by the atmosphere around us. If we have sattva in us and if we are in a place where sattva is dominant, where the atmosphere is governed by sattva, then there is free play between [the atmosphere and] our sattva, and development prospers. But if we are placed in a situation where tamas is dominant and everything is governed by tamas, then our sattva is subjected to tamas and there is no rise of sattva in those surroundings. It's quite possible that the common man would just add more tamas and lose sattva there. When there is no dominance of sattva or no dominance of tamas we can see ourselves as we are; we act as we are made, according to our natural assets. So the outward effect, the atmosphere which contains sattva in itself, is partly responsible for the development of sattva in human beings.

All the gunas are everywhere in the world—sattva is everywhere, tamas is everywhere, rajas is everywhere. But when particular situations arouse dominance of one, then we feel it. Even in the West, where good people assemble, one can see the rising of sattva and experience it. He quotes as an example that whenever we go to a temple or a holy place in the jungle or along the bank of a river—whatever we are in our natural state with as much sattva as may be, the particles of sattva which form the atmosphere around these places, around the realized man, along the banks of the sacred river, around the temple in the jungle, they unite with the sattva in us, and with this unity, happiness and bliss are created; and this subscribes to the development of sattva. This is the sympathetic situation; in unsympathetic situations we are starved of sattva.

Dr.R. So, little progress is possible in unsympathetic situations.

One wants to try to collect in a situation as much of this sympathy as possible.

H.H. Of course it's one of the important matters for the human race. But common men, ordinary men cannot do this; they are just controlled by the atmosphere, by the external situations. But men who are on the Ladder, who have realized the possibilities to some extent, who can outweigh the situation with their own sattva, they can influence the situation and improve the atmosphere with the sattva that is in them. But common men just follow the stream.

* * *

Dr.R. One part of our teaching is about the three components—three gunas—in each activity. And it says that it's not only the proportion of the three gunas that matters but their order of action which gives either this result or that result. In His Holiness's system is there anything equivalent to that?

H.H. There are two things, the outer and the inner: The inner is the feeling or motive, and then there is the outward action—and the interplay of these two can determine the result of the action. The interplay can be quite different; even if the motive is good and the action is wrong, it might lead to wrong results. Or if the action is good and the motive is wrong, it will lead to different wrong results. We can see the relation of these two and understand to some extent how our actions take shape. As an example, if you are angry with a student and you give him some punishment, you know that the result is going to be good. Another instance: You know that a certain person is your enemy. You talk sweetly with him just to get the information, and you know the result is going to be a fight between you and your enemy. So all these situations, these types of actions, have different types of effect.

A man of understanding knows everything, and he is most attentive, so he can see everything, can decide the mode of action and know the result as well. The common man who does not know all these things, acts like a machine. To him the inner and the outer are just one thing. For a realized person, he knows the result he wants and adjusts the genesis of the action in his thought to the performance of the action, so as to give the desired results. And there lies his efficiency in diagnosing the action and getting the results.

* * *

Dr.R. Will your Holiness speak of how to increase the concentration of sattva in the body? Is the company and example of a saint important or essential?

H.H. There are two ways of increasing sattva guna. One is, as you say, the company of a saint; and this is as important as the other, which lies in *right conduct* during the day in respect to actions, feelings, and thoughts.

If these are good one day, one may achieve the balance of sattva, rajas and tamas, and sattva will prevail over the others. If they or one of them is bad, then the gunas are unbalanced with either rajas or tamas prevailing. But the effect of these good actions, feelings, and thoughts would be to create more sattva and help to restore the balance. If either actions, feelings or thoughts remain bad, the balance will be further upset and will lead to bad effects on oneself and other people.

The criterion of the "good" as used here is whether the effect is increase of happiness merging into eternal happiness. The actions, feelings and thoughts are bad if the effect is only temporary happiness leading to unhappiness later.

* * *

Q. What is the relation between *memory and consciousness*? Moments of consciousness seem to bring very vivid memory of quite a different nature from ordinary memory of details.

H.H. The memory in a period of consciousness is complete. You see and you remember everything as a whole. But memories depending on physical or sensory experience are never whole; so they are changeable, distorted and short-lived and never real.

Dr.R. The sort of memory I mean, that is associated with Consciousness, is like the memory Lakshman lost when he dived into the water.

H.H. Gives a description of three types of memory: Memory imbued with tamas is lost immediately; you lose everything that you have observed; the impressions vanish out of the mind. Memory with rajas is sharp, but short-lived, and may be distorted. It's always on the move; it's not *yours*, and will go away. The third type of memory arises from the sattva. That is the memory that people hold, even in dreams. Most dreams we don't remember when we wake up [Tamas]; other dreams associated with rajas we remember some of them; and there are again certain dreams which we never forget. They are the dreams that come from sattva. So memory, too, depends on the three gunas.

Dr.R. So the memory the aspirant must have for the realized man —the most important kind of memory, being imbued with, and coming from sattva, might persist?

H.H. The aspirant's relation to the realized man can have different flavors. If one word spoken by the realized man to the aspirant is taken with sattva [love], it will be fixed in the memory; if with rajas, some will be distorted or forgotten, but even what is forgotten will have gone deep into his heart and will arise sometime. They won't lose their power or effect. Even with tamas, it may seem that some words have not been taken by the aspirant, but when a suitable time comes they will grow up like seeds and have the required effect on him.

Dr.R. Even in ordinary human relationships memory can be important. One can hurt somebody very much by forgetting. Memory does play a part, doesn't it, in ordinary human affairs as well as in the big relation of aspirant to realized man?

H.H. These days forgetfulness has become a habit with people. But in the case of aspirants this is not the usual thing which happens. If it *does* happen, the realized man will see that if he begins to forget things, he will be given a shock to get his memory back. A learner who goes to swim in the water is held by the instructor who holds him at a level suitable for learning to swim, but at moments the instructor lets him go down so he gulps some water. But the instructor knows all about it, and if something goes wrong he will simply pull him out. It's all for learning to swim. Just so the realized man always keeps the balance of the situation in his hands and knows what's going on; if something begins to go wrong, he will see that everything is put right.

* * *

Q. We all want more of the sattva, but is its presence or absence in any way related to the right balance of rajas and tamas, and if so what form do they take?

H.H. Presence of sattva has nothing to do with the balance of rajas and tamas. When sattva presents itself the others diminish with their absence. Sattva comes in more. If sattva is absent, then rajas will prevail alternating with tamas. But one should know that balance of rajas and tamas has nothing to do with absence or presence of sattva. If one comes, the others go. He gives the example of two people who are in the presence of the realized man; they have come to hear him; but one is attentive, what he hears he holds and uses later on. The other who is weary and tired and in the grip of tamas, his body is there but he's not listening; he's neither getting rest nor attending to the talk, so he's wasting his time. That is the difference; but sattva prevails only when others diminish; if they are there in quantity, sattva can't come in, and if it does come in, it has to clear the way for itself by pushing out rajas and tamas.

Dr.R. Does it follow that if somebody is very busy with "rushing round life" there'll be no room for sattva? Unless he changes his form of life—has more quiet rest—will he not find it difficult to meditate?

H.H. It is not necessary to change the mode of life. If somebody has a world which needs rushing around, he should just go along with it. But when he comes to meditation, if he has acquired the practice of going deep, he will get the relief, the physical relief also, as the happy peaceful feeling. But if one does not have that practice, then of necessity he will go to sleep or half-sleep, because a tired body is not well-trained for it. But these people, it is essential that they have some rest before they start meditation; let them have their physical rest and then they can go for it; otherwise it will be waste of time and nothing more.

Q. One knows the different manifestations of all three in thought, all three in feeling, and all three in action. So when one speaks of "more sattva" what is meant?

H.H. When we talk of "more sattva" we mean more "positive emotion," and more energy. By sattva, outwardly we get pleasure, happiness. Inwardly we are calm, undisturbed, never tired, always fresh to act. If we have "more sattva" we have the energy to do as much as we want to do—and we will do everything happily. By "more sattva" we simply mean "plugging in" to Eternal Bliss and unending energy.

Q. Can you please tell us something about the movement of the three gunas experienced during meditation?

H.H. In meditation there is no movement of rajas and tamas: It is the sattva which takes you inside into the Atman, into the energy of Eternal Bliss; and when you come out of meditation sattva brings you out into the outer world. Rajas and tamas do not prevail in right meditation. After meditation most people go into action which is rajas. Some people can hold sattva for a longer period than others. Some people immediately after realizing some degree of happiness go straight into action and lose the sattva and forget the happiness. As you go higher on the Ladder you start keeping the bliss [positive emotion] with you for longer periods of the day. The fully realized person keeps it almost continuously. He has to do some work to renew it and then be active with rajas and take some rest with tamas; because without taking rest you cannot move into sattva. It is not possible to go from rajas to sattva instantly.

So in meditation there is no movement of rajas and tamas, they are subordinated to sattva.

* * *

Q. It would seem that the heavenly Ladder can only be climbed by the use of right triads. If the goal is reached, that particular octave will not recur.

H.H. Yes, right use of three gunas can lead us on the Way, enable us to climb the Ladder. If they are not properly used they will slowly bring you down. The right use of the three gunas is good. Once we reach the top of the Ladder, which we conceive of as liberation, there is no question of going back, repeating the octave at all!

By meditation when we rise on the Ladder we do away with our "False I's" and establish the "Real I." Once we establish the "Real I" the three gunas are properly used, that is naturally.

There is never absence of these three gunas. It is a question of right use of them. He gives an example of the stomach. The heat in the stomach deals with the diet, reduces food to its smallest particles for distribution through the blood all around the body. If there is too much heat in the stomach, it appears as fever and we have to suffer for it. But once we take some medicine and bring it back to balance to the right temperature, then the system returns to normal.

Gunas II

Dr.R. How are the three gunas brought into equilibrium in a man or in a situation?

H.H. The creation starts with agitation in the equilibrium of gunas, and it exists as long as there is agitation or un-equilibrium. It will of course merge in equilibrium at the end. So there is no question of achieving equilibrium in a man, or a situation or in creation. That will be the last thing to happen. We all live in that agitated state which calls for imbalance of these gunas. Gunas make up the material world. Atman is not made of gunas. So Atman, when fully realized, is out of the bonds of these gunas. It is peaceful and blissful and it can stay like that undisturbed.

Dr.R. What introduces the imbalance which allows one guna to predominate?

H.H. There are two reasons. One is the common and the other is special. The first reason is the essence which is responsible for our direction in life. The other is the company. One could get into good company or a bad one and that will play its part toward imbalance, which allows predominance of one guna. A man of good essence may fall into bad company and become a lowly creature devoid of all sattva and come to live in tamas. Likewise a most violent being with worst essence in good company would change the composition.

* * *

Dr.R. In Allahabad H.H. spoke about attention and sattva. Could he say more about their relation?

H.H. Attention and sattva are very much related. There are two stages of sattva. One is the pure and the other is mixed with rajas. People [at the ceremonies for the birth of Krishna] were attentive and there was a lot of activity going on, while there was a sprinkling of sattva all around and people seemed to float in the stream of good emotion. This attention is through action toward sattva. The other is an attention which one feels in deep meditation which comes with pure sattva. In pure sattva there is complete attention, which also brings in peace and bliss.

* * *

Dr.R. In sattva the meditation seems to work perfectly naturally. So does one allow some sattva to collect for sometime when one comes in a hurry?

H.H. All our activities, all our movements are in rajas. To go in for meditation one must stop the rajas from within and without. Meditation is also an activity, but this has very little rajas and it leads one to sattva. It is therefore necessary that we give a little time for rajas to cease. When the engine of a car is stopped, the motor still goes on moving due to the speed and force. It would take a little time before it can stop. You may switch off the fan, but it will not stop immediately; it will keep on moving due to its momentum and slowly come to a stop. The same happens to us. One is expected to give a few minutes rest between two actions.

In the Eighteenth Chapter of the *Bhagavad Gita* Shri Krishna tells Arjuna about the sattvic, rajasic and tamasic activities and their results. The sattvic activities are painful in the beginning because of discipline—unless the discipline becomes natural. The pain is only felt by body, senses, mind and Buddhi. The result of these activities is eternal pleasure to all and bliss to Atman.

For example, infants find it difficult to learn the alphabet and they look around at the walls and sky, or scratch the ground because they find it difficult. Once they have learned the language, reading and writing is an unending source of pleasure. A disciple has to train his body, senses, mind and Buddhi to conform to the discipline and it is painful indeed, but leading toward pleasure and bliss!

Tamasic activities lead toward sleep. A tamasic activity gives the pleasure of not doing this and that work and allows the body, senses, mind and also Buddhi to be lazy and thus rot away. All activities are rajas. It is the direction to sattva or tamas which sets the pattern. Tamasic activities give pleasure in the beginning but end up in destruction and death, bad health, poverty. A pure Buddhi takes one toward sattva and impure will take one toward tamas. One who has a strong, clear, pure and decisive Buddhi, he doesn't have to worry, he will be on the right path, the path of sattva.

Those in tamas are lazy. They think they enjoy sleep, but too much sleep reduces blood into a watery substance and they lose all energy of body, mind and Buddhi which adds to their fall. This is how people destroy themselves. A man of higher level can of course go into sattvic activity without having to allow body and mind to still. He dives immediately and gets to the Source, which in turn relieves all fatigue and tired feeling. He always comes out fresh for more activity. Hard work is not only for disciples but necessary even for realized men—even if not for themselves, then for others.

A faithful wife will always recognize the voice of her husband in a multitude, and a true disciple will also recognize the voice of his teacher in a multitude. Shri Vyasa, who collected the *Bhagavad Gita*, recognized and heard the voice of Shri Krishna on the battlefield of Mahabharata which was filled with war cries and the clash of arms and many voices. In the same way one who is really searching for the Atman will hear and recognize the voice of the Atman amid the multitude of desires, ambitions and duties created by the mind. This all is possible because of love and devotion.

* * *

H.H. Although it is true to say that sattva helps to stabilize and purify the Buddhi it is not fully true [Buddhi can't be sattvic all the time] because sattva, rajas and tamas are the influences which can submerge Buddhi, and Buddhi thus becomes sattvic, rajasic and tamasic. It would be difficult to differentiate at the moment. The beauty of our living is that we have to rise above them.

Sattva may predominate at one time and rajas or tamas at other times; for example, in good company or in the company of a realized man Buddhi would take sattvic influence. In active life one has to use rajas for there can't be any activity without rajas, and when going to bed one has to go to sleep in tamas. In fact none of these at their proper place is bad, so one doesn't have to feel guilty about the predominance of any of the three at a given moment. One should use them at the proper place and time. A driver drives his car slowly in traffic and goes fast when out of traffic by changing his gear according to the need. He is not really concerned about the gear but about his destination. This is the attitude we should have, using sattva, rajas or tamas as the need may be and not getting involved with them. One has to rise above them, even rise above sattva.

* * *

Dr.R. In my group we felt recently that we had been making a mistake about the three gunas. We began to dislike rajas and tamas and to long for sattva. There was much talk about sattva, and we became very attached to it. Then I came across Lord Krishna's words again:

"He who shuns not the guna which is present nor longs for that which is absent, and he who rises above the gunas, shall become one with the Eternal." This helped several people. Yesterday your Holiness seemed to be saying the same thing. The simile of the car driver not concerned with his gears but with his destination is very enlightening. Does the rise above gunas mean first not to be attached to our actions and their result?

H.H. The creation is full of these three gunas. Everything is evolved out of these three gunas, and nobody can escape them. What we can escape is the clamoring for them and once we have escaped clamoring for any of the gunas, things should be easy; but it would be impossible either to collect one of them and leave the others, or use one of them or leave them. This will be impossible because every man, every action and every thing is full of the three gunas. No one can escape and we have to work in conformity according to the need.

Attachment in any form with anything is bound to bring misery and bondage, so keep off the attachment, even to sattva.

To meditate is to be in sattva, but after meditation when you walk away from the place or in any activity you take to, you come into rajas; when you go to sleep you have to come under tamas. To be in the world, to live in this creation, one has to use sattva for a certain period, rajas and tamas for certain periods. One should not think that because sattva is better one should have it all the time. It would be against nature and it will not be possible. So if one sees that sattva is good, one should attempt meditation with more feeling and attention compared with other activities.

The creation is full of this trinity of sattva, rajas, and tamas. This is the primal factor. The same three forces are repeated all through the creation to its grossest form. For example, knowledge, change, and ignorance; evolution [creation], existence, and dissolution; in Sanskrit grammar: first, second and third person, or masculine, feminine and neuter gender, and so on. The pattern of three [is] created right through the first impulse in creation to the end product. A discriminating [person] should be able to see more of it in every form of creation. But one thing must be kept in mind that, although these three forces are working through the creation, there is another factor which only observes the coming and going of three forces reacting on each other.

There was a certain man who kept a placard with a reminder before him that "Even this will pass." All experiences and impressions were followed by this reminder, and he ultimately became only the observer of events, without any reaction of pain or pleasure.

Although we like to have sattva which is pleasant and better than others, let us not hanker after it and be greedy about it. When sattva comes we see it, and when others come we again just see them work and move on. Conclusion is that we must not be "attached" to any of them, and keep observing.

* * *

Q. At certain times things are so low that even remembering the realized man, God or meditation does not change this lowly state into a happy one.

H.H. This desperate situation arises out of an overwhelming excess of tamas. As long as tamas dominates it would be difficult to do anything. There are three sources to contribute to this tamasic situation. First the place, second, the situation [time], and third, the being itself. One can help it by giving a little time, which like everything passes away. One should not be much disturbed by it and need not relive it. It is just a passing phase.

Dr.R. Tamas in such cases seems not to be confined only to a situation of sleep and inertia, but appears in a person who carries negative emotion and impatient or rebellious attitude.

H.H. The situation which Dr. R. has described is tamas mixed with rajas. There is in this tamas some activity going on. This is more like early morning or evening when there is neither day nor night, light nor dark, a mixture of both. One should just see the situation as it is and observe what is happening, and in doing so perhaps you will find a moment which would bring forth solace and pleasure. Knowing that everything changes, we know that this situation is also going to change; there will be a turn for the better.

* * *

Dr.R. The last few days I have found great help in practice from your words "Buddhi must be stilled." This is achieved now during meditation and is so also when I wake at night. But any mental activity sets it moving again, and it takes time once more to still it. How to keep it quieter?

H.H. We want to still Buddhi because Buddhi is in motion. Of course it is in motion because every activity is basically rajas. Whenever you have activity Buddhi will have to work and so move. When in meditation Buddhi is still, that is fine. Nothing wrong. What one needs is to see that one has to activate Buddhi for certain work but when not required one stills it. You can enjoy Buddhi either still, in meditation, or properly active in work. Meditation has three qualities, its use can be described in three ways: first, nourishment; second, cleansing; third, healing. We need food every six hours to keep the body going, a bath every twenty-four hours to keep it clean, medicine every so often if ill—if homeopathic, every seven days! As body needs these things, so the whole system needs this service, except Atman which in fact does not need anything, being complete in itself. But activities of rajas and tamas collect impurities. Meditation cleans them out. If no impurities, no need for meditation. Meditation is not an end in itself. Bliss is the ultimate end. It is the nature of the Atman to be blissful, but rajas and tamas deprive it of bliss. Meditation cleans out everything so that Atman reaches its natural state of bliss.

* * *

Q. All the great teachings have as their main theme the unity of men with each other and with God. Why is it that so simple a truth has always been difficult to grasp, never more so than today?

H.H. Simple truth has always been there. The pace at which men live and the rajas that this speed produces has made men forget this simple truth. The speed increases all the time creating ever more rajas. We now go so fast that fewer than ever have time to remember. In fact we now go so fast that the impression is given that it is we who are stable. It is of course the knowledge and truth which are stable, and we who are rushing. You put something valuable and important away in a safe place in your house. Then you go out into the rush of the world's activities and, lo, you cannot remember where you put the thing you value. Only when you stop and stay still will you recall where you put it. We go on making more rajas and are devoid of sufficient sattva. We must try to make more sattva. This we do through keeping good company, keeping contact with realized man. A man sees the need for rest of tamas after hard work. If he could in a like way see the need for sattva after the rajas which surrounds him, he would grasp the truth.

Q. Can mankind as a whole slow down the acceleration of rajas, or is it part of the divine drama?

H.H. Yes, mankind can do this—the foregoing was about individuals, and, at that level, half-hour meditation after tamas gives enough energy for the day. At night, too, between rajas and tamas, another half-hour is necessary. Thus, if we punctuate work with rest, we will build up sattva and slow rajas. As regards the grand scale of creation, the human race is governed by certain combinations of the gunas. When those combinations are favorable everything is well and there is not much rajas. When some big law changes the combinations of the gunas and things become unfavorable much rajas is created. This carries mankind along willy-nilly and individuals can't do much about it. A special person is however eventually sent to check the movement.

* * *

H.H. The body and the pranas, they feed on tamas; because of the activity of rajas during the day they slide down into tamas at night to recover themselves and become fresh. The mind and the heart—they take rest in sattva. So whenever one gets tired in the evening and goes to bed and the sattva is still there, this sort of thing [waking up and being wide awake in the middle of the night] is possible to happen. But the body and the Manas will be colored with tamas. It is natural that a little conscious effort should be good enough to disperse that tamas so that the whole body, mind, and heart is left without it to have rest in sattva. In the night when somebody wakes up and the whole world is sleeping in tamas, the atmosphere is very clean and pure. That is the best time; if one can make just a little effort at that time and do a little meditation one will be rewarded much more than at the usual time of meditation.

* * *

Q. I greatly value connection with realized man and wish to ask about union between the downward current of creation—nature or the drama—and the upward current of the aspirant's return to the Source, the Unity.

H.H. In the Fifteenth Chapter of the *Bhagavad Gita*, Lord Krishna describes the downward current of creation. This tree of creation is upside down where the roots are above, the trunk and branches pointing downward, and expanding in all directions. The fruits of the tree being the True Knowledge are decorated with leaves and flowers. The whole creation becomes gross in the gunas, in which human beings are bound by their actions.

Just as one sees a tree on the earth with roots in the ground, through which their food is found, this tree of creation gets its food, i.e., the energy, from the Absolute. The way to the Source is to climb the tree from the branches. Only the accumulation of sattva can help one free oneself from the bondage and go upward.

* * *

Q. Are the majority of people predominantly one way or the other, or the majority of people evenly balanced with the gunas?

H.H. The nature of these three gunas is such that one of them is bound to be in predominance in every situation. The equilibrium of gunas means dissolution of the creation or the person which is not possible. These gunas are not constant in their relation all the time. They keep on changing their quantity. One might be in predominance now and the other might be predominant later, due to desires, attachments or outer influences. The job of the school in guiding people is to see the predominance of gunas and arrange them in such a way that one is helpful to the other and not causing troubles.

Dr.R. I want to be clear, when His Holiness refers to somebody as predominantly rajas. From the point of the three rooms of the house, he could drive fast cars, want to be active in sports, excitable in feeling or emotionally, or mentally be talkative or domineering. There are many manifestations. Does predominance refer to any room or just one room of the house?

H.H. The talkative intellectuals, excitable temperamentals, sentimentals and those who become angry quickly are weak compared to those who can perform quick actions and are efficient. Those who drive fast cars, like quick sports and quick actions and can perform them efficiently, are with rajas, so they do better meditation.

There was a tradesman who used to get excited very much and was in the habit of thinking without purpose, calculating his designs and so on. One of his well-wishers took him to a satsang. There he sat behind in the last row and due to complete lack of interest he was soon fiddling with the shirt of the person sitting in front of him. Later on he was asleep, and in his dream he was selling his cloth. After discussions with the client in the dream, he was asked by his client to tear a piece of cloth of few yards in length. Having heard this, the fiddling fingers got busy and tore the shirt of the person sitting in front, and soon opened his eyes to see what he had done. The other man was furious. The tradesman promised to give him six yards of new cloth and begged him not to make a fuss. He then also realized the futility of too much thinking and calculating.

* * *

H.H. The nature starts from the subtlest form of Buddhi and descends to the grossest manifest forms in the universe. The act of meditation is the reverse because you start with coarse and end with subtle material. If one could keep balance and allow interplay of these two aspects of living, one would sail happily through life.

Even a realized man is not free from such phenomena and as long as he lives in the manifest world he has to work with the nature. He acts from the foundation of peace, from Para-Prakriti, and faces the situations and, after doing the needful, forgets them. The aspirant likes to suppress the disturbance forever by staging a final fight! But there is no final fight with the nature. It is a continuous process of refinement.

In the Fourteenth Chapter of the *Gita*, Shri Krishna says to Arjuna that this Prakriti has three qualities [gunas] known as sattva, rajas, and tamas. The effect of these is experienced as light, activity, and limitation or bondage. Light is the effect of sattva and it has knowledge, purity, and love contained in it. Out of this all the thoughts, images and creative faculties arise in the individual mind or the Universal Mind. The rajas shows effects as activity or disturbance. This is the period between the sattva and tamas, or between "ideal matter" which is sattva and the "material idea" which is tamas and experienced as the manifest world. Tamas is the frozen idea which has become nothing but bondage or law working in the creation. The realized man sees everything in its true form and does the needful without being attached to any of the gunas.

* * *

Dr.R. His Holiness saw yesterday a dark cloud of ignorance rising up, based I'm sure on a kind of intellectual pride. Head thinks it knows, but heart knows better. When you give so generously of the knowledge why should some individual take it as his own? How to tell quickly enough the moment when sattva has gone, and rajas and tamas take over?

H.H. To observe as to how rajas and tamas takes over sattva, one has to watch what one thinks, says, and does. If all these three correspond to each other, then the person must be good, and if there is disparity between them, then the person is evil; in fact the rajas and tamas take over and disparity in thinking, talking, and doing begins. Manas and Buddhi are the main factors to govern one's actions. Buddhi is rational so it does not like to do wrong, but if it is weak and impure then Manas, supported by senses, rules the man and one would see that even without one's own consent one is doing wrong actions to please the senses. When the Buddhi is strong and pure, then one would reason before embarking on any action, and that would give one a better understanding of the situation to do only the right action, and one soon learns to feel, think and act rightly. The key is within each individual and one has to ask oneself, and even if the Buddhi gives way under pressure, it echoes its reason. To this one must learn to listen, howsoever feeble it may be. On the basis of this, one can decide whether the action was taken over by rajas and tamas or not.

Dr.R. The Manas is always inventing thousands of ways of excusing what Buddhi knows is wrong.

H.H. In such circumstances when Manas can take over and give excuses to carry on his way, one must look at the result. If the action is followed by misery, loss of energy, anger or anguish etc., to oneself or others, then the action could not have been reasonable, and if the result is good for himself and others for all time, then it must be reasonable.

* * *

Dr.R. Some of your stories concern a "holy man and his servant." With sattva one gets some insight into the meaning of this in oneself.

You, yourself, have said that the term "holy man" denotes "Buddhi when seeing with the eye of Atman." Would "servant" mean Manas looking toward outer world?

H.H. Buddhi is very much like a realized person provided that it is pure and still. For Buddhi is also subject to three gunas; when imbued with sattva then it is taken as the realized man. In this context Atman would stand for the Absolute.

The difference here lies in how these two deal with the others that come under their domain. A realized man never resorts to other than sattvic means; so whether he is dealing with his servants, dependants, or disciples, he will always seek the reasonable and peaceful ways of correcting them. But as far as the Absolute is concerned, it is not essential that He must always follow the line of peace and pursuit of reason, because the Absolute can also take charge of a situation and inflict terrible punishment upon all those who do not follow the Law. Particularly he mentioned the demons, who when they become powerful, have got to be dealt with by force, and this force is always applied by the Absolute. But a realized man would never resort to violent means for the creation or the correction of disciples.

* * *

Dr.R. In the West we have mostly been brought up in the Christian Tradition so that Christ's stories in the Gospels are very familiar, and we recognize some of them as happening within ourselves. These stories surely are contained in His Holiness's Tradition also; it would help us to understand H.H.'s terminology of Buddhi, Manas, Chitta, and Atman in this particular story I would like to re-tell.

A man had two sons. The younger asked for his portion of the inheritance and went to a far country where he "wasted his substance in riotous living." Now there came a great famine on the land, and being reduced to condition of a swineherd he would even desire to eat the pigs' food; but when "he came to himSelf he said, 'How many hired servants of my father's have food enough and to spare and yet I perish with hunger. I will arise and go to my father,'" and when he was yet a great way off his father met him and kissed him and made the servants put the best robe on him and prepare a feast. But the elder son was working in the fields and when "he was told what was happening, he complained that though he was always faithful, his father never made a feast for *him*." But the father said, "Son, you are always with me and all that I have is yours, but this your brother, was dead and is alive again; he was lost and is found."

If father was the Atman, who are the sons, and who receives the "good impulse"?

H.H. The father is the Atman or the Absolute. Sons are men, one with understanding and one with ignorance. The son without understanding associates himself with the body and its claims. So he asks the father to give him his portion. In doing so he only establishes a boundary within the creation which he could call his own. He then goes out into the search of pleasure far removed from the center of happiness into the realm of material world.

This "far country" is the country where the physical laws prevail and when the physical body has spent up the substance, there comes a famine due to lack of rest and real bliss. Utter confusion is the misery, and then not being able to see further he looks back or looks within. He remembers to look within because of the great misery. He remembers the wealth and abundance of his father's house where everyone is happy, and discriminates his situation from others. He is then met by his father in the midway and is given the robe. The giving of the robe is the dawn of discrimination of the True Knowledge, and then all become happy and make a feast. He starts a new life because a transformation has taken place due to discrimination and True Knowledge. When the other son asks as to why was he never given a feast, he is told that the feasts are given to those who have been separated. Those who are united with the father, they are always celebrating. There is not a moment when there is no happiness in the company of the father. The outer celebration is only for the separated ones, and since the younger was separated from wisdom he was being given a special treatment to start afresh. One who is with the father is without blemish, and one who is without blemish is indeed the Absolute. In Absolute [Brahman] there is fullness and completeness, and in fullness there is no blemish.

* * *

Dr.R. A practical point is that when we are trying to be *One*, it is marvelous to think of a single inner organ like the Antahkaran, whereby all the other functions get programmed, rather than analyzing one's psychology into different parts. This would be a very refreshing idea in the West—the idea of an inner organ with four gears or aspects depending on the concentration of three forces, and on a higher level synchromeshed or "integrated." Can we take this as correct?

H.H. [He] agrees that this simile is quite suitable. The whole engine and its power would be much like the Atman Himself, together with the Antahkaran, from which all the forces are derived that motivate the car. And then the engine can be divided into mechanisms such as these four gears—Ahankar, Chitta, Buddhi, and Manas.

Now he goes on to Ahankar and says there are two major divisions: one is nirvikalpa, the state in which the feeling of "I" is not related to one separate individual, nor his mind, nor his body, nor any separate thing; but has the feeling of the Universal "I" with no qualification of any kind.

Now the other ego or the feeling of "I" comes under the threefold division: If a man has sattva in abundance, he will have a sattvic feeling of "I" which is very close to the Atman. If it is full of rajas, it will imagine the ego to be composed of Atman or Buddhi or Manas or any instruments of the inner body. If the Ahankar is weighted down by tamas, then the ego feeling will be equated with the body and its senses. So for him "I," the Self, will become only that; he looks only after that, and does not bother about anything. This is how the feeling of "I" gets its threefold construction—the same kind of threefold construction as supplied to Chitta, Buddhi, and Manas also.

This is how the threefold division enters into these four. There are thus twelve possibilities for these four parts or four kinds of gear. With sattva you start the engine and then with the accelerator you apply rajas and go up through the gears; then tamas is like applying the brakes or even going into reverse.

* * *

Dr.R. I am asking not for myself alone but because in Western cities, like London and New York, the cry from among our more experienced people is always for more sattva. They know very well by now that if they had abundant sattva, things would become right. How to answer this cry? Does it involve a way of living, reading Scriptures, helping each other, thinking of the realized man?

H.H. The sattva is described mostly as light—a light which is a steady light. So one of the major manifestations of the presence of sattva is this illumination in any type of work one takes on. If one finds one is afraid to tackle a new situation or one has doubts on certain types of subject, they instantly mean lack of sattva.

What can one do to change the situation so that there is abundance of sattva in one's being? The collection of certain good qualities is very essential. The good qualities are these:

1) One should always love to speak the Truth: so there is no disparity between what one thinks and what one says; or between what one says and what one does. There should be complete correspondence of ideas with activities.

2) Cultivate the love of people, encouraging them in turn to express their love through certain types of activity.

3) Be magnanimous in dealing with those around you, and the other things which come within the influence of a realized man.

With increase of these good qualities one would see that the sattva is increased.

One of the major factors is that Manas, Buddhi, and Chitta must all come together and stand simultaneously; there should be no division between these three; that one should run on one line of action and the other should run on another line of action. So there must be complete unity of heart and mind and activity. It is only through these means that it is possible to increase sattva. And then one could see that whatever the situation, howsoever new they might seem to be, one would handle them with great patience and love, without putting a foot on any wrong lines at all.

* * *

Q. (from Mexico) Does the possibility contained in any moment depend upon remembering the Atman?

H.H. Remembering Atman is certainly essential, but if at the beginning, at the end and somewhere in the middle one remembers the Atman, then the activity will be supported by sattva or the truth. It is not necessary to keep on remembering the Atman all through the activity related to any moment. What one needs is to start the activity by remembering the Atman, and thus the initial sattva will be available with which one would be able to perform the activity to its full and true effect. One may again remember Atman in the middle of the activity and at the close. If the activity is performed without remembering the Atman, then it is quite possible that rajas or tamas would take over, and one would not face the occasion with enough sattva and miss realizing all the possibilities of that moment.

* * *

Q. Sometimes one reaches the bliss of deep meditation when one is in difficult circumstances and is lacking in sattva. Is this some special gift or grace from a source outside oneself?

H.H. One should not think that because one is lacking in sattva, one will not get bliss in meditation. It is not only the person who is responsible for creating such a situation, but time and place also play important parts with their own release of gunas. This means that if in difficult circumstances one had a blissful meditation and found it as a gift or grace without having deserved it, this is a wrong presumption. The gift or the grace of the Absolute is always and everywhere available; and anyone, when tuned-in to it, would avail himself of it. Time and place are the other two factors also, such as morning and evening periods in good places would be more fruitful than the afternoons in noisy places.

* * *

Q. During meditation, repetition of the mantra sometimes brings a wish, a desire to meditate upon the Atman, the God within. Can H.H. give any advice about this?

H.H. He says whatever one meditates on he becomes. So if one were to meditate on the God which one has within oneself, one would see that the qualities [attributes] of that God will take appearance in oneSelf.

But there are thousands of ideas and pictures of gods; so one must make sure as to which and what type of god, is really the God. One has to make sure, before "meditating on God," that one has got the real concept of the Absolute, and not as explained by people here or there.

Since meditation is the sattvic activity, it achieves whatever one aims at. One can meditate upon God, or Atman, or individual, or anything whatsoever, and one will experience the dawning of those qualities within oneself, if the meditation is right. In fact however, we have not been introduced to the concept of meditating *upon anyone*, because in the meditation even if only for a short time, *all cognition is removed*; and then we are giving up even the subtlest activity which could go on.

Q. One has this feeling *in the heart* of wanting to reach out toward the Creator; but perhaps, from what he has said, it is not profitable to make more concrete or actualize this view?

H.H. The purpose of meditation is to bring the individual to the great stability. Stability [equilibrium] is the quality of the sattva. Once the individual has achieved this complete equilibrium, and has done away with all ideas, even of meditation, meditator, and mantra, so that he has achieved equality or unity; *only then*, if one does take to this feeling and meditates on that, could it be useful. He says the meditation is only to achieve stability, but if someone feels like meditating upon God, he is free to do so, but it will always be within the limitation of whatever idea of the God one holds.

The meditation is a discipline designed to produce the sattva and the stability which comes with sattva. Once you have got some sattva out of meditation you have to use it. You have to choose the way you wish to use it either by loving people, or by helping people or doing some other activity pleasing to God. You will see that whatever you do, you will do it with more efficiency and goodness within it. And so the activity of meditation is not for the sake of meditation itself, otherwise it will become void. It produces sattva, and the sattva has to be used for the type of activity which one chooses to take on in the worship of God or any other activity for the spiritual advancement of the individual.

* * *

Q. (from Mexico) Is it possible that meditation removes harmful tendencies from past lives, so that more can be achieved in this life?

H.H. The System of Meditation is to create sattva. Sattva [being the repository of light] does away with the darkness. The harmful tendencies of one's past lives come in the sanskara [essence of previous life's deeds]—the harmful sanskar. But if meditation has been fully established and is done properly, then enough sattva will be available to neutralize these harmful tendencies and gain the victory over them. Even if there is something bad which is very predominant in one's sanskar, this harm will be lessened and lose its strength through the effects of sattva and meditation.

The method of meditation is somehow related to all three times, past, present, and future. It doesn't only correct the harmful tendencies of this present life related to the past life, but the meditation and sattva take care of third dimension of time—the future—and cleans everything. The effect of sattva on rajas and tamas is greater than the effects of rajas and tamas on sattva. This means that sattva produced by meditation wins over the harmful tendencies and allows most possibilities to be realized in this life; and removes harmful tendencies for the future.

One of the examples which could be seen is when harmful tendencies of past lives have caused a disease in this life. A disease is in three phases. The first is when it attacks the patient, the second when it has gained hold on the patient, and the third when the disease is passing from the patient due to time or other factors. In the normal case these three phases of the disease act on the patient varyingly, and he goes up and down.

But a person who has mature meditation going on will be affected only on one level. Without much difficulty, though the body may be suffering, the Manas and Buddhi will be unaffected by what is going on in the body. Most of his activities will be performed without pain or complaint. He will be able to withstand the pain well compared with those who don't meditate.

* * *

H.H. If there is any query arising out of the discussions here or in London suggesting that the words of the Indian system cannot be fully understood in the English language, he rules out this problem. This isn't the problem because the main principle of this discipline is the meditation. Meditation is designed to improve the level of sattva. Once the sattva has become more abundant in the individual, then a light will appear within himself. If he has not been given full treatment on the intellectual level, if he is not satisfied about certain ideas, then he himself will be able to look at his problems and find the answers because of the sattva within. In fact it is a human problem and not a linguistic problem. The main attention is to be given to the human problem and discussions aimed at the particular individual difficulties. If one vital question in an individual life is solved somehow, then the man will be able to guide himself and learn whatever he needs. The best thing is to meditate properly.

Happiness

H.H. Birds have two wings by nature and it is the interplay of both the wings that allows them to fly high in the sky. If one of the wings is cut off or put out of action, then the bird is forced to stay on the earth and it can not fly any more.

Similarly, there are two wings of our existence—the material and the spiritual. Somehow, people seem to prefer the use of one wing only and either cling on to the material wing or the spiritual wing. Since both are naturally necessary there is much strife in search of bliss. Unless people do realize the need to use both wings and refrain from being partial, the Atman will be deprived of freedom and bliss, which all seek. Unless this truth is realized the work can't pick up speed nor can the flight into the spiritual world materialize.

* * *

H.H. The whole of our mind has for so long been associated with the outer world that it has quite forgotten the existence, let alone the language of the inner world. The moving mind looks for happiness in getting and experiencing things. These do not suffice, for, when the mind has one thing, it immediately rushes after another. The still mind finds happiness in everything.

This kingdom within or the heaven within is the reservoir of peace and bliss. No violence can reach there. Devotion is the gentle art of unity.

In our worldly life we look for pleasure, and we strive hard to snatch those moments of pleasure. Once you get an atom of bliss, you long for more. The craving for pleasure becomes less because of the depth and strength of joy in bliss. For example, you don't care about the well when you get to a lake or river. Bigger and better things reduce the importance of small and inferior things. Dive

Happiness

in with devotion and swim around gently in that blissful heaven which is within you.

* * *

Dr.R. Yesterday you showed me the place in the heart where Atman lives. This is the place where I want to stay and go out to work and come back. The mantra now goes straight to this place. Could he advise further since we have only a week with him?

H.H. All the creatures in the world are running after the bliss, happiness. This is the great eternal chase. We run with our subtle body and also with the coarse body. The coarse body gets recharged if it gets rest, and there are many levels of rest. A running man gets rest by standing, the standing man gets rest by sitting, the sitting man gets more rest by lying down on the bed, and one gets the complete rest by having a deep sleep. This is how one gets his used-up energies back. Similarly, the meditation is to give rest to the subtle body.

The mind is also running for happiness. Some run fast and others faster. With meditation some just stand, have the little rest; some sit or lie down, and some are fortunate enough to dive deep and have the complete rest. According to the level of meditation, they derive their benefits. As one goes deeper and deeper one adds to peace and happiness. The test of a good meditation is the abundance of happiness available then and there. The test of a good deep sleep is that one gets up fresh and energetic. The benefits of the meditation is not only happiness, but also that the physical body responds to efficient, precise work. This we must watch.

* * *

H.H. If you want deeper happiness, you will have to go through hard work—sometimes difficult work—and because things are difficult they require more attention, and it [the word] brings out more knowledge and ultimately creates more and deeper happiness. This alone is the natural way—the education has missed it. Give a better education; let children grow under these ideas.

* * *

H.H. This whole creation is the creative act of the Absolute and it is an artistic creation. It is full of various tastes. [The Sanskrit word is "Rasa"; previously he has said there are in India "Nine Rasas" like the Nine Muses in ancient Greece, the mother of whom was Mnemosyne (Memory)]. Literature is created in which there are many styles and these styles create different effects. These effects are appreciated by those who read the literature, see the painting, or go to the theater and see the play. If all artists produced one type of work, then people would be tired or bored, even if it was a blissful painting. So there must be variety; variety is the spice of life. And what people usually call misery is a part of this variety; it is one of the tastes of life. It is created so that you can enjoy the other tastes. If somebody wanted always to be happy, they would get fed-up with happiness. This is the law of our lives.

* * *

Q. Why does God allow poverty and suffering and cruelty?

H.H. After all, what is misery? Give someone one suit of clothing or a hundred, will they be satisfied? Will they not hanker for different or better ones? Happiness and misery are not caused by lack of food or clothing. They are both a product of the mind. As long as one allows oneself to be identified, one can be miserable without food or with plenty of food. Who *really* knows that the poor, the weak, or the unsheltered are living in misery? Equally, who knows that the rich are happy? As often as not, they lack the zest to enjoy things they buy, or can't digest their food, or lack health to enjoy natural surroundings. One should not judge the condition of the Atman by poverty or sickness. One should look always to the cause —what brings misery? It may be covered in silk or it may be naked. Nor should one conclude that death is the ultimate answer for the relief of misery. Release from misery comes from True Knowledge which takes no account of riches or poverty, sickness or health. Discrimination is the key. Through it one can see one's own desires for things one lacks, and one can also see that those who have the things one covets are not happy. Neither happiness nor misery dwell in things, but in one's own decision, made through discrimination, that acquisition of worldly things will bring neither. Following that decision detachment comes, releasing from misery and bringing happiness.

* * *

Q. I have been asked by the BBC to join a panel of people discussing *happiness*. It sounds promising, doesn't it?

H.H. One should keep in mind that people have forgotten the real meaning of happiness. People take pleasure for happiness. Pleasure and pain are derived from material things and their association with one's state of mind [ego]. Pleasure and pain chase each other like day and night. Man's relation to pleasure and pain is always temporary and always changing, and everyone gets his share of these two like a daily ration from the ration shop. Happiness [anand] is one of the natural manifestations of the Atman (Self). There are three states: Bliss [happiness], Consciousness, and Truth. The real Self can never exist without these three aspects. This is a higher state of Consciousness. When one reduces the real Self to a mere petty desire or associations, then one gets pleasure when desire is fulfilled and pain when it is not fulfilled. This may also contain happiness but only to the extent of the truth involved in that desire or association. Some happily subject themselves to pain for a purpose. This purpose would in that case have a grain of truth. This happiness is always just above pleasure and pain. You go to a theater and see actors in laughter and tears and because you are only watching and observing the play without being involved in it, you come out happy. So happiness is that which is derived from truth and consciousness. In the case of the play, from the true characterization and conscious plan, you enjoy truth and consciousness. One should be very careful not to confuse happiness with pain and pleasure.

* * *

Q. How can one help others to intensify their desire?

H.H. Every human being drives toward happiness. It is natural for him to do this. If he gets a little taste of it, he wants more—again natural. Anyone who has made even a little progress in the Way and who has taken to meditation must have had at least some taste. Two things are to be done to encourage the taste further, and also to attract those who have not yet tasted. First, an example: If people see you leading a good productive life and see that you are in a good and peaceful state, they will be attracted. They will want to know what you have got and they will ask. The second thing is to explain the knowledge to others so that Buddhi can be transformed. Without this change of Buddhi, nothing will happen. If you drop grains of sugar here and there, ants will follow the trail till they reach the source. Once anyone has been induced to get a glimpse, they will not forget and will want more. So the efficiency with which you deliver the message and your personal example will be the grains of sugar which will bring people to Self-realization.

There were two ants who lived one on a salt mountain, and one on a sugar mountain. [We will call them Sally and Sue respectively.] They met one day and invited each other home. Sally said, "My place is nearest so come to me first." On arrival Sally naturally offered Sue something to eat, which was of course salt. "What ghastly stuff," said Sue, "how can you eat it?" "It's very good," retorted Sally, "I've eaten it for ages. It has done me fine and I like it." Shortly Sue suggested that Sally should return with her to her mountain of sugar. "When you get some of my sugar," she said, "you will never want to touch salt again; it is so wonderful." As she was leaving Sally felt that she did not want the day to go without some of the pleasure of salt, so she stuffed a grain or two in the corner of her mouth and off they went. On arrival, Sue gave Sally some sugar, but Sally would only admit that it was quite nice, certainly not as nice as Sue had made out. Then Sue saw the grains of salt still in Sally's mouth. She took the grains out, then Sally had the true taste of sugar and never wanted anything else again. It is the same with human beings; even if we are offered the sugar of True Knowledge, we will not taste its true flavor if we retain the craving for the salt of material things and worldly desires. Remove this salt and enjoy the pure sweetness of sugar, then you will want nothing else.

* * *

Dr.R. One often needs two minutes rest when a day is filled with people's complicated questions like, "Should one marry one wife, two wives, someone else's wife, this one or that one, or no one?" One needs to have a clear mind to deal with such things wisely.

H.H. All such people who have such doubts, anxieties, and troubles as to whom one should marry, etc., they haven't found a proper definition of happiness. They cannot locate where their happiness resides. They need some sort of knowledge that the source of all happiness is not in the things of the world around them, not in the beautiful or ugly forms confronting them, but it is within themselves. Once they know and have a taste of this happiness within, they would then like to refer to their own Self to decide what they should have and what they should not have. If one cannot do it by himself, he must go to a person whom he thinks is happy and satisfied and get some direction. Those who have to guide would simply ask him to turn inward and resolve the problems for himself.

* * *

Q. In the life of the householder, when he sees everything going on around him as a great drama and he plays his allotted role without identification, then happiness arises. Is this what the Shankaracharya meant when he spoke of happiness being a sort of food for Atman?

H.H. If it is due to some external object, then it is certain that at one time or other, the external object will go away. Whatever you get externally will also get lost. It is true that there is some happiness when you get your desired object, but that happiness is transitory.

The happiness which is associated from inside—which comes from inside—that is the real happiness. That will stay for a long time. And that is the real food for Atman. The happiness which you get from inside, that being of a particular nature—that is the food for Atman.

Heart

Q. The Shakaracharya said that knowledge was never lost. Is it right that only a certain quantity of knowledge is permitted at any one time and so it has to be rationed? At the same time is it true that there is an inexhaustible supply of love?

H.H. The supply of knowledge is unlimited and available at all times. It manifests itself according to the need of the time. It is only available when the need arises. As for love, the stream of truth is one, but when man catches it by heart or mind he catches it in two different ways. By heart he means his love, by mind he means his knowledge. But in fact it is always the same. It is always present in the world, will always be present in the world, but people will only take as much as they are destined, or they need.

Because of the nature of people, the way they look for this spiritual manifestation—those who look through the heart get love, those who look through the mind get knowledge. In any event, if they reach the top or a very high level, everyone realizes that both are the same. There is no difference either through the way of heart or through the way of mind.

* * *

Q. This bringing together of the idea, the knowledge and the experience, is this the right linking of head and heart that he spoke of to Dr. Roles?

H.H. Yes, that is certainly so—the union or the unity of head and heart is essential. When this unity takes place it is the sattvic Antahkaran—the individual is full of sattva and it is only under sattva that something good can prevail. Those who cannot bring their head and heart together—if they are not aligned—then the distortions take place and no discipline is actually fruitful nor are discussions understood by them.

There are two types of people: those who work predominantly with head, and those predominantly with heart. Those who work with head are usually prone to too much discussion. Those who work with heart accept the discipline or the discourse without any reasoning and like to get along with the work. But neither of them are really complete because the rational man, or the one who simply keeps on discussing and does not practice the discipline which is being given would not attain any level further, so he would not be able to reason in a better way and about subtler levels. The person who takes to the discipline just on trust—if he faces a person of the other sort he would not be able to match up to him. Then if he cannot match up, he will have some inward doubt in his own heart about the discipline. It is quite possible that under the stress of the opposing ideas he might give it up. Here is a story to illustrate this.

Two people were going to bathe in the Ganges, and while they were walking the man [belonging to the line of] the head said to the other, "Look at this Creator—he must be a fool because he never knew what he was doing." While they were going along they passed two types of trees—one was pumpkin growing on the sandy soil above the river with many big pumpkins, and six feet away was a mango tree. So the man [belonging to the line of the head] said: "This is such a small plant and the Creator put such big fruits on it, and if you look at the mango tree, which is such a big tree it has such small fruits. So he must be a nut to have done such a thing."

The other man, belonging to the line of the heart, couldn't reply and couldn't say that, after all, the Absolute was not so foolish in doing this, but anyway he kept quiet and felt sorry for himself.

When they were returning after the bath, on their way home they were tired and they thought they would have a little rest under a tree, and they happened to sit under the mango tree. While they were dozing, one of the ripe mangoes fell on the nose of the man who was the intellectual. It hit him hard and he felt a lot of pain, but the moment [this happened] he exclaimed to the other chap that now he understood why the Absolute made such small fruit on big trees. "If He had acted according to me, I would have been nowhere!"

The moral is that both ways are insufficient. The real way is to bring these two together, and in unison the life is better and purposeful.

* * *

H.H. Emotions and intellect are our two servants [helpers]. Their seats are the heart and the head. Good thoughts and good emotions are good for development. They keep us safe from impurities. In lonely, thick jungles, hermits usually keep a fire ring around them which keeps even the most ferocious and violent animals away. They never dare enter the ring. So it is also possible to create fire rings of good emotions [love], and intellect [right thoughts] to keep the Self safe, wherein there be peace and possibility of right action.

* * *

Dr.R. Does essential effort mean work on Buddhi, and is devotion the way to prepare oneself for that?

H.H. Buddhi works from emotional center as well as from intellect. The intellectual effort is very important, for whatever one gets into the emotional center is derived only from the head. Once your emotional center is properly charged, then it helps very much.

* * *

Dr.R. Is it that in pure Buddhi intellect and emotion are *one* and one can know the Truth by intuition?

H.H. Buddhi, the pure intellect, is the active principle. It earns for the Self and passes the valuables to the heart which holds the treasury. Every one of these valuables come only through Buddhi. It is the only instrument we have through which the values of everything seen or unseen are derived and also given away as well. The heart, which is the seat of emotion, keeps the treasure. At the moments when one finds unity with the outer world, Buddhi allows the heart to respond directly. When one is saturated with sattva and Buddhi is pure and the heart is responding, then truth is flashed by intuition or one gets inspiration under [their] state of being. One can't command such situations.

Dr.R. Does Manas carry out the commands of Buddhi?

H.H. There are four streams which constitute the inner world.

Manas is the mouthpiece of desires; through this all desires are expressed before the senses take over to act. *Buddhi* gives directions as to what is useful and harmful to the Self.

Chitta [Memory] is the store where continuity is maintained in order to fulfill the desire. It always keeps [one] reminded of the line of action.

Ahamkar [Individual Ego] is the Individual Self which gives the feeling of existence. The feeling of "I"—"I am doing," etc.—is established by it.

These are the four main streams which have multifarious minor channels of their own through which the life of a man sails along the world. All these four are subject to corruption and weakness. Once they become weak, things usually go the wrong way. A weak Buddhi loses control over Manas, and the man becomes a slave to momentary desires of pleasure. If one is prone to such desires, the Buddhi will protest according to its strength. If it failed and Manas had his way to momentary pleasure and having seen the bad result of the desired action, Buddhi would once again remind of the harm done to the Self. A weak man forgets all this again and does the same harmful but momentarily pleasant act again and again. Such men are doomed. If one's Buddhi is pure and strong, it will keep check on the Manas and allow only those desires to be acted upon which are useful to the Self. All these streams are connected to the heart.

Q. What are the principal centers of Chitta and Ahamkar in our body?

H.H. Ahamkar is the feeling of "I"—"I am this," or "I am talking." This pervades all over the body from top to toe. Chitta, which stores all resolves and thoughts and keeps them alive continually, is centered in the heart.

Dr.R. This feeling of expansion here comes through an idea—the idea of drama, or the same substance of Creator in creation. Can the feeling of expansion be created by exercise or other means?

H.H. No, this is the activity which is beyond physical activity, and is in the sphere of ideas. Through the idea, the mental activity can be brought about. One should understand this thing—that all our physical and bodily functions are governed by that substance which pervades the realm of the ideas. From the realm of thoughts all activities take origin. When we talk of expansion, we give an impulse to the heart, and expansion starts taking place; and in that light a unity is achieved with the substance which prevails everywhere. The creation begotten by the Absolute is itself Truth, Consciousness and Bliss. In expansion a connection with this is established and you feel the whole cosmos as your own Self.

Dr.R. When he said "heart" just now, can there not be emotional parts of intellect, body, movements, and all functions?

H.H. We have been told about four activities—the activity of Ahamkar, Chitta, Buddhi and Manas. They all get impulses through the heart. Every activity in that realm which is not physical originates in impulses from the heart. But these impulses are manifested in different places: For instance, Buddhi acts here in the head. The impulse will start from the heart, the activity will take place in the head; and the same with Ahamkar. When you think that you are Dr. Roles and you are this and that, it all happens in the head because the manifestation of that activity is supposed to be located where the machine is there to do the job.

Two other activities usually happen there in the heart itself, although one's mind, once again, takes the message immediately after that.

The activity of Manas and Chitta arise in the heart, so one would not be able to differentiate in this respect that one acts in the Buddhi, or the other in the head away from the heart. In fact, it all originates in the heart.

Buddhi, or mental activity which goes on in our head, is the secondary station. The original station is the heart and they are manifested somewhere else; to see this take a person who has lost his mental activities yet he goes on living; but no one can live if deprived of his heartbeats. Everything would end there.

Dr.R. How can one be sure [at the time of action] whether the activity on which one is engaged is useful or not?

H.H. The effect is due to gunas. The balance in gunas would decide whether the activity is useful to Atman or not. And if one doesn't have enough sattva and Buddhi is active, one is subject to so many influences and diversions. Any ordinary event or people around him might influence his activities, bodily and mental. Once one has reached the maturity of Chitta [Consciousness], stills his Buddhi, and cleanses them both, then outside influences don't have any hold on that person. He can move around anywhere and still be free without taking any impulses from bad sources.

* * *

H.H. When anything is related to the thought or thinking process, then certainly the brain comes into action. But whenever we have a desire, the brain is not activated. It is somewhere near the heart that the desires arise, as a spark of the consciousness, whatever form it takes. That is truly Manas. When one feels one's own ego, as we know about these Ahankaras, there again the brain is partially linked to this feeling, but it is not completely through the brain that we feel our ego. Whatever we call the thought process—Buddhi, reason, logic, or thinking—it is certainly the field in which the brain is activated. As far as Chitta is concerned, it is directly related to Chaitanya, which is the consciousness, the experience. This Chaitanya is also not directly related to the brain; it is somewhere in the area of the solar plexus. This is the division which we make —the four aspects within the Antahkarana, and brain is just one aspect of thought process.

Take an example of the material, practical experience—we see through the eyes but we never speak through them, we never taste through them. The only work which we can do through the eyes is to see the world. But even seeing implies many sorts of activities —if we have to look into the far distance we may have to use some magnifying lenses, so that we can see the scene which is a great distance away, which our natural eye cannot see. Sometimes when we have to read we need glasses to be able to read properly. If there is very bright sun, then we may need dark glasses on our eyes so that they can see without damage by the sun. So there are various ways the eye can do one particular thing. The design of the Antahkarana is very much like our eyes, but on a larger scale. It can be used in a great variety of ways although there are two seats through which this works—one seat is the brain, the other is the heart. As was said previously, the force which comes into experience is only singular, it is one, it is the force of consciousness which works through all these four agencies—four agencies working through the same consciousness and being activated at two different places—the brain and the heart. When the consciousness wants to think, manipulate the thought process, it certainly goes to the brain—that is where all the necessary ingredients for thought process are available. It will do its activity in the brain and resolve whatever is necessary, and this we call Buddhi. But it would be presumptuous to say that Buddhi resolves. It is the consciousness which resolves through the Buddhi, which is one factor of the Antahkarana. The same applies to all the other three factors. When we feel our ego, Ahankar, and this Ahankar could be of anything—of being a doctor, professor, or being a lady—this certainly arises with the help of the brain; that is where all the knowledge and information about oneself and the world lies. The rise of the desire is through the Manas and it comes through the heart. So these four factors are very different and yet using the force of the consciousness.

There is a quotation from the *Gita* which says that there is not a moment when the Antahkarana, the inner part of our being, is at rest. As long as it is awake it is doing one thing or the other, and we have to keep it engaged on one or another work. The meditation and discipline have been given so that we can eliminate all unnecessary work, so that the power of the Self which is available to us can be channeled into positive actions for better results and improvement of the being.

Q. Can I ask H.H. whether it is related to the physical heart, as we relate Buddhi to the physical brain?

H.H. The rise of a desire is related to the samskara, and it is the quality of the samskara that gives form to a desire. If it is good and pure samskara, the desires will be pure; if it is impure, the desires will be impure. Desire has nothing to do with the physical at all; it is the emanation of the consciousness which we feel as a desire. So whatever we desire is after all the consciousness itself.

* * *

H.H. Antahkarana is basically located near the heart, although certain activity of the Antahkarana which is composed of four factors —Manas, Buddhi, Chitta and Ahankara—some functions are performed here in the brain (pointing to the spot between the eyebrows). When meditation is done, and the mantra is activated, it is initiated there (central forehead). When we start thinking we do start in the head, but the pre-condition of our thinking process is not in the head, but is activated right from the heart; this, the heart, is the original place where the first movement takes place in the consciousness which activates this part (back of head) where the memory is held. Then the picture arises in linguistic form, said or unsaid. All thought process takes place here (forehead). In the course of this yogic tradition (of which we have been given all these six chakras), by the application of this whole system, if at the source of energy—which is the Muladhara—the conscious energy has been activated, then it goes right.

* * *

Q. When through grace one comprehends a big idea, what must one do to preserve it?

H.H. Whenever one gets something in the physical world which seems valuable, one likes to keep it in a safe place, in such a place that one can easily make use of it, or look at it whenever one feels like it and get some pleasure from it. One sometimes puts them into safes, and whenever the need arises, one takes them out and uses them.

In the same way when we get some big or good idea either from the grace of the Absolute, or from the grace of realized man or from the Scriptures, or from satsang, the best thing to do to preserve it is to keep in a safe place. The safest place is the heart itself. That is where one can keep it and then make use of it later. Only the wise can keep it in their heart because the fool assembles all the rubbish which he collects and keeps that in his heart. So when he gets a really valuable thing he has no room left to keep it in his heart, thus he cannot hold it and he cannot make any further use of it. The important thing when one does get some such thing by any grace is the love, and the importance which one gives to that idea. This will decide what one does with it. If one loves something one will not forget it—this is the natural thing. If one attaches importance to something, it will not be lost from the phenomenal mind and thus can be used and preserved.

Q. What exactly is meant by keeping it in the heart?

H.H. Anything that we *remember again and again and seek for*—that must be in the heart. This is how one can check if the thing has been placed in the heart or not. As to how to attach importance to something so that it may reside in the heart and one would remember it again and again, this can only be done by satsang. There are the three types of satsang: satsang of the Self, satsang with the realized man, or satsang with colleagues or companions. It is only through this continuous effort with the satsang that an attitude of importance could be established toward a certain idea. If one gets that by grace, one would be able to preserve the idea.

* * *

Q. In the example of the telephone exchange, His Holiness said you only have to ask and the line will be made available to you, provided you ask from the heart. This is not quite the same as resolution, is it? We form questions in the mind, but how do we communicate in this way from the heart?

H.H. The good resolutions from the heart spring from within, and that which springs from within keeps on reminding one again and again. The other type of resolution, which flashes into the mind, is the result of certain external situations and associations. When these associations and situations are gone, then those resolutions are also lost in time. So one has to see if some idea or resolution is reminding one again and again in spite of all difficulties and opposing situations; then this is proved to be coming from the heart and must be kept going and, in fact, you will be forced to keep this going simply because it comes from the heart.

As an example: If you have to go to a far distant city in a car, when you come to a small town you have to slow down the speed of the car because of the traffic conditions in the town. In the heart of the city you have to go slower still, and you may even have to stop for some time and start again. When the road is clear, you can go faster to reach your destination. In the same way, when resolutions come from the heart, situations may delay their fulfillment, but the speed can be increased again when better circumstances allow it. However, if it comes from the mind, and is checked, you will not remember it and it will be lost.

* * *

H.H. The physical help which one gets within the limits of time and space is fairly small, but H.H.'s mind is always open to help us a hundred times over. Not only that, his heart is always ready a thousand times over to help all of us. He keeps us in his heart and mind all the time. The physical limitations are certainly very coarse and not much can be done, as one can see from ordinary daily life experience.

For instance, people who walk on the street have to face so many obstacles and the motor cars driving on the road have to meet so many obstacles that their passage is not always clear. But for an airplane it is all very clear because there are not many obstacles for it. There may be a cloud or mist, or some bird flying might collide with it, but these are very insignificant.

So even on the mental level though there may be difficulties these are so small that they can just be forgotten. The speed of mind is far quicker than can ever be achieved by physical means; one simply remembers someone and one is just there. The speed of emotions [the heart] is far faster still, and H.H. keeps his open for all of us all the time. To connect to such a case is simply to remember.

For instance, if one wants to talk to somebody by telephone one simply has to dial the number in such a way that the connection is made and one can have a talk.

It is simply necessary on the spiritual line to remember the person to whom one would like to be connected and it is so instantaneous that there is no obstacle of any sort.

Householder

Dr.R. How to make use of the eight hours of our active life for Self-realization? Is there some instruction you could give, perhaps on the lines of Chapter Three of the *Gita*, where it is said, "Action is the product of the gunas, inherent in nature. It is only the ignorant man, who misled by personal egotism, says, 'I am the Doer'"?

H.H. Whatever has been described in *Bhagavad Gita* in Chapter Three originates from the Vedic system, the threefold system. One is the path of Wisdom—Knowledge; the second is the path of Love, worship, service and devotion; and the third is the path of Action. The path of Action is mostly for the householder. It is according to the three fundamental aspects of the human being. Every being has one aspect out of the three, which is predominant, and because of the predominance of this element in his being, he takes to one particular path. Their aims differ, according to the system. Everybody takes to any action [as we had been told some time ago] for some sort of reward. The householder's path is predominantly on this line. They look toward active life in the world with efficiency and their influence in society, and also preparing for the other world. They are not entirely devoted to either of them but would like to aim at both simultaneously.

The path of Love is aimed at trying to establish unity and connection with the lover, the Absolute, and in that direction all his activities are performed. We have been told that on this path he surrenders everything—whatever he has, inside and out.

The aim or the ultimate end of a man on the path of Action is heaven, and for the man on the path of Love it is merging with the lover, or having experience of the love, the Absolute, physical —mostly. But in the case of the man on the path of Knowledge, he simply wants to realize the abstract form of the Absolute; reaching

Householder

the highest level, that is the absolute end of all his endeavors. And that is achieved through the path of Wisdom or Understanding also, which is a combination of all three.

In the *Bhagavad Gita* the first six chapters speak about the path of Action. Practically everything is related to that in those six chapters—how this path is built up and how one has to act. The next six chapters deal with the path of Devotion, Love. In this part all attributes of the Lord, His compassion for people, His association, His love and how He comes to rescue them in case of need—all these things are described. And in the third part—from the thirteenth to the eighteenth chapters—the path of Knowledge is described, which deals with abstract ideas about the Absolute and His relation to creation. After describing all these Lord Krishna asked Arjuna, "Now since everything has been described to you, has it removed your attachment? Have your doubts been discarded? Are you ready for your duties?" And then Arjuna says, "Yes, my doubts are removed, and my attachments are no more with me, and I am ready to do my duty—to take the law [dharma] in hand. Whatever is needed will be done."

When the Creator gives the impulse for creation to start, first comes Brahma. To him is imparted Knowledge, True Knowledge. From him different manifestations of creation start and come to the gross form, which we are. Brahma possesses the Knowledge, and this Knowledge is said to be the three Vedas, which are said to be composed of 100,000 shlokas. These 100,000 shlokas are divided into three sections—80,000 shlokas dealing with the path of Action, in which different types of work are prescribed and [the shlokas] also related which work would bring what sort of reward. So everything is delegated to this—the householder to take up the daily activities and duties.

The second chapter, which has 16,000 shlokas, deals with the path of Love, and their attributes are described. The third chapter, the last one, which is composed of only 4,000 shlokas, deals with wisdom—the True Knowledge. So it is not only the *Gita*, but the original Knowledge which is described in the Vedas which is revered very much in India. [It is] supposed to be the path of God

—not made by man, although seen by men. These three aspects can be seen. These are original recordings.

Dr.R. Among the people we meet in the West there are no extreme types. We are all very much the same. We want some knowledge, have a little love, and demand some action. Is the system of meditation a fourth path to provide the people who have something of everything but not enough?

H.H. Meditation is the medium to acquire force—power—which makes everything move, move in the sense that if you have a power, you can use it to do any work. We have been told about these three paths—the path of Knowledge, the path of Devotion, and the path of Action. One can see in the world there are many knowledgeable people—so-called learned; but since their mind is not still, and their being is not high, nothing really works through them. They can speak a lie just for a little gain, irrespective of the greatness of their knowledge. They are the people who have just the flash of knowledge without having the heart of it. Meditation stills the mind, stills the Buddhi, and in that stillness the possibility of this power being used properly arises. So meditation is useful to those who go on the path of Knowledge, also to [those who go on] the other two paths.

If you are in love and you want to bring the form of the lover into your heart, but if it is moving, always mobile, where will he take the seat and get peace? So even for those who go on the path of Love, they have to still themselves. Without stilling the being, it will not be possible really to love anything.

For the men of action—one can see so many acrobats performing different types of asanas. These asanas are devised on the basis of yoga to acquire complete control over the body, so that the subtle forces, Manas and Buddhi, can be stilled. But in fact these people, these acrobats, have no recourse to those powers. They just exhibit their talent and get some money for their livelihood. One can see that efficiency or love or knowledge devoid of a still Buddhi is not fruitful. It does not lead toward unity with the Absolute. So meditation is the path through which all the paths become possible.

* * *

Q. In Fourth Way is knowledge essential?

H.H. Of course it is. The Way of the Householder is in action. There must be knowledge for any action. We need all knowledge in the worldly life. But one must keep this in mind, that the nature of this knowledge brings in pain and pleasure. What we need is to coordinate and harmonize our life with True Knowledge. This should be able to help us to do actions better and more precisely, at the same time binding us no more with pain or pleasure.

* * *

H.H. Sadhana is a *system*. It creates a force so that the individual, who has forgotten the natural and proper way of living in the pattern in which he was originally evolved, can correct his deviation from it. Sadhana is created to put him on the right line so that he can rise step-by-step to achieve the purpose for which he was created. Sadhana empowers us to meet both aspects of our life, the practical aspect of dealing with all worldly affairs, and the other, which we have to create for the next world. For example, in the military system, the men are trained to march in step; hundreds of feet rise and fall together. In the same way, all people must be educated so that they can express themselves in short, appropriate, rhythmical and beautiful fashion. But the message should be delivered without much fuss. In doing any work, there is always a better way which brings better results to the pleasure of all. So Sadhana is only a way by which better and quicker results can be achieved.

Q. For the householder, therefore, there is no opposition between Sadhana and his family life? He doesn't keep up his own discipline and come back to beat up his family!

H.H. Those who are free in their Sadhana certainly would eventually find it easy and speedy to go further on the Way, compared with those who are governed by too many rigid rules and regulations. As far as cruelty is concerned, if somebody has cruelty in his nature, it could express itself anywhere, to his relatives as well as to others. Sadhana is only to control the lack of balance. Cruelty would be banished from the person who does his Sadhana properly.

Q. What is love? The word "love" is given many meanings. What is the meaning of the word H.H. uses? The seven stages of Self-realization seem to describe the way of being through knowledge.

H.H. Knowledge comes through Buddhi, for only Buddhi can discriminate and give decisions. That is why on the Way of Knowledge we have definite levels. Out of the seven levels the first five come under proper light and the levels can be seen; beyond them the experiences become more inward and not discernible from outside and not possible to discuss and explain. This way the disciple takes in knowledge and develops being and releases barriers around Self and thus comes closer to Self-realization.

The Way of Love is different from the Way of Knowledge. Love is based on the emotional center and is a sort of stream in which the disciple surrenders himself to the mercy of the stream. On this way he or she takes in nothing but gives up everything and in doing so merges into the stream and unites in love with the lover [object of love]. Being a Way of Love, knowledge is rather secondary and unimportant. It is a field of experience beyond Buddhi. That is why there are no stepping-stones or steps of the Ladder to be seen and marked. Anyone who would venture to mark them would not have direct experience, so it will only be guesswork and will be based on knowledge and devoid of love. One should not and could not establish the levels on this way.

Dr.R. I would like to ask, when he says that on the way of love it is by giving up everything, does it mean for the householder, if it is possible to go that way, that he gives up *everything inside* himself?

H.H. Love starts with emotional surrender. *Everything* containing one's possessions, in and out. A householder has to live in the world and use everything. The lover uses them as if they belonged to the beloved. This doesn't mean to part from them. You give up possession of everything.

Dr.R. In order to love, one has to give up just one's own ego, one's own possessions and in trying to do that one would give up self-love.

H.H. Householder on the way knows only one thing—that the whole creation is the manifestation of his beloved, and he uses everything at his disposal not for himself but for the service of the beloved. It is not physical giving up as one may give money to some other person. The question of giving up things really comes to him who possesses them.

* * *

Dr.R. I feel sorry that I get pulled away from Atman. I would like to do things more from my center.

H.H. If you feel you are removed from the center, that is the most important thing. This is the strength of sattva. To be active in the world is no bad thing, for this is your destiny. For example, if someone works hard in the heat of the sun, he is doubly appreciative of the shade of the tree. If you are very busy in your ordinary life, go on doing it, but the moment you come back to meditation, the pleasure and peace will be especially deep. All who want to give this peace to others have a special responsibility. They must not withdraw from the active world. If they did, people would think that they are trying to escape from the active world. That is not what the meditation is for. Go into activity, exert yourself, exhaust yourself if need be, but keep alive the thread leading to sattva which calls on you to come back home to meditate and get the energy for next time.

* * *

Q. The householder following Bhakti sees no difference between the guru and Param Atman. How should the householder following Jnana see the guru?

H.H. It is more necessary for a person who is following the Jnana of the householder, who is following the path of Jnana, to feel that there is no difference between the guru and Param Atman. Of course this is desirable for those who are Bhaktimargh [householder] but even for those who are Jnanamargh it is more necessary for them to feel that there is no difference between Param Atman and guru.

For the householder who is following Jnana, the guru, Param Atman, and Atman are one and the same thing; so, also for Bhakti. But for those who are following Bhakti, they get liberation after they leave the body, after they die; but those who are following Jnana, they get liberated even before death, leave the body, for they are taught to practice that they are not the body.

* * *

Q. Last Wednesday the guru referred to the search for spirituality through the medium of action and the medium of renunciation. Could he say more about the medium of action?

H.H. As I said before, there arc two different ways of approaching the liberation of mankind from human form. One is through activity toward liberation, and the other is by renunciation—complete renunciation of the worldly life, and withdrawing oneself into such corners where one is not obliged to attend to any activity of the world. Of course he will take to the activities related to liberation, but not related to the world. There are certain examples of this: Rama, Vashishtha, and Janaka.

[*Note*: Rama was the incarnation of God who was the hero of the great Hindu epic the *Ramayana*. King Janaka you have heard of through the stories His Holiness tells about him. Vashishtha we know little about, but the following words of Sri Ramakrishna refer to him.

Ramakrishna: He who has knowledge has ignorance also. "How amazing!" said Lakshman to Rama, "even a sage like Vashishtha was stricken with grief because of the death of his sons!" "My brother," replied Rama, "he who has knowledge has ignorance also. Therefore go beyond both knowledge and ignorance."]

These three examples are exponents of this philosophy of liberation through activity. They were householders who were very famous men. One of the main facets of worldly anxiety is the fear and pressure attached to birth and death. By themselves they have nothing to do with any sort of bondage; it's only when one takes them very seriously and treats them as real, then the bondage starts and the trouble appears. A man of activity would learn to discern what the reality behind the appearance is and, although he would act in the appearance, he would always hold on to the reality and thus avoid the conflict of pleasure and displeasure which seem to appear through birth and death.

For example, one knows, and everyone knows that one is a human being, and this human being, neither in his awake state, nor in his dream state, or sleep state or any other state would ever think that he was not a man; he would never think himself a beast of any sort. In the same way, if one knew precisely and decisively that one is the Atman or the Absolute, then there is no reason to bypass any worldly activities; one can sail through them by the virtue of reason, *discernment*, and act as the situation demands and hold no sanskar for it.

It is the birthright of human beings to walk on the earth but it is not necessary that they must also swim in the water, but they can learn to swim, and if they have learned to swim, they can walk or swim, whatever the circumstances may be; they will be able to do their job or cross the land or river whenever it is necessary. It is in exactly the same way that the human being can learn to swim through the world into the liberated land and act whenever the action is needed from him. This is the householder's way.

* * *

Q. It seems obvious that there is a world of consciousness as well as a world of movement. One wonders why it takes so long to discover it when it is so obvious that in that world of consciousness there is stillness and one cannot be moved.

H.H. Birds have two wings by nature and it is the interplay of both the wings that allows them to fly high in the sky. If one of the wings is cut off or put out of action, then the bird is forced to stay on the earth and it can not fly any more. Similarly, there are two wings of our existence—the material and the spiritual. Somehow people seem to prefer the use of one wing only and either cling on to the material wing or the spiritual wing. Since both are naturally necessary there is much strife in search of bliss. Unless people do realize the need to use both wings and refrain from being partial, the Atman will be deprived of freedom and bliss which all seek. Unless this truth is realized the work can't pick up speed nor can the flight into the spiritual world materialize.

Knowledge

Dr.R. Does the word Sadhana include both feeling and intellect, both devotion and imposed discipline, and does it include a "way of life" as well as a "system of knowledge"?

H.H. Sadhana is a *system*. It creates a force so that the individual, who has forgotten the natural and proper way of living in the pattern in which he was originally evolved, can correct his deviation from it. Sadhana is created to put him on the right line so that he can rise step-by-step to achieve the purpose for which he was created. Sadhana empowers us to meet both aspects of our life, the practical aspect of dealing with all worldly affairs, and the other which we have to create for the next world. For example, in the military system, the men are trained to march in step; hundreds of feet rise and fall together. In the same way all people must be educated so that they can express themselves in short, appropriate, rhythmical and beautiful fashion. But the message should be delivered without much fuss. In doing any work, there is always a better way which brings better results to the pleasure of all. So Sadhana is only a way by which better and quicker results can be achieved.

* * *

Dr.R. I wonder if I was keeping my light dim by always thinking of myself in my little ego. In my reaching out towards the Atman, helping by love and devotion might quicken the way to disperse the cloud.

H.H. (Laughing) No, Doctor, you don't have to surrender!

Thrilled with the same idea, our Indian friends never try to tread the Way of Knowledge. They leave everything to the Absolute. It really never breaks through the cloud properly. Devotion is necessary, but Knowledge is equally necessary. For example, think that you have to go to Badrinath. On the way you come to a place which looks like Badrinath and stay there. But if you have a map, then you can know where you are and where is Badrinath. One needs devotion and also the Knowledge to make sure you don't stop at the lower level. One needs True Knowledge so that one may not be deluded on the Way before reaching the goal.

* * *

H.H. The knowledge of anything is the source of pleasure or pain. With knowledge we associate ourselves with things or events and then derive pain and pleasure. This is the nature of worldly knowledge. In ignorance there is no pain and no pleasure, no bliss. But behind the structure of knowledge flows the True Knowledge which does not bind us. This is spiritual knowledge. With this we rise above the results of pain and pleasure and enjoy bliss even in the midst of actions.

Q. In the Fourth Way is knowledge essential?

H.H. Of course it is. The Way of the Householder is in action. There must be knowledge for any action. We need all knowledge in the worldly life. But one must keep this in mind: that the nature of this knowledge brings in pain and pleasure. What we need is to coordinate and harmonize our life with True Knowledge. This should be able to help us to do actions better and more precisely, at the same time binding us no more with pain or pleasure.

* * *

H.H. In the spiritual world there are books to give you knowledge, but more knowledge doesn't make you a realized man. You need experience. Unless you go on the path, knowledge of the path is useless. What books can't give you, a teacher will do for you. But above everything, you can get almost anything from others, but realization you must experience yourself.

* * *

H.H. The different ailments in the field of the spiritual world are manifestations of one real ailment, the ailment of IGNORANCE. That is the root of all ailments by which common men suffer. For a guide it is necessary to know that all different types of needs with which individuals come are based on ignorance, and the remedy is knowledge. Some would be cured by the knowledge of meditation, some by particular types of music or knowledge. Everyone is running after more happiness. The materialist or the spiritualist, all are trying their wits for more happiness. The materialist also gets his share, but it is momentary and temporary, but the spiritualist gets lasting and permanent happiness. The need is the same, ailments are different, but the remedy is also the same. Give them the Knowledge. In antiquity there lived a very materialistic race. They worshipped matter and man as he is. They believed in what they saw and no more. A prince of the dynasty took to meditation, and small boys used to assemble and meditate together. This showed them the right path and they turned to a better way of life. These people were called Asura, which means "opposed to Divine way." The prince was called Prahlad. In short, if you are assigned to look after the needs of aspirants, cut the roots of ignorance first.

* * *

H.H. This [music & chanting] is called "Keertan" and it is a form of devotion. When we chant the word of God with devotion an atmosphere is created which establishes relation with the energy of God. There are different ways of devotion: to study spiritual literature, to sing spiritual songs, to give physical help to others, to worship, to pray, or to meditate. One has only to see that we do it inwardly as well as outwardly. One can get Self-realization through Bhakti [Devotion], through [True] Knowledge, and [Right] Actions. The Vedas give three systems, i.e. Devotion, Knowledge and Actions.

The system of Self-realization through Action is to do everything right and do it for the sake of God.

The second is through Devotion. By this way the devotee keeps God in memory, prays, adores and does everything in praise of God with his heart and body, and when he takes his meals, he takes the food and drink as a gift from God, which in turn helps his being to be more devotional.

The third is the Way of Knowledge. The general questions of our origin, or origin of anything, lead to speculation about the unknown. True and constant search on this line also leads to realization.

In short, out of many ways, these are the three main systems of Self-realization or union with God. For example, we have different roads leading to Allahabad and some of them are the main roads. We simply need to be on one of the ways and it will take us to Allahabad. In the same way, if we take to one of these Systems according to our inclinations, it would eventually lead us to Self-realization. There are three main systems of Action, Worship and Reason.

* * *

H.H. Music has the power to give bliss because the vibrations emanating from rightly composed notes form certain patterns of particles which create bliss. Composition of *Bhagavad Gita* is based on certain meters which create sattvic effect.

Bhagavad Gita is the cream of all Indian knowledge. It contains four Ways:
The Way of Knowledge,
The Way of Devotion,
The Way of Yoga, and
The Way of Action.

In the Way of Action you work in the world but never get involved in it. Meditation is common to all these four Ways. It would be worthwhile referring to some *Upanishads* and particularly "Mandukya."

Everything is vibration. In vibrations live all words and Knowledge. One can hear the words of past also. The True Knowledge is sometimes passed on to aspirant even without word of mouth. This ensures the continuity of True Knowledge. Time and space don't stand as barriers in imparting True Knowledge.

* * *

Q. In our System great importance is attached to *understanding*, which is brought about by a combination of all three parts of a man: head, heart and bodily instinct. Do you agree?

H.H. Agrees with your description of understanding and gives an example.

Just as an efficient and good doctor knows everything about the disease a person has and about the man himself, and prescribes the right remedy, so a realized person, a man of full understanding, knows everything about the world and can diagnose any situation any time.

Q. Further, understanding is said to be the result of both a man's knowledge and his being—what he knows and what he is. If either is deficient or if the two are not balanced, his understanding would be weak.

H.H. Of course there are two sides of understanding—one is knowledge, the other is being. Without the coming together of the two, one could not have full Understanding. As an example taken from an ordinary person taking up a trade—he may know the theory of the trade, but not its practice, though that is covered by the theory. Another person may be trained in the technique or practice but would not be able to explain the theory. Both of these are weak in understanding of the subject. But of the two, the man with practical ability but without the theory is preferable to the theorist; which means that the man of being is preferable to the man of knowledge.

* * *

Q. Can a man *temporarily* in a higher state receive knowledge from that level?

H.H. Although it is possible, it is unnatural. If someone sits with a realized man, it is possible that the particles of knowledge from the realized man will move round the other man giving him an uplift. He might come to a stage temporarily to have his knowledge increased beyond his being. He might be uplifted, but the moment the realized man goes away those particles will lose hold because there will be no further supply. He will slip back to the level he was at before. Example: The natural abode for birds is a garden and trees. If a boat comes into the port some of the birds go and sit on the ship. This is not their natural abode and when the ship starts moving they fly off. As the ship goes further one by one all the birds come back to their natural abode in the tree in the garden. The same thing applies here; one may be uplifted temporarily to a very high level, but that is unnatural and not much use can be made of such knowledge.

Q. Is this because the man lacks the memory in which he can store this knowledge?

H.H. In our System, if a man is sleeping he won't know anything. A man of Consciousness, if he is awake, has the ability to catch those particles and keep them. A man in sleep might have it by being in association. He will get it but he will lose it very soon so it is a question of being awake or being asleep that will decide. Further to that, if a man is awake—if he is conscious—it is not necessary that he come very close to the realized man; he has the power to receive it from a distance as well.

* * *

H.H. There are three hindrances to meditation—Dirt [Impurity], Sheath, Tension. They are mental hindrances and can be overcome by meditation itself. "Sheath," is misunderstanding. It means thinking black is white or East is West. If a traveler is going East when he thought he was going West, this was misunderstanding. If he were told he was going the opposite way to what he wanted he should check his direction by the sun or the stars, or by what he saw around him. When he established that he was going the wrong way, he would turn round and go in the right direction.

For the spiritual traveler knowledge is the sun and ignorance is what misguided him. The traveler should not be rushed. He should be told to release his burden and relax awhile before being told the proper way.

Q. Why should man suffer from misunderstanding?

H.H. It is because of movement which is caused by different desires.

If a light were continually moved from one point to another, it would make patterns that prevented you from using the light or understanding what it looked like. If it were still, you could understand what the light was and use it.

Impure thoughts make the mind opaque. If you put red in a glass of water you see things through it as red. If you add green, it becomes more difficult to see through at all. Add more color and the water becomes so thick and dirty that you can see nothing. The mind is like water, and you can't see the Atman through it unless it is clear. Meditation clears it.

* * *

Q. What is love? The word "love" is given many meanings. What is the meaning of the word H.H. uses? The seven stages of Self-realization seem to describe the way of being through knowledge. Is there also a description of the Way of Love?

H.H. Knowledge comes through Buddhi, for only Buddhi can discriminate and give decisions. That is why on the Way of Knowledge we have definite levels. Out of the seven levels the first five come under proper light and the levels can be seen; beyond them the experiences become more inward and not discernible from outside and not possible to discuss and explain. This way the disciple takes in knowledge and develops being and releases barriers around Self and thus comes closer to Self-realization.

The Way of Love is different from the Way of Knowledge. Love is based on the emotional center and is a sort of stream in which the disciple surrenders himself to the mercy of the stream. On this way he or she takes in nothing but gives up everything and in doing so merges into the stream and unites in Love with the lover [object of love]. Being a Way of Love, knowledge is rather secondary and unimportant. It is a field of experience beyond Buddhi. That is why there are no stepping stones or steps of the ladder to be seen and marked. Anyone who would venture to mark them would not have direct experience so it will only be guesswork and will be based on knowledge and devoid of love. One should not and could not establish the levels on this way.

* * *

Dr.R. Does the Shastra provide all knowledge necessary to live?

H.H. Yes, but there are two types of Shastra. One type points the direction and orders what should be done. The other type offers counsel only and never demands or commands.

Dr.R. Does it help a man to take an interest in and know about the great world of the stars and the little world within himself?

H.H. Knowledge of the higher and inner worlds is necessary, for by knowing the laws of those worlds one can escape from them. Knowledge of this kind is always good but one should be careful that it is complete. A little knowledge is dangerous. Nearly all the mistakes made are through limited knowledge. Some don't need knowledge for they go by the emotional way. Someone can tell them about this and off they go. They do not need to acquire this knowledge by themselves as do those who follow the path of Knowledge.

* * *

Dr.R. asked about True and differentiated knowledge, and whether it is stored in Buddhi?

H.H. In Buddhi True Knowledge is reflected through Manas, the mind and body. As True Knowledge is appreciated by Buddhi, so also is differentiated knowledge. The first glimpse of both is felt in Buddhi; later it is felt elsewhere in other ways.

Q. Have we known the Param Atman before? Is it memory of that [which] makes us make effort and also tells us whether we are on the right path?

H.H. The knowledge in the Absolute and the Self [Atman] is always the same. The Atman within the individual has that part of knowledge which belongs to the Absolute. If by analogy the True

Knowledge were taken to be a store in the Absolute, the individuals possess a part of it. The worldly activities and daily struggle for a living, all desires and volitions create certain obstacles and sheaths and due to the habit of being involved in them we forget the True Knowledge. Those people who train us for the world lead us to that differentiated knowledge and the mechanical routine which makes it possible so that for some time we have no direct access to knowledge which belongs to us. Sometime when you come across some people who have the connection, the impulse from them reminds you once again, and the memory of that experience is always there; and once aroused it would be impossible to forget in this life. The forgetting is possible only to us human beings; the Absolute never forgets, for if He did, all mediums of communication would come to an end. Once reminded you may not make much effort —that is different—but you will recognize that the knowledge is there. It is up to you to take action or not. For example, if you stand by a river under a tree and gaze at the flowing water, you will experience the feeling that you are moving and the water is still. If you look away from the river, then you will find in fact that you are not moving, and it is only the water that is in movement. The same applies to our relationship with the world. When we turn inside then we find stability in ourselves and can observe that all the movement is in the world. If we get involved with the world, then we lose our stability and find the world stable and ourselves making all movements of activity.

Dr.R. Is the undifferentiated knowledge which we get from the Atman stored in Buddhi? And is the differentiated knowledge in Manas, etc.?

H.H. In Buddhi the True Knowledge reflects. The Manas, senses and body are affected by knowledge. Just as True Knowledge can be appreciated by Buddhi, the differentiated knowledge is also taken up by Buddhi. It is the clarity and stillness that will define what type of knowledge he has got.

Dr.R. H.H. has said that before anything is done an image is first formed. The same is true for an artist, a sculptor who makes a statue, a composer who makes music. Is that image formed in Buddhi?

H.H. Though the image and the concept are formed in Buddhi yet it is only a reflection of the Atman. For example, the governor of a state is responsible for doing everything, for looking after high and low and the general welfare within his state. He gets the authority from the King, and he simply carries it through.

Dr.R. One asks all this because one wants to create an ever-present image of oneSelf, the Atman, or of His appointed fully-realized man. Is this done in Buddhi if it is stilled and purified?

H.H. Yes, this is the point of it, and it is done if Buddhi is still and pure, but where there is tamas one cannot keep the image one wants. He says Buddhi is the element which discriminates, but the actual store of all the knowledge is Chitta. For instance, a man goes to the market and earns his livelihood and when he comes home he either gives the money to his wife or puts it in the safe. Buddhi also gets knowledge by discrimination and stores it in Chitta. But Chitta, which is a sort of filing system, can file things wrongly; or things may get mixed up in the filing cabinet. So Buddhi cannot get the right thing at the right moment when wanted. It is very important to improve the filing and store our references systematically and keep them separate and classified so that Buddhi can make the best use of knowledge stored. Of course Buddhi also absorbs unwanted and even dangerous things when it is not still, when moving about with Manas.

* * *

Dr.R. Would you tell us some more about the idea of the drama of creation as a means of developing non-attachment?

H.H. The Creator starts the creation as a play with the help of Maya. The relationship of the Creator and Maya is the same as the relation of an individual [Atman] to ignorance. The ignorance is a shadow of Maya, just as the individual is a reflection of the Absolute. The Absolute plays with Maya and knows it to be play and thus amuses Himself; the individual doesn't know that because of ignorance. So he has to take recourse to Knowledge [True Knowledge]. With this True Knowledge—which is again all about Maya—he gets to know Maya, and then he understands that all that play in the universe is only a drama. The knowledge of this is True Knowledge. In the moving aspect of our Chitta [Consciousness] and because of the impurities around it, Chitta is deprived of that Knowledge. Lakshman saw the impurity and speed of Chitta in his dip.

* * *

Dr.R. Many people want to hear more about the Tradition of the meditation, and particularly about the first Shankaracharya and his predecessor. We have some material but we would like to know more.

H.H. When we talk about the first Shankaracharya and the Tradition of Shankaracharya we don't really mean that this Tradition was produced and created by Shankaracharya. It was only made available through him at a certain point in our history. The Tradition starts right from the beginning of creation, starting from Narayan, coming through Brahma, Vashishtha, Shakti, Parashar, Vyasa, Gandpadacharya and Shankaracharya. Since the first Shankaracharya we have the tradition of four seats of Shankaracharyas for the last 2,500 years. The Knowledge does not come from men at all, whether Shankaracharya or any other leader of other religions. The Knowledge belongs to the Absolute and the Atman. These leaders simply only catch the ideas and expound them according to the need of the time, place and the people. He clothes the Knowledge in a fashion that suits the standard of people living at the time and place where he happens to be. This is why the religions differ. Fundamentals are always the same, but details are always different. Some say it in crude form, another uses a subtle language, whereas the third might give a synthesis of the two. All the religions of the world like Christianity, Islam or Hinduism, etc. are not really what is meant by dharma [righteous way of living]. They are only fabrications round the dharma. Humanity is one, so human beings can have only one dharma, and that is the system of True Knowledge which has found different manifestation in different religions. It is the desire and need of the time and place which crystallizes into one single person, who becomes a vehicle to express the True Knowledge in his own way. Neither the present nor the first Shankaracharya nor anyone else has created the True Knowledge. It simply happens to pass through certain individuals.

* * *

Dr.R. I was thinking also of preserving ideas from the Holy Tradition which have been kept clean for so long and kept alive; and thinking of the best way of preserving those. They must not get muddled, for I know how easy it is to misunderstand an idea which is clothed in Indian dress!

H.H. gives an example of the way the Indian dress can be twisted. This study of the Self or the Truth needs three years. But anyone who thinks he knows everything after three years, in fact knows nothing. On the contrary: The man who feels that from this point, after three years, starts the True Knowledge, so his thirst for knowledge continues unabated, then he would be the man who has understood something about the practical continuation of this work.

You and the other Europeans who were in the RAM NAGAR expedition—when these sixty-to-seventy people were set an examination of 20 questions—12–16 correctly-answered questions was the pass mark. To your misfortune you failed the examination! But as the twist of this Indian nature plays its act on most of its aspirants, those who passed didn't develop this thirst at all and have been lost for good and all. But the one who failed is somehow kept alive and is still striving in this line of search.

If anyone thinks he had learned enough spiritual knowledge and knows all the answers by himself, then he has done nothing in this line of study and will meet with failure in his life, particularly along this line of spiritual endeavor. Tulsidas [the great poet] once said, "If anyone has had enough of the prayers and recitations

Knowledge 241

about Rama, he has learned nothing about Rama." [Rama was his deity.] The same idea has been explained in the Upanishads—that one who claims to have known Brahma, has not known Brahma. The one who says he doesn't know Brahma will also not know Brahma. But who then does know the Brahman?

In the course of his life, a certain king set aside 100 cows laden with gold to be the prize for the man who could claim to be the wisest in the assembly. The great rishis had assembled—one was Yajnavalkya, one of these rishis. Without claiming to be the wisest man, he asked his disciples to drive these cows to his ashram. A wise woman called Gargi [his wife] rose up and asked Yajnavalkya, "Do you claim to be the wisest of all?" Yajnavalkya replied, "I always pay my respects to the wise men, but if you have any questions, you can ask me. But do not ask me an impertinent question." So she asks the question: "Where is the phenomenal or Earth-world world?" He replies, "This Earth-world is in the water." "Where is this world of water?" she asks. And so the questions go on through fire, air, and ether [space]. The question comes back to the answer that everything stems from the Brahman.

He continues, "There is no cause of the cause so don't ask further questions. If you do ask, you will be impertinent and your head will fall from your body!" This is how the Rishi Yajnavalkya took away the cows without claiming to be the wisest of all the contesting teachers.

H.H. continues: If there is any query arising out of the discussions here or in London suggesting that the words of the Indian system cannot be fully understood in the English language, he rules out this problem. This isn't the problem because the main principle of this discipline is the meditation. Meditation is designed to improve the level of sattva. Once the sattva has become more abundant in the individual then a light will appear within himself. If he has not been given full treatment on the intellectual level, if he is not satisfied about certain ideas, then he himself will be able to look at his problems and find the answers because of the sattva within. In fact it is a human problem and not a linguistic problem. The main attention is to be given to the human problem and discussions aimed at the particular individual difficulties. If one vital question in an individual life is solved somehow, then the man will be able to guide himself and learn whatever he needs. The best thing is to meditate properly!

* * *

Q. So on the way discrimination is necessary between these forms and elements and the pure Atman, and this must take place whether in meditation or about our affairs?

H.H. We naturally live in the world of names and forms and we are surrounded by them, and even the being we call ourself has as many names and forms. People have name, form, and also the Atman; thus it seems everything is everywhere, but because of ignorance people get involved in only the world of name and form. Usually they take their 6-foot body as their Ultimate Being. The System of Knowledge and the method of meditation is to remove the narrowness of that boundary and bondage and allow people to discriminate and see the unlimited and unbounded Atman which cannot be brought into the limits of names and forms. Here is an example.

Someone went to a holy man and asked to be introduced to God. The holy man said that when I go to Him, He will ask about you. What shall I say about you? So first give me some details of your own credentials. The man pointed to his body and told his name. The holy man said that all this is made of flesh and bones which is always subject to growth and decay. How could this be you? It is only your body and name. Get me your proper credentials. The man thinks and says that perhaps his thoughts, desires, feelings were his proper credentials. The holy man again observed that even more rapidly than the bodily form these are changing all the time. Give me your proper and fixed credentials. In this way this man was led to recognize his own True Self and then he did not go around seeking any more introductions.

The System of Knowledge and method of meditation are simply to lead people to discriminate between the transitory and the eternal, between formal and informal, between words and the Spirit, so that one can enjoy forms, words and also the real Being.

* * *

H.H. What takes the time is that the knowledge of such ideas must first be appreciated enough to put it into practice—such as the idea which was taken by your Buddhi [i.e. intellectually only] that the flesh, bones, Manas and Antahkarana are *not the Self*. For these relate to the five sheaths described by the first Shri Shankara in "The Crest Jewel," and anyone will have to penetrate through these sheaths and detach one after another by faithful practice in order to realize the Self.

Unless this theoretical knowledge, which at most is just good information, is put into constant and continuous use, it never becomes real or realized knowledge. And only when that knowledge is realized does the individual become realized.

* * *

Dr.R. Does this concentration of the sattva which often follows attention also lead to sudden moments of truth which also feel like "waking up," as when you wake up and see that yourself and also the people of the world are asleep and all their troubles come from being and doing in sleep?

H.H. The effect of sattva is new awakening. It comes with a new opening and one is opened up to what actually exists and not to what pictures we have in the mind. People wake up and see whatever there is. Just as with an oil lamp which is about to go out due to lack of oil, and when supplied with oil it brightens up. Whenever there is a wave of sattva in the being it arouses a new awakening. How this new awakening is used entirely depends upon the essence [sanskar] and the being. If only a casual drop of sattva has crept in, the awakening is followed by sleep and the effect of sattva is lost. If the presence of sattva is constant and the essence is good, the True Knowledge and meditation available, then it can lead to higher consciousness, and use of awakening can be made to help oneself, and others too. Naturally one can't have sattva all the time. Most of our day is governed by rajas and tamas. At most one could be under the influence of sattva for two or three hours.

Q. Like some others, often I have the feeling that I have lived before and I have lived many lives, and then I know what is going to happen because the situation is familiar.

H.H. This effect is due to increase of sattva. Those who are fortunate enough to have abundance of sattva, they can retain the knowledge and also revive the knowledge of the past or see the future events. Those with too much rajas and tamas they cannot even retain what they hear. They keep on hearing and also keep on forgetting. Due to the lack of sattva nothing is retained. It is the sattva that holds the knowledge.

The quantity of sattva is also subject to increase and loss. It depends upon how does one live his life. If he is under the influence of True Knowledge and practices meditation, the possibilities are more; when the life is directed only to sensual enjoyment and material gains, the sattva will be reduced.

* * *

Q. Is it possible to put a question in relation to the real world and the unreal world? If the wakeful state is as it were the lower level of the consciousness of the real world, what are the higher states in this world?

H.H. It would be good to refer to details of the Seven Steps of Knowledge which had been given long ago. After leaving the three steps behind, when one comes to the Fourth Step of "Pull of the Way" then the sattva starts building up, and in that state many good things seem to happen such as, if one said something, it might come true; one might see future events or have some visions or read the mind of other people whenever there is influx of sattva. When you reach the Fifth Step of "Insight" then the attraction of the physical world starts losing its hold. The good things of the material world become easily available, but one doesn't wish to use them even though the physical forces for such use of them are working. Due to presence of the sattva and the True Knowledge, one just prefers to ignore them. One also develops a sense of "seeing through" the things and situations. The next stage is of the "Abundance." In this stage one begins to experience the Self in all things. Instead of looking at the outer form of matter, one looks into the heart of matter where the Absolute abides. This is practically the highest state in the world. Beyond it is "Turiya" when no cognition of any duality is possible. Everything is just one, and even the knowledge of the manifested world seems to be lost, for one sees only unity, and the world of manifestation and division is no longer seen. Turiya state doesn't last for long. It is mostly preceded by samadhi. There is no idea, no form and no word in this state. It is all One.

Q. There are scientists, busy with their efforts, who look into nature's laws step-by-step and give us knowledge about them. They also harness the discovered laws for the benefit of the masses. What difference does it make for a man who has taken to the system of True Knowledge and meditation when compared to the scientist who hasn't?

H.H. The basis of all scientific work is the elements. They discover their laws and use them for quicker and faster use of the material world. The pace of life is thus made to be faster. The electricity or an airplane will take men high into the sky, but they have to come back for the rest to the earth because without it they cannot live. The quicker pace of life is quickening everything, and in this process the natural balance is being lost. But the men on the path of knowledge and meditation work for peace and happiness. In doing so they become natural and thus enjoy everything. The scientist runs after the effect and *we* look for the cause.

Dr.R. I was not referring to the scientific world when I asked my last question. I meant the sattva shows the inner connection between things that one doesn't see in ordinary sleep state; for instance, ordinarily we see just two things—duality. I meant that in the stage of "Pull of the Way" [Sattvapatti] you begin to see the third element in everything. You begin to see the Law of Three. Because you have sattva, do you not begin to see the three forces and not duality?

H.H. The physical world with all its laws is there and the physical faculties are also there to appreciate the physical laws for each of us. It is the quality of these faculties which determines how much one can make use of the physical laws and the elements of matter. This is a common factor and common knowledge for which there are schools and colleges to provide such knowledge, and anyone who wants them can have them. The difference between this type of knowledge and ours is this, that if having resorted to pursue and use the physical laws you find yourself torn into pieces, disturbed and miserable, then beyond this physical world there is another world and its laws which are known to us, and we can comfort you with them and lead to peace and happiness. We will also initiate you to make you able to go to the source of knowledge and energy with which you still further your life with peace, happiness, efficiency and precision. The appreciation of the Law of Three or seeing the third force is just part of the knowledge of this world.

Just as there is someone present to give water to a thirsty man or if someone is hungry, there will be someone to cook for him; likewise there is always someone ready to supply what is needed. In being with the physical world and working on the physical world you take what you need; and in taking all that you want or which you think you want, if you find that you are in trouble, then there is someone to give you peace and happiness. That is the reason for our existence. We give what science cannot give or what science cannot evolve or what would never come out of their effort.

* * *

H.H. Practice and discipline always lead toward truth and purification [refinement].

You, Dr. Roles, are predominantly emotional. But this has to go hand-in-hand with discourses and knowledge of Truth, by which emotional center [Bhawana] and intellectual center [viveka]

Knowledge 247

are brought together. Only then is it possible that a person would move on the Way easily and with precision. That is why it is essential that discourses must take place to clear out any errors in the mind or anything not fully understood. True Knowledge is the only means to free one from any doubt, or whatever could arise, as a setback on the way of Liberation.

* * *

Q. Could H.H. say something about anand? Is it something that comes as a result of development on the Way, or is it a state which one can induce?

H.H. Anand is the natural state of the Atman when all other things and obstacles are removed, then the Atman exists in the anand; no one in the creation can exist without some anand. One might feel that as one develops on the Way and makes progress, so one feels that anand is also improving or developing, but this is only illusory. The real state is that anand is always with the Atman and so unchanging. It is only our view of it which has changed.

So it is very much like what we have always been given about the Absolute as Sat-Chit-Anand: that Sat is that which is always there, which remains always the same and which is Truth. Then he defined the Chit which is Consciousness or Knowledge, none of these three ever changes.

Men as they are born are not given any particular knowledge, but all the knowledge resides in the Atman, so in all individuals. This has got to be aroused by somebody who seems to be giving the knowledge, but in fact nobody gives any knowledge to anyone. One becomes an instrument to arouse the knowledge which is in everyone. When these two come together, Sat and Chit, then the outflow of anand takes place immediately; with the Truth and Consciousness, the anand flows in. One would not say that there is any improvement or any excess availability of anand because one is going on the Way, but it is clearing of all unnecessary obstacles which allows the anand to flow into the life of individuals.

The nature of water is liquid and cool, but if other sources are applied to make it hot, the nature which is cool is no longer available with the water, so, this natural state of the Atman which is anand can change into some other thing, just as we can experience with water.

In that relation, when people attach themselves by seeking pleasure rather than anand from worldly things, then certainly they are not experiencing Atman in its natural state.

Just as when one goes to sleep, and the sleep is good and profound, when one wakes up then one knows that the sleep was good and one experienced a happy state of sleep. The same applies to all other activities. Unless you take the food you would not be able to experience the happiness or joy of eating it.

Similarly, unless you meet the person you would not be able to derive the happiness, so this experience of happiness is possible only when some activity has been performed. It is only by coming together that anand is possible.

* * *

Q. Do the orange-colored robes worn by mahatmas attract sattva?

H.H. (The question made His Holiness smile.) Yes it attracts sattva. Orange, and more precisely yellow, is the color worn by Lord Vishnu. Devotees also wear this color for its purifying effect on the mind.

Sannyasis who have renounced the world, however, wear hematite color instead of orange which contains a greater proportion of red than orange. This is because it is the color of fire. Fire burns all worldly things whether good or bad. Not only that, but it also changes everything into its own shape, fire; and fire is a great purifier. Similarly, a renounced person burns all his worldly impulses whether good or bad, transforming them all into his own pure Self. The fire in this case is True Knowledge. This fire of True Knowledge burns away the entire false illusion of the world, "so this is good, this is bad," and all that is left subsequently is pure reality.

The wearing of the orange or hematite color is meant to remind the wearer constantly of his duty, just as wearing a uniform reminds a policeman or a soldier of his duty.

* * *

Dr.R. Chitta will then release consciousness in proportion to the importance of the occasion? [H.H. assents.] Bank managers often say we are overdrawn. [People laugh.]

H.H. But *this* wealth is of a special kind. The more you take out, the more is available without end and in abundance—unless it is spent in purposes of rajas and tamas. If it is used for sattvic work, there will be plenty available. Then one can never overdraw.

The energy of a sattvic person or a person who purveys knowledge of the truth is of this kind. However much he engages himself in discourse to explain the truth to his pupils, or those needing his discipline, the more he does, the more he gets; there is no debit and the expenses are not out-going, but self-evolving; so he always adds more, and more becomes available.

Knowledge in Action

H.H. My blessings and goodwill for the well-being of the Society which was started by a great man who hailed from Russia, and who was loved by Dr. Roles. When he was about to leave his mortal body he instructed Dr. Roles to find the teacher in India. This tradition is ancient, and the tree planted and nourished by Dr. Roles cannot be harmed by any turbulence.

* * *

A real tradition is not the relic of a past that is irretrievably gone; it is a living force that animates and informs the present.... Far from implying the repetition of what has been, tradition presupposes the reality of what endures. It appears as an heirloom, a heritage that one receives on condition of making it bear fruit before passing it on to one's descendants.

Igor Stravinsky

Dr.R. I don't know if you have heard the story of the great teacher to whom people used to come from miles around. Before he spoke to the people he would go into the forest, light a fire and say a prayer; then he would come back and speak to them. He died, and his successor used to go into the forest, light a fire, but couldn't remember the prayer! After a time this teacher, too, died and his successor just went into the forest; he had lost the art of lighting a fire or saying a prayer, but came back and spoke to the people; and finally his successor did not even bother to go into the forest, but just sat and taught the people, and that was the end!

And Dr. Roles adds: So there you have the life history of "C Influence" and what happens to it if people just repeat the words without working on their being.

H.H. As for the remembering of the teacher, it again does not mean the flesh and bones, but the knowledge and the Way, which he represents. Having remembered the teacher, one must once again remember all his teachings and that he only represents them because he has put them into practice. *Ultimately knowledge in action is all that matters.*

As previously told to you, there are those who only know that they exist and partake of "Sat." They live at a very low level. Others think and know, so they can reason and with that regulate their lives. They partake of "Sat" and "Chit." A third kind have known Sat and Chit, and get Ananda also. For them the world is full. They experience the Self as threefold [Sat-Chit-Ananda]. Ananda is the happiness that comes from practice of knowledge through action and in perfection. [When any job is done nicely, there is ananda or satisfaction at a "job well done."] So action on the basis of available knowledge is the keynote.

* * *

Q. So does His Holiness mean by "going deeper" into the subject, more and more study of the information or something rather different?

H.H. His Holiness says three things are necessary for complete realization. First is that you have to listen or study. This means do the study, shravana. Now the second thing is concentration on what you have studied—go on thinking about it, reflection upon it. That we call the manana. First you have to listen; and second is manana, concentration and reflection; and third is nididhyasana which means that you will have, after considering it for some time, to sit quietly and get absorbed in it.

Q. We might call that "contemplation."

H.H. Yes.

Q. And is there any method to be employed in the art of contemplation?

H.H. His Holiness says there are two things to be done. You are asking what is the machinery of contemplation. There are two things.

One is that one has to be attentive—attentive whether during study or listening. This is the first part. Studying, or listening is the first part and one has to be attentive in it, then alone the contemplation part will come. If one is not attentive, and one is only listening with a part of the mind, as it were, then the process of contemplation will not start. It will not be possible to indulge or employ oneself in that process.

The other thing is that one has to have a feeling of its greatness, of its utility. One has to be impressed about the greatness or the utility of the information then alone will that process be employed. So there are two things, one is attention and the other is a feeling of greatness or of its utility.

Q. And so is the knowledge of its utility a product of the desire to know?

Translator Exactly. This was the point, which I myself raised. Shankaracharya has already replied to that part. That desire to know is when a man asked the question for the first time, but when he repeats that question, then that desire has already been satisfied. Now there is only this thing of contemplation, thinking about that question again and again. So the desire part is finished; this is now manana—the thinking part.

H.H. We see so many things. We don't remember them all. Unless we see things with attention, then we remember. We listen to many things. We do not remember them all. There are certain things, which we heard many years ago, and we still remember them because we heard them with attention. And we thought that they were worth remembering, we had a feeling about their utility. Therefore we continue to remember them. Similarly in this spiritual work, then you will listen to things and you will study things, you will be able to contemplate when you listen or read with attention and when you have a knowledge of their utility.

Q. Yes, by way of example, when I was here before, three years ago, His Holiness said, "That little sattva which you have is worth more than all the things of the world about you," and that was heard with the heart and has been of great utility. So, this especial attention can, I think, be practiced so that one hears more and hears better, but then one would need discrimination, what to attend to and what not to attend to.

Knowledge in Action

H.H. His Holiness said that discrimination is what you can use; this is the utility of a thing, which is more useful—and when you know the usefulness of a thing, then your practice will be automatic, you won't have to seek it, it will come of itself. You will be more attentive to those things which you think will be useful to you. Unless you have this feeling that this will be more useful toward you, you will not be able to practice attention toward that. The knowledge itself decides the utility.

Q. When you acquire the knowledge then you will know which is useful and which is not useful. That I think, may be obscured by desire, because if I want to know about this I will attend to this, and if I want know about that then I will attend to that. And so there is first to be made a discrimination, but if the desire is too strong—for the world shall we say—then how does a man proceed from that position?

H.H. Your question was that the desire for the world, if there is a great desire for the world, then how will you get away from it, and the reply is: It is natural for a person to be walking on earth, but some people practice and they can learn to swim, so they can swim in water. That's not natural. Man is by nature supposed to walk, not by nature to swim, but he can acquire that knowledge [of the] art of swimming so that he can go in the water. Similarly [there is] this rather natural tendency of mankind to have a feeling of utility of the worldly things but by practice he can acquire the power of knowing the utility of things other than those of the world—the ultimate things. Now while you have a feeling of the knowledge of utility of the things of the world you can also acquire the knowledge of the utility of the things of God and spirituality.

His Holiness further illustrates: The woman loves her son, her child. Also she loves her husband. But the quality of love and affection differs. She has a different sort of affection for the husband than for the child. But she can love both. Similarly a person can have a knowledge of the utility of the things of the world as well as a relationship with God Himself.

The only point is that it is slightly different! The base is the same. External affection is the same, but its nature is slightly different.

So your knowledge of utility is the same, the base is there, whereas we want to get this measure, as it were, for the world and differently for the God.

Q. Yes, this is very useful because many people argue that you have to choose one or the other and don't understand that the two can proceed side-by-side.

Q. Shankaracharya told us yesterday that we should keep our treasure in the heart where it could be used as necessary. I would like to ask further what can we do to ensure that the understanding of an important idea is ever present throughout the day, coloring our thoughts and actions?

H.H. One has to decide what are good thoughts and what are bad thoughts. This is a decision one has to make. Once a decision is made then one ought to stick to the good thought and remind oneself of it as often as one can. After some time it will have a place in the heart and all activities would be colored by it. Whatever is not good judged by one's own decisions, should not be toyed with. If any such does appear before the individual he should never give any support to it—just drop it. At those moments one can encourage good thoughts supporting and sustaining them. Only through this would it be possible to live up to the good idea.

There was a certain realized man, a holy man, to whom an elderly lady went with a small boy who was addicted to eating sweets. She wanted the influence of the holy man to remove this bad habit. When the holy man heard about this he asked the old woman to come back in a fortnight. After a fortnight when the old woman went there, this holy man simply said to the boy that eating sweets is not a very good habit, it will result in some sort of disease later on, "So, my good boy—you should give them up." The old woman said, "If that's all you had to say, you needn't have bothered me to come back after a fortnight." The holy man said he could not have done this the other day because he himself was in the habit of eating sweets and had no authority to ask any one else to give them up. So he had to give up eating sweets for this full fortnight and control his own self because if he did not control it he could have no authority, and even if he had said this to the boy it would have had no effect. In fact just these few words did do the trick. So ultimately it comes down to the individual.

If by the application of this knowledge, this company or the satsang and use of one's reason one has definitely found some truth somewhere, then the only thing one has to do is to put it into constant practice. One should never indulge in anything, which stands opposed to that goodness. Unless one does that there would never be any moral authority for preaching. So whatever one has decided is wrong, one should not entertain at all, and all that has been decided to be good should always be entertained and realized only by practice. By doing this one would see that the effect on the community, or the people around you, is positive and goodness will prevail.

Ladder

Dr.R. Our System [from Mr. Ouspensky] says that all the laws governing this manifest universe can be reduced to two fundamental cosmic laws: the law of three forces and the law of octaves. The law of three governs the birth of each single event, one example being the three gunas which control the physical and spiritual life of man. The law of octaves—or "law of seven"—governs every succession of events whether ascending or descending. Understanding of the interaction of these two laws is that of a man who has achieved all possible human knowledge in a state of cosmic consciousness. We have a universal symbol based on a circle of nine points which can explain this interaction and therefore all knowledge can be found in it. Would you tell us whether this outline is correct and whether, in your opinion, our system could at one time have branched off from your meditation tradition itself?

H.H. There is no difference at all in this broad outline between your system and ours. Since he has already spoken fully about the law of three and described, with examples, the interaction of the three gunas, he will now give a description of the law of seven.

The law of seven is a repetitive motion which goes on mechanically unless there is escape from the circle through full realization; otherwise the movement goes on repeating again and again. As an example the quest for Self fulfillment has been described as a *Ladder of Seven Steps.*

* * *

The NYAYA LADDER (after further research on the root meanings of the Sanskrit names of the seven steps)

The First Stage, SHUBHEKSHA: pious desire, longing, auspicious urge. The desire for liberation or unity by one who has some degree of attention as a result of his unselfish deeds and discipline in his life up to then. The manifestation is the start of an inquiry into one's own Self—a search for the Atman.

H.H. says: This is the good intention, the rising up of right desire. This is the start which leads to:

The Second Stage, SUVICHARNA (Suvicara—right company): good reflection, thought, investigation, circumspection. The act of investigation and thinking about all that one has gathered concerning the desire for liberation or unity.

H.H. says: The coming to a decision by which rationally [by reasoning] he comes to the point where he can go further without doubt. The Way appears to be in line with his intention and his conviction.

The Third Stage, TANUMANSA (Tanumanasi—threadlike attention): lessening of outward mental movements. Entry into the knowledge of Self. Regular practice in experience of the unity of Self and Atman and righteous living leads the mind to go naturally inward rather than outward.

H.H. says: When the particles in the body start the striving toward Sattva.

The Fourth Stage or *SATTVAPATTI*: the dawn of true Self; having gone inward he comprehends his Self as it really is. The doubts and reflections cease and the real Self with right knowledge begins to appear.

H.H. says: This is when the Pull of the Way pulls him from the outside world of sensory impressions which begin to lose their power over him.

Long before he experiences the full strength of will [Atman], the third and fourth stage determine that he is getting quite strong will in himself; and by the time he crosses the fourth stage he has attained so much will that there is no question of that aspirant coming down the Ladder at all.

The Fourth Stage increases the sattva guna [Divine Love in this context]. The increase of sattva guna determines this stage for the aspirant so that the pull of the spiritual world becomes greater than that of the sensory world. Even very important activities in the material world no longer have so much pull for the aspirant as do his endeavors in the spiritual field. He saves time from them to complete the work on the spiritual line. It is this stage which determines that the disciple would rather complete that work than leave the Way.

The Fifth Stage, ASAMSHAKTI (Asamsakti—detached insight, complete non-attachment to worldly objects): loss of attachment. After regular glimpses of the Real Self, the attachment of self to body or possessions fades away. At this point there remains no identification, association or attachment of self to anything else. [Also ASAKTA = unattached]

About this H.H. says: This stage denotes that the man starts looking at things *as they are*. He gets right values for everything; he realizes about things what they are, how they are constituted, what their properties are.

The fifth stage is that in which the person ceases to consider all that is in the world as outside himself. He starts getting glimpses of the fact that he and the "outside world" are one thing. It is quite possible, even before the fourth stage, to have glimpses of the next stage ahead, but, as in ordinary education, you have to pass from Primary to Graduation stage-by-stage, just so you have to take these steps. Unless you pass one, you cannot go on to the next. Thus the completion of the fourth stage determines that the disciple does not turn back or leave the Work. The realization of the fifth stage gives a feeling of unity with the material world— unity of spirit with materiality. He realizes, for instance, that the clay is not different from the [design of the] pot. He sees the unity, the causal aspect within all the material things we register in our daily impressions. He sees the root cause and the effects of that cause together—sees them as one thing.

The Sixth Stage, PADARTHA BHAWANA, means the absence of duality, or "Pure Bliss." At this stage one realizes the presence or existence of Atman in everything, everything in Atman. This is equated with samadhi.

H.H. says: This is the stage when the outward pull is nearly gone, and he comes close to pure sattva and abundance of sattva. Asked further about loss of the sense of duality, he replied with the example of a real elephant and an artificial one made of felt. They may look alike, but with the real elephant we watch out for our safety as we might do with the artificial one if we didn't realize it was unreal. The coarse material world of the senses is like the artificial elephant; once we know all that is artificial then we know the real; we establish relation with the real, and we don't bother about the artificial.

The last or *Seventh Stage* is *TURIYA*: the fourth, the mighty. The fourth[†] state of Consciousness when the Self becomes one with the Atman.

H.H. says: Turiya is the stage of the realized man when he knows himself, he knows everything, he knows how to DO, and whatever he does is just the right thing—right action, right thoughts and right feeling—everything all combined.

He said there are other, exceptional, states of consciousness beside the four described, e.g. fainting or unconsciousness of body from whatever cause, hypnosis, trance state, and finally there is samadhi where all outward and inward impressions stop for the disciple, who simply exists in bliss but keeps his consciousness by will. But Turiya is none of these and yet all of them. All the degrees and kinds of consciousness are like colors which merge in the white light.

* * *

H.H. You asked about the good impulses and all the good resolutions which come in one's everyday life and then are not usually carried through. One has to differentiate between two types of good resolutions and good impulses. One is born of the mind [Manas] and is the effect of time and place, certain situations or certain influences which come from outside—we seem to be in those situations, so we resolve to do certain things. The other is born of understanding [Buddhi], which comprehends that in such and such a situation we have this much energy or capacity; and so, with this capacity, we resolve to take up an activity or any one of

---

[†]This refers to four states of consciousness met with on the Ladder: 1) Dreamless Sleep; 2) Dream; 3) Waking; 4) Unity, Enlightenment.

the good resolutions, and then we carry it through, we just do not drop it because times have changed, the atmosphere is gone, or our energy is dissipated. So one has to decide by one's own reason as to whether the resolutions to be taken are worthwhile, whether they can be carried through; and then, once having decided, we should keep to those resolutions.

* * *

Q. Is it right to think that Effort, the third step on the ladder, is the effort needed to practice attention, and that this is no longer necessary when one feels the Pull of the Way? Is this in line with what His Holiness has told us that dharana [concentration] goes into dhyana [meditation] and dhyana goes into samadhi? Is true will, or the will of the Atman, needed in order to practice attention?

H.H. The difference between true will and ordinary will is that true will concerns the Truth, whereas ordinary will concerns itself with worldly matters. Truth in its purest form is that individual and Brahman are the same.

Attention is necessary for every type of action, worldly or spiritual. People attend naturally to what pleases them but the pleasant is not necessarily the same thing as the good. The good is that which leads to realization that you are the Absolute. To move toward the good one needs discipline. The ladder of knowledge and the system of yoga are two ways which prepare and provide the way to Self-realization.

* * *

H.H. Only when a decision is accomplished can the aspirant move with attention and some devotion to make systematic efforts [tanumansa]. Through these efforts impediments fall away and the Pull of the Way [sattvapatti] is established. This happens due to increase of sattva in one's being and knowledge. This then clears the intellect so much that Insight and Abundance follow, leading to Turiya.

The Pull of the Way materializes because elements of sattva

have cleared the intellect and the way is clearly seen. Although confusion and doubts are mostly cleared away and a natural and steady progress on the way is possible, attention is still needed. By this time the true will of the Atman would have taken root as in dharana, when stability of the mind has become obvious. Only with the help of attention can Insight, Abundance and Turiya be reached. Turiya is the only point when will and Atman become one, as in samadhi.

* * *

Q. Where is the act of consciousness on the Ladder of Self-realization?

H.H. It starts from step number five. As has been said, first step is the impulse to find a way; the second is considering the pros and cons with plenty of bad thoughts still. Third, bad thoughts get weaker and in the fourth they are gone. On the fifth step where the pull of the way to Atman is felt, self-realization begins. On the sixth step, the name and forms by which we see the outer world cease to exist. The seventh step is equilibrium where the "I" becomes dissolved and everything becomes one.

* * *

H.H. stresses that the realized man maintains his consciousness and his will even in samadhi and in Turiya, and this is the important part—that he should always remember himself and not disappear into a trance where he is no longer conscious, for that leads nowhere.

* * *

H.H. Turiya is a state which even ordinary men experience, but that happens in momentary flashes. They may be intermittent in our life. But the state which is the Seventh Step on the Ladder is the state one would experience forever, following on after Self-realization. For a householder it is not necessary that they must have that state. They may get glimpses and that is enough.

* * *

Dr.R. Over the years we have made some discoveries for ourselves about this ladder. As shown in the diagram these seven steps are already in existence along any radius "Now" from the periphery to the center. But because the repetitive movement of "passing time" is imposed on the body of the individual from without, so "time" in hours, days, years seems to take command over a union which by its nature is instantaneous or continuous like the spectrum of white light. The individual [Jiva] must not be upset or deluded by "passing time" which belongs to the sensory world and does not apply, on higher levels or to pure Consciousness itself.

And finally while the intellect is always demanding precise definitions, descriptions, rules and regulations, a heart, full of joy and gladness can transcend such artificial barriers though the mind must be present as a conscious observer. (See diagram.)

The Ladder of Seven Steps according to the Nyaya or Nai System

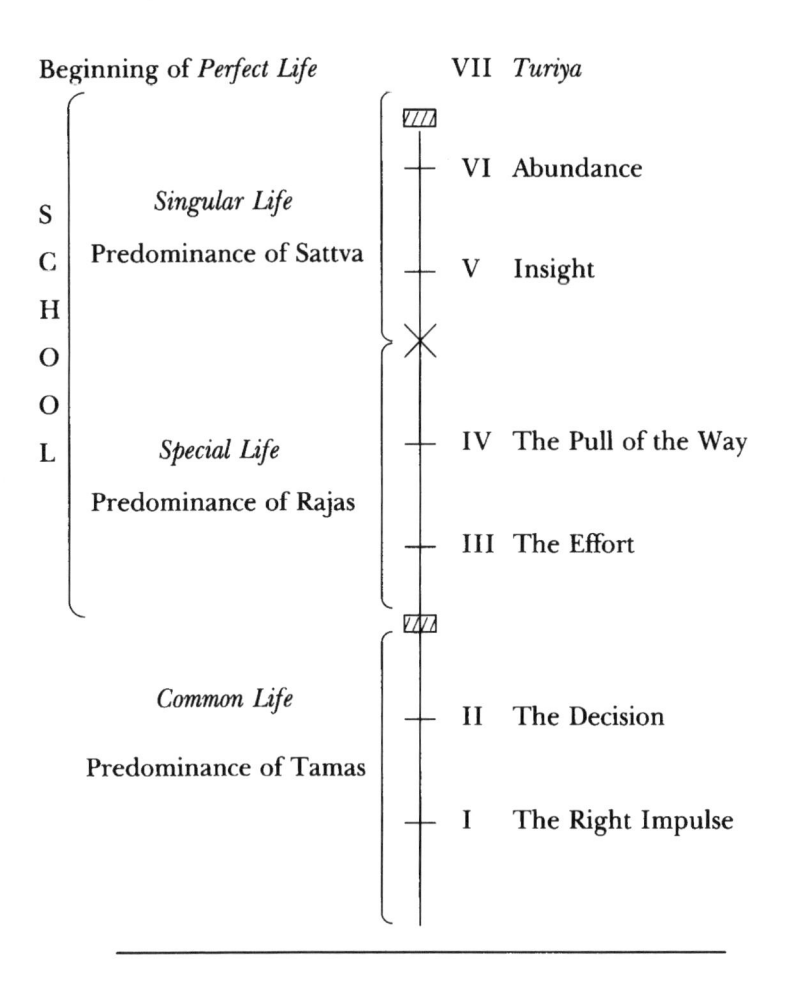

	Beginning of *Perfect Life*	VII	*Turiya*
S		VI	Abundance
C	*Singular Life*		
H	Predominance of Sattva	V	Insight
O			
O			
L	*Special Life*	IV	The Pull of the Way
	Predominance of Rajas		
		III	The Effort
	Common Life		
		II	The Decision
	Predominance of Tamas		
		I	The Right Impulse

Level of ordinary life .... "Street Level"

Laws

Dr.R. What is the chief difficulty with many people was answered in a talk H.H. gave here fairly recently where he says that Param Atman gives to each person what is good for him—what they deserve, and what is good for them. We see all kinds of tragedies around; they cannot understand that and this drives many people away from God, a misunderstanding.

H.H. One has to understand the two facets here, one is Samashti and the other is Vyashti; and the presiding Deity [or the responsible Being] of Samashti is the Param Atman Himself, and the responsible person of Vyashti is the Jiva, oneself. There are two sets of laws responsible for the government of these two levels. The set of laws, which govern the individual [Vyashti] are the outcome of the activities which have been performed by that individual in the cycles of birth and death. The reward for the deeds which he has performed in his previous life will be presented to him in this life. For instance, one might be going along the street and be involved in an accident and fall dead or be seriously injured there. Obviously there is nothing to indicate the responsibility of the individual for being knocked down in the street. The only causal explanation that could be given for such accidents is that he may have done something in his previous life for which he is paying the price today, according to his prarabdha [which is unknown to him].

This set of laws are there to govern the individual and they will keep on governing; whatever happens is the reward of one's own deeds. One should understand these laws. Having understood the laws, the misery following any seeming accident would be reduced.

Then there are the laws which govern large numbers within the Samashti [the Universe]. For instance, fifty people may be sitting in a boat and the boat might sink in the river, and one cannot say that all fifty deserve the same fate. There may be one who deserves it or none, but this is at the level of the Samashti—there have to be certain accidents. Because of the Samashti activity and the prarabdha all these things happen: Trains collide and hundreds of people die; a war comes and thousands of people die; at the frontier the forces from two different nations face each other and shoot and kill each other. This does not come about because of the deeds of the individual—although for everything that happens on either level, payment has to be made by individuals everywhere. The presiding deity of the Samashti is the Param Atman Himself but He responds by neither sorrow nor pleasure; so far as He is concerned it is only a play—a drama which is being enacted—and He is not involved in the justice of what is being performed, but He must act because the laws are there and His laws must be carried on. Since it comes back to the individual either on the Vyashti level or on the Samashti level, then the need for understanding is doubly necessary.

If one understands these two sets of laws, then one refrains from attaching oneself to whatever result comes in life, either by oneself or as part of the universal laws of nature.

The same principle has been explained in the Fourth Chapter of the *Bhagavad Gita* [V.6-12] in which Krishna says that "this Universe is created by Me and in this there are four castes and they work according to the laws, but I attach no importance to any of it. I keep going without any attachment to whatever happens in this world, but individuals have to take whatever comes their way. If they understand these laws, then they will come to realize that this Universe and whatever happens in it is an act, a drama." Just as in a drama, having performed all the different activities, behind the curtain the individual remains the same, having no attachment of any sort, and he does not react to the pleasures or misery of the drama on the stage. This is all one has to understand. If one understands these two sets of laws and detaches oneself from the resulting miseries and sorrows, then one would simply live according to the laws, both of which are regulated by the Absolute in either way.

In the universe there will never be a time when everything will be going smoothly. In the nature of things there will always be some agitation, for the creation itself is the product of agitation. There will be imbalance all the time. But for the individual there is a way of escape from this agitated state of the universe and that has been suggested to you all in the meditation, samadhi and deep sleep. Having gone deep into meditation then you come to a state of equilibrium where the laws do not contaminate you—they do not touch you. That is the only moment of equilibrium available, apart from deep sleep, otherwise there will always be disturbances in the universe and we ought to learn to face them with detachment so that their effect in misery, ecstasy, or pleasure does not bind us.

* * *

Dr.R. To come near to the Samashti H.H. said, "the individual must become very light"—drop his burden of worries about the past and future. So now what to ask? We now have a firm faith in the immanence of the threefold unity, but cannot manifest this worthily, cannot carry out His will, and "say what we feel and do what we say." Are there further instructions?

H.H. The first thing to understand is that one should never consider one's shortcomings on this Way, one should always take the positive aspect that whatever glory is made available in the form of force or energy, power, intelligence, wisdom, should be put into action. I will explain the distribution of energy emanating from the Absolute in this universe,

The universe is designed in such a way that each being has its place and is empowered with certain limited force. Within this limit, they will have to carry on the act which is most suitable to them. It is true that they can do it better or worse, but always within certain limits. So each being is provided with certain things within his Antahkarana, which he has to make use of for himself, his family, for his society, in his nation, and so on. Each one has to understand how much energy is available to him to manipulate in a particular place and at a particular time.

In the *Gita*, Krishna says the action should be performed with pleasure, not by coercion, not by compulsion, not by bondage of any sort; so whatever emanates from the state of one's being should be performed and then should be forgotten, so that the next opportunity may be taken and then performed.

This relates to the principle that one does not have to think about what one *cannot* do, one should always keep on thinking about what one *can* do.

The bliss is the sort of measure, the limit, which is implanted in each being, and this creates the force in each individual. From this, everything has to manifest. If anyone wants to transcend this limit—with goodwill, of course—with ambition to have extra power to manifest the extra glory of the Absolute, then one would find oneself in trouble!

Take the example of someone who had to travel about ten miles away to attend to some urgent work, and it was late at night and pitch dark. He took his lantern and came out of the house. He looked out and saw the pitch darkness, which prevailed the whole ten miles to his destination. He thought of his small lantern and wondered how he could tread this ten miles of darkness. He thought his own light would not be capable of leading him ten miles. Fortunately a holy man passed by and he inquired why the man was standing at the threshold. The man expressed his fears of finding his way ten miles with a light, which only shone ten feet. The holy man told him not to worry because the moment he stepped forward, the light would also move forward. The light would always be ten feet ahead of him, so don't worry—just proceed. So he did, and reached his destination.

This only established that whatever power within the laws of the universe—the laws of Samashti and Vyashti—has been enshrined in the individual, he has to make use of it in the best possible way. Electricity is made available through all the connections and wires, but if anyone tries to put 250 watts through a 100 watt bulb, it will fuse of itself. This means that individuals, having certain limits to manifest the glory, *cannot* claim, cannot have any extra power because they are not designed like that; and this, each of us has to realize.

The ant has a particular measure of power and within those

limits it will have to perform its activities. The elephant has a different measure of power and accordingly a different body, so it will always use the power which is available to it; neither can the ant perform the deeds of the elephant, nor can the elephant perform the deeds of the ant.

It is not only these so-called sub-human and ordinary human beings who are limited by a particular measure, but even the incarnations come down to earth with limited powers. The incarnations, which are described in India, are said to have descended with certain powers and they are regulated to certain numbers. Krishna, supposed to be the ultimate, descended with sixteen measures—that means full measure; but others did not have full measure—they had ten, or six, or four or three—whatever it was. This means there are limits in this universe, but within those limits, much can be done. The more you keep on doing, the more power will be available, so we should not worry that we "cannot do," but we should be concerned about what glory we manifest and be happy with it. One should, of course, take precautions not to fall below one's standard.

* * *

Q. H.H. referred to the two laws responsible for the government of the two levels of Samashti and Vyashti and said that we should understand them. How can we do this?

H.H. It is a very vast field; it needs much time to go deep into the subject, but one can give some indications about this problem. The laws are the same for all—both Samashti and Vyashti—but there is a difference in the way these laws are obeyed by Samashti and Vyashti. The laws are fully obeyed by Samashti all the time; there is no inclination to forget, ignore or disobey, only to obey what has been ordained. There is no possible desire or like or dislike, but only the will of the Absolute, and it alone prevails in Samashti. But this is not so in relation to Vyashti. In Vyashti the opportunity has been given to consider and obey, or hesitate to obey or disobey; there are all these alternatives to choose, and it would seem that the inferior rather than the superior way is followed much more in one's life, because Vyashti has forgotten its nature.

So there are other rules applied in Vyashti, which are not seen in Samashti at all; these extra laws, the retributive ones, are cause and effect. If you did A you will be rewarded by the fruits of A, and if you did B you will have the corresponding effect, so this keeps on going and makes the life of an individual much more complex than it was designed to be in his nature. This complexity arises from the free will which has been given to the Vyashti, particularly human beings.

Freedom is given, but this does not mean that one should become willful to do whatever one likes to do. The incarnations come into this world and they are certainly free—they are not bound by anyone. Yet it is seen that whatever shape or form the incarnation descends in, he always keeps to the laws available to that particular form. When he descends as a boar, he follows the laws of the boar. If he comes as a human being, he follows the laws of the human being—he does not transcend them at all. It is in the nature of the incarnations that they will do exactly what is needful and whatever is natural. The same applies to those who are wise people. They use their freedom to carry out the Will of the Absolute, not their own, which means they respond to the universal laws which govern the individual and also the universal.

A foreman in a factory signs the register himself, but the ordinary worker must punch his card to ensure time. If workers were allowed the same freedom, it would never be known if they were late or absent.

There are three types of people: the pure and the wise who naturally carry out the laws without any hesitation; whatever seems to come to them they will not bother about the effect, but they will carry out the law which is given to them. Then there are those who willfully disobey; they know that what they are doing is not right, but they will not do the right, they will willfully go against it. This creates confusion, and the common man is led by this confusion, so sometimes he does the right thing and sometimes he does the wrong thing. This is the majority in society, so it is up to the wise man, the pure man, to gather as many people as he can, carry out the pure will of the Absolute, and allow its effect to be absorbed by those around who have not yet become natural. It is only through this that the natural laws of the Samashti level can be performed at the Vyashti level.

The sun, which is governed by the Samashti law, has never seen darkness. It is in the nature of the sun that it will never come across darkness at all; but the individual being, though he has Atman within him which is much more brilliant than the physical sun, seems to see all sorts of darkness in this physical world, so let the wise man keep doing what is right, collect others to follow his example, and keep guiding the young ones.

* * *

Dr.R. Are not the laws of nature themselves powerful enough to punish those who break them? Why did you say yesterday that the Absolute Himself intervenes to punish?

H.H. Rules of nature? Nature is of the Absolute. So if nature proscribes anything against the law-breaker, it is only from the Absolute itself. So there is no difference between what nature does and what the Absolute does. It is all from the same agency.

Dr.R. Why do I keep worrying about the laws of nature: I don't like them very much—all these exploding stars and storms and floods. I would like to think that the subtle and spiritual levels are proof against all that.

H.H. In the Eleventh Chapter of the *Bhagavad Gita* there is the episode described where Krishna shows Arjuna his Great Self.

"In this Great Self all sorts of things are going on—one devouring another, killing and explosion, and realized man preaching, and all sorts of activity which one can think of in the world were being performed in the Great Self of Lord Krishna."

Arjuna said, "I am frightened to see all this, why is it so?"

Lord Krishna said "You think *you* are going to kill these great warriors facing you as enemies and *you* are going to be the cause of victory over all these enemies. But you can see that all these things happening here in my body are happening automatically, in the sense that this body of mine is the symbol of time. In time all these things are happening. You are only a stooge, an instrument! In fact you do nothing. In fact, everything is being done by the Absolute Himself."

Arjuna nodded in appreciation, but yet he said, "All that you [Krishna] have said is true, but I still prefer your peaceful incarnation to come in front of me again. Please take this frightening scene away!"

A lion can be seen in different moods. Sometimes he roars to frighten animals or attacks fiercely. Also he can be seen loving his offspring. The offspring can experience both the loving and the fierce moods. But the cub is never frightened because he is the son of the lion.

* * *

H.H. There are two kinds of Laws: One category is called dharma —*natural laws, laws of nature*; the other is called *Neeti*—*man-made laws*. The relation between them is like that between husband and wife. If both agree, there is peace, prosperity and contentment. But if there is conflict between husband and wife, there will never be much peace in the house—just eternal conflict!

The men who understand the laws of nature, and the men who administer the man-made laws, are respectively like a lame man who can see but cannot move, and a blind man who is very active but cannot see in what direction he is going or what will come out of his activities. So a way must be found for these two kinds of people to work together—the blind man should take the lame on his shoulder. The lame kind advises the blind which way to walk and the blind can be got around and do the job. But in the case of conflict nothing can be done; the blind will run the wrong way, and the lame will only talk. That should also be the relation of the realized men, to the public men—men at the market or the government. If that relation could be maintained, the house of the nation would have peace. Otherwise the nation will in the end disintegrate.

* * *

H.H. This modern time is such that the material gain is the foremost thing in the mind of people everywhere; but again, in India, there are still certain people engaged in keeping this tradition alive and making these influences available only to those who want them. When the proper time comes, then these influences will increase in India. In the same way, if you collect influences from here and have more contact with people, then the influences can be spread at your place.

In the worldly life the combination of these two [the lame man and the blind man] is necessary, so that the movement toward the achievement of the Self-realization and of the Liberation is possible —only by the union of the lame and blind. It works because, by this union, the regulations become a little more gentle and the people can move with the gentler touch of the natural law, rather than being forced by man-made regulations to do certain things under force. The achievements are bigger with the man-made laws, but they do not last long.

* * *

H.H. Creation is governed by the laws of nature, which are the expression of love. Nature assists those who seek transformation and punishes those who are attached to rigidity and do not want to change. This is the lesson.

* * *

H.H. According to [our] system, all our actions are governed by four principles, [?] laws:
 1. Time
 2. Our own nature
 3. The nature of the action
 4. The three gunas.

The interplay of all these decides the nature of our activities— where we are and what we will be doing.

H.H. goes on to give quite a lengthy description of *time* according to the traditional astronomy of India. In the rainy season you find worms springing up and dying in a day—2 hours, 3 hours—and that's their cycle of life. We men have 30 days in the month, 24 hours in a day, 60 minutes in an hour, and a month is one day for Indra. And for the ancestral men who live beyond the earth in the subtle body, 15 of our days is a day for them. A hundred years of Indra—on the basis of a day of one month—is only 2 moments for Brahma. And a hundred years of Brahma is just the twinkling of an eye for Vishnu, and a hundred years of Vishnu is nothing but a passing desire for the Great Absolute Brahma.

Now one can see the relation of speed of time to different types; there is no movement of time for Brahma the Absolute—it is still, not moving. You can see the relative speeds of common man and worm; they simply go on repeating their cycle, but at the end they will have to meet somewhere with Vishnu when the whole Creation will be taken back, and that's the way it goes on.

Dr.R. At important points in the whole history of humanity (for Humanity, too, must live again and again within Vishnu), suppose realized men were there to help, would humanity perhaps not take these wrong turnings—[where] religious life become[s] separate from the ordinary life of the householder, for instance—until perhaps even Adam might realize himself enough not to eat the apple and be expelled from Paradise?

H.H. When we think of creation, and resolution of creation, we see only the external physical changes; the coarse matter taking different shapes, merging one into the other; but being without all that, Atman and the Knowledge are Eternal, they never die. So what they hold always remains there; it's always there. They don't have to go anywhere to collect it. For them time and space is immaterial, so if a creation is made and dissolved, for them it is nothing but just a play going on and on. Atman holds the knowledge.

In the creation certain people prepared themselves to receive this knowledge, the incarnation of Vishnu. This passes into certain men who are prepared to receive it so as to make the knowledge known to humanity. This is how the Eternal Knowledge is being passed from creation to creation.

* * *

H.H. In the scheme ["process"] of this creation "Time" stakes its own claim. In "Time" events are generated, grow, and mature; when mature, actions are fast.

Obstacles [to quick and efficient action when called upon] arise from two sources inward and outward. Outward obstacles are not so difficult as the inward ones which arise from excess of rajas and tamas in one's own being. All disciplines and trainings are aimed at elimination or reduction of this excess to give place to sattva.

The transformation of the gunas into one another is inherent in the natural order. When the right "time" arrives, the work is done easily, but at any other time it hardly gets done even with great effort. In the early stage of discipline [meditation] also, when rajas and tamas get reduced, both worldly and spiritual work become easier; because sattva [being increased] gives light, removes fear, and inspires all to their duties. That is why the *Gita* says that the True Knowledge is easy and comforting to practice; when sattva is abundant the work will be done faster too.

Dr.R. There are two chief meanings given to our one word "time" as commonly used—a "period or stretch of time" and the right *moment* or "moment of opportunity." The wise teacher (who is named in Ecclesiastes as Solomon, son of David) expresses this in Chapter Three: "To everything there is a season (Chronos) and a time (Kairos) to every purpose under the heaven—a time to cast away stones, and a time to gather stones together; a time to embrace and a time to refrain from embracing."

This distinction—much forgotten nowadays on all scales—underlies also the recognition of those moments during every day, when "natural samadhi" is possible. It's much more difficult at any other "time." They are moments of opportunity, which we mostly don't notice.

* * *

H.H. describes what he means by *Our Own Nature*. The lower type or people who are under accident or chance have two possibilities. These accidents sometimes lead a man into good company, sometimes into bad company. Even if a boy is placed in a completely foreign environment, his essence could change the place and time and the culture and the environment in which he is to live. Sometimes even a good man may be led into bad ways because of the environment and circumstances. That is the level of ordinary men. If they get good company there is chance of improvement; if they get bad company there is no chance.

The other type are the people who are not governed by any environment at all. They have a germ which is individual. They *will have their own way*. They may not affect others, but surely they themselves will not be affected by others. That is their quality and those are the people who come to the System; they become the aspirants or the disciples, here, there or anywhere, the Ladder is for those people.

Dr.R. You mean it is the inner growth of something inside them, which makes them independent of public trends or opinion?

H.H. Yes. These people have such a strong quality of their essence. Take for example the great runner; many people run but some few run faster and beat all of them. The people who go for discipleship or go on the Way have something in their essence very strong which is quite different from the ordinary material of which essences are made; and that will shine and that will lead them to some way—whatever comes within range.

* * *

Dr.R. Will your Holiness speak of how to increase the concentration of sattva in the body? Is the company and example of a saint important or essential?

H.H. There are two ways of increasing sattva guna. One is, as you say, the company of a saint; and this is as important as the other, which lies in *right conduct* during the day in respect of actions, feelings and thoughts.

If these are good one day, one may achieve the balance of sattva, rajas and tamas, and sattva will prevail over the others; if they or one of them is bad, then the gunas are unbalanced with either rajas or tamas prevailing. But the effect of these good actions, feelings and thoughts would be to create more sattva and help to restore the balance. If either actions, feelings or thoughts remain bad, the balance will be further upset and will lead to bad effects on oneself and other people.

The criterion of the "good" as used here is whether the effect is increase of happiness merging into eternal happiness. The actions, feelings and thoughts are bad if the effect is only temporary happiness leading to unhappiness later.

Dr.R. Does the night reveal what the day's actions, feelings and thoughts have been?

H.H. Yes, for ordinary people. People come into different categories in this respect. The *realized man*, having during the day performed good actions and enjoyed good feelings and thoughts, collects them all to one point in himself and goes to sleep without bothering with anything but sleep. When the time comes he just goes to sleep, and nothing more. He doesn't know his dreams.

But the *ordinary man* might during the day have good actions, feelings and thoughts just because of certain outside influences, but in the night his own inward nature comes out and brings about bad thoughts and bad dreams. And in still another category are the partly unrealized men who do good during the day, and have good thoughts and dreams at night, noticing these, and not completely refreshed by dreamless sleep. Each one can see from this in which category he stands.

Dr.R. Then it is not advised to give an account to yourself at the end of the day of actions good or bad?

H.H. It becomes unnecessary once you are on the Way. Then you are not troubled by such things. You do what you have to do, but you do not cling to it.

Dr.R. Since you have said that the first action of the meditation is to bind together the inner and the outer divisions of the mind (the reasoning part and the feeling part), does it mean that a man who has good days and bad nights is not meditating happily or fully?

H.H. In ordinary man actions, feelings and thoughts are produced from without. Meditation brings about a situation where these functions arise and are governed from within.

* * *

H.H. In relation to Self-realization, [let's relate the Law of Three] to the three gunas. Of the three, two of them in this case are the poles [sattva and tamas] and rajas is the interaction of sattva with tamas. This simply goes on like the three times, of which he says there is past and there is future; what we call present is the interaction of these two. The future being passed on into the past is called present. Such is the position of rajas or present—though it is always there, it is not dominant. Man either lives in tamas or lives in sattva, but rajas is always there, which signifies all activity of the present moment.

Sattva is the natural state of man, while tamas is the outcome of inertia. Rajas is needed to give them a push, give them impulse to go ahead, to move toward sattva. But fortunately or unfortunately many people once again come back to inertia, very few go on to the natural state of sattva. He gives us an example that in the process of eating the action is rajas. The effect of the eating can be of two kinds: If it is a moderate and well-regulated diet it gives a good effect and leads to happiness and good health, which we could say is sattva; but if it is not a regular and moderate diet, it can lead to indigestion and some other diseases which could be compared with tamas. So, action is very little, but the effect is prolonged either as tamas or sattva; rajas is the intermediate period of action.

* * *

Dr.R. Can H.H. say more about the criterion of goodness in thoughts and actions and feelings, especially actions? Many actions are necessary—part of one's duty, not just for selfishness, yet not because they lead to spiritual things. But they could lead the way to what he calls "good actions," couldn't they?

H.H. All the actions in the world *can* be related to the good actions and should be. They could all be made by the realized man to lead in the end toward consciousness. The actions of the ordinary man have no significance, but the actions of a conscious man even if they seem outwardly to be evil are designed to lead towards goodness; so, action is not wrong if it is done by a conscious man. If he [H.H.] punishes someone it is for his benefit, to correct his wrong.

Dr.R. All that you are saying agrees with what our system says, "There can be no conscious evil."

H.H. Consciousness can relate all types of action to goodness.

Dr.R. In our teaching, actions are said to be different in their genesis and result according to the nature and proportion of the gunas contained in the action. Do you agree?

H.H. On a lower level, actions can be classified according to gunas. But, in the higher stages of consciousness all action emanates from consciousness for goodness.

* * *

H.H. All activities of the *human* race are governed by sattva, rajas and tamas, these three gunas. Whatever the activity may be, these interplay in that with our nature, our essence, whatever essence we have; with our natural self we are governed by the atmosphere around us. If we have sattva in us, and if we are in a place where sattva is dominant, where the atmosphere is governed by sattva, then there is free play between our sattva and development prospers. But if we are placed in a situation where tamas is dominant and everything is governed by tamas, then our sattva is subjected to tamas and there is no rise of sattva in those surroundings. It's quite possible that the common man would just add more tamas and lose sattva there. When there is no dominance of sattva or no dominance of tamas we can see ourselves as we are; we act as we are made, according to our natural assets. So the outward effect, the atmosphere, which contains sattva in itself, is partly responsible for the development of sattva in human beings.

All the gunas are everywhere in the world—sattva is everywhere, tamas is everywhere, rajas is everywhere. But when particular situations arouse dominance of one, then we feel it. Even in the West, where good people assemble, one can see the rising of sattva and experience it. He quotes as an example that whenever we go to a temple or holy place in the jungle or along the bank of a river, whatever we are in our natural state with as much sattva as may be, the particles of sattva which form the atmosphere round these places, around the realized man, along the banks of the sacred river, around the temple in the jungle, they unite with the sattva in us, and with this, unity, happiness and bliss are created, and this subscribes to the development of sattva. This is the sympathetic situation; in unsympathetic situations we are starved of sattva.

Dr.R. So, little progress is possible in unsympathetic situations. One wants to try to collect in a situation as much of this sympathy as possible.

H.H. Of course it's one of the important matters for the human race. But common men, ordinary men cannot do this; they are just controlled by the atmosphere, by the external situations. But, men who are on the Ladder, who have realized the possibilities to some extent, who can outweigh the situation with their own sattva, they can influence the situation and improve the atmosphere with the sattva that is in them. But common men just follow the stream.

* * *

H.H. The Law of Three or the cycle of sattva, rajas and tamas cannot be ignored but with stillness it will be brought to a good balance without disturbing the still nature of the Atman. The physical body is composed of tamas aspect of nature; the organs of knowledge and actions are composed of rajasic aspect of nature while the Antahkarana of Manas, Buddhi and Ahankar is made from the sattvic part of nature. Thus our whole being is a mixture of these gunas, which can rest in tamas, act in rajas, and meditate, be still and enlightened in sattva. The machine is primarily finely balanced but not properly used without meditation and sattva.

Love

H.H. Love is the motive force behind all the processes at work in the world to sustain it. The world could never be sustained without love. In the case of human life its examples are the love of parents, the love of brothers, the love of friends and colleagues etc. Even the behavior of insects and moths seem to be based on some form of love. So much so, that the ultimate cause of hostility is also love, because hostility springs up when love is hindered. Thus a duality of love and hostility prevails everywhere. We want a thing we love; if we do not get it, we turn hostile.

A love free from the above duality is true love. The whole drama enacted by Param Atman depicts this one thing only. But there is none to understand it.

A perennial game of hide-and-seek seems to be going on. We are all seeking something. Some seek it in annihilation, some in creation, some in light, some in darkness, some in intellect, etc. Actually it is Param Atman that all are seeking, and Param Atman is hidden in all these and in everything else. But while seeking, people have forgotten what it is that they are seeking.

A man wanted to go to his father-in-law's place to meet his wife. He went to the railway station where the train was standing at the platform, and he shouted at the booking clerk, "A ticket to my father-in-law's place, please!"

"Where on earth is that?" asked the booking clerk.

"Oh, my father-in-law's place! Please! Please! Quick!"

"Just tell me the name of the place."

"I'm telling you, my father-in-law's place. For God's sake be quick! The train is about to leave!"

And the train started, leaving the man behind. Something like that is happening to all of us.

* * *

Q. H.H. once said to Dr. Roles that love was the motive force of the universe. Please can H.H. help us in our longing to act only from love?

H.H. In the *Vedas* it says of Brahman "Before the beginning of time the Absolute existed alone so His desire was to create many."

The entire motive force, which manifests this creation of animate and inanimate variety is love or bliss. The galaxies, stars, planets, creatures and everything else are set in motion by this conscious force—love. Every bit of creation is part of the Creator, and everything is playing its part according to the conscious charge, which animates it. The Leela [play] is for the pleasure and satisfaction of the Absolute, taking place with Him and within Him. While this play is proceeding, some forget their part and the source of the motive force. The result is limitation [by superimposition]. Love for one turns into hate for another. All limitations are governed by limitations of time, space and qualities [the gunas]. Through ignorance these limitations become hard, binding and complex. Only True Knowledge, love and devotion can dissolve them, and in simplicity the troubles arising from complexity disappear. The universe is one and perfect within the Absolute, and it is His will that it should remain so. But in illusion and agitation everything seems incomplete, separated and alienated. The fullness, the perfection and the unity held in love is then shattered, and in this ignorance everything looks small. In order to escape from this, meditation, True Knowledge, love and devotion are the way to unity. But these ways do not belong to any one individual, group, society or nation for all such concepts are limited and binding. They are in truth universal. Everyone in this universe is looking for love and deserves it, and must get it.

The Absolute is "Premaswaroopa," "Jnanaswaroopa" and "Bhakswaroopa" [the embodiment of love, knowledge and devotion]. It is limitless in every sense and its door is always open. The universe is one and full of love, and everything is motivated by love. Let love flow without hindrance from any direction.

* * *

Q. I would like to ask H.H. how to improve the quality of my attention by better concentration in meditation, as I feel this would be a way to increase my capacity of love for the Param Atman?

H.H. Although individuals do feel a separate identity, in reality there is only one identity, and that is the Param Atman. In our Antahkaran—the inner body, and the subtle body—we have this individual Being, and because of ignorance and other influences it seems to feel a difference from the Param Atman, and that is why it wants to unite with the Param Atman. For this unity of the individual and the Universal it seems as if the effort is being made by the individual himself. The individual, if indeed he does anything at all, only removes the impediments which block his vision of his unity with the Param Atman. In fact, the movement is only from the Param Atman's side. It is Param Atman who reaches out to the individual Himself. The love or devotion should be developed by removing the impediments and that, of course, is possible through the meditation and the attention which one brings into one's life; and this, in a way, removes the separate identity of the individual which is composed of his name, his form and his so-called nature. All these things have got to be given up for real Unity or for real Love toward the Param Atman. The effort is of course, made by the individual, but he makes little effort. The greater effort is made by the Param Atman, just as a small being or child has small legs, so he can take only small steps. The big man can walk quicker and cover more ground. The same applies to the individual who is a very small being, and the Param Atman, which has no limit. This is how the unity of the individual and the Param Atman should be made.

All individuals are the Absolute themselves, and so are you. It is only a question of realizing that one is the Absolute. To realize that, one has to do away with those impediments, and to illustrate this, here is a story about the lion cub.

Once, in the forest, the lioness who had several cubs went off to search for food, and while she was away one of the cubs strayed and got into the middle of a flock of sheep. The cub followed the sheep, and the shepherd, seeing the cub with the sheep, kept him. The cub behaved like the sheep because of the company of the sheep. The shepherd thought that if he remained in this forest, then one day the lioness will roar, and the cub, hearing the roar would remember it was a lion and would attack the sheep. So he took the flock with the cub to another forest where he believed there were no lions.

One day, a lion did roar in this other forest, and all the sheep ran away, and the cub also tried to run away. The lion—in lion language!—asked the cub to stop, and said, "Why are you afraid of me? There is no need. You are not a sheep. You are a lion like me. If you are not sure I can show you." So he took him to a pond and the little lion saw in the reflection that he had the same face and same characteristics as the one who roared. Then the lion asked him to roar with him, so he learned how to roar, and the whole personality and individuality of this little lion was completely changed and he started roaring like a grown lion.

All our efforts in the world are learning the language of the world, which is like the language of the sheep and the life of sheep. By good company—the company of Saints—and through the discourses, we learn to give up the language of the world and take to the language of the spirit. Once we have learned, and have seen how the saintly persons—who are much nearer the Absolute—how they conduct their lives, we can also be like this young lion and start behaving like a proper lion, because we are all proper lions by nature.

* * *

Dr.R. I was going to ask [that] if desires arise in the mind, what is the loving mind?

H.H. The ordinary desires arise from the Manas, but the center of love is the Atman. It is from the Atman that love arises; although it is also expressed through Manas, which is the agency through which all these desires are expressed.

Now there are two types of love in Sanskrit. These are prem and moha. One would see that the expression of these two types of love [prem and moha] might have the same form and manifestations toward the beloved, but one is motivated, the other is not. The true love has no motive. It is all-forgiving to the beloved; the whole life becomes a service so that the beloved may be pleased, and it will be for his pleasure that everything will be done, without demanding anything at all; and if there is any difficulty of time and space or meeting between the two, it does not diminish or lessen. It rather increases; speed becomes more. But in the case of the other love [which also works through this emotional center], it is used only for the achievement of certain results; and if the result is not forthcoming, then this love turns into bitterness and anger. This is how one can see, that if love turns negative it is impure love. If no tension rises and the devotion is always in stream, then one can say it is pure love.

Dr.R. Is it possible that a true love overtaken by Manas and Buddhi in time may turn into impure love?

H.H. Love would not become impure because it has been taken over by Manas, but certainly rajas and tamas coming in between would bring about some illusion of ignorance, so that the whole thing would take a different turn. For instance: If we see a piece of rope we know that it is a rope and that is the end of it; but if there was only a little light when we happen to come to that place, then there may be two thoughts prevailing at the same time —whether it is a rope or a snake. At the moment when this idea comes to mind that it could be a snake, the physical body gets into agitation and sets itself to react in a certain position, because of the fear that it is a snake; but throw light there and that fear will be gone. As long as the knowledge is not pure or complete, this is quite possible. Once the knowledge is complete, the love which is always pure will shine through in purity. But if the knowledge is incomplete this might bring in illusion and might direct you to the other type of love which is called moha.

Dr.R. A Christian saint [Augustine] once said: "A man becomes what he loves. If he loves a stone he becomes a stone; if he loves mankind, he becomes a man, and if he loves God, I dare not say more for you might stone me."

H.H. He says, according to his System it would mean: If you worship a stone as a stone, you become a stone. But if you worship the stone as the Absolute, then you become the Absolute. There is nothing like a mere stone in this creation. The stone is one form of the same substance which is taken everywhere in creation. It is the same force working through men, vegetation or minerals. All that we see—the Samsara [the process of worldly life], the stone, the man and everything—is not real. The reality behind everything is the same Sat, Chit, Ananda—Truth, Consciousness, and Bliss. Once you have separated and purified it, and removed the limitation of the eyes in ignorance, you would be able to see that Truth, Consciousness and Bliss even in the stone.

We have a beautiful story of a saint from South India. He was called Saint Ramdas, and he had quite a good following of thousands of disciples. One day he decided to test his disciples, so he pretended to be sick due to a boil in his leg. What he did was to take a mango and tie it to his leg and put a bandage around so that people would see that there was something swelling inside. He said, "Well now, I am suffering from this poisonous boil. I do not think I will survive and it seems my end is near, but there is a possibility that if someone sucked the poison out of this boil, I might be saved; but this unfortunate man will have to die from the poison." Everyone started looking at each other but none came forward.

After quite a long time the educated disciples who used to look after the theological part and the administration of all his work throughout India assembled and said to him, "Swami, since you have come near your end and there is no other possibility, would you like to dictate the terms to form a trust, so that the management of these disciples and the deliberations may be carried on?" They did not mention anything else. But from among them one person came forward and said, "I am ready to do anything for you in whatever way you please." Then Ramdas told him that he will have to suck the poison, but he will die. He replied, "If thousands of people are going to derive wisdom from your survival, then my loss of life will be a real gain to me. I will be happy to give my life for a purpose like this"; and before anybody could check him he forcibly went near him and started sucking the poison, but to his great surprise it was a sweet mango. The trick was thus exposed and most of them felt the shame of not rising to the occasion and only pretending to love. Only very few really love, for love is something very rare. One can see these two types of love—prem and moha—in simple terms. If you want happiness or pleasure from the beloved, then your love toward him is deluded attachment; and if you are sacrificing everything for the pleasure of the beloved, then it is Love.

* * *

Q. You said yesterday that in meditation "the source of love has become blocked; only the external actions are going on." You gave me a way to help this problem in meditation; could you advise further in relation to daily life?

H.H. For strengthening the feeling of love, an emotional attitude, essential for love, is required. Purity of thought [Buddhi] is necessary in order to strengthen this feeling. We should make ourselves as liberal-minded as we can; while emotional attitude is essential, purity of action also lends a helping hand.

Suppose there is a man for whom we have great respect. The more we become acquainted with him, the greater will be our love and respect. Our love does not diminish with increasing acquaintance.

In this case, the man is the Atman. To know something about the Atman (such as how the Atman behaves) is necessary for the development of love. What is the Atman? How to recognize it? To gain the knowledge of this Atman, we require a *steady state of mind.* The more one's mind is at peace, the more we shall know about the Atman.

* * *

Q. H.H. said it requires sincerity and love to get anywhere. One can be sincere through the practice of disciplining oneself, one can get knowledge through attention, but how can one get love?

H.H. Whenever one takes to any discipline with a view to do by one's own efforts and achieve these ends which one has in view, then this is impregnated with some sort of egoistic, individualistic approach, and as long as this approach is there in undertaking any work, even spiritual work, the result will be such that it will not be with love, for the success and failure will affect further effort. When you have some sort of love the effect is that you bring enthusiasm into the work so keep it continuous. To bring about this situation he says that if we think and try to impress upon ourselves that all the work which we are undertaking for any result is only in the service of the Absolute so that whatever we do we offer as our service, then the individualistic approach, or the egoistic approach would not intervene in the work. Whenever there is individualistic approach the effect of the work falls on the body and mind also, for people get tired physically and mentally—both; and if they get tired physically and mentally they would not be able to continue the work. The other way, when you serve the cause of the Absolute, because there is no egoistic approach the body and the mind is never tired, and if it is not tired, one would be able to continue with the work and to do as much as is necessary. That is the true way and one should see that one serves the Absolute, and does not think to achieve things by one's own deeds.

Manas

Dr.R. In our System we call the uncontrolled activities of mind as "imaginings." We had no way to get out of it. Your suggestions have been very useful in this direction.

H.H. The activities of mind are twofold. One directed to the useful work for the Atman and the other against it. The useful activity for Atman results in usefulness of Buddhi, senses and body also; and the useless, or activities directed against the Atman, result in destruction of Buddhi, senses and body. The "imaginings" are the useless and harmful activities. They use our energy for our own destruction. For common men, all that which is useless and harmful is pleasant to senses and they run after it without realizing that it is not useful. So the mind becomes the boss and the being is recklessly used in pleasure-hunt and self-destruction. If Buddhi is allowed to control the mind, the direction of activities will be toward the usefulness. [Here mind is used for Manas.]

A sick person usually likes to eat food which he is asked not to eat by a doctor, because the effect will be damaging. People today are sick; they don't know what they should have and what should be left alone. In running after only the pleasure they allow mind to go toward ruin.

Dr.R. It has been found that mind is either running into past or future and not making use of the present moment for Self-realization.

H.H. There was a lawyer; he got married and after some time they both started planning their future. The lawyer suggested that when they will have a son, they should bring him up and educate him to make him a lawyer, even better than his father. The wife had something else in mind. She wanted her son to become a doctor because her parents were in the medical profession. The arguments started and they got heated up. While they were fighting for their arguments a holy man happened to appear and asked them why they were fighting. The husband put [forth] his ambitions and the wife explained her ambitions. The holy man asked them to call the boy and inquire as to what he would like to be. The couple said, "The child is not yet born." The holy man laughed at the stupid planning even before the child is born. Such future plans have no substance. Such desires are not useful. Pure Buddhi suppresses such foolish desires and imaginings around them like a snake charmer who presses down any snake who raises his head unnecessarily. Desires are not bad; too many of them are bad and all superfluous constructions [imaginings] around desires are bad. They are utterly useless.

* * *

Dr.R. Most people's minds in the West keep on running and that advice is just what they need.

H.H. Mind doesn't naturally run; it is encouraged to run. When Buddhi allows it to run, then it runs. A weak Buddhi is overruled by it. Don't allow the Buddhi to be weak or impure. Few desires and no imaginings are good for disciples. This keeps them in good form.

A running engine uses up the battery, which then needs recharging. A running mind uses all our energy which must be recharged. In meditation we recharge the energy, but why misuse it? Use it for better purpose. Use it for Atman and then even body and senses will get their share of real happiness. If energy is used too much or too little then there is always the danger of the engine wearing out or getting rusted. So one must have a measure to use proper energy in a balanced way.

Dr.R. I would like to find which are the people who do recharge the energy but leave their engines running too!

H.H. It is only a matter of habit. Some people while away their time in playing cards. These habits are neither useful in the material world nor Spiritual world. If one has to have habit, one should have good habit. Although habits are no good for Atman, yet a good habit will at least put one on the better side of the fence. One should never allow the mind to establish his kingdom of pleasure.

There was a disciple attending a holy man. He used to go to the town to collect alms to prepare meal for both. Once he saw a marriage procession. On inquiring about it he was told that a girl and a boy are getting married and they will live in love and live together in peace and happiness. On the way he stopped by a well and to get over his tiredness, he tried to take a nap. In his dream he saw himself being married and took his bride home and was sleeping with her. The wife asked him to move over a little and he did, and fell into the well! The people in the town brought him out and asked what happened. How did he fall into the well in the daylight? He told of his dream to the great pleasure of the people and went back to hermitage with the resolution not to allow the mind to create his own kingdom. People fall in the well just for nothing.

* * *

Dr.R. H.H. has said that distraction during meditation can be avoided by the feeling of expansion. How does this work when body is still and eyes closed?

H.H. Body and eyes are the two main sources to attract the Manas [mind]. Once the body is still and the eyes closed most of the distractions are over. When one starts meditation the mind is turned to attention and at that time even a small sound feels like a loud one. The mind immediately runs to the spot and, nobody can stop this because mind is tremendously fast. So one should let it go. What one really needs to do at that moment is not be bothered about the mind. Mind is a servant, and if you didn't care as to where he is going or gone he will soon come back to the master knowing his disapproval. Master must not run with the mind [servant]. By doing this one will be really still. This does not mean that all the distractions will vanish. No! They will always be there. Many things are happening in the body simultaneously and we never get angry or disturbed for we know that it is happening in me. When you expand your self and embrace everything around you, these distractions become just a part of you and their harshness disappears. Having one's body still, eyes closed, mind unattended and with the feeling of expansion, the meditation becomes easy and fruitful.

Dr.R. I feel that the world being vibrations and the vibrations passing through me are blocked by my thoughts.

H.H. The vibrations first reach the senses, then mind and later on Buddhi. Buddhi is the inner gate where all this stops and doesn't reach up to Atman which is in fact apart from that and holds us apart. One should watch this Buddhi. It can be a barrier. Once this barrier is removed the passage is clear.

* * *

Dr.R. The clouds seem to have disappeared now, but I know that if I allow my mind a free ride it will form the mist again very quickly!

H.H. One should never allow the Manas [mind] to go free. It is a very important link in our being, so it must always be under control of pure Buddhi. Body is easily trained and that can be made free after some period of discipline. One can of course have some trials and tests to see the level of one's mind and Buddhi and for that purpose allow them a little freedom. If they naturally go toward activities useful to Atman, then they can qualify for freedom, but not before. In schools boys are given freedom to write what they feel in an exam and thus their level is determined. One of the easy tests is one's dreams. In dreams people are mostly in their natural state of mind and the type of dreams can reveal the working of their mind.

H.H. One has to be always on the alert and not allow everything to happen as they want. This is down the stream. The way of development needs watch and discipline. If one has lost his opportunity of the company of good men or discipline, one may as well let oneself loose to suffer for long. The human form is the platform where discipline is available; miss your chance and you go repeating the same miserable life in eternity. The mind (Manas) thinks that the world is true and likes to live with it in ignorance. This is illusion, and to cure this illusion the discipline is prescribed. Now even this discipline shouldn't be taken to be true! The Truth is that one really is Atman and the Absolute, but one doesn't know this secret because of ignorance. Once you realize your Real Self the discipline also becomes useless. If you have a thorn in the foot, you take it out with the help of another thorn and throw both thorns away after use! So in some way even the discipline is illusion, but this illusion only will undo the fundamental illusion of ignorance.

There was a dhobi [washerman]. He used many donkeys to carry his load. One day he fell ill and asked his son to load the donkeys and take them with the washing. He loaded them and tried to move them towards the river but they didn't budge an inch. Seeing they weren't tied up at all, he was surprised at what happened and went to ask his father. The father said, "Oh, I should have told you this also. In the evening I touch their feet as if I am trying to bind them with a rope, and in the morning touch them again as if I have undone them." The boy also did the same, and then each donkey started to move. The fact is that the donkeys all thought that they were not freed and therefore they couldn't walk! So is the condition of all human beings. The ignorance is illusionary, and to remove this one must undergo another illusion in order to realize one's real state; but this is very essential and one has no choice to evade it.

The Absolute creates the creation when He looks outward. When He is looking within no creation takes place. So the creation is outward-bound and, due to the nature of creation, body, mind and [?] Buddhi become outward-bound too. Discipline turns them toward the "within." In Self it is all Bliss, Consciousness and Truth.

* * *

Q. Should one guard the eyes from wandering glances in order to maintain contact with the Self? I feel that they steal treasure from me.

H.H. These wandering glances do give away treasure, because with the glance goes the mind [Manas], which is followed by Buddhi.

Thus everything is given up and one becomes destitute. To stop this there are two ways:

First is to see everything without any attachment; and the *second* way is to look at things which are artistic and represent aspects of Divine nature. By doing so one would learn to see beauty of the Absolute in everything one perceives.

Dr.R. This answer is very interesting because this woman herself goes to museums and other places for Oriental and Indian art. Perhaps she has got the idea.

H.H. tells a story of a holy man who was passing through a road where he saw a very beautiful woman. Having seen the beauty he stopped for some time and couldn't take away his gaze from her. Some people asked him as to why should a holy man indulge in staring at a woman? The holy man said: "I am looking at that which is behind the face, for He takes fascinating shapes to show Himself. Beauty is of the nature of God."

The holy man in that story sees things through the eye of the Atman, which is knowledge of the Absolute.

* * *

H.H. From earth and right up to the ether one could see the interplay of elemental material although the first three are formal and the last two without form, but they are part of the manifest world. Beyond these five elements is the Mahat-Tattva, which literally means the great principle or the universal or individual being. From this principle manifests the five elements, their five qualities and also the five senses of knowledge and five organs of action. The senses collect the knowledge of the qualities of the elements, just as ears collect the quality of sound, which belongs to ether, skin or sense of touch appreciates the air, eyes appreciate the form and color, tongue appreciates the taste which is the quality of water, and the nose appreciates the quality of smell which comes from the earth. The act of appreciation is going on simultaneously and all the time in the universal being through the Mahat-Tattva and also in the individual being through the Manas.

Though Manas can appreciate all the five qualities, it does so only one at a time. It is only due to this reason that one can really know anything; otherwise there would be knowledge of a mixture of five qualities all our life. This is done by Manas in individual level, and the same is known as the Mahat-Tattva on the universal level. This is the intermediary. It takes in knowledge of the phenomenal world through the senses and passes them on to the inner being, and it also passes the orders from the inner being to the organs of action. This works both on individual and universal level. In the universal level, the desire of the Absolute is being passed to the phenomenal world through this Mahat-Tattva which allows manifestation of all forms, and it is only through this Mahat-Tattva also that all the knowledge of the phenomenal world is passed to the Absolute being.

* * *

H.H. Manas is in the middle of the inner and outer worlds. The desire of the Absolute is bound into forms through this medium, and all bound forms are liberated into ideas—or the source of all knowledge, which is the Atman—only through the Manas. So Manas [mind] can be the cause of bondage or liberation. It is very much like the interpreter. If the interpreter is attached to one or the other side, then he cannot do his job properly. He must fully understand both sides and be unattached to both. All misery in the world is caused by this attachment. Some minds are attached to the physical world, and like to dwell only in physical forms and pleasure. They only enjoy coarse world and remain poor and bound to the low level. Some minds are attached to the inner world and resign from the physical world and don't like to take to active participation in the world. Such people are usually lazy, inactive, unproductive, and live like parasites. They are known as virakta. Although they are attached to the inner spiritual world, they are also not right and do not conform to the natural laws of the universe. We do not approve of such people. The really good life is unattached to both and yet working with both the physical and spiritual world.

***

H.H. The first of the *Upanishads* ["Isa Upanishad"] begins: "Whatever lives is full of the Lord. Claim nothing; enjoy, do not covet His property. Then hope for a hundred years of life doing your duty." They do not ask us to live a hundred years of misery. However, our life does become a life of misery because of our feeling of *attachment* to worldly objects, and this feeling of attachment to worthless things is the root of all miseries. The world, as it really is, has no miseries at all. It is we who manufacture them by harboring an attachment to worldly objects.

Attachment means, to consider as "ours" what really belongs to God: our body, our house, our wealth, our son, etc. Give up this feeling, and you get rid of all troubles.

Do not think that the world around you, i.e., your house, your money, your body, etc., are unsubstantial. Rather, it is your feeling of attachment to them that is unsubstantial. Whatever is happening around you is right, but what is wrong about it is the view you are taking of it. If you could correct your viewpoint, you would be happy.

The world is a great show, which God is staging around you in the shape of the universe. But it is a mere show. Your birth is a show; your death is a show. Actually there is neither birth nor death. Know that, and you would be happy.

The common outlook is that the world is everything, and that Param Atman is nothing. It is a crime to hold this view, and the punishment for it is to be imprisoned in this physical body. You can't be happy while undergoing a term of imprisonment.

Our mind has the property of thinking of something or other all the time; it cannot remain idle. If it does not remember the Param Atman, it would think of the world. Remembering the Param Atman leads to happiness, and thinking of the world leads to unhappiness. It is true that people do not find it easy to hold the Param Atman in mind. The reason for that is lack of practice. As long as the ability has not been acquired, there would be difficulty. But the ability can certainly be acquired.

A baby cannot eat solid food in the beginning because the ability has not been acquired. But this ability comes quite easily later when he tries (after he has some teeth!).

Acquiring the ability to think of the Param Atman is as easy as that.

Someone went to a Mahatma and said that he would like to serve him, but he added that he must have something to do all the time, as he could not remain idle. The Mahatma asked him to go and cut a long piece of bamboo. When he did so, he asked him to fix it in the ground. This done, he asked him to climb to the top of it, then come down, climb again, come down again, and so on. Thus he had constant work to do.

Similarly, keep the mind occupied, otherwise you would go mad.

You have a mind, you have a body, and you have intelligence. Let the mind be trained to remember the Param Atman, let the body do service to Him, and let the intelligence discriminate.

Observer

Q. If we had known the Absolute before, is it the memory of this that makes us make efforts and also tells us whether we are on the right path?

H.H. Knowledge is the same everywhere in the Absolute and in Atman. Atman's knowledge of the Absolute is direct. As True Knowledge is stored in the Absolute, Atman has direct access to it. When we become too involved, however, in worldly activities and ambitions, we forget about that True Knowledge. Eventually the habits grown from this involvement create clouds which block out True Knowledge altogether. Then we have no access to True Knowledge. When one comes across someone who has that access, our memory is stirred and we remember True Knowledge. Once that memory is stirred it is impossible to forget in this life. One will always remember that True Knowledge is there, and it is up to one whether to take it or not. For example if you stand under a tree on a river bank and look at the water, you will see and feel movement yourself, but a glance at the bank will show you that it is the water and not you which is moving. In the same way, if we get involved in worldly things we come to think that it is they which are stable, whereas if we have an observer, a glance inward will show that it is we ourselves, the Atman, which is stable and the worldly things are moving.

* * *

Q. What is Self-realization?

H.H. "I am"; I am out of everything. These are the two poles between which creation revolves. To realize this, that the creation is in myself and still I am out of it, is the sole purpose of Self-realization. To become only the Observer, and allow everything to happen as it has to happen. One has to realize "I am" before "everything is." Today I am this in this puny form and have existed long before its creation, and also will live on when it is destroyed. To this vastness through eternity is the journey of Self-realization. After having a form and body, people limit the self to the body and the world around without getting a glimpse of the vastness of eternity. Once you realize the greatness of what is not before you, then you find right value of what lies before you. To find this proper value is the work of Self-realization.

* * *

H.H. Man has got more and more separated from the source of creation and has to find his way back. That is what all these techniques are designed for, the cornerstone being that he has to become the Observer. The eyes, for instance, could not observe by themselves, they needed the sensory organization; the sensory organization observed the eyes and was in turn observed by the intellect that told it what it saw—the meaning. But the intellect in turn was observed by the ego, and the ego in turn observed by the Atman. It is only the Atman which is not observed by anything else. So when a man reaches the Ultimate Observer, he reaches the Atman who just watches what goes on without becoming involved.

Dr.R. My own teacher kept saying, "Observe, observe"; without a method I did not seem to be able to do it.

H.H. Nevertheless, your teacher was absolutely right, that was the true direction. But the house we live in is a big one with seven rooms: First a living room [the body], then the dining room given over to eating, then a withdrawing room, then a social room for entertainment, then a study, then a bedroom, but in all those rooms a man can be interrupted and his peace disturbed. So he begins to look, and the eyes explain to him the existence of a seventh room where his peace cannot be disturbed. Meditation is the best way to get to that seventh room and become detached from everything and just observe.

Dr.R. But even after a good meditation, in quiet surroundings and with nothing particular to do, I find it difficult to remain a detached onlooker for more than about two hours. But when in action in a busy life interrupted by people and telephones I don't see how you do it!

H.H. But you don't have to be saying all the time, "I am observing, I am observing." Suppose you can swim, you don't go about on the dry land saying all the time, "I can swim, I can swim." You just remember it enough so that if there is a flood you swim automatically. Even so, whenever there is a free moment you remember the Atman with the help of the mantra; so you turn to the spiritual life at any moment when possible or necessary.

The quickness with which you can do this comes with experience and practice in the meditation so you gradually get its full value. The beginner learning to drive a car takes a long time and much noise to change gears; the expert does it instantaneously.

* * *

Dr.R. The last few days I have found great help in practice from your words "Buddhi must be stilled." This is achieved now during meditation and is so also when I wake at night. But any mental activity sets it moving again, and it takes time once more to still it. How to keep it quieter?

H.H. We want to still Buddhi because Buddhi is in motion. Of course it is in motion because every activity is basically rajas. Whenever you have activity Buddhi will have to work and so move. When in meditation Buddhi is still, that is fine. Nothing wrong. What one needs to observe is that one has to activate Buddhi for certain work but when not required one stills it. You can enjoy Buddhi either still in meditation or properly active in work. Meditation has three qualities; its use can be described in three ways: first, nourishment; second, cleansing; third, healing. We need food every six hours to keep the body going, a bath every twenty-four hours to keep it clean, medicine every so often if ill— if homeopathic every seven days! As body needs these things, so whole system needs this service, except Atman which in fact does not need anything, being complete in itself. But activities of rajas and tamas collect impurities. Meditation cleans them out. If no impurities, no need for meditation. Meditation is not an end in itself. Bliss is the ultimate end. It is the nature of the Atman to be blissful, but rajas and tamas deprive it of bliss. Meditation cleans out everything so that Atman reaches its natural state of bliss.

* * *

Dr.R. Doing one's duty is no problem, but one gets up to a lot of mischief and uses energy on useless work and useless pleasure.

H.H. All work that is useful to Atman is all right—go ahead with it. Some work which is useless to the Atman may be dictated by attachment, other [work] by time, place and situation or circumstances. Provided you know that this is useless work you are safe. You are observing, not doing it intentionally, not identified. You may be forced by circumstances to do these things, so provided you know what is happening you need not worry. For example, no one likes to be sick, but sometimes we do get sick for reasons outside our control. Medicine cures the sickness but one does not dwell on it, one enjoys the freedom of good health. As long as one keeps coming back to useful work, one is all right. In fact one is fortunate, for common people do not know what they are doing, whether it is useful or not.

* * *

H.H. Always and everywhere the Observer is present even if these five sheaths are experienced or not. There are five states of our consciousness—the awake, dreaming, sleep, unconsciousness and samadhi. In three of those states—samadhi, deep sleep, and unconsciousness—there is very little experience. Although the five sheaths exist in these states, practically nothing is observed. Only in the awake and the dreaming states do we have direct experience of these five sheaths. In samadhi, it is only the consciousness in equilibrium that is experienced. Some weak persons experience the unconscious state, but here there is no experience of anything but ignorance. Among all these sheaths and states through which the individual goes, there is only one element which is not involved —the Observer, the Atman—which is Eternal. One should rise and go beyond the sheaths.

* * *

Dr.R. Is there any further advice His Holiness can give on the subject that the Atman alone is real and looks on all the changing events and situations as a passing show, without getting involved?

H.H. In order to appreciate the Self described in the *Upanishads* one needs simple methods. Many such descriptions have been given in the past, but more light can now be thrown on the subject. The states of consciousness experienced in deep sleep, dreams, the daytime state, spiritual awakening, samadhi, etc., are governed by the influx of sattva, rajas and tamas from people, situations and events. These all undergo change, but the Observer who sees them all as a "passing show" always remains the same. This Observer never registers any change in itself; if any modification appears, then this must happen to the individual [Ahankar] since change is its very nature.

For example, pure gold always remains gold while its uses and shapes and forms are liable to many modifications. The sky remains the same, while storms, clouds, rain and snow keep on changing our view of it, and yet do not affect the sky in any way. [One experiences this vividly every time a plane takes us up above the cloud ceiling.] The waves of the sea cause no loss or gain to it, the waves are only on the surface; at the bottom of the deep blue sea there is complete stillness. In the same way all these passing shows of the gunas do not change the Atman, but only provide variety in its appearance.

* * *

Dr.R. Recently I told the story of the parrot and his master, the intellectual man, who did not put into practice his instructions. Following this, I tried to carry out certain of His Holiness's instructions to me. Next morning, I woke up with a clear and happy feeling as if I saw the whole of my ego or personality, like that of the intellectual, as from the point of view of the liberated parrot sitting in the tree!

I still have the feeling and keep noticing that there is an incessant commentary going on in the mind about what one sees—approving, disapproving, etc. Is not this a useless function of the mind which could be made to observe impartially like an interpreter?

H.H. The incessant commentary going on in the mind about what one sees—approving, disapproving, etc.—is certainly a useless function of the mind. One method to avoid it is to observe impartially, considering yourself as separate from the mind, as you yourself said. The other method is to keep the mind engaged on good thoughts only, so that it gets no opportunity to entertain wrong ideas. This amounts to keeping the mind under control as you would a servant. Let your mind be the servant and you its master.

* * *

Q. The remembrance of Param Atman during the day is an increasing comfort and nowadays everything is more pleasant. Even unpleasant things seem less important than before. However, one feels on a dreamy plateau where, because of the pleasant life, the *need* to keep moving on the path is less sharp. One is not complaining about the increased happiness, but though one feels the greater presence during the day, one's meditation does not seem deep enough and one seems more caught in a dreamy phase. Can His Holiness advise?

H.H. One of the fundamental characteristics of life on this earth is the worldly illusion of being the independent doer, of having free will. It is very difficult to maintain that individuals are the doers of anything, for the whole creation is a manifestation of the Absolute who is the real doer. He has made His whole show in such a beautiful pattern that it keeps changing from one moment to another, and must keep on multiplying also. The whole thing is going on by virtue of the creative impulse given by the Absolute; He is the independent one, He is the free one, and He is the real doer.

Part of the show is our human nature with its capacities of memory and thinking which, if one takes the load of the "past" and the "future" upon oneself, makes the journey hard and treacherous; for the "past" and the "future" appear terribly big, and it is very difficult to walk along the Path if one carries this load. "If such and such actions were taken," we think, "then a particular result could be achieved"; or "If I hadn't acted the way I did, I could have saved myself from these effects." One should always keep oneself light-hearted and free of that burden.

In fact, the load is on the mind [Buddhi] itself; the physical body has nothing to do with it; but because the mind governs the physical body, the physical body also suffers.

One of the best analogies is the shadow play of puppets. There is someone holding the strings and moving them, but they appear to be moving themselves and to be the real doers. The whole of creation is very much like a puppet show, with the strings being held by somebody else. In another simile he gives the example of the cinema show, where the film is being shown on the screen and the people keep on looking at these moving pictures. On the screen you see mountains, buildings, seas, and fights, love scenes and religious scenes. All types of scenes are being enacted on this screen. Some people watching are like the puppets, and they get animated by the scenes.

One should be able to see the things which are happening in the world—but only as a silent observer. See all the pleasures on the screen, but don't be involved and moved off course.

* * *

H.H. You mentioned the dream state. There are five states of consciousness, from *relative unconsciousness* (1) in *deep and dreamless sleep*, through the *dreaming State* (2), the ordinary daytime state of *relative consciousness* or waking sleep (3), to the *awakened state* or "*Self-consciousness*" (4), of which we all get glimpses (which we would like to last 5 minutes, half-hour, a day), and *turiya* (5) *enlightenment* or *"Cosmic Consciousness."*

All these five states belong to the mysterious creative art of the Absolute. Each of these states is part of the manifested creation for the pleasure of the Self. In fact each state is a useful state for one or another purpose. There is nothing to choose between one or the other. One doesn't have to choose anything, but stand at the middle and see both sides, the outer and the inner. Or stay in the present and watch the passing life—the play of "past" and "future." Each state is part of the Absolute, and one does not have to select one of these situations. One has to become the impartial and silent Observer of whatever happens, may it be samadhi, waking, dream or sleep. If *that* is achieved, it is beyond all these states of the world we live in, and in effect everything is Sat-Chit-Ananda—the Absolute. Even the most ordinary work, such as digging, then gives bliss or Ananda.

* * *

Q. His Holiness has said that we should look at every thing in the creation from the viewpoint of the Observer. It appears to me that only the Self can glimpse the Self [there cannot be two selves]. When this happens it seems like being conscious of consciousness. What prevents this from being continuous?

H.H. There is not one observer, but thousands of observers—unlimited observers. But in every Antahkarana there is an observer, so that in the eyes of one Antahkarana the other is what is being observed—it is a matter of observation. Each Antahkarana is observing the other, so that in the eyes of that one observer the other person is the object being observed. In the eyes of the other person who is being observed by the observer, the first observer is the object being observed. In that way there are unlimited observers but there is one Observer in the eyes of whom everything is being observed. So for him there is only one like that for whom everything else is the object of observation.

The Ahankar part of the Antahkarana is responsible for this

distinction between the observer and the object being observed. But when there is no Ahankar—there is only one—and there is no distinction between Observer and the observed. A person asked a realized person—a sage—that when one Atman, which is pure and absolute, is pervading everywhere, then where is the need for any practice of Sadhana, because Atman is pure and is pervading everywhere. Why this Sadhana? What for? The sage replied that only by Sadhana you will be able to realize that this is pure and is pervading everywhere.

* * *

H.H. The witness or the Observer is the Atman and He doesn't do anything. He simply knows everything. He becomes conscious of what is happening. In meditation when one has gone to the deepest layer, where there is no activity, then the Atman is experiencing Himself. That is a state of complete bliss or happiness. The activities have their being only on the physical plane or the mental plane [inner body of Manas, Buddhi, Chitta and Ahankar]. According to the level of meditation one will find comparative slowness of the activity, and at the end there is no activity. There it is only the Observer; there is nothing for which one needs to be moved. Quantity of meditation is not important. The quality of meditation is more important. It is much more possible to derive great benefit from little meditation than by long or unlimited meditation. One has to be watchful for sincere meditation, and the test of the sincere meditation is that one reaches into the realm of no activity and comes out with satisfaction and bliss.

* * *

Q. At a certain stage in the development of meditation there seems to be a barrier blocking final unity. Is this illusion? If so, can one destroy it? If not, how can one overcome the barrier?

H.H. The last barrier to the Atman is Ahankar, the feeling of "I" —I, the one who is meditating, or I am the one who is about to go over the barrier into the unity. As long as one sticks to this the unity is impossible. We have to learn this and make sure in oneself that when one reaches to a spot of this nature, one should drop even the idea of the feeling of "I." Everything is to be given up, even the sense of I. Once the sense or feeling of I is given up, then only the unity is possible.

A certain man went to a holy man to be initiated in meditation. He was asked as to what things he saw on the way. He said that among all those things I saw I remember a donkey very well. He was then asked to remove him from his memory. The poor man tried hard, but failed, and expressed his inability to do so. The holy man said that the art is to drop the memory. This memory or the feeling of "I" is the greatest and the last barrier to meditation. The man who meditates or the man who observes must be dropped so that he is able to merge into one.

Obstacles

Q. To sharpen Buddhi and strengthen its resolve to serve the Atman seems very important. Can His Holiness give more guidance?

H.H. The best way to strengthen and sharpen Buddhi is to refrain from entertaining too many desires. As long as one holds on to hundreds of concepts, alternatives and ambitions in one's mind, Buddhi will be blunt and weak from over exhaustion. Therefore, one must limit the number of desires. The vikshepa, or agitation in the mind, makes Buddhi ineffectual. How can law and order prevail when a riot is going on in the mind? When problems are few and the mind is not agitated the light of Atman can fall on Buddhi to resolve problems. A steady mind has a strong and sharp Buddhi. Buddhi gets its power from the Atman and it can be used in any direction—for better or worse. In the light of True Knowledge Buddhi works positively, but if the mind has absorbed attachments and hatred then all its functions work negatively. Attachment helps to further a cause one loves even if it is wrong, and hatred reinforces the rejection and destruction of the cause one hates. Viveka is neutral and transparent. It favors nothing, and hinders nothing, but furthers the cause of unity, purity and universality, which are associated with the Atman. To serve the Atman is to serve the universe by establishing unity, purity, love and equality. The test of viveka is that it leads from individual to universal. To use Buddhi for the individual rather than the universal is the wrong use of Buddhi.

* * *

Q. Could H.H. tell us more about the cultivation of pure reason? There seem to be two types of analyzing of ideas: The usual one is an active thinking about ideas, which leads away from, or replaces "practice." One would like to ensure that when we meet in our groups the discussion leads *toward* Self-realization. The same thing happens when ideas of Truth come to one alone. Without right use of reason one seems to be carried away from the "present moment."

H.H. The discipline of pure reason is that one should first of all get the information [system], and then relate it to one's own experiences which might present certain doubts [questions] regarding the propositions put before one. If you work in this way the function of pure reason is possible. Otherwise if somebody takes the discipline without reasoning, which means without putting up any personal experiences and questions arising out of them, that would be taken as a kashaya [veil]. This is one of the three coverings—mala, vikshepa, kashaya—a sort of cover, which you put over yourself and block out reason. That is not really very useful or good, so every discipline, which is given must be reasoned, and the way to reason is to relate to experiences and the questions and doubts arising out of them. The other way, which leads towards futile discussion, is when the reason or the logic is not related to experience or diverts from the subject itself. So if the subject is kept in mind, and if the experience is reflected, only then is pure reason possible.

H.H. continues: About the three types of coverings, which we have —because of these coverings communication is hampered and is not possible between the disciple and the teacher. One of them is usually predominant in each individual. The first one is mala [literally translated as the "dirt"] the opaque dirt, which prevents all penetration into the Antahkaran of the individual, so that he doesn't understand anything of what is being preached, or the way being shown to him. The second is the vikshepa [distraction] which is when the discourse is taking place and someone is giving the teaching, the attention of the individual goes somewhere else just after catching the first sentence, and so he cannot listen to what is being said. And the third one is kashaya [veil], which is the sort of covering out of which, there is practically no impression gained by the individual. This kashaya is due to sticking to certain ideas which have been taken without any reason—[sort of blind belief]. These are the three ways due to which communication of pure reasoning is not possible. One has to get rid of these before reason can prevail.

Dr.R. What did H.H. particularly mean when he said on Monday, "You have faith but nothing much comes out of it?"

Of course I agree completely; I just want to have something come from it!

H.H. In pursuit of spiritual development, people usually meet two types of leader. The first type belongs to the Yogic System. They have gone through the Eightfold System and through that arduous "discipline" they have achieved certain powers, which they can use for their disciples or even for their own end. They can show certain miraculous performances; and their disciples love them and have faith in them; and as long as the miracles work their followers keep hanging on to them. Later however, either they break away, or sincerely take to the "discipline" themselves and work out their emancipation, or achieve some miraculous powers for their own use and satisfaction. There they stop.

The other type is the wise man or holy man who does not care for external or physical miracles and works through knowledge, being, meditation or devotion. He works on the removal of mala, vikshepa and kashaya of his disciple, knowing that Atman does not need any development, for it is the Absolute itself; but only ignorance in the form of mala [opaque dirt], vikshepa [distraction] and kashaya [veil] surround him, and the real Self cannot exercise its Truth, Consciousness and Bliss. To achieve the removal of these causes of ignorance [or samskara], he prescribes certain "disciplines" for the conduct of life; gives them knowledge by which they can arouse reason and put right their mistakes themselves; and also arouses emotion to lead them to devote their energies to the Universal Self. He has to keep the momentum going continuously, and often applies a little fire to make the disciple stronger.

Just as a potter makes different objects from wet clay and then fires them to make them dry and hard, and only then can these objects be made use of; similarly heat must be applied to the disciples so that they have more strength to keep toward truth and not break under temptations. This work goes on till the disciple himself feels that he has arrived or he is out and free or he now knows. Once a disciple came to ask if I could say that he now knows. One could only laugh at such a situation for it is like looking for the Sun with the light of a lamp. How can anyone else judge the Self? If someone knows, then he never asks anyone's approval. Self-realization can't be proved by certificates, recommendations or affirmations by anyone, whosoever it may be. When the Self knows itself to be free, only then is it free. If anyone pretends to be free then he is only deceiving himself, not realizing.

Dr.R. Why has this taken more than eight years in spite of all the wonderful instruction and help received? Is one just too stupid to succeed?

H.H. The eight years have not been wasted, for a good thing has been now known. In this work on spirit, there can never be a time-limit for full realization. It depends on the state of the Antahkarana of the individual. If it is ready-made at a high level then realization is very quick, otherwise unless the cleansing process is complete, the realization would not come about. It may very well take ten or twenty years for some people. Apart from the time factor, the knowledge of such ideas must first be appreciated. This would be a common knowledge ["common" equals "not put into practice"] such as that idea taken by Buddhi that the flesh, bones, Manas, Antahkarana are not the Self. These relate to the five sheaths [Annamaya, Pranamaya, Manomaya, Vijnanamaya, Anandamaya koshas]. A person has to penetrate through these sheaths, and, by practice, to detach one after the other to realize the Self. The realization means putting this superficial knowledge into practice. Unless this available knowledge, which at most is good information, is put into use, and indeed constant and continuous use, it never becomes real or realized knowledge. Only when the knowledge is realized does the individual become realized. The work of realization is to clean out the kashaya; kashaya is some habit, which must be removed (and there may be many of these). A bad habit must first be replaced by a good habit, and then even the good habits can be given up. This replacement of bad by good habit is so very necessary. Some people learn to speak as a great man would speak, but they can't really do anything, for they haven't realized the Self. This ultimate knowledge derived from practice is like seeds of knowledge out of which all dignified acts arise.

The available or common knowledge is like a well near a river; when the river is full, then the well is full; and if the river is dry, then the well is dry. Common knowledge is available for use as personal knowledge. In contrast, the True Knowledge is always present [in existence] but is not available; it is made available through a wise man, a realized man or a qualified teacher.

* * *

Q. On our last visit H.H. talked about the three graces; one knows from experience that the guru's grace and guidance is always available, yet one does not seek it enough. Can we be told more about asking for help?

H.H. There are three graces, which are always available; they are constant and ever active, and they emanate from the Param Atman, the guru and the Shastras [the Scriptures]. There is no hindrance within these three sources as far as the availability of the graces is concerned. Although all these three graces are available yet they do not reach the individual, and that is the difficulty. There is this fourth aspect of grace, which is the aspect of the Self—oneSelf—the Atman. The reason for the hindrance in making use of the graces is because there are three coverings, mala [thick dirt], vikshepa [disturbance], and kashaya [attachment], all due to avarana [ignorance]. These are the three layers, which prevent the availability of these ever-present graces of the Absolute, the guru, the Scriptures, and the Atman.

These work as follows: Mala is that which always takes one in the opposite direction to whatever is available. So even if the scripture is available, even if the guidance of the guru is available, one will turn one's face in the opposite direction and will not heed at all. This is the layer of mala, that's how it acts on the individual.

Vikshepa is that which creates temporary hindrances, so instead of attending to one thing, one attends to another—not necessarily opposite. It may be analogous but it will never be on the point one should act on or attend to. This is because of movement in the Manas. This vikshepa comes; the mind gets agitated and impedes the flow of these graces. The third one is kashaya. [These are] all caused by ignorance, universal ignorance [avarana]. Although there may be a little light of knowledge available, the thickness of the universal ignorance will prevent the availability of all these graces to the individual.

To undo these three hindrances the only course is viveka, discrimination, True Knowledge. It is only through discrimination that all these three hindrances could be removed. This is a gradual process, which will work in time—there cannot be instantaneous removal of all these three hindrances. It will be gradual. The more they are removed the more you will find that you appreciate and respond to these three graces. If these hindrances are completely removed, then you will see that you have no need to ask for any help, because you will reach the central point, and all universal graces—which are always available—will be yours; and you will act through them without any need for questions or asking for help—the grace will be everywhere, and all the time available without any break.

* * *

Q. H.H. has been quoted as saying that there is ignorance in the causal body and that for the normal man the causal body is not pure, and is responsible for making him mistake the illusion as real. Could H.H. tell us more about this?

H.H. There are three types of covering: One is transparent, the other is translucent, and the third is opaque. If you build a house of glass you can see inside from outside and outside from inside. Although there is a barrier, a structure or form which divides the inside from the outside, yet the appreciation of both is possible from both sides. In the case of the translucent covering, something of the inside can be seen from the outside and some of the outside can also be seen from the inside! But it is hazy, it's not defined—it's not clear. The third is opaque, where the division between outside and inside is very firm and complete. If you are out, you can't see anything inside and if you are inside, you cannot see anything of the outside. These are three types of covering we find in Antahkarana, the inner organ of the individual. They arise from the samskara and mala, vikshepa and avarana, which have been mentioned before, as these three types of covering. Mala is the opaque; it simply doesn't allow anyone to see inside from outside, or outside from inside. Vikshepa, which is the product of rajas, [and] a predominance of rajas allows you to get a glimpse, but it is very hazy and indecisive, not clear. Avarana is like the glass, transparent. If the avarana is clean, then you can get a clean picture of the outside and the inside. These three relate to the three gunas; mala is the product of tamasic samskara, vikshepa arises from rajas and avarana is the sattva. If the avarana is thoroughly clean by the predominance of sattva, then one can see the truth inside or outside, as it really is. In vikshepa he can see some truth, but he misses quite a lot, so it is a mixture of truth and untruth. In mala he takes truth for untruth and gets untruth for truth.

Note

Mala: The opaque dirt, which prevents all penetration into the Antahkaran of the individual, so that he doesn't understand anything of what is being preached, or the way being shown to him.

That which always takes one in the opposite direction to whatever is available. So even if the scripture is available, even if the guidance of the guru is available, one will turn one's face in the opposite direction and will not heed at all.

Mala is the opaque; it simply doesn't allow anyone to see inside from outside, or outside from inside. Mala is the product of tamasic samskara.

In Mala he takes truth for untruth and gets untruth for truth, defects, impurities and other undesirable things.

Vikshepa: Agitation in the mind. Distraction, which is when the discourse is taking place and someone is giving the teaching, the attention of the individual goes somewhere else just after catching the first sentence, so he cannot listen to what is being said.

That which creates temporary hindrances, so instead of attending to one thing, one attends to another—not necessarily opposite. It may be analogous but it will never be on the point one should act on or attend to. This is because of movement in the Manas.

Is the product of rajas; a predominance of rajas allows you to get a glimpse [of truth], but it is very hazy and indecisive, not clear. Vikshepa is that which keeps on reminding us again and again of attachment to experience.

Vikshepa is not mala but thoughts of past and future. We are sitting still but the Chitta is running very fast; this is vikshepa.

Kashaya: Veil—which is the sort of covering out of which, there is practically no impression gained by the individual. This kashaya is due to sticking to certain ideas which have been taken without any reason [sort of blind belief].

Some habit, which must be removed [and there may be many of these]. A bad habit must first be replaced by a good habit, and then even the good habits can be given up.

Attachment. Taking the discipline without reasoning, which means without putting up any personal experiences and questions arising out of them.

Kashaya is a kind of forgetfulness which is neither mala nor vikshepa. Emptiness means: "I am neither remembering anything nor imagining anything but am feeling vacant."

Avarana: Ignorance. Universal Ignorance. Avarana is like the glass, transparent. If the avarana is clean, then you can get a clean picture of the outside and the inside.

Avarana is the sattva. If the avarana is thoroughly clean by the predominance of sattva, then one can see the truth inside or outside, as it really is.

Avarana is a sort of circle, which we keep on turning again and again.

Obstacles to Meditation

Q. What can the meditation do for us?

H.H. There are three things: mala, vikshepa and avarana. Mala is the dirt which we accumulate. Vikshepa is that which keeps on reminding us again and again of attachment to experience, and the avarana is a sort of circle, which we keep on turning again and again. These are the three types of things, which the mantra removes. The best way of removing all these three is the meditation.

* * *

Q. How far in the different levels is the sway of the gunas maintained? Does it end somewhere on the levels; does it go as far as the causal level?

H.H. The three gunas are accumulated by three processes. One is the process of action, which produces tamas. The emotional acts create rajas, which is the vikshepa; and intellectual work creates sattva, which is avarana. Because this is the way these are produced, exactly on the same lines they can be dissolved. If you take up a life of service, to the world, or to the universe, or to a teacher or anywhere—if you serve people—then the tamas, or the mala, will be dissolved. This dissolves tamas guna. If you take to meditation and allow the emotional feelings to be pure, that will get you some sort of attention and cut down the vikshepa, which is flickering attention; and through the light of True Knowledge it is possible to dissolve the avarana which is transparent—the product of sattva. Combine it all and you are free of all the gunas.

* * *

Q. Concerning meditation—I understand that there are some obstacles to the deep dive and these are: torpidity, distraction and bliss.

H.H. How is bliss an obstruction to the deep dive?

Q. I will explain. There is this state where everything is enjoyed. There is everything there to be enjoyed and one stays about in that state and hesitates, waits to take the deep dive into what I believe is called turiya, where there is nothing. This blissful state is like floating; everything is there, one is aware of existence, the body, the world, everything, but it is nothing. One fails to take that further step to nothing. One is still aware of the body and surroundings as well as at the same time the bliss.

H.H. One thing is mala. Things like laziness, which constitute papa [sin], which means defects, impurities and other undesirable things. Vikshepa is not mala but thoughts of past and future. We are sitting still but the Chitta is running very fast, this is vikshepa. Kashaya is a kind of forgetfulness, which is neither mala nor vikshepa. Emptiness means: "I am neither remembering anything nor imagining anything but am feeling vacant," [a vismriti meaning inability to remember (smriti = memory; vismriti = loss of memory)]; sunyata, "I am not remembering anything, I do not even know that I am meditating." Ananda is losing ourselves in joy and forgetting even what is ours and not ours. The joy is so intense that we forget what we are, what is ours, even what is Atman and what is Param Atman, that is ananda. Kashaya is due to wrong samskaras, the mind does not stay steady.

Q. Is it distinct from mala?

H.H. Mala is such a defect that meditation cannot begin at all on account of it—not feeling a sort of joy in meditation. Kashaya is a middle stage between vikshepa and sunyata.

Kashaya is the inability of the mind to enjoy meditation—a middle stage, which is neither emptiness nor vikshepa. [It is the] inability to realize what is real. Rather we should say it is as if when some people say that they have understood while they have not.

Sunyata [an absolute lack of knowledge] is under the influence of tamas [inertia].

Q. Is it like sleep?

H.H. The blankness of sleep is total tamas; but this is a stage with a mixture of tamasguna. Holy actions remove the defect of mala [dirtiness]. Kashaya is not understanding while understanding. Take the example of a light. Around the light there is always darkness—the light is surrounded by darkness. This is kashaya. It is light covered by a curtain of darkness or a curtain of darkness covering the light. That curtain can be removed by dhyana—through dhyana and steadiness. Removal of kashaya is by concentration. To lift the mind off sunyata [the void], as soon as sunyata comes you think of the mantra and this will take it toward ananda.

The sign of sunyata is that the body inclines or bends. During dhyana the body remains perfectly vertical. We enter ananda even if we do not feel it. It has got so much power that it does not let the body bend this way or that. Time spent in sunyata is wasted time. We should remove the mind from this state of sunyata and take it toward dhyana. Ananda is coming but it is not apparent. One kind of ananda is this—we like a thing and we get it. Another kind of ananda is that which is not separate from us and we come to know it only after we have got it. One is the ananda of having a thing—fulfillment—while the other is of not having a thing. One is external the other internal.

One form of joy is created by a thing while the other form is not created by anything. That joy which is not dependent on anything is the natural joy of the Atman. Atman is separate from this joy [ananda]. It is enjoying and is not the joy itself. Ananda, it is revelation. The joy is coming to us but we ourselves are not the joy, we are the knower of even ananda. The viewer of turiya is the Atman. Ananda is a state while Atman is not a state. Take the example of a banana: Fruit is a banana, but if we put the question to someone, "What is banana?" they will say, "It is a fruit called banana." The skin, the pulp, the root, the leaves of banana all these are of banana, but not banana. What is banana? The final answer we are going to get is that banana is a fruit—a delusion of words, and all the names belonging to it. All these five—mala, vikshepa, kashaya, sunyata, ananda, are due to the gunas; some to rajas and some to tamas. Who is it that is experiencing the ananda, sunyata etc.? The thing to which all these things are happening is the Ahankara and the thing to which nothing is happening is the Atman.

Q. It is mostly a matter of having signposts during meditation.

H.H. When the four things are finished—mala, vikshepa, kashaya, sunyata—and only ananda remains, there comes a sense of extreme gratification and we wonder where to find a place that can accommodate that great ananda which we have got.

* * *

H.H. Supposing there is water and a light is thrown on that water and the water is not still, it is rippling; in that case the reflection will not be clear. But when the water becomes still, then you will be able to see the image reflected clearly. Similarly, when the concentration is deep, there is stillness; the greater the concentration, the greater the stillness, and in the stillness the reflection of the samashti is clear.

Antahkarana is made to stand still by the process of dhyana and the greater the stillness which is achieved the greater is the force of samashti—the oneness with the samashti is being experienced.

But this is only half the answer, because there are two things—mala and vikshepa—while Antahkarana is just like a pool of water. If the water is not still, Antahkarana is not still; then the reflection will be poor. At the same time if there is mud, if it is dirty, then too —even if it is still—then the reflection will be poor. So the dhyana helps to do both things: It removes the mobility or the rippling of the water—it removes vikshepa—as well as cleansing, which means the removal of the mala.

Q. What in man concentrates?

H.H. Chitta. This is responsible for doing all the concentration. It is Chitta, which is affected by mala and vikshepa. Mala is caused by previous samskaras—previous connections—and vikshepa is there because of present connections, not separate.

* * *

Vedanta Meditation

Stages:

(1) *Pratyahara*: Withdrawal of the sensory faculties from their fields of objects to the interior, so that they may be put at rest.

(2) *Dharana*: Firmly fixing the inner attention on the "One-without-a-second."

(3) *Dhyana*: Deep meditation, an intermittent activity of the inner attention after it has become fixed on the "One-without-a-second"; an oscillation that proceeds like a stream that temporarily ceases and flows on again.

This preliminary realization of the Self is followed by:

(4) *Samadhi*: Absorption; which is of two kinds: *Savikalpa*, which is absorption with the continued awareness of the duality of the perceiver with the thing perceived, and *Nirvikalpa*, which is non-dual absorption, absolutely devoid of any awareness of a distinction between perceiver and object.

Four states of mind stand as obstacles to the attainment of nirvikalpa samadhi:

(1) *Laya*: Deep dreamless sleep. Instead of passing on to turiya; the "fourth," the mind lapses into unconsciousness, and the person mistakes this melting [laya] for that of the mergence in the Self.

(2) *Vikshepa*: Distraction. The oscillation of the mind cannot be brought to the single-pointedness that leads in the end to samadhi, and thus remains as receptacle of transitory floating contents.

(3) *Kashaya*: Gum, resin, extract or exudation from a tree, dirt, uncleanness. With reference to the psyche its mean-

ing is: "Attachment to worldly objects; passion, dullness, stupidity." "Something sticky, provided with a strong flavor or aroma which darkens clarity."

(4) *Rasa-asvada*: The tasting or enjoying of the sap or flavor [rasa] of the Self. This obstacle arises when the mind has not the strength to give up the bliss of identifying with the Self and to become annihilate.

Nirvikalpa samadhi is known when those four obstacles are passed; the attention then stands unmoved—like the flame of a lamp protected from the wind. "The normal eagerness of the subtle body to take the shape of every name, reminiscence, or sensation is allayed, has found its "rest."

Param Atman

H.H. In the ageless continuum of time, it seems so futile to take account of all the events that go on making and unmaking themselves in an unending chain. A little while ago we were preparing to set up this Mela. Now we are preparing to wind it up. Thus, anything that begins has to end, and anybody who comes into the world has to go.

Many people say that there is no rebirth. Actually each birth writes down the destiny of death, and each death writes down the destiny of birth. The *Gita* says that there is neither any "birth" nor any "death," but it is merely a cycle, an apparent change, that is going on all the time. One who sees a changelessness in all the changes that are going on, sees correctly. It is a body that is born and dies. The Atman itself which inhabits the body is birthless and deathless. *It is enough to understand only this much of the subject, because in trying to understand everything we often end by understanding nothing at all.*

* * *

H.H. The first of the *Upanishads* ["Isa Upanishad"] begins: "Whatever lives is full of the Lord. Claim nothing; enjoy, do not covet His property. Then hope for a hundred years of life doing your duty." They do not ask us to live a hundred years of misery. However, our life does become a life of misery because of our feeling of *attachment* to worldly objects, and this feeling of attachment to worthless things is the root of all miseries. The world as it really is has no miseries at all. It is we who manufacture them by harboring an attachment to worldly objects.

Attachment means to consider as "ours" what really belongs to God—our body, our house, our wealth, our son, etc. Give up this feeling and you get rid of all troubles.

Do not think that the world around you, i.e. your house, your money, your body, etc., are unsubstantial. Rather, it is your feeling of attachment to them that is unsubstantial. Whatever is happening around you is right, but what is wrong about it is the *view* you are taking of it. If you could correct your viewpoint, you would be happy.

The world is a great show which God is staging around you in the shape of the universe. But it is a mere show. Your birth is a show; your death is a show. Actually there is neither birth nor death. Know that, and you would be happy.

The common outlook is that the world is everything and that Param Atman is nothing. It is a crime to hold this view, and the punishment for it is to be imprisoned in this physical body. You cannot be happy while undergoing a term of imprisonment.

Our mind has the property of thinking of something or other all the time; it cannot remain idle. If it does not remember the Param Atman it would think of the world. Remembering the Param Atman leads to happiness, and thinking of the world leads to unhappiness.

It is true that people do not find it easy to hold the Param Atman in mind. The reason for that is lack of practice. As long as the ability has not been acquired, there would be difficulty. But the ability can certainly be acquired.

* * *

H.H. Gokarna says in the *Shrimadbhagwatan*: "This body is only flesh and bones; cease to be attached to it." Transfer your attachment to the Atman. Because Atman is part of the Param Atman, there is no difference between the two. Both are able to cut worldly bondages.

This body is the vehicle and the Atman is the rider. Treat the rider separately from the vehicle. It is not easy to do so. It requires years of practice. We practice by thinking this body is God's property, not ours. This mind is God's property, not ours; everything is God's, and nothing is ours. In this way we free ourselves from all attachments, all constraints. Again, this concept is difficult for those who think that "I" is the physical body.

***

Q. How can I improve the quality of my attention by better concentration in meditation, as I feel this would be a way to increase my capacity of love for the Param Atman?

H.H. Although individuals do feel a separate identity, in reality there is only one identity, and that is the Param Atman. In our Antahkaran—the inner body and the subtle body—we have this individual being; and because of ignorance and other influences it seems to feel a difference from the Param Atman, and that is why it wants to unite with the Param Atman. For this unity of the individual and the Universal it seems as if the effort is being made by the individual himself. The individual, if indeed he does anything at all, only removes the impediments which block his vision of his unity with the Param Atman. In fact, the movement is only from the Param Atman's side. It is Param Atman Himself who reaches out to the individual. The love or devotion should be developed by removing the impediments and that, of course, is possible through the meditation and the attention which one brings into one's life. This, in a way, removes the separate identity of the individual which is composed of his name, his form and his so-called nature. All these things have got to be given up for the real unity or for the real love toward the Param Atman. The effort is, of course, made by the individual, but he makes little effort. The greater effort is made by the Param Atman, just as a small being or child has small legs, so he can take only small steps. The big man can walk quicker and cover more ground. The same applies to the individual who is a very small being, and the Param Atman which has no limit. This is how the unity of the individual and the Param Atman should be made.

All individuals are the Absolute themselves, and so are you. It is only a question of realizing that one is the Absolute. To realize *that*, one has to do away with those impediments, and to illustrate this, here is a story about the lion cub.

Once, in the forest, the lioness who had several cubs went off to search for food, and while she was away one of the cubs strayed and got into the middle of a flock of sheep. The cub followed the sheep and the shepherd, seeing the cub with the sheep, kept him. The cub behaved like the sheep because of the company of the sheep. The shepherd thought that if he remained in this forest, then one day the lioness will roar, and the cub, hearing the roar would remember it was a lion and would attack the sheep. So he took the flock with the cub to another forest where he believed there were no lions.

One day, a lion *did* roar in this other forest, and all the sheep ran away, and the cub also tried to run away. The lion—in lion language!—asked the cub to stop, and said, "Why are you afraid of me? There is no need. You are not a sheep. You are a lion like me. If you are not sure I can show you." So he took him to a pond and the little lion saw in the reflection that he had the same face and same characteristics as the one who roared. Then the lion asked him to roar with him, so he learned how to roar and the whole personality and individuality of this little lion was completely changed and he started roaring like a grown-up lion.

All our efforts in the world are learning the language of the world, which is like the language of the sheep and the life of sheep. By good company—the company of Saints—and through the discourses, we learn to give up the language of the world and take to the language of the spirit. Once we have learned, and have seen how the saintly persons (who are much nearer the Absolute) conduct their lives, we can also be like this young lion and start behaving like a proper lion, because we are all proper lions by nature.

* * *

H.H. Normally, it should be the incomplete who would seek the complete. Therefore, one who is already complete should have no necessity to seek the complete. But, strangely, it is only the completed being that would seek the complete Param Atman. It is so because it can only be the completed Self which would automatically go into the thought of Param Atman as soon as it sits down quietly. As long as anything else can attract you be sure that

Param Atman is far away. After all you cannot ride two horses at the same time.

As Param Atman is all-powerful and limitless, it is obvious that no bondage could tie Him. But it is strange, again, that strings of love and Bhakti can do so. We know that only acquaintance can create love. Param Atman is so beautiful that the more we get acquainted with Him, the more we get filled with joy—this creates Bhakti automatically and necessarily. Then, acts of worship become redundant. They, however, constitute a preliminary necessity.

It should be understood here that that so-called "devotion" (which we can attempt before acquaintance), is a forced phenomenon and unreal, while that which sets in inevitably after acquaintance is real. Then our body, mind and all the possessions become dedicated to Param Atman, and this dedication itself becomes the worship of Param Atman. Then we eat, drink, act, etc. for the sake of Param Atman and do nothing for ourselves. Everywhere and in everything we see nothing but Param Atman. This is a stage of absolute intimacy with Param Atman, and Bhakti is just another word for this stage.

Now let us revert to the question of acquaintance once again. Without being acquainted with a thing, any love or worship offered to it would be insincere. The question, therefore, is how to acquire this acquaintance. Worldly acquaintances can be got by trying. But Param Atman is outside the worldly sphere. So human attempts to catch Him all fail, unless and until He brings Himself within our grasp. This He does as soon as He sees that we deserve it. So, what we should do is to deserve it.

Holy company provides a training ground for all this. One of the things we learn from it is that the deepest possible relationship that can exist between two things is that which exists between our Self and Param Atman. All other relationships are less. A realization of this fact can give a lot of Bhakti, and we reach our goal.

* * *

H.H. The Holy Scriptures lay down that at all times—in the beginning, in the middle and in the end—all over the past, the present and the future, one should always think of Param Atman, because we do not know when the end may come. But we cannot do this without forming a habit. However, it is wrong to imagine, as some people do, that they would form this habit in their old age. If we do not cultivate this habit in our younger days, it is difficult to do so when we are old. But if you only manage to remember Param Atman in old age, though not when you were young, He would be satisfied even then!

This world wants your body. Well, serve the world with your body. But Param Atman wants your love only. If you love Param Atman, it would be Param Atman who would then begin to serve you.

* * *

Dr.R. I find it comparatively easy to *think* about the Param Atman particularly in connection with the laws of nature in the universe and in man, and in seeing that all that is going on in the outside world—whether it looks good or bad—is a part of One Param Atman. But I would greatly appreciate help in developing a love or devotion to the Param Atman through what I suppose would be the practice of Bhakti. My capacity for love seems to be such a feeble thing and it is shown in the way I keep making demands upon you as our Teacher, instead of feeling for you and your wishes as Shankaracharya and living up to the Holy Tradition.

H.H. You have asked for help in developing love or devotion to the Param Atman through the practice of Bhakti, stating that your own capacity for love seems feeble. You should not worry on this account. Rather, you should remind yourself that the path of Love is that very path on which Param Atman is pouring all His favors and blessings all the time. Love is not an action; it is a feeling. Love and True Knowledge are two names for one and the same thing, which is a natural manifestation of the Atman, and it comes to the surface spontaneously when the Antahkaran concentrates. Then you get the "feel" of it.

Through your beneficial and holy efforts, let your own fullness see the fullness of the Param Atman, and let the practice, the practitioner and the object of practice merge together to form one single identity. Then the world as such disappears and the Param Atman appears in its place. This summarizes the philosophy of Bhakti through love.

* * *

H.H. If we do not see Param Atman everywhere in the vast field of creation, and do not enjoy its sweetness, and are not filled with joy by it, then we really see nothing at all. Then our practice lacks impetus. So Param Atman is in everything. Let your heart be filled with joy on seeing how Param Atman manifests in everything. Then, if Param Atman lives in your whole vision, He also lives in your heart.

* * *

H.H. No worldly action, however good, can be entirely free from evil. No worldly pleasure can be obtained without causing pain to someone. Every sinner has a virtue. Should we, then, abstain from action in order to get away from evil?

The way to rid oneself from evil is to cultivate the attitude that it is nature that is acting through the body, and not the Self. The body is the machine of nature to produce action. Your Self is only the witness, and not the doer. It is through nature that Param Atman is making the whole universe dance, but He does not dance Himself. He makes our Manas, Buddhi, etc., dance; but none can make Him dance. He is the Reality and the Truth, and there is no place where He is lacking. The states of Chitta are not the states of Atman. Meditation, practice, samadhi, etc., are all states of Chitta. Even digging the ground for the service of Param Atman is heavenly, while even worship of Param Atman for worldly ends is hellish. For practicing remembrance of Param Atman, do not wait for a suitable opportunity. Do not think of today or tomorrow. You can do it whenever a feeling of devotion arises in your heart, paying no heed to the hindrances present.

* * *

H.H. We want to meditate on the Param Atman. As it is the source of all greatness, its own greatness must be infinite. As it is the source of all happiness, its own happiness must be boundless. As it is the source of all beauty, its own beauty must be—we do not know. But how could we ever meditate on such a Param Atman, whose qualities and nature are thus beyond the utmost stretch of human imagination?

This was the question which was naturally put by Arjuna to the Lord Krishna, and the answer is contained in the *Bhagavad-Gita*, Chapter 10, verses 20–42.

Here is a translation of a few of those verses:

> O Arjuna! I am the Self, seated in the hearts of all beings; I am the beginning, and the Life, and I am the end of them all.
>
> Of the Scriptures I am the Hymns; I am the Electric Force in the powers of Nature; of the senses I am the registering mind; and I am the Intelligence in all that lives.
>
> Among the vital forces I am Life itself; I am Mammon to the heathen and godless; I am the energy of fire, earth, wind, heaven, sun, moon and planets.
>
> I am all-devouring Death; I am the Origin of all that may happen; I am fame, fortune, speech, memory, intellect, constancy and forgiveness.
>
> I am the gambling of the cheat, and the splendour of the splendid; I am Victory; I am Effort; and I am the Purity of the pure.
>
> Whatever is glorious, excellent, beautiful or mighty, be assured that it comes from only a part of My splendour.
>
> But what is the use of all these details to you? O Arjuna! Enough that I sustain all this world with only a fragment of Myself!

All this implies that by thinking of the most powerful manifest thing as only a tiny particle of Param Atman's power; by thinking of the most beautiful object we can and then treating it as a mere atom of Param Atman's beauty and so on, we can gradually find our way to the Param Atman. Thus, starting from sensory objects and rising higher and higher, we reach a state where all difference between sensory and ultra-sensory, between definable and indefinable has faded away from us.

Then, what to ordinary people are *different* forms and shapes, are to a fully-realized person all manifestations of one and the same Param Atman. What he sees then around himself and within himself, is Param Atman, and *not* the mirage which we call "the world." Such a man would welcome heat and cold, pleasure and pain, fortune and misfortune—all alike—because all are manifestations of Param Atman.

* * *

H.H. There are four sources of the knowledge of Param Atman. The first is the Vedas, the Scriptures; the second is the word of the guru; third is the illustrations which have been given; and the fourth is one's own experience. When all these four sources combine together, then one gets the real knowledge. Unless a harmony is reached in all these four, then there will be no clear understanding of the Param Atman and one will have to start again to obtain that harmony.

* * *

Q. What is the relationship of Atman to Vyashti; and of Atman to Jiva?

H.H. The relationship between Atman and Vyashti is this: The Lord of Vyashti is Jivatman; the Lord of Samashti is Param Atman. So that Vyashti is the individual; Samashti is the entire cosmos. Now, Atman is the Lord of Jiva. The Lord of the Cosmos is Param Atman; the Lord of the Jiva is Atman.

* * *

Q. I see. The Lord of the cosmos looks after everything; everything would obey Him without question.

H.H. There are three essentials—omniscience, omnipresence and omnipotence. These are the three great qualities of the Param Atman, the God of the Cosmos.

In a theatrical performance various roles are allotted to various actors and some of those actors sometimes start feeling that they *are* the persons whose part they are playing. Others remember that they are not what they are depicting themselves to be, but they are something different from the character which they are only just enacting. So the one who remembers that he is enacting a part is different from the one who actually starts feeling that he is the person whose part he is playing.

Param Atman is the person who remembers that He is Himself and is not actually the person whose part he is playing—He is someone different, but He is depicting someone else. But the Jivatman starts feeling that he is the person whose part he is playing; so that makes all the difference. That's why the Param Atman is not bound, has not got any bondage, although he also comes and takes birth. Even then He doesn't feel the bondage—just like Arjuna and Krishna.

* * *

Q. Vikshepa is like the snake in H.H.'s story, and, like the mongoose, we have to return to the attack again and again with the help of the special plant. Would this herb be remembrance of Param Atman?

H.H. Yes, the name of Param Atman or the remembrance of Param Atman is like a talisman—if you put it very close to iron, then iron turns into gold. The name of Param Atman is the only thing which can bring about any transformation in situations, or in oneself.

* * *

Q. As a business man, during the day the mind is continually active, dealing with one problem after the other. There are times when one can work with an underlying stillness and a feeling of the presence of Param Atman. As soon as there is a brief pause the mind naturally returns to this stillness. On other days there is no memory and the mind wanders. Can His Holiness explain why it should be different on different days and advise how to increase the tendency of the mind to return to the memory of Param Atman when finished with an activity, rather than wandering into the past or future?

H.H. It is not always necessary to be always remembering the Param Atman. If you do it for a few minutes every day, then you will be carrying the memory of that. Having thought of Param Atman in the morning, or at one time, for the rest of the day that memory will carry you throughout the day.

Just as the wife meets the husband for a little time, then for the rest of the time she has the memory of being united with her husband for the rest of the day; that's enough. It's not necessary that she should be thinking of him all the time. While you are doing your work—business—during the rest of the day it is immaterial whether at that time also you are thinking of the Param Atman or not. If you do think of him, of the Param Atman, once a day, that will be enough.

* * *

H.H. When we prescribe rest on the subtle or the causal level, we are not meant to keep at rest all these faculties and the subtle body itself. We only need from time to time, as has been prescribed to us during two half-hours, to go into the treasury, to go into this stream where the energy is available and make ourselves fresh. So all we need to remember is to go into this stream of the Param Atman twice a day and let it happen as we have been told, so that the energies are recharged. Then, come out into the world and act as the situation demands.

How to act in the world is again regulated by the True Knowledge which is being given to individuals: One can waste the energy in fruitless activity or one can use the energy to good purpose. So one should use Buddhi, one should use Manas and the eyes, the ears, the body and make the best use of all faculties according to the True Knowledge. Then, having spent one's energy, go back in meditation—two half-hours every day—and recharge oneself with the pure energy which is available from the subtle or the causal level.

* * *

Dr.R. In trying to dedicate one's actions to the Param Atman, one finds there is much unworthiness in our thoughts, our words and our casual postures and actions that one could not possibly dedicate to the Supreme Self. If one wants to do what one says and say what one thinks, it seems to be a full-time job!

H.H. In dedicating to the Absolute or to the Self, the most important part is the *heart* and that is very simple. If that is properly achieved in its simplicity, all the rest should not bother one because nothing else is very important. One can see from so many examples that this is so. Here is one:

There was a great elephant who was proud of his size and strength, but when he went for a bathe he was caught by a crocodile in midstream and dragged out of his depth into the deep water. He was helpless and couldn't do anything; but just when he was about to be drowned he happened to catch with his trunk a lotus flower floating on the river, and offering that flower to the Absolute, to his God, he begged Him to save his life. So pure was his offering, that the God came running barefoot from his throne.

One might wonder how one could dislodge the Absolute and cause Him to come barefoot from His throne by just a little flower! But it was not the flower, it was the spirit behind the flower—it was the heart which prayed.

The same is true of Draupadi. On one occasion she had given a Saddhu a very small piece of cloth. Then occurred the episode when she was being dragged into court to be stripped by one of the Kauravas. That little piece of cloth came to her rescue. It enlarged in length so much that those who wished to undress her grew tired and gave up the attempt. Her honor was saved by just that tiny strip of cloth.

There is another story of a saint called Rantideva, who took just a little water and offered this small amount of water and, in doing so, achieved Liberation—only a pot of water as against full Realization!

* * *

Q. His Holiness explained the other day that it was the force of Param Atman flowing through everyone that caused subtle communication to take place. He said it was due to sattva. I understand love as the outpouring of Param Atman. How is love related to sattva?

H.H. Love is the natural quality of Param Atman. And it is exhibited in sattva, so the natural quality comes out only in sattva, otherwise it is all artificial.

Q. Is it there that the force or power of sattva is reflected?

H.H. Yes. There are two effects of sattva: One is the stillness and the other is light; and when the two are present one can experience Param Atman. Light means knowledge. When there is light and stillness then the Antahkarana will experience the Param Atman; there is nothing in Vyashti which is not in Samashti.

* * *

Q. We have been told that the nature of the Param Atman is Sat-Chit-Ananda. Does this fundamental threefold nature have a manifest and un-manifest aspect? If so, could His Holiness say something about it?

H.H. It is correct to say that the threefold nature manifests sometimes and is un-manifest at other times. Sat-Chit-Ananda are the qualities of Param Atman, which means that these qualities pertain to the nature of Param Atman. Param Atman himself is not Sat-Chit-Ananda, but it is the nature (Prakriti) of Param Atman which is Sat-Chit-Ananda. Param Atman is always pure, there is no change in him; all changes come in the nature.

It is just like a play where there is rest before the play and rest after; the play is not for the sake of playing. There is rest before and after the play, the play is in the middle. The Param Atman has a desire to play, not for the sake of playing but for the sake of rest; one plays because one wants to take rest; rest is before and rest is afterwards, and the activity is in between. Dhyana is able to understand that this is only a play; one does not feel that this is reality. It is all Maya. So in deep sleep, when one is resting, the Prakriti, Sat-Chit-Ananda is un-manifest, and when there is activity, then it is manifest. So these three qualities manifest and remain un-manifest, but dhyana clarifies. Even when it is being manifested, even then it is all the doing of the Maya, otherwise Param Atman is pure, there is no change in Him; He is Absolute, no manifestation or un-manifestation, nothing of that sort—He is Absolute.

* * *

H.H. There are two types of Ahankar. One is pure Ahankar and the other is impure Ahankar. Now pure Ahankar relates to Atman and impure relates to the body, so the purer your Ahankar is, the more it is associated with the Param Atman. If it is impure, it is related to the body. It is desirable to eliminate the impure Ahankar. The idea that "I am Atman" cultivates pure Ahankar. Your realization that you are Atman is also Ahankar, in this case it is pure Ahankar.

The key word is Aham, which means "sense of individuality." If this ego is connected with the body, then it becomes Ahankar. [*Kar* is "vehicle."] So if the bodily vehicle is attached to Aham, then it is Ahankar [it is impure], but if it is attached to your Soul [Param Atman] then it is pure Aham.

* * *

Q. Yesterday H.H. also said that the way to weaken identification of the Ahankar with the body was to identify myself with the Atman. This identification with the Atman seems to have two aspects: one related to knowledge and one related to action. First, I need to *know* I am Atman. I need to *know* that I was not born; I need to *know* that everything is going on within me. This is the knowledge aspect; and second, I need to act in relation to my occupation in the marketplace. How does one act while remembering the Param Atman?

H.H. The disassociation of yourself with the body will kill your false Ahankar [ego] in both these respects: in the respect of knowledge, and in respect of action. Because, when you do something and you consider it is being done not by you as doer, but because it is your duty—it being a service—you are doing it because somebody else has desired you to do it. Therefore you are not the doer of it; you are only carrying it out at the behest of someone else.

* * *

Dr.R. In a talk here this time last year we are told that His Holiness said, "One of the benefits of holy company is that we learn from it that the deepest possible relationship that can exist between two things is that which exists between Ahankar and Param Atman." So no wonder we could not define it in words! Only experience in the presence of a realized man could reveal it?

H.H. In the realm of Bhakti—devotion—this relationship exists very closely between the Param Atman and the Ahankar, and is used in the most positive manner. The individual in this realm looks at the Param Atman in its manifest form and makes it the object of his worship. He sings the praise of this Lord [whom he wishes to worship] by proclaiming all the glories which are enshrined in this God and, because he tries to become one with Him through his emotion, he subdues or merges his Ahankar into the Being of the Absolute—the God. Then it seems that, because of this Unity, the qualities and the glories of the God are shared by the devotee himself.

Take Tulsidas who, in one of his couplets, says that whenever you try to unite with any particular being (it could be a God or anything else), and you devote yourself entirely to the service of that particular being, then all the characteristics of that particular being will be shared by you. When a devotee merges his Ahankar into God, then he starts sharing the qualities of God.

When you, for instance, take to the ideal of being a man, then immediately all the qualities associated with manhood are separated from those of all other beings. One feels shy and ashamed of not being able to measure up to these qualities associated with being a man, so one refrains from being like an animal. One always keeps that standard before oneself, because this manifestation of the Absolute as a man—"the ideal man"—stays very close to the Ahankar of the individual, and then he behaves as a man should.

This is how one can see that through the Ahankar when it is sattvic, the qualities of the gods descend on the man. When it is rajasic, then he takes it as his own body—his own doing—and does not get the finer qualities of the Absolute. When he takes over the tamasic aspects in his Ahankar, then he acts in a very cruel and rigid way and, in fact, he becomes less than a man should be. If the Ahankar is sattvic then the relationship with the gods will also be sattvic.

* * *

Q. Is the Atman the reflection of the Param Atman in the Antahkarana?

H.H. There is sun and there is light of the sun. Now, the light is different from the sun in the sense that here you get the light but not the sun. But there can't be any light without the sun, so the two are one and yet they are different.

Similarly, Atman is part and parcel of Param Atman. Yet it is different. It is here as well as there. In the Antahkarana, there is Atman; it is part and parcel of Param Atman, and yet Param Atman is something far away also. Atman is not the entire Param Atman, it is only a part of Param Atman and yet it has got all the properties of Param Atman. It is small in size and yet it has got all the qualities of Param Atman. It is part and parcel of Param Atman, yet it has all the qualities.

* * *

Q. Is it in the causal body that Atman and Param Atman are united when the Antahkarana is stilled?

H.H. This will be very clear to you if you think of two pots full of water placed together: One is small and the other is bigger. Now, if you place them in the sunshine the sun will be reflected in both of them, the small pot as well as the bigger pot. But the thing which is being reflected is the same; only one sun is being reflected in the small one as well as the bigger one.

Similarly, that which is being reflected in the Antahkarana of Samashti is known as Param Atman, and that which is being reflected in the Antahkarana of the smaller Vyashti, that is Atman. But in reality Atman is not different from Param Atman and the thing which is being reflected is only one.

If the water of the smaller pot is dirty or not still, then the reflection will be also of the same kind; if it is colored the reflection will be colored so that it is an illusion; we say that the light which is being reflected is colored or is dim or such, but there is no difference in the light, light is the same. The difficulty is with the water. So with Antahkarana of the Vyashti: As and when it is cleansed, you do not have to feel that the light which is coming in the Vyashti is the same as the Samashti—there is no difference. If any difference is being felt it is because of the impurity of the Antahkarana of the Vyashti.

I will raise a question on your behalf. The next question would be, "What is the relationship between Atman and Param Atman?" The reply is contained in the Vedas where it has been said that when you feel that Atman and Param Atman are one, it is Brahman; there is one Brahman. When you feel they are different, then it is Param Atman and Atman.

Prakriti

Dr.R. What is needed to transform Prakriti (which I take to be the individual Antahkaran on the causal level when the four gears are all one engine)?

H.H. Before one can transform Prakriti, it is essential to understand what Prakriti is. Prakriti is the combination of all these four functions, which are known as Ahankara, Chitta, Buddhi and Manas. Ahankara is that which gives the feeling of "I," based on any relationship of Self and non-self; Chitta is that which holds all the knowledge of the individual and cherishes certain thoughts; Buddhi is that which discriminates between useful and not useful; and Manas is that through which one has desires and counter-desires.

If the Prakriti is good and pure, then all these four functions will also be good and pure because Prakriti is the force which works through these four. When the force is good the instruments function properly. In this way the Ahankara will stand for Atman, the True Self, and not other things like body or mind; this will be pure Ahankar, which will be universal. The Chitta will have good knowledge in store and cherish good ideas. Buddhi will be pure and would rightly decide what is good for the Atman and refuse other considerations; and Manas will have good desires for one's development only.

If Prakriti is wrong or bad, then all these functions will be reversed and result in poverty. In such cases the Ahankara will not be for the Self, but only for one's body, strength, mind, intelligence, beauty and wisdom which one claims to have, and one would say, "I am the wise, the beautiful," and so on. Chitta will cherish evil thoughts [distorted pictures], and bad knowledge only will be in store. Buddhi will always take wrong as right and leave the right and good, considering them useless. Manas will always have desires of sensual things, more and more of them.

One need only look at oneself, at what one desires, decides, cherishes and claims for the Atman, and one would find out what one's Prakriti is; and then through the help of True Knowledge, good company, scriptures, discussions, realized man, one should try to turn away and work with attention so that one always desires good, decides for good, cherishes goodness, and only stands for the Atman which is everywhere. This particular work is only done by the aspirant himself and for himself. The inner help comes from the Atman Himself.

Prakriti is the being of the Self [that is, "Jiva"]. Suppose there is a householder with two sons. One son obeys the parents, learns the trade, serves the parents, and assumes the responsibilities of the household; he increases the trade by his hard and intelligent work and brings in prosperity and goodwill. This will relieve the work and toil of the parents and they could happily enjoy their old age in peace. The other, having a bad Prakriti, takes his share of wealth, squanders it in useless pursuits, gets into debt and then becomes a burden to his brother.

This is how the two kinds of Prakriti work. One is for advancement, the other [leads to] destitution.

* * *

Dr.R. Would H.H. please help me once more in how to dismiss the Buddhi (intellect) at the critical point (experienced by me again last night) when Buddhi has sign-posted the way to Atman but now husband and wife (Param Atman and Jivatman) may be left alone together?

H.H. Buddhi is like a gate and can lead you to the signposts on it, beyond which one has to enter inside to have communion. It would be necessary for some force to take over the leading role from Buddhi at this stage. This force is the Prakriti or "nature" of the individual. Prakriti is the combined name for Manas, Buddhi, Chitta and Ahankara. So it is different from Buddhi alone. If this Prakriti of the individual is good then it will be helpful; otherwise it will become a hindrance to communion. So Prakriti or nature of an individual must be made good and useful and ready for union.

When one goes to one's work or business away from home, one meets different types of people; situations and interests clash, and a lot of rajas comes into play. When one gets back from such humdrum surroundings to one's home one needs rest and comfort. Here the wife represents one's Prakriti. If she is a good wife, she will make you comfortable, cheer you up, and give advice when needed, give consolation, encouragement, and best of all would make you at ease. This ease will help you recover all the vitality lost during the day, and next morning you will be a new, forceful, fresh and alive man again. If the wife is not good, then the moment you enter the house she starts nagging, creates irritation and agitation and would like to rule the house in her own way. In that way one would never regain the lost vitality and would become depressed and weak and even more run-down.

It seems then that one really needs a good Prakriti or wife. To those who are recluses and have no wife to comfort them, they get comfort from their own Prakriti, which has been transformed and purified and made beautiful. In fact their general need is fulfilled by their nature which is a part of the Universal Nature or Prakriti. Under the present circumstances one needs to transform one's Prakriti, and systematic practice is the only way. Systems may be manifold, like work, prayers, songs of praise, scriptures, meditation and so on. Through these one may transform, purify and beautify one's own Prakriti, which will lead to the real communion.

Dr.R. My troubles both in meditation and in outside problems seem to come from too much rajas due to that unholy alliance between false Ahankara and Buddhi. You have previously said that, "The joy which Buddhi experiences is only temporary," and also "that purification of Buddhi through the medium of holy thoughts is the best remedy." When holy company is available, as here, everything is put right. But, say, in England, is the remedy to keep reading his discourses and the scriptures? Is there further advice connected with the melting of the heart?

H.H. The process of changeover from hardness to melting of the heart is gradual and would take time according to the degree of hardness. *Abundance of rajas or hardened heart* is the outcome of certain kinds of activity which have been practiced in the past, and has become the nature, "Prakriti," of the individual, so that it is now habitual and is a springboard for all his actions when he is not awake and attentive. The company of a wise man or even the scriptures can make it obvious for him where his actions go wrong. This knowledge of mechanical behavior is only the beginning; for unless this knowledge is transformed into his nature it is not of much use. To do this one simply needs to practice that which will undo the previous practice. To get out of the rajasic practice one needs sattvic practice, which means to do good deeds and meditation and all other actions which create sattva. If the rajas and tamas come up sometimes, then don't be disturbed for they have a rightful place in you.

For example, if someone wanted his house cleared of a troublesome tenant, then he must give him some notice, persuade him; and if he does not go then, you take legal action. Even the judge will give him time before eviction. If he does not then comply with the judgment, only then is he forcibly removed.

In all cases time is very necessary. The long-living tenant of rajas will take a long time to get rid of. One must keep on doing those same things again and again which will produce more of sattva to melt the heart.

Suppose someone has been sick for some time and the doctor has cured him; but during convalescence he will still be weak and must take a prescribed diet, which will eventually come to full meals. If he thinks that good food in greater quantity will make him strong *sooner*, then he might get into further trouble. He must go slow to allow his digestive system to pick up strength slowly, and only after a good restful time will he regain his health. One has to learn the right measures and must have patience for nature to reform itself.

* * *

Dr.R. Would H.H. say something more about Chetan Shakti? Isn't Shakti one of the names of the Divine Mother-Nature, which assumes multifarious forms? Does this refer to Purush and Maya?

H.H. This Chetan Shakti is certainly the Maya. The Maya or "Nature" of the Absolute or Purush. This Maya is of two kinds: the first is Vidya and the second is Avidya. They are also known as Para- and Apara-Prakriti. Vidya means literally "knowledge" and Avidya means "ignorance." *Para* means beyond and *Apara* means immanent, here and now—present right in the front of one's being. The difference between these two is that the Para or Vidya, which is composed of pure sattva, is mostly known as the Chetan Shakti. The Apara or Avidya keeps changing because [it is] involved with the three gunas, sattva, rajas and tamas. Because of all this the multifarious forms are evolved in this Apara-Prakriti.

This Apara-Prakriti is divided into eight levels—earth, water, fire, air and ether, and Manas, Buddhi and Ahankar. These eight compose the Apara-Prakriti, out of which multifarious forms are evolved in the course of this creation.

He gives another example of the relationship between the two as follows:

Picture a lump of ice having form and whiteness. It can be touched and experienced as a solid. It is very rigid in its form, but when heat is applied it will melt into water. Water has no form, is always mobile, and has no color. In the same way the Vidya or Para-Prakriti is related to Avidya or Apara-Prakriti, which has form, color and taste and these five elements and their qualities governing these forms, which it takes on.

It would seem that although the pure Chetan Shakti is the Para-Prakriti or Vidya, yet all the physical world and the world of subtle forms and causal forms are also governed by Avidya or Apara-Prakriti which is the lower Chetan Shakti, not pure but impure.

* * *

H.H. In Dehradun, in an ashram, an old woman of 80 used to go for satsanga. She would merge herself in bhajan and kirtan, do all other work of the ashram; she seemed a good devotee and was treated as such. But she had a habit of stealing from childhood.

One day she stole the alarm clock and then pretended to search, acclaimed horror for [the] satsangi who stole it and made such a show that no one could ever think of her being the thief. Anyway, the satsanga started and very soon the alarm went off. She was right in the front row and the clock was recovered from her handbag!

Such people are plentiful for they are everywhere. However much practice and "discipline" they do, things turn back to the same point unless this Prakriti is changed. Change is possible only when there is a real desire for change—there must arise one paramount desire for truth, which will permeate this Prakriti and transform it. A real desire is that for which one would not stop anywhere short of fulfillment.

Prakriti, being the basis of the individual, is the most subtle of all causes of motivation. The coarse and subtle aspects of our life can be erased by "disciplines" of physical or intellectual type, but to remove the most subtle nature hidden very deep in one's being is, of course, very hard. This is that most refined sort of sweet longing, which lies very [deep] and springs up only at odd moments when one may not be too vigilant. This alone is the cause for all those disciples who don't get real bliss in their devotional work. Here reason fails, but a strong desire can succeed.

* * *

Dr.R. H.H. showed me so beautifully yesterday how to proceed to dig out the roots. On the basis of his illustrations (especially the "householder's two sons and the good-looking thief") I was searching for any two characteristics by which I could recognize the bad one.

H.H. It is good to hear this. A good disciple is one who is inquiring, devout and, in being so, he tries to find out his shortcomings and then remove them. Ordinarily people can see the obvious shortcomings and, with attention, they are corrected; but the basic and deeply-rooted faults in the Prakriti are very hard to see, so it is to the benefit of the disciple to look for them thoroughly and remove them completely. It has been noticed that many who come into this Work usually get over large or great defects and yet conceal or ignore their little defects, which remain hidden. With all their work on being and knowledge, they stay at a low level. To remove these they have to take another birth; for without disposing of them they can't be liberated. When Arjuna asked Lord Krishna about what happens to the Yogi who falls short of full realization and dies, Lord Krishna said that such people are born in better and more favorable conditions where they start work early, and then achieve full realization soon by removing all shortcomings of Prakriti. But it is not necessary to wait for the next life when this can be done in the present life itself.

Dr.R. Noticing in the night an angry thought which accompanied a mechanical train of actions, together with internal body movements such as changes of breathing and stomach, it became clear that one could root out the cause, namely the angry thought. Can't one gradually find the thief in this way and put him in prison?

H.H. Apart from anger arising from frustrations in the chase after sensual or other desires, under such situations where one is trying to look at the root causes of one's Prakriti and trying to remove them, it is equally possible that after working deliberately and with attention, one sees that the roots do not seem to be displaced easily; and one becomes desperate, impatient, and a bit angry. But this type of feeling, which combines desperation, impatience and anger all together, is not entirely bad, for it gives extra strength and determination to the individual in his attempt to root them out. One must keep on and should not give up the vigilance, or the process of uprooting will stop.

Dr.R. I was beginning to practice systematically and logically, but then it became emotional, and this helped to make the practice sattvic—that is, emotional but wakeful, not desperate. Another aspect which has come to be seen is that the signs of bad Prakriti are features of which one is ashamed and hides away, so they come up in moments when one is off one's guard. Is this so? Does one really know the thief very well after all? When one doesn't say what one thinks and do what one says? When one loves a lie and not the truth? We have a saying: "A man winnows another's faults like grain, but his own faults he hides as a cheat hides the marked card in his sleeve."

H.H. There are different ways to uproot the bad Prakriti. If even after successive attempts one doesn't succeed in displacing the more subtle bad Prakriti, one may hit hard by hard discipline. Another is the rational way by satisfying one's Manas and Buddhi, and then resolve that such and such types of work are not useful and then give them up. Yet still there is the emotional approach to the problem by diminishing it through love and devotion. Any of these can be tried. It all depends which of them is going to do the job of uprooting. Even all of them can be tried. It is like in management of national affairs that either counsel, finance, confrontation or division-making policies work in tackling the wicked or the enemy. The end is to tackle the enemy and it should be once and for all by combined effort.

In alchemy the chemicals or metals are refined for use as medicine. [The] deeper the disease, [the] finer the chemical. The chemical or the metal is heated and then cooled; again the heating and cooling process is repeated and continues until the desired refinement or maturity in the medicine is achieved. So does the disciple keep on trying and keep on gathering more strength until he finally succeeds in uprooting the evil.

* * *

Dr.R. Thinking often of the story of that "one man who went through the seven gates to get the keys of the Kingdom from the King himself," I had understood H.H. to say that this "one man" was the individual Atman and the King was the Param Atman. Is this correct?

H.H. The seven gates are the seven covering layers of Prakriti or manifested nature, such as the five elements—earth, water, etc. —and the two aspects of mind, Manas and Buddhi enclosing in the most inaccessible layer of the Antahkarana [Soul] the Jivatman and Param Atman. The Jivatman actually sits in the lap of the Param Atman; but the trouble is that Jivatman, in spite of such close proximity, possesses an external outlook, and worries about those external layers of Prakriti, i.e., the seven gates. If Jivatman could turn its eyes inward through meditation, then it would see where it is, namely in the very lap of Param Atman. Then the seven gates cease to matter, and there is a state of unbroken joy all round.

* * *

H.H. All the disturbances which arise in any man's life or in the universe are destined to end in peace. They all arise from peace and end in peace. If one finds disturbance one should be happy that another chance of peace is near at hand.

All this is perfectly natural. There are two aspects of Nature known as Para-Prakriti and Apara-Prakriti. Para is naturally peaceful and unified and the Apara is experienced through movement, agitation which is [the] cause of all manifest creation. This is how the peaceful Para is naturally agitated to give way to the creation and manifestation. Each of us is a part of this creation, which is governed by Para and Apara-Prakriti. None can escape this law. The Para-Prakriti within each individual is peaceful and by its own nature turns into agitation to bring in another bit of peace.

Thus agitation or disturbance is neither wrong nor sinful. Each one of us gets hungry every day and takes food to satisfy this need. How could one say that hunger is wrong or sinful? It is only a natural phenomenon.

* * *

H.H. The Prakriti is always trying to please the Purusha and presents herself in ever new and changing forms in her own way and in her own time. Having had some pleasure with her, the Purusha [individual in this case] develops a taste for that and then likes to have it more often. This is bhoga, enjoying the richness of the creation, or desiring the enjoyment of the creation. By getting into the habit of such enjoyment, he may fall into moha which is deep attachment. Prakriti goes her way, and when Purusha [individual] forces her his way then the trouble starts. When the demands on Prakriti become hard and rigid, then she can't do what she wants to do, which is to please the Purusha. This makes the situation miserable either on individual or universal level.

The way of True Love (prema) is in a sense the process to reverse this miserable situation. In love you always give and don't demand in return. By giving you allow things to happen. Love of Absolute will not make it possible for one to enjoy the riches of the creation, for all *that* would have already been offered to the beloved which is Absolute. In this way bhoga and moha would not be possible. Those who learn to give up bhoga and moha break their bondage and emancipate themselves, or realize themselves. The devotee who went to the mosque was not really in love, for he only wanted a physical communion and got the bag of peanuts according to his worth. True lovers never go to sleep while waiting for the beloved! One must learn this lesson well—that one never demands anything for one's love and then, only, does one get all one needs for a happy and good life.

* * *

Q. Would H.H. please say how the daily activities of a job in life can be brought more under the influence of sattva? There are rare and wonderful times when a feeling of only being the instrument in trying to help people is felt. How to make these more frequent?

H.H. Suppose one is engaged in caring for infants or small children, then there is never a sense of duty, work, service, obligation, help, sacrifice or any other form of Ahankara [ego], for it is only play. This play is due to love, which is like an ocean in which two bodies are engaged in a certain type of movement. There is nothing beside love; no idea of personality or ego arises from either side.

This is real work. Here persons are only instruments and the creation is bliss. If one could establish the same relationship in daily work, then the doer is an instrument and the receiver is also an instrument, and the two Atmans become One. The unity thus achieved becomes a fountain of happiness. We all experience such moments of joy when we remove our covers of individuality or personality or any type of Ahankara. The remedy is simple. Give up all idea of being the doer and it will all be bliss everywhere.

Rest

H.H. In the physical world everyone needs food, water, clothes, a house and so on to live happy. These are being produced as a result of the study of the laws of physical substances.

If all the luxuries of the world were provided except the sleep, in three or four days a man will go crazy for want of rest. What is this rest which is so very important compared to the luxuries of life? *To rest is to give up.* This is a law. One must give up if one has taken any thing; and in this giving up, one is re-charged to take further. A man can manage to live with less food, no house and very little clothing, but he cannot live without rest, and the *rest must be full*. Rest is to give up, so he must *give up in full*. The physical world will crumble down if this law is not obeyed. The same applies to the other world, the spiritual world. One can go on looking for things and ideas which you think are useful and you go on accumulating them, but by accumulation of all this, when you are by yourself you don't find peace because of lack of rest. What do these people become? They go crazy, become mad or attempt suicide. This is all because they haven't had rest. Unless one has rest in love and happiness one cannot survive, just as one cannot [survive] without sleep. This system of work is to provide the rest.

To take people to bliss is simply giving them rest, to rest with the Self so that they may have new and fresh mornings of life. Without this life is not peaceful, and it is no wonder there is much chaos in the world.

* * *

H.H. There are three types of rest: the bodily rest of the physical realm, the mental rest of the subtle realm, and the spiritual rest of the causal realm. As far as the *physical realm* is concerned, every one knows that after a full day's work one must get rest during the night. Even after exertion during the day one must stop to rest and *gain* energy to start again. Most people know about it, although not every one knows the art of physical rest.

The rest at the *subtle level* appears between the end of fulfillment of one desire and initiation of the next desire. This is the state of non-desire, which provides rest of the subtle level. One stops all hankerings, and the thinking process comes to stillness.

The rest at the *spiritual or causal level* is available when all activities of the physical and subtle body—the desires, the thinking process and even the feelings and emotions—are stilled. The body, Manas, Buddhi, and Chitta are all stilled. Buddhi and Chitta at the causal level are the ultimate initiators of all activity, and when complete satisfaction with everything and every situation is materialized and there is no hankering after any further needs, then one gets the rest of the spiritual realm. In that rest the Atman appears as the sole witness in its luminous glory; and observes the great stillness of the whole universe as one single unit where there is no play of physical movement, mental movement, or even emotional movement. This could be described as "complete surrender," or "complete faith in the will of the Absolute." One simply accepts everything without any rejection or opposition. These are the three types or levels of rest, which the school should provide for its members according to the varying needs of individuals.

* * *

H.H. As an introductory observation on the relation of meditation to mental activity there are two factors to be remembered: First, whenever any fresh activity has to be started, it can only be initiated from a point of *rest*. If one is not at rest psychologically [that is on the "subtle level"], then since there is already mental activity going on, there won't be any question of being able to *initiate* any other different activity.

The second factor is that the progress and success of any constructive mental activity will depend on the forces available at the point of rest. So the *available energy* forms the capital (in the individual's bank account) and governs the quality and the amount of any mental work he will be able to carry on.

This is the pre-condition of successful meditation, and also of all (first-class) mental as well as physical activity.

H.H. There are *three forces of rest* available for the individual known —according to the guna preponderating at the time—as sattvic, rajasic or tamasic rest. When tamas or rajas preponderate, not much increase of energy is provided as far as the mind is concerned. So, unless sattvic rest is made available for those people who are deficient in mental energy, it would be difficult to change the content and direction of their mind. So we shall have to look into the relation between rest and mental energy under these three conditions.

* * *

Dr.R. At this audience questions were also asked about the three types of rest, which H.H. had mentioned in the first audience.

H.H. The law of three prevails at every stage and is involved in every event of life. There isn't anything that escapes the law of three. And the same law of three was previously discussed as physical, subtle and causal in relation to rest, and also yesterday as tamasic, rajasic and sattvic. Whatever event you like to see, visualize, or analyze, you will find the law of three works. In relation to the Ahankar, each individual who has a unified concept of himself and a picture evolving out of this unified concept of the world as he sees it and the way he behaves, is governed by this law of three. If the person is tamasic, then he sees himself within the tamas and is seen to be composed mostly of tamasic elements. He will see the world in a tamasic way; similarly, rajasic or sattvic, which we have discussed many times.

* * *

H.H. When tamas predominates, he sees himself imprisoned by tiredness and lethargy and needing extra sleep, which however does not refresh him; for his intake of energy through impressions is much reduced and he finds little to interest him outside himself.

With rajas predominant: You keep on having all sorts of worries in your mind, and creating dreams or weaving desires and plans for "future" achievements, so that you waste the time set apart for sleep and never get the rest you need before engaging yourself in further activity. But the man who goes by the way of sattva and devotion to the Absolute immediately goes to sleep the moment he is in bed and wakes fully fresh. He is not identified with any particular desires and therefore has no conflicts, nor does he worry about results to be achieved. He is only concerned with doing *what needs to be done* in the best [most "artistic"] way he can; and increasing moments when he can attend entirely to the Absolute, the Atman. Thus he becomes a really healthy person happy to perform any vigorous physical or mental work demanded of him.

* * *

Q. I am rather confused by your answer at our second audience about samadhi being available between desires. I had always understood that samadhi was an exceptional and definite state to which one aspires and which is only available after much work.

H.H. There are two types of samadhi. One is the natural and the other is the Yogic. Yogic samadhi is achieved by the eightfold discipline which we have previously been given, and even in that system there are different stages. Natural samadhi is not designed by anyone; it is provided by nature itself. Common man experiences it every day, but he *doesn't know that he is* experiencing it. But this is the source through which he gets some sort of steadiness, energy and happiness and it is *automatic*. The wise have understood the importance of this samadhi provided by nature and by understanding that this, *which is available all the time*, can also be put into further use, so they try to increase the extent (or duration) of this samadhi. In this samadhi the idea is that after a desire has been fulfilled, there is a little gap before the start of the next desire. Let us extend this time, which is natural free time. If we can extend it, *nature will certainly provide the necessary further extra energy*. Nature has made this automatic, so that everybody is re-charged every time they have completed their desire.

During this samadhi—if we can extend this period of rest between two desires—what we can save is more powerful than what we can get out of eight hours of rest in sleep.

* * *

Q. Could we hear what we really need to do in the pauses so that we can extend this period of availability of energy as in samadhi?

H.H. All desires arise in consciousness, although this consciousness is not appreciated or not registered by the common man; but one who knows, or who has taken to discipline, does realize that there is a moment when a desire arises, and of course everyone knows when the desire is fulfilled. So with ordinary man the cycle of desires and their fulfillment goes unnoticed—although it happens in consciousness, it is not registered. It can be registered if we want to register it, and those who are following the discipline certainly would be able to do that. Because it is done in consciousness, when a desire is fulfilled, everyone can see for himself that there is a moment when he puts up a new desire. If you appreciate the moment of lack of all desires, then at that moment you will not have a desire, because only one thing can happen at a time—either there is a desire or there is no desire registered by you; you cannot register lack of desire and desire both at the same time. That is the moment to catch, and by practice it is possible to extend this moment.

H.H. Take the example of a canal: When it is constructed to irrigate the fields, hundreds of small openings are made into the canal to feed the water into the fields. But, if you have hundreds of openings then the amount of water being put into the fields will be less than if you had only ten openings. The application of meditation is just one such way to curtail our desires, because you give some time to it and it takes you away from your lovely desires. The extension of this moment of samadhi between two desires is another way. Understand this central point that consciousness is consumed only through desires—the fewer the desires, the better the use of consciousness can be made. All the disciplines which we have been given are to lead in this direction. If we practice the extended moment of samadhi between two desires, we can by practice, extend it and get the full benefit of this process.

* * *

Dr.R. In the "natural samadhi" which he [H.H.] is describing to us, the thread of consciousness and memory is—with practice—not only retained but increased. This again is of two kinds, under rajas or under sattva.

H.H. Here the more usual kind is the "rajasic samadhi" when you get peace after finishing some activity, but after only a little peace you once again hurry into action and so keep repeating the cycle of activity and peace. That keeps you going, but it does not improve the situation, though of course there may not be any loss either.

Dr.R. As an example of "sattvic samadhi" he [H.H.] describes a scene from the Krishna dance drama Rasa-Leela.

H.H. The Rasa-Leela is the enactment of Creation itself in which the Absolute desires to "play" and so from One he becomes many, Krishna is represented as the Self, his consort Radha is his Buddhi [reason], the Maya is the desire to "play" which will create all these beings that take part; the gopis [milkmaids, for Krishna began as a cowherd] are his own ideas or manifest desires stirred up by Cupid, the god of attraction or passionate love; and Chitta is the playground or stage. Radha will see that Krishna will come out free from attachment.

H.H. The Lord Krishna as a youth used to dance with the gopi girls [milkmaids] in the lovely forest of Vrindevan near his birthplace by the river Yamuna. One of the scenes depicted is that of the final stages of the dance, when the gopis stand in a circle and between every two gopi girls there is a Krishna; and this is a picturesque view of the natural samadhi where, between two desires [the gopi girls], there is always the restful Krishna, the Absolute.

* * *

H.H. The realm of desires and their fulfillment is the common realm. Some people have more desires than others, and certainly through all the disciplines we can learn to minimize our desires and the more they are minimized the more force of consciousness we would be able to use through our desires.

There is a way whereby there is no cessation of activity and yet there is no desire. There is no concept of achievement; there is no entanglement, no attachment to any activity, and yet there is a ready response to do whatever nature calls for, whatever the moment demands of you. Now this surrender to the activity generated by the nature itself is a state where there is no hankering by the individual—whatever is wanted he picks it up and puts it down instantly when the time to stop has come. He thinks no more about it, and he may pick it up later on if he is called upon to do exactly the same thing again. Ordinarily it might seem very odd because in common life most of us like to complete the job, because completion of the work is related to achievement—fulfillment of the desire.

Summary

H.H. The rest at the *physical level* provides enough energy to employ in eight or nine hours of activity for any individual. This is how the human race keeps going without much trouble. At least people with common sense appreciate this and provide themselves with physical rest, and keep in good health and normal activity.

The rest at the *subtle level*, by cessation of conflicting desires, brings another dimension to the idea of rest. In this dimension of rest efficiency arises, and this works through all activities—ordinary physical work or artistic work. Thus, rest at this level between fulfillment of one desire and initiation of another, will be rewarded with efficiency.

The third or *causal level* of rest, which is profound stillness or total immobility, is in the realm of the Absolute. Since the causal realm cannot be described, one learns about it from its effects. One can see it in the activities and dispositions of such men who provide themselves with *spiritual* rest. There are three prominent features:

Firstly, they show love and affection toward everything they encounter. All activities will be initiated with love, and then held and nourished with love till they come to their fulfillment. All relationships with individuals or activities, direct or indirect, will be lighted and guided only by love and affection.

Secondly, their ideas, intentions or motives will be pure and simple. Purity and simplicity widen the horizon, and they think and work for the whole of humanity and only through the Laws of the Absolute. The divisions of groups, races or nations disappear and only natural Laws are employed. Their thoughts naturally encompass the whole of the human family, and its intrinsic goodness.

Thirdly, the physical movements of such people are only geared to the natural rhythm, and the result is simplicity and economy of movement. They never rush into any situation; are never agitated; and perform all actions in an efficient, sublime, and refined way.

Whatever they do will emerge from stillness, be held in stillness, and again submerge in the same stillness, which they experience in this great total immobility.

Samskara

Q. When His Holiness speaks about level, is it chiefly level of being or anything else?

H.H. The levels are the levels of being which are based upon the concept of samskar. Samskars vary, hence the variety of levels. But these levels of being are not totally fixed for the whole life. If they were, then change in being would be impossible. Thus there is a provision of pratibha which can, under certain circumstances such as good company, override the samskar and lead to transformation, or even fall from a fairly high level of being. Pratibha is a part of Buddhi, which musters emotional power as well. In a way it is the reflection of consciousness. If it is not used rightly then one can keep on living a mechanical life totally ruled by samskar.

* * *

Q. Can it be understood that as His Holiness said earlier—[there is] something that everybody has that he can do and only he can do well in that particular way?

H.H. Talent depends on samskar. Some people have done that job before in their previous life also, so that they have the knack of doing things. They are getting that from their previous lives; they will be able to do it well and they can progress further. Some people will have to be taught for the first time in this very life to do a particular job so they will be creating samskar in this life, which will be helpful to them in their next life.

Q. Several years ago I experienced a flash in the mind in which I was shown the way to liberation of the householder. I find it hard to formulate all that was shown in that moment, but here seem to be the key points:

Firstly, one should think of Param Atman at all times.

Secondly, one should conduct or spend one's life as though watching a show.

These two statements appear to contain the essence of the Way of the Householder.

I have practiced total acceptance of each moment as it unfolds. Letting go of ideas as they arise in the mind in certain situations and letting go of fear when the mind gradually becomes empty of thought, a state of not knowing. Can discussion of actual experiences to remember Param Atman in small groups help? Could His Holiness give guidance on all that I have said?

H.H. This is right: These two things contain the essence of the Way of the Householder. It is also right about the total acceptance of each moment; however I would like to throw some light on this aspect. Happenings can be of two kinds, good and bad. The good happenings come from the side of the Atman or the Param Atman while the bad ones come as a result of our previous samskar. I emphasize the point that we should accept the good happenings and we should show our indifference to the bad things. We should accept the good things and be indifferent to the bad things; by bad things I mean those things which appear to be misfortune and the like.

Experiences relate to that which has already happened, so discussions won't help. We can do nothing about them. What has happened cannot be undone but remembering Param Atman is good in all circumstances whether alone or in groups. Here is an example:

A learned man went to a gathering to give a talk. The first sentence he said was, "Does this audience here present understand me?" Everybody raised their hand in the affirmative. He said, "All right, since everyone understands me, there is no need for me to say anything else." Next day he repeated the same question, "Does everybody understand me?" Everybody said, "No." "Since nobody understands me, there is no need to say anything else."

This is about group discussions and happenings. When good things happen—good experiences—they are the result of Atman or Param Atman, because they are incapable of doing anything bad. Whenever anything bad happens it is the result of our own samskaras.

Modern man gives undue thought to what has happened in the past. From a spiritual point of view this is useless, we should rather think of how to behave in the future.

* * *

H.H. Discrimination is not natural. We became acquainted with it since we began understanding things. Before these things—prior to them—is the one who knows. That knower was always there and always will be. All these good and bad things have come up in between, but they come and go like the waves in the ocean while the ocean ever remains the same. Atman is like the ocean.

Nothing is good or bad; it is due only to our samskaras that things appear good and bad. If the attitude to see is good then everything appears good. Intrinsically, considering the fundamental nature, nothing is good or bad. For example, one man likes food, another man does not like food. So whether a thing is good or bad, the root of this kind of discrimination lies in the mind of the person, not in the thing itself. As regards Atman, what is the thing that is good or bad for the Atman, liked or disliked by the Atman? Everything can be good for it; everything can be bad for it. For example: take provisions, whether when cooked they will produce good or bad dishes depends on the cooking. Provisions themselves may be good, but if not cooked properly they will not appear to be good, so the result will depend on how they are cooked.

* * *

Q. We know that impressions rain on all five senses; would these be selected in accordance with the purity of Buddhi? We know many of these impressions are stored in the memory at the subtle level; some remain for a short time, and some for life. Would any impression of great intensity, such as artists sometimes receive, and which His Holiness spoke about when describing the "Golden Universe," would such an impression reach and get stored in the causal level, thereby affecting a future life?

H.H. In an individual's life, or in the life of an artist, there is a capital deposit within the essence, samskar, which is already created and crystallized. It is of two types: It can be conducive to good fortune or misfortune—they are both there. The world itself presents all these situations with the golden covering; but it's not always golden either! If this individual happens to be in bad company, then whatever his samskar (essence) may be, he will have to face this situation, which is basically bad. His good essence will be misused much more than it ought to be, and his bad essence will be encouraged and will increase because of the bad company. So the good will be suppressed and the bad will increase. On the other hand, if it happens that our man finds good company, then even if he has bad samskar it will not arise; it will be suppressed by the company he keeps, and encouragement to his good samskar will be possible in this company. Likewise there can be many combinations.

In Yogavasistha (a monumental work on the Vedanta) it is said that there are two natural streams flowing in every individual—one is pure and the other impure, or one of them is auspicious and the other inauspicious—and it is in the combination of the worldly accidents which come to this individual that he finds how he sails. If he is in good company and is always supplied with certain material which gives him encouragement to go on a better path, then he will be able to sail all through the auspicious or inauspicious circumstances to improve his lot. The satsang is created only for this—a constant reminder—so that whatever your samskar may be, you should always be able to keep yourself in the stream which is auspicious.

Take the example of agriculture: when you sow the seed in the field and irrigate it. After some time you will see that the rice plant grows, but with it there are some weeds and grasses which do not need sowing; they are already there like our samskar. They will come up and it may seem that the grass and weeds grow much faster and stronger than the rice plant itself. A good farmer takes care of this by uprooting the grass and weeds and throwing them away. With the aid of the water supply the plant is allowed to grow faster because there is now no competition for the food from the soil. Later on the grasses and weeds will appear again, but by that time the real plant will have grown big enough and the heat of this plant will dissolve these little grasses and weeds and you don't have to bother about them.

The same happens in satsang. A good teacher uproots all these grasses and weeds, or the worldly involvement, and then allows the good samskar to prevail and grow. After some time it becomes natural, so that even if you have some bad samskar, it won't be able to affect you and you will be able to rise on the ladder.

* * *

Dr.R. I was told kashaya came from a Sanskrit word meaning the sticky gum of a plant from which one cannot free oneself, like a fly on flypaper.

H.H. Yes, in the system about the samskar, which we have been given previously, we can see that on the physical realm there is some sticky material to which flies or anything can be stuck, and one can keep on adding to it and making it thick. But as far as the body of samskar is concerned, one does not see anything physical in that realm at all; it is only the idea which gets stuck in one's being, and if you play with the same idea again and again, then the impression is much deeper and stronger. To undo any such samskar we cannot eliminate anything just by itself, the elimination takes place by putting in better thoughts, righteous thoughts. If one wants to do away with kashaya, all one has to do is to implant good thoughts in one's being and keep company with them so that one by one they will make their mark and one can implant better being, better samskar.

* * *

H.H. It is actually the Atman which is the motive force behind the three bodies. I say this in order to throw some light on what Atman is and how it keeps the functions of this body going. This body is like a replica or model of the Atman, and in relation to this it is Atman, which gives power to this body. When we make our mind steady then we come face-to-face with the Atman.

Through some easy method we have to settle down in meditation in order to arrive at a steady state. Manas, Chitta, Buddhi and Ahankar, all four are very, very restless, always moving on to this side and that. So meditation is nothing but to bring these four forces to rest. When this has been achieved then we are able to see Atman.

If a mirror is covered with dirt you will not be able to see your face as it actually is. On account of our past—samskaras—the mirror of our mind has become dirty, so we are not able to see the picture of Atman correctly, and as a result the mind becomes bored. This boredom drives you away from meditation. When you begin to clean the mind you start to see Atman, and then you will start to derive pleasure in meditation. In this case the question of boredom or running away will not arise. This cleaning of Chitta is essential for glimpsing the Atman. It is cleaning the mirror. This is only achieved by meditation. The steadier the mind the cleaner the mirror and the clearer will be the image of the Atman. Then you will begin to derive pleasure in meditation. Without this pleasure the mind will get bored.

* * *

H.H. The real cause of the different effects of the meditation in different people is the distribution and proportion of the three gunas in their own nature; in no two men are they alike. It depends on the former life.

[The word used was SAMSKAR, the "essence of the individual life," into which is collected the joint effects of all these thoughts, feelings and actions]

* * *

H.H. The rise of a desire is related to the samskara and it is the quality of the samskara that gives form to a desire. If it is good and pure samskara, the desires will be pure; if it is impure, the desires will be impure. Desire has nothing to do with the physical at all; it is the emanation of the consciousness, which we feel as a desire. So whatever we desire is after all the consciousness itself.

* * *

Dr.R. As I was just going off to sleep, after pronouncing the mantra, I suddenly had a wonderful feeling and saw the meeting of the chariot of Arjuna as the Jivatman and the chariot of Lord Krishna as Param Atman between the two armies, good and bad. This came as a result of the Krishna play. It gives a feeling of sattva whenever I think of it since.

H.H. It is from good samskara [essence] that such a vision or experience arises. The Absolute or the Atman is free, all-knowing and ever blissful. His creation is His "leela" [play], which is also blissful. His play is eternal, and whosoever participates in that leela will also partake of the goodness, freedom and bliss. When, during sleep or waking, one thinks or gets glimpses of His play and His goodness, one is supported by sattva, which is due to His good samskar or essence. When the mind is made to rest then the essence or samskar takes over to project subjects or visions from within. Good projection comes from good samskar and bad projections from bad samskar. The meditation is also made to do just that, so the individual has more sattva and may get more energy for advancement.

In the Fourth Chapter of the *Gita,* Krishna says that although the fourfold caste [system] was created by Me through the differentiation of gunas and karma, I am the changeless non-doer. Actions don't taint Me nor do I have thirst for results. Whoever knows Me thus is also not fettered by action. This means that to indulge in such good thoughts or visions would not in any way be a bond-producing activity, for all this purifies the individual and leads him to freedom. The creation comes forth and is sustained and ultimately withdrawn back into the Absolute; and men who see all this as Leela [a play] participate in this creation, sustaining and merging in Sat, Chit and Ananda.

* * *

Q. Is there a chief feature in everyone's make up, particular to themselves, which is their main obstacle to climbing the ladder? Does each individual have to find out what this is for themselves?

For example, it is most distressing to observe how fragile my good states continue to be, and in spite of all my efforts over the years, how vulnerable I still remain to attacks from petty vanities and arrogance. These seem to have crystallized into a formidable obstacle, which prevents me from climbing the ladder.

H.H. The Antahkaran has two active elements apart from others, which are Manas and Buddhi. Manas is the means of expression of desires to initiate actions. Buddhi is the means of discrimination of what is useful or harmful for the Self. Manas is usually dynamic, whereas Buddhi is reflective and needs wisdom to operate its discriminative force. If Buddhi has been sharpened with reason then before it can offer restrictive commands the dynamic Manas can quickly get the body into action. Whatever is pleasant to the senses Manas is ready to repeat very spontaneously. Therefore, all that is necessary is that Buddhi must be made sharper and stronger to control Manas before it gets into action on impulse. Those who seek True Knowledge are usually blessed with reason, which can remove all those obstacles on the way. One needs to be patient and persistent. Sooner or later reason will prevail.

There may be an element of samskar from birth, which may burst out at unguarded moments to claim its share of pleasure. Those who are not provided with True Knowledge and reason do not know what causes these eruptions. They even justify them. Men of reason have the capacity to recognize them. This recognition of failing is itself the proof that Buddhi is active. Action done cannot be undone, but men of reason feel sorry to have seen it take place unintentionally. This sense of feeling sorry sets up vigilance, and in the light of reason such samskar loosens its strength and in the course of time disappears.

There is no such obstacle which cannot be removed by reason and wisdom. After all, consciousness is not supreme for nothing. Vanity and arrogance are no exceptions. Reason can dissolve them only when one sees the obstacle and feels sorry to have stumbled.

There is no eternal obstacle, for obstacles are nothing more than a wrong measure of the goodness provided by the Absolute.

* * *

Dr.R. At step number five, or high up the Ladder, would Chitta be capable of remembering the previous life?

H.H. Step number five on the Ladder of Self-realization is a step where old influences of the past have apparently melted away completely. By then those influences have been washed and cleaned away so they no longer exist. In their place new influences have made their home, and these new influences are of a different order. There are two types of influences which are accumulated in samskar [essence]: one which leads toward activity, and the other which leads toward non-activity.

But there are two kinds of activity: One is useful activity, which is called "good" activity; the other is useless activity, which is "bad" activity. So the activity or the influences which lead toward activity may be good or bad. The bad have been washed away by the new influences through this system of meditation and the knowledge; and because the new influences have come in, the old ones cannot arise because they no longer exist there. Of course anybody might have had these new influences some time ago, and then have forgotten them. So at stage number five there would be no question of remembering anything about what has passed.

Q. In his first answer His Holiness mentioned nations, societies and religions in relation to coming toward love. We have found questions arising, in considering samskar, as to whether samskar is involved in larger groups or nations? Some people seem subject to the effects of their nations, quite apart from the effects of their own deeds. Can H.H. help us to understand this level which is larger than the individual?

H.H. Samskar relates to individuals. It is individuals with their samskars which form societies and nations. Societies or nations express the predominant samskars of the majority of their individuals. Societies and nations are composed of individuals. Only an individual can acquire or dissolve a samskar. When the majority within a nation manifests malicious or benevolent samskar we ascribe it to that nation, but a nation is not a being but a group of beings. Thus the question of samskar concerns individuals. A society which is actively engaged in the search for truth and disciplined by the practice of meditation will sooner or later dissolve the unwanted samskars in most of its members.

For example if you go to clean a room you begin to clean individual items like a chair, table, curtains, windows, walls, floor or ceiling. The dust and dirt is held by these individual items and that is where the cleaning has to start. Once the items are clean, you can say the room is clean. But in relation to samskars they are not dissolved by physical means—they have to be dissolved at the mental level of the Antahkaran. When the mind and intellect are clean it leads to cleanliness at every level. To help a nation one must start with individuals. With detachment, the feeling of not being the doer and following the discipline given, one can remove all samskars. The nation is purified by purifying its individuals and then the world can be enjoyed.

Q. Surrendering to the Param Atman and giving up the sense of being "the doer" seems to be the shortcut to "no samskar." Could H.H. say something more about this?

H.H. In this creation everything is moving and every movement leaves a trace or effect. These effects are the samskars, and because of the movement they are subject to change—good or bad. New samskars arise in place of old. Some are deep and strong so last longer. They all exist in the Antahkaran.

Take the example of Valmiki who, in the early part of his life, was a robber. He used to rob people for himself and his family. He was also violent and his deeds caused misery and loss of life. With these samskars, one day he met some sages who were passing through a forest. The sages influenced his mind and he was ready to listen and act on what he heard. He was given a mantra on which to meditate; due to his sincerity and devotion his violent samskars were dissolved and he turned toward purity, beauty and truth. He became a poet and his Sanskrit *Ramayana* is so beautiful and full of feeling that he was called the "Adikavi" or First Poet.

Thus all samskars can be changed from the worst to the best, but as long as one is participating in the ever changing creation some samskars will always be there. They give form to existence. They arise in connection with objects, persons and actions. Good company offers good samskars and bad company brings in bad. In good company one hears spiritual texts, analyzes through reason and participates in the stream of love and devotion; then all previous samskars of selfish pleasures, pride and prejudices begin to be dissolved, and new ones of purity, beauty, justice and love prevail.

This leads one toward universality and one begins to see the whole world as one's own family. This is how one moves from the limited towards the unlimited, from imperfection to perfection. Everyone is full of pure and loving samskars because that is the desire of the Creator, but for some reason they are overlaid by the selfish, material and divisive samskars. All one needs is to shed these superimposed evil samskars and once they are eliminated the pure motive force of love will take over. This one cannot remove for it gives form to the universe and all in it. This is natural and ordained by the Absolute. It is part of the ocean of bliss expressed by waves of bliss. In this no one experiences separation, conflict, misery or sorrow. With detachment our actions will bear no fruit and the laws of nature or the process of ever changing samskar will make no mark and thus one stays free. This is what is referred to as "no samskar."

Sanatan Dharma

Q. Seekers after truth follow different traditions in different parts of the world. It has been said that the essence of all these traditions lies in Sanatan. Will H.H. say something about this with particular reference to Western Christian traditions?

H.H. Human beings everywhere are the same and so they have common desires and aspirations. One of the most universal of these aspirations is happiness. All religions everywhere have as their aim the achievement of happiness or bliss. The differences in religions are not to be found in their aim but in their rituals. These rituals have different forms and characters according to the geographical place and historical time of their origin. If one looks behind these rituals one can see that the fundamental spiritual activities of man are practically the same everywhere. If one recognizes and overlooks the physical differences of the rituals one can see that the essence of the religions is practically the same also.

* * *

Dr.R. Can one enter into Sanatan religion by inner understanding of it, or must one be admitted into it and adopt its rituals?

H.H. It is not necessary at all to embrace our Sanatan Dharma. Every religion contains Sanatan Dharma. If each one follows his own religion truthfully he would for certain be following Sanatan Dharma. It is the basis of all religions and their center. There is no need to change anybody's present religion. [Dharma is that quality which everything naturally contains in itself for its existence = intrinsic goodness.]

Dr.R. What is the meaning of Sanatan?

H.H. The word Sanatan is made up of two words: *Sada* and *Tan*. *Tan* means the body, inner body. *Sada* means eternal, the "body of eternal religion," that is, Sanatan Dharma. Sanatan Dharma is the religion of the Atman—the Natural Laws of the Atman. An example of a Natural Law is that if somebody wants to speak lies *all* day, he just can't do it. It is impossible because it is not the nature of the Atman to speak a lie.

But if somebody wants to speak the truth all day one *can* do it, it is not impossible.

This is so because the nature of Atman is to be truthful—Atman is Truth. The Sanatan Dharma is the original, the root of all religions, and of the religions which we see today. The *different* religions—Hinduism, Islam, Christianity, Jainism, and so on—have somehow come out of this and taken different shapes. Another example: With the help of the Great Man, lesser men continue to be helped a bit; so with the help of the Atman and the Religion of Atman, any other religion can also benefit. The original, which is eternal, without beginning and without end, will go on. Another example is that of a boy who has to learn something. The initial stages of learning are difficult; he has got to work hard. Once he gets over that initial stage, things become easier and he doesn't have to go on learning all his life; he learns for a short time and then he has to put into practice what he has learned, and over a much longer period. Just so, the creation of Sanatan: The initial laws of Atman are of course difficult, but once one gets hold of all these laws, life becomes easier and without troubles.

Q. Who founded the Tradition of Sanatan Dharma and how was it supported?

H.H. The Tradition was founded by all those men whose names you pronounce at Initiation—Narayanam, the first one, and all those realized men who followed him have been supporting; and they are the real men behind Sanatan Dharma. When we use their names we want their blessing so that they can help us on the Way. In the world if we go on a long tour we take some companion[s] and in the tour to Atman these people are our companions.

Once a King announced that he would give his kingdom to any person who would come to him by 4 o'clock. Everybody heard it and thought it a good idea to go and meet him at 4 o'clock. But what the King did was this: In his capital city he put beautiful shops containing everything that can be had, jewelry, gold, silks, and toys, everything that anybody could want to have. And at every gate and in every quarter, there were people to give away all these things, without payment, all free! Thousands of people started out to go and get the kingdom, which the King had promised to give away, but they were persuaded to go to the shops and take whatever they wanted free, and enjoy themselves. So they lost themselves among the golden ornaments, silks and jewels, beautiful clothes.

But one man didn't listen to any one of these people; he went straight without letting anyone dissuade him. He just went through and met the King at the appointed time and demanded the kingdom, which the King duly gave him. The moment he took over the government, he issued an edict to arrest all those people who were taking things without paying for them!

The same can be related to our Work. If somebody wants the kingdom he has to go straight inward for it and get it; but unfortunately the pleasures and beauties of the world tempt nearly everyone away. That is the kingdom about which Sanatan Dharma tells.

* * *

Dr.R. I see this as from two approaches: through the temple and through the audience chamber. I have understood that Sanatan referred to the temple side—prayer, religious exercises and rituals. Am I right?

H.H. The Sanatan Dharma today has two aspects: One is the local aspect which belongs to land, society, and the traditions; and the other is the universal aspect which belongs to humanity or mankind. In the first one, which belongs to the traditions, there are many things that Indians do which others do not. For instance, they worship idols, go to the Ganges for a bath, go to temples to see the deity or have kirtan and bhajan, sandhya and many other ritualistic activities. The other aspect, which is the good company, listening to realized man or man of higher level, meditation or prayers [these] are universal in their nature. This aspect is not limited to land or society. These activities are universal in their nature so can be used by everybody, because they wouldn't present any problems of tradition. But it would be difficult to do everything as Indians do and anyway it is not necessary. It should be left to the local people and sources in their own traditions, so that new activities fit in properly. Whatever you think about Sanatan is practically right, keeping these two aspects of activities in mind.

Dr.R. The word Sanatan then covers everything?

H.H. The real meaning of Sanatan is eternal, which will dissolve or disappear with the dissolution of creation itself. It starts with the creation, exists with it and dissolves with it; but even in dissolution this will exist as the knowledge of the Absolute. These are the natural laws.

In the ordinary aspect of the word, Sanatan, for common man it is taken as meaning to prepare a man for two orders of activities: one of the worldly activity and the other of the world beyond. These would prepare you to discharge the worldly activities and also prepare yourself, here in this life, for the next journey. This is Sanatan Dharma.

One can see this as laws given by the Absolute. When the creation starts it runs on certain laws and exists on laws given by the Absolute. These laws are seen by certain people, laws as they are. This may be seen here or anywhere else according to other religions—Mohammed who realized Allah, or Christ who realized God, or anywhere. They are the people whose level is so high that they can see the natural law direct from the Absolute working through creation. There would be no difference as to these laws seen by an Indian or anybody else. They are the basic principles. But there are numerous secondary laws which are enacted according to the land and time—man-made on the basis of those original laws. They differ because you see them through traditions and different types of culture all over the world. But, in a sense, the Sanatan Dharma is the knowledge of the Absolute. It comes into existence with the creation and is seen by different people, and after the cessation of this creation it dissolves again into the Absolute.

Dr.R. So it is by no means limited to Way of Love or Religious Way, but includes both Way of Knowledge and Way of Love?

H.H. There is a general law that everybody wants to know something, and after knowing it wants to unite with it or get it. So all the knowledge in the world is not for only the sake of knowledge, but it leads to that other part of human activity, which is to get united. The first act of knowing is the Way of Knowledge. The other act is the love, which is aimed at unity. This is a natural thing and basic to everybody.

Dr.R. This is going to make for clarity in London where there is this discussion going on, and this has made everything clear.

H.H. All these discussions show that nobody has fully experienced either way. The effort should be made to go on *one* Way earnestly; and once you have reached the end of the Way, immediately you are on the second Way and you don't have to work too much and start from the beginning again, because by the time you have reached and fulfilled the Way of Knowledge, you would be quite a long way on the Way of Love as well. The desire and thirst for the other Way will be so intense, and your being will be so high, that everything will happen very quickly. If you take the Way of Knowledge, don't think that you would be satisfied with these words—not at all. Once you have really understood things love will spring up. You cannot do without it.

So it applies the other way round too. The people who have really loved something, they will see that knowledge is not far away, and it will always be available to them whenever they need it. The best thing is to keep on one track sincerely.

The Absolute, which exists and wishes to expand itself, starts with the Prakriti. The Absolute is called Purush. This Absolute is consciousness and knowledge; and the emanation, which follows from this desire, which is termed as Prakriti—Nature—is the aspect of love. So the moment creation starts this knowledge and love just keep on expanding and they exist as long as creation is there. The same applies to us.

Take a man and a woman. The dharma of a woman is to serve the husband, and the dharma of the man is to keep safe and care for the woman—protecting in all aspects. This protecting is the quality of knowledge. This sense of protection is arrived at through the knowledge, whereas the service to the man comes from love. These are the two streams which are brought together in a marriage. If both work properly and both play their part in life harmoniously, they enjoy life; and then they depart to whatever place they belong after their life is complete. This is the ideal man-woman relationship.

In India, for all those who are celibate and love no wife, as H.H. himself, Buddhi is supposed to be their wife. They look after Buddhi, protect it, and Buddhi serves them and keeps them going. They are the husband of the Buddhi.

* * *

Q. Still staying with the question of the role of our Society in the world, we would like to ask His Holiness if He could tell us more about Sanatan Dharma being the root religion of all religions?

H.H. Sanatan Dharma is not bound by space and time or division of the human race at all. It is for the human race as a whole. Other religions, and development of different cultures, arise from the talents expressed in a certain place; and then the culture evolves from that talent. Some individual arises in a place who has a vision and through that vision he produces a philosophy, ideas, or a religion, and a culture arises on those basic factors, established by that particular individual.

For instance Christianity, although basically coming from the Jewish culture, was reinterpreted by the ideas given by Christ— this was how the religion arose.

You will not find anything of this sort in Sanatan Dharma. It was not created or evolved by human mind as it is known today. There is no reference to any individual in Sanatan Dharma. One does find in India that there are various ways where principles of Sanatan Dharma have been applied, but Hinduism is not a religion in the sense we understand Christianity. It is a conglomeration of many different types of approaches, and in fact we do have quite a number of religions, which you could equate with Christianity but all these religions are supported on the basic idea of Sanatan Dharma.

There are concepts, which one finds in Hinduism and divisions of Hinduism, Christianity, Islam, Buddhism, Jainism or any other religion or culture, and you will find all these ideas there in Sanatan Dharma, but they have been developed in different ways. The basic concept of Sanatan Dharma has been summed up in ten principles:

The *first* [Dhrh] is concerned with having confidence and patience. If there is no confidence, there can't be patience. These two are united in this Sanskrit word *Dhrh*. So, Sanatan Dharma wants individuals to develop Dhrh.

The *second* [Kshama] means having consideration, and giving pardon and being tolerant of all the difficulties and awkwardness and faults of others, so that you provide them space, and in due course when they see [that] there is no reaction they may learn something better which you hold very dear to yourself.

The *third* [Dhama] means the senses are very fast, and if the mind is turbulent, receiving impressions from different sources, it is quite probable that sensual hunger and thirst may be enflamed because of the beautiful things being seen in the world, so every individual needs to have some control over their sensory appetite and expressions.

The *fourth* [Asteya] states that you should take only what you deserve, and consider everyone else equally deserving. So, do not take anything extra—all that you accumulate extra is theft. You steal from the universe and you deprive other people. So do not keep anything more than what should be equally available to everybody else.

The *fifth* [Shaucha] is about the cleanliness of body and mind. One has to learn to clean one's body, one's mind and one's heart and for that one has to find a system through a teacher.

The *sixth* [Indriya Nigraha] is to do with the senses. There is a natural course of use of the senses and these can be regulated, and the rules are prescribed in every tradition, and from these one has to learn how to use one's senses within those limitations. One does not curb the use of the senses but regulates them. The curbing of excessive use will then take place naturally.

The *seventh* [Dhee] refers to the use of intellect, Buddhi or reason, and one is expected to use one's intellect and find out the causes of things and use them as necessity may arise.

The *eighth* [Vidya] is based on the need to acquire the knowledge, which is made manifest as far as Sanatan Dharma is concerned through the Vedas, which are supposed to be not manmade. Who made them nobody knows, so one has to acquire the knowledge of the Scriptures.

The *ninth* [Satya] is about the truth. There is only one truth about an aspect; there can't be two different truths about the same subject. Everybody in the world is hankering for truth, but it happens that people want their particular brand of truth; they are not eager or ready to accept that there can be something different. One may be right or wrong, and then rationalization is very necessary. Even thieves, robbers and evil men, they also wish that the people with whom they cooperate should speak the truth so that they do not get caught by the police! So truth is important not only for people in a highly developed and cultured society, but the need is everywhere, but somehow people like to serve their own ends through their own concept of truth.

The *tenth* [Akrodha] states that one should never get agitated under any circumstances. There may be occasions when a hard line is very necessary, usually for the sake of education, but taking a hard line is not necessarily getting agitated. One can tell the difference between righteous agitation or wrong agitation. If one is wrongly agitated one cannot take right action, so this has to be avoided.

Considering all these ten factors one can see that they do not only apply to the Hindus of India. They are for all human beings. That is how basic religion, or the concept of human religion is Sanatan Dharma, and the meaning of Sanatan is that the root of this concept, or idea, or religion has no end or beginning; it was not started by any particular man, and it will never end whatever happens. As long as human beings exist these concepts will prevail. There is a Sanskrit shloka which says that if one learns to understand that one is part of this universe and one has equal status with everyone else, then give to others what you would like given to you. What pleases you should be made available for the pleasure of others—or "Do as you would be done by." This sums up the concept of Sanatan Dharma. It is not a religion; it is a concept for humanity.

Self

Q. H.H. has told us much about meditation and has given us guidance for other ways of working on our being. But it seems that this alone is not enough and that one needs also to work with and for other people who share the same aim of Self-realization. Would H.H. speak about this and give guidance as to how the two ways of working may be kept in balance?

H.H. The first duty is to work on Self, knowing that the Self is everything; our first aim is to see ourselves on the way of development. After that (not that we can't start without being fully realized) as we get guidance we can help guide others who desire self-development [realization]. Working on these two lines one would see that the third line is being worked automatically. He emphasizes most the first line. On the second line one can take the knowledge to others who are eager and have questions and doubts for clearance. One should deal with them and clear their minds and keep them in their fold. He did not specifically say much about the third line, but he mentioned that by working on the two lines the third is accomplished.

The work on the Self and work for the neighbor and the work for the sake of the work [universal work] are the three lines of work. To see which comes first he gives an illustration. If someone had a boil, he might get fever, which will be followed by general weakness in the body. How to tackle these three? Should one treat the weakness or the fever or the boil? The answer would be to tackle the causal boil on which the others depend. Once the boil is under cure, the fever will vanish and after full cure strength will be regained. So first job is the work on the Self. If you have undergone some change your neighbors would like to know how. Give them what you know and the process goes on and the third line works without anyone knowing about it.

* * *

H.H. Meditation [dhyan] is made up of a root verb called *dhi*, which means to hold and contemplate. In meditation the moving mind is held and contemplates. What is that which one should hold and contemplate? And how can one do so? These are the questions one asks.

We can appreciate a thing only if we know about it. The more we know the more is the possibility of liking (if it is likeable). We have our senses and their subjects. We see, touch, hear, smell and taste. We sometimes like and sometimes dislike and, moreover we have no control over the subjects of senses. They seem to change all the year round and so become the cause of pain and pleasure —both. The mind is also so very mobile and intellect seems to change very often due to change of time and place, and thus we find that all these senses, mind and intellect have changing nature. What else is left in us then?

There is that unchanging, eternal, blissful, conscious, peaceful entity called the Self, the Atman, and that is what we try to hold and contemplate during meditation. We should know more about it. We might like it.

* * *

Q. How to bring about expansion?

H.H. By feelings and thoughts. The microcosm is made of the same substance that made macrocosm. The body is made of elements of earth, water, air, fire, ether, mind, intellect and Atman. The universe is also made of the same. In consciousness the elements are united and the body expands to embrace the universe. This is possible only when full Knowledge of microcosm and macrocosm is given to aspirant, and then there is the element of all-flowing love. Once we create feeling of love we are connected to everything we love. Feeling and thought processes can bring about expansion. In doing so one doesn't have to run around the Universe, but just gradually to expand oneSelf to embrace all that is in the Universe. Running around is only done by the mind, which is not needed.

Keep hold of center, which is the Self, and expand it to embrace all that is the Absolute.

* * *

Dr.R. I wish to saturate my Buddhi with sattva so that it would be stronger. I find that worry eats up the sattva and faith improves it.

H.H. The natural state of the Self is sattvic. All modifications in sattva are rajas and everything opposed to sattva is tamas. One must make it sure and clear that the Self is sattvic by nature, and we don't intend to make it sattvic because there is no need to do so. What we try to do is undo the cloud and impurities, which surround it and make it look multifarious and rajasic. This is due to bad company—the physical and the mental company. If one has the company of good people and True Knowledge the way is clear and the distinction is right. At times of reduced sattva one can always avoid the bad company. A day in bad company is more harmful than a day in good company is useful. If one has acquired influences from bad company, one can always remove it with the knowledge of the Self. When one walks in the street and lands on some dirty material, one doesn't amputate the dirty feet but washes the dirt away with clean water. All bad influences are dirt and [can] be washed by True Knowledge and meditation.

Once sattva is predominant and you live naturally in sattva, then even company makes no difference because no bad influence can penetrate you any more. For example, sandalwood tree is surrounded by poisonous snakes, but no poison affects it. Company of good people and True Knowledge stabilizes faith and ensures sattva.

Keep this central idea always in your mind: that nothing can really affect the Self. We only need good company and true knowledge to dispel the cloud surrounding the Self.

* * *

H.H. Self-realization is to see oneSelf. But the question is *how* to see the Self and what is the instrument or the agency through which to see Him? One can see things in light, in sunlight or moonlight if one is fortunate enough to have proper eyes to see. If the eyes are bad, even the luminous bodies like the sun can't help anyone. But the Self is a subject which can't even be lit by the sun or other bright lights, so how could one see this? When you look at creation and see everything as an observer, then you start getting glimpses: That I am not the ego, but the ego belongs to me; the Manas, the body, or the chair is not my *Self*, but *for* my Self. Likewise when you see everything as the Observer then you get a glimpse of the Self. When this becomes permanent then it could be Self-realization.

The miracle of this substance is not only that it lights up the object it knows, but it also lights up the unknown. For it is only up to Atman to say that it does not know a certain thing. If I did not know the working of a machine, who will determine the ignorance? Only the Self is capable of doing so. For example, you enter a dark chamber and you may not see your hands or body or anything, but you have no doubt about yourself being there. That is the subject, which is to be realized.

* * *

Dr.R. Is there any further advice His Holiness can give on the subject that the Atman alone is real and looks on all the changing events and situations as a passing show, without getting involved?

H.H. In order to appreciate the Self, described in the *Upanishads*, one needs simple methods. Many such descriptions have been given in the past, but more light can now be thrown on the subject. The states of consciousness experienced in deep sleep, dreams, the daytime state, spiritual awakening, samadhi, etc., are governed by the influx of sattva, rajas and tamas from people, situations and events. These all undergo change, but the Observer who sees them all as a "passing show," always remains the same. This Observer never registers any change in itself. If any modification appears, then this must happen to the individual ego [Ahankar] since change is its very nature.

For example, pure gold always remains gold while its uses and shapes and forms are liable to many modifications. The sky remains the same, while storms, clouds, rain and snow keep on changing our view of it, and yet do not affect the sky in any way. [One experiences this vividly every time a plane takes us up above the cloud ceiling.] The waves of the sea cause no loss or gain to it. In the same way all these passing shows of the gunas, do not change the Atman, but only provide variety in its appearance.

* * *

H.H. The three forces, which are acting through the creation in us, in all other things or events which come before us, and [which] present a gloomy picture, all emanate from the same source. This is the interplay of these three forces which goes on in creation. If one could detach oneself and see the interplay of these forces, one would find that they are powerless to disturb you because your Self is away and only observing, and not participating by attachment. Thus in pleasant situations you are neither overwhelmed, nor distressed by gloom. Being forceful is here not attached to its force.

The Atman is, and the forces are, free in their own right. The bondage is felt when Atman is said to be associated with matter. When one thinks that the body is the Self, or his mind or Buddhi are the Self, then he feels pain and pleasure. By discrimination one has to see the freedom of Atman, who has nothing to do with pain and pleasure. An example is given of how discrimination is made useful for the master.

Once about 70 years ago under the British Raj, someone built a carriage driven by four horses. When he drove through the city, he was stopped by a policeman and charged for breaking the law, for no one could drive a carriage driven by four horses without special permission. A summons was issued and he was called to court to answer why he should not be punished. He consulted many lawyers but only one came forward and asked to inspect the carriage, horses and everything. He took his defense for Rs. 10,000. In court he pleaded not guilty, and showed that there were in fact three mares and only one horse to drive the carriage, not four horses as prohibited. The man went free. One must make use of Buddhi in proper way to find freedom. Discrimination is very necessary.

* * *

Q. I know and understand that Atman is universal Self, and this affects my life. I do not fully *experience* this in meditation, though I often seem on the brink. What stops me there?

H.H. In everyone's life one does experience unity with the Atman but one does not know. During deep sleep the self merges with the Universal Self. This happens in ignorance but is a natural phenomenon. If during active life or meditation one does not feel this merging, it is because of a sheath. This sheath is natural too. The unity which is experienced is the light thrown by the Atman on this sheath, and recognized by the Antahkaran. If the sheath is transparent and pure, then all is well, but if it is cloudy or dirty, one only gets a glimmer. This is the brink of direct experience. If the water in the Ganges were Universal Atman, then water taken from the Ganges and put into a bottle would be the individualized self, although the water is the same. Once you open or break the bottle letting the water flow back into the Ganges you would no longer see any difference, and you would not be able to take that water back, for it will have merged with the Ganges again and forever. The only thing that has made it different is the sheath. So Antahkaran separates the individual Atman from the Universal Atman.

* * *

Q. Is Self-realization the same as merging into the Absolute?

H.H. Self-realization means to see the Self, the Atman. But the Atman is not a subject to be seen only, but one to be known. The Atman comes to know itself—that is Self-realization. The merging into the Absolute or Param Atman is different from Self-realization. Param Atman is a state—it is devoid of action. It is the merging of desire and action into equilibrium. In Self-realization activity has not stopped.

* * *

Q. His Holiness has given us so much wonderful knowledge, and we would like to make best use of this. From what he has seen of us by our questions, could he say what might be the best line of study for us to continue when we return to London?

H.H. Before studying anything else one has to study the Self. One has to study one's physical body and one's subtle body, and look within to the causal body. There is nothing else to study so no line of study is prescribed. Whatever may be useful according to the place and time, and the type of literature, which pleases you or seems to satisfy you, you can get help from them. It can come from any source, it makes no difference. The emphasis is the Self and the non-Self. One has to study the Self so as to separate the non-Self; one has to experience happiness so as to leave behind misery and unhappiness. One has to find Truth to leave behind untruth. One has to find what is useful to the Atman and make use of it and discard what is not useful to the Atman. These are the ways one can study.

Referring to Atman and non-Atman: If one took Ganges water in a bottle it will be clear and pure. If one added a drop of red color then the whole water would be red. If one added a drop of green it would become brown, and if one went on adding more and more colors, after a time one would find it looked brownish-gray, and one would not be able to recognize the pure clear Ganges water. One could leave this water and the dust might subside, but the color would not disappear. One has to add some sort of alum to decolorize or clarify the whole thing and only then would one be able to see pure clean Ganges water. The Atman is very much like Ganges water which is pure and clean, but it is surrounded by Antahkaran, Chitta, Buddhi, Manas, the senses of knowledge, the senses of action and the elements, and everything one has taken from society. One has to undo that, but for that to be done we have to use something like alum—the alum of discrimination. One has to put in discrimination and shake the bottle—bring in some discussions based on personal observations—not bookish knowledge.

It is only through that one would be able to decolorize oneself and see the pure Atman taking charge of all situations.

The color, which we see added to the pure clean Ganges water, is the color of all desires. We are surrounded by our desires and we are producing them every day and covering ourselves with a multitude of desires. One after the other these colors are being added to this pure being and it is not being seen because of our desires. Because these desires are multiple, they are usually opposed to each other, and a desire, which meets opposition raises doubt. So one lives with desires and doubts and because of this it is very difficult to take direct or conscious action. Discrimination, as has been said, is the remedy.

There are three lines to work on: One is the meditation which should be done with faithfulness and sincerity. It should be done regularly and continuously twice a day every day. And then we can take to satsang [good company]. Meditation is also one part of satsang, the company of the Self or Truth. Second comes the company of those beings who have decided to go on the way of development or Self-realization or liberation. In this group falls the realized man—his company or the company of people who are very similar to oneself, and who would like to bring in their personal experiences and discuss them, and who would like to apply discrimination in all their actions.

To help all these we can take the help of the Scriptures. Those Scriptures which discuss the question of the Self and the non-Self, and all those books, which throw some light on these subjects, can be picked up from any source.

Working on these three lines—the True Knowledge, the company of truth-seeking persons and the company of the Self—these are the three types of satsang which would lead one to the pure Self and do away with all the colors and minimize all our desires except the one desire of the Absolute. Appreciate the desire of the Absolute and then let the Self act.

The real satsang is the company of the Absolute, the company of Truth, Consciousness and Bliss. On the subtle level where the company is based on True Knowledge one can see some difference.

If there are people who are looking for the truth and try to conduct the affair themselves, it would be much like a class where there is no teacher and progress would be very hard and slow. So it is necessary to put somebody of heavier weight with a group to lead them, and these chains of heavier grades should also be associated with the purest knowledge available. Now this purest knowledge is available everywhere but in certain cases it is caught up with the color and one sees difference, but within the differences the truth is always present. One has to discover the color and then one would be able to see the pure Self everywhere.

If there were 100 bottles of Ganges water and they were brought together, it will be the same Ganges water; one would not be able to say that there are 100 types of Ganges water, but only that there are 100 types of color of Ganges water. The design of the bottles may differ and the shape. Wherever difference is being experienced it is only in the realm of ignorance; in Truth there is no difference anywhere.

The True Knowledge which has been transmitted right from the Creator—Narayan to Brahma and to this date has been kept clear, and one has to find out the clarity and purity where one lives; and with the help of a teacher one should try to find one's way based on all these three maxims:

The company of the Self—meditation

The company of Knowledge—a group

The company of literature—knowledge outside and through discussions, questions and answers.

Dr.R. The first time we heard this story at Rishikesh [ten men crossing a river], His Holiness went on to tell us: "Before we could know who we are, we have to learn to come out of what we are not." We have begun to see some of the things we are not, but how can we begin to say what we are?

H.H. Whenever one has lost something in the physical sense one has to get some light to look for it and find it. There are many different types of light of which one can make use—a small lamp, a lantern, electric light, moonlight and sunlight. One of them would do according to the type of thing, which one is looking for. They are sufficient for the physical world.

In the subtle world of Manas, Buddhi and Chitta, if one has lost anything there one has to get the Light of Knowledge, the light of the subtle world, and with that Light one can find what one has lost. As far as the Self is concerned, the Self is always experienced by everyone, whether one is lost in the physical darkness, or within the subtle darkness of ignorance. In each case the Self is always experienced and present—one does not need any other agency to find out the Self and experience the Self, and no one can deny the existence of the Self, because there is no other means of denying it except the Self! The situation is that the Self is always available and whatever is available and experienced does not need any extra light. The light we need is only on the physical and subtle levels. For that we can take the physical light or the subtle light of knowledge from the Scriptures, from a realized man, or teachers. Even with knowledge, if the knowledge is not complete we still cannot transcend the subtle world, and in that way transcend the reality beyond this subtle world, so the proper experience of the Self is not constant and continuous. The Self is eternal and the Self is the Light of Lights. The Self is Consciousness, and the Self is Happiness. It is eternal and it is Truth, and all these things are never lost because they are ever present everywhere. One has simply to dispel the physical darkness or the subtle darkness which is prevailing, because the Self is always with each of us. Let the Self prevail, there is no need to search for it.

Sheaths

H.H. We naturally live in the world of names and forms and we are surrounded by them, and even the being we call ourself has as many names and forms. People have name, form, and also the Atman; thus it seems everything is everywhere, but because of ignorance people get involved in only the world of name and form. Usually they take their six-foot body as their Ultimate Being. The System of Knowledge and the method of meditation is to remove the narrowness of that boundary and bondage, and allow people to discriminate and see the unlimited and unbounded Atman, which cannot be brought into the limits of names and forms. Here is an example:

Someone went to a holy man and asked to be introduced to God. The holy man said that when I go to Him, He will ask about you. What shall I say about you? So first give me some details of your own credentials. The man pointed to his body and told his name. The holy man said that all this is made of flesh and bones which is always subject to growth and decay. How could this be you? It is only your body and name. Get me your proper credentials. The man thinks and says that perhaps his thoughts, desires, feelings were his proper credentials. The holy man again observed that even more rapidly than the bodily form these are changing all the time. Give me your proper and fixed credentials. In this way this man was led to recognize his own True Self and then he did not go around seeking any more introductions.

The System of Knowledge and method of meditation are simply to lead people to discriminate between the transitory and the eternal, between formal and informal, between words and the spirit, so that one can enjoy forms, words and also the real Being.

* * *

Dr.R. (quoting from *Crest Jewel*) "When the five sheaths are removed because of their unreality, I do not see, O Master, that anything remains but universal negation. What then remains to be known?"

H.H. The third section [of the *Crest Jewel*] speaks about the five sheaths—Annamaya, Pranamaya, Manomaya, Vijnanamaya, and Anandamaya. These are the five sheaths which surround the Self, the Atman. Ordinary men think that this body, which is made out of food, is the ultimate. They try to look after it and have no sense to go further. Or, at the most, they try to take care of the Pranamaya kosha [sheath] which is supported by air and water. These are the two limits which common men usually find. The third sheath, the Manomaya, is composed of Manas. We find that mind is always changing hither and thither, moving all the time. It is never the same. So it should be concluded that mind cannot be that individual which *I am*, but it is an instrument to serve that individual. And the same applies to the fourth one—Vijnanamaya—which works on the level of Buddhi. We know that even if one doesn't have Buddhi one still survives, and nobody uses Buddhi all the time. Sometimes it is still; sometimes it is in use; sometimes it is not in use. Then one looks upwards to the fifth sheath, the most subtle of all—the Anandamaya—composed of happiness; but then again, you find that happiness is also one of those elements which comes and you feel one with it, and then the atmosphere changes, circumstances change, and you go back to some other state. In fact, all these sheaths from gross to subtle are not that One who experiences. The disciple asks "What then is it which experiences?" That which is beyond these sheaths—that is Atman.

Always and everywhere the Observer is present even if these five sheaths are experienced or not. There are five states of our consciousness: the awake, dreaming, sleep, unconsciousness and samadhi. In three of those states—samadhi, deep sleep, and unconsciousness—there is very little experience. Although the five sheaths exist in these states, practically nothing is observed. Only in the awake [conscious] and the dreaming states do we have direct experience of these five sheaths. In samadhi, it is only the consciousness in equilibrium that is experienced. Some weak persons experience the unconscious state, but here there is no experience of anything but ignorance. Among all these sheaths and states through which the individual goes, there is only one element which is not involved—the Observer, the Atman—which is Eternal. One should rise and go beyond the sheaths.

* * *

Q. May we ask for clarity about the elements you spoke of and which we have to discriminate in relation to Manas, Buddhi, Chitta and Ahankar?

H.H. When we relate the five veils with elements we must keep in mind the difference. Two veils are formed with the coarse material which are the Annamayakosha and Pranamayakosha. The other three—Manomaya, Vijnanamaya, and the Anandamayakosha—are formed of the subtle body. This subtle body is made of conscious material, and it is only through these we become conscious of the phenomenal world.

Q. We have a beautiful description of the five sheaths in the book called *Crest Jewel of Wisdom*. Can we ask H.H. to tell us how these actually show themselves, how they manifest and how are they recognized so that we can be led to discriminate between them?

H.H. The *physical body* is formed with five elements and is also maintained with them. The body is supplied with food and water, heat and air which we get from the elements. In the body there is a certain proportion of earth, water, fire, air and ether. We take some of these every day, and they are transformed into new tissues and energy, and the unwanted portion is discarded. This is how one always keeps a workable balance, and whenever the balance is lost, we have discomfort and disease. The other [the subtle] body is made of Manas, Buddhi, Chitta and Ahankar. This, with the coarse body, constitute the five veils. The Annamaya veil is made of earth, water and heat; the Pranamaya veil with air and ether; the Manomaya veil with Manas; the Vijnanamaya veil with Buddhi; and the Anandamaya veil with the Chitta. Just as the element of earth is produced from water, and water from heat, heat from air, and air from ether, and in each step the matter is finer, in the same way Pranamaya veil is finer than Annamaya and Manomaya is finer than Pranamaya, and so on. In searching for Truth, the Atman, one has to rise to appreciate finest from the coarse till one reaches the finest, which is Atman. This process is called discrimination. To discriminate is to discriminate Atman from the non-Atman.

* * *

Dr.R. [speaking at a London meeting in reference to the previous question]

There followed a fairly full description which was recorded on tape and subsequently translated. But R. was not attending. He thought: "O Lord, all these Indian names!" and dismissed them all from his mind.

But three nights later he had a strange experience in the form of a very vivid dream which woke him up about one a.m. into clear Consciousness. In the dream there was a big audience hall with many people present, and he was just one of the audience. On the dais was the first Shankara, a commanding figure with robes and banner. The figure was quite impersonal and the features could not be distinguished, but the form resembled the statue of Sankara in the shrine in the ashram grounds seen two years before. He was explaining the five veils with the utmost simplicity and clarity and R. felt there was no difficulty at all in understanding them.

The essence of the description was that there are five forms of Maya or imagination, five veils of illusion which obscure for each man his "Real I" and which have successively to be torn away before a man can see himself and become himself.

The *first (Annamaya)* is the illusion that the body of flesh and bones, of cells and organs and systems is himSelf. (This is the materialist view of man that fills all our text-books of medicine, and accounts for the feverish desire to keep the body alive at all costs by artificial respiration, organ transplantation and the rest.) In the ordinary Westerner it obtrudes itself especially in times of pain and illness, or physical urges like hunger and thirst and sexual desire; and then he is apt to forget altogether that he is something more than a piece of flesh.

The *second (Pranamaya)* arises from the autonomic nervous system with the changes of respiration and circulation and the endocrine cycles and rhythms. It is manifested by changing physical vitality and by chemical cycles and reactions between people. It is the physical motivation that keeps the heavy body in movement.

The next three veils arise in the subtle body (what we call our "minds") and account for all our psychology and mental warfare.

The first of these, the *third veil or (Manomaya)*, is the ceaseless mental activity so prominent in the West at present, whereby the mind chases after sensory impressions, labeling, relating and associating them; the mind that forms opinions, talks and writes books, looks up references, consults encyclopedias and forms theories. It thinks of itself as "objective," but really is mixed with dreams and much influenced by the subtle body and the chemical weather. It never can relate the part to the whole, but takes the part for the whole.

The *fourth veil (Vijnanamaya)*, is that which surrounds Buddhi, governing the main tendencies of a man's life. It makes one man go after trade or money, makes another join a certain religion and still another become a crook. It sets the general pattern of successive lives in which particular tendencies grow or diminish.

Even when this is torn aside, there is *still a fifth veil* which I did not understand. Its name, *Anandamaya*, suggests that even in the state of ecstasy there is still a veil preventing final union, still a mistaken point of view about the Real "I," still some kind of duality.

Sankara concluded his discourse with the answer to a question: "When the five veils are torn away because of their unreality, I do not see that anything remains but universal negation. What then remains to be known?" As he replied: "That which remains unchanged among changing things, that by which everything is known, though unknown by anything else, realize that knower to be ...." I woke right up, got out of bed and read the account in the *Crest Jewel*.

* * *

Q. I would like to ask a question from Dr. Roles. He asks how to get rid of the Vijnanamaya sheath (as described in *Viveka Chudamani*) which seems to be the chief block which prevents the ananda that we so often experience now from shining forth in our thoughts, words and deeds, for all to see and hear? His Holiness has said we must distinguish between the bodies or vehicles and the rider —the luminous Atman. In that way would the Buddhi be doing its right job?

H.H. It is enough for you to feel that the Vijnanamaya sheath is something separate from you. In fact, you are not the Vijnanamaya sheath; it belongs to you. While you are in meditation, experiencing ananda, the Vijnanamaya sheath will not bother you even though it is being experienced. When you are not meditating, then you are reminded of your worldly thoughts, words and deeds. They become a sort of barrier. The knowledge of these worldly affairs forms a barrier to our experience of ananda. If we remember that this knowledge of the Vijnanamaya sheath is *ours* to use whenever we wish, then even when we are doing things we will continue to experience ananda. There should be no difficulty. But this we must always remember—all the knowledge is separate from us. We are not the knowledge itself, but the knowledge belongs to us.

* * *

Q. With the question earlier on Vijnanamaya sheath, in connection with that, is Anandamaya kosha where the man has in some way limited the feeling of bliss, or ananda, to himself, rather than the bliss that is everywhere and in everything?

H.H. A light is thrown on the mirror, the mirror reflects that light. Now we say that this light is coming from the mirror. It is not true. Light comes from somewhere else; it is being reflected by the mirror. Similarly the ananda: We get pleasure (a morsel of bliss) when we see a guava, for example; now the bliss (pleasure) is not in the guava, it is in us; it is actually in the Ananda kosha and the Ananda kosha reflects it onto this guava, and then we feel that pleasure; but this is also not in Anandamaya kosha—we are not Anandamaya kosha—we are Ananda, and from us it goes to the Anandamaya kosha, the Anandamaya kosha reflects it on the object and then we feel the pleasure; so that we are neither the Vijnanamaya kosha or the Anandamaya kosha—we are something separate from either of these two, and what are we? We are an incarnation of Ananda. We are ourselves Ananda, we are Bliss incarnate, and we feel Ananda in various objects by the process of reflection.

* * *

Q. Is there a simple way that we can distinguish between Manomaya sheath and Vijnanamaya sheath?

H.H. The function of Manomaya kosha is to say that we like this or we do not like this—Sankalpa, Vikalpa. We want this, we do not want this. We like this, we do not like this, we love this, we hate this. All this is Manomaya sheath.

Q. Is desire related to this?

H.H. Yes; and Vijnanamaya sheath says: "This we should do, this we should not do." This is the function of Vijnanamaya sheath. It is the knowledge of what we should do and should not do. This function is known as Vijnanamaya sheath.

Q. And the error is to be ignorant of the fact that we are not the doer? If we remember and remain ourselves, then these are like one's servants?

H.H. The distinction between the two is rather subtle. It can be understood in this way: In Manomaya sheath you say," I want this, I would like to have this, I don't want this." Vijnanamaya sheath decides, "You may want it all right but will it be good or not for you to have it?" This decision is taken by Vijnanamaya sheath. The desiring part is the Manomaya sheath, while the deciding part is the Vijnanamaya.

* * *

Q. Does the Jiva's sense of individuality, when he forgets the Atman—this forgetting that he is the Atman—does this arise in the Vijnanamaya kosha?

H.H. When the individual forgets that he is the Atman and considers himself to be the body, then he is Jiva. When he remembers that he is Atman, then he is Atman.

Q. When he claims the knowledge that belongs to Vijnanamaya, is this Ahankar? When he doesn't claim and knows that the knowledge belongs to Atman, is that Aham?

H.H. That is correct. When there is Ahankar, then he becomes Jiva, but when he is devoid of Ahankar, then he is Atman.

Stillness

H.H. The sound of a mela in Indian villages seems so roaring from a distance, but once you go in to the mela this roaring sound seems to disappear because you become a part of the mela. Likewise during meditation the distracting noises seem very harsh, but if one expands oneself so as to cover everything, then these distractions become very minor things for they are part of yourself. One would hear them and be aware, but not disturbed.

In the same way in scientific terms, when any thing passes by another object in great speed, then it seems that both are moving. Trains are examples. People sitting in a moving train find that the motionless train is also moving, but in fact it is not. If you are in the motionless train and you don't pay attention to the moving train, then you feel motionless; but the moment your attention is drawn toward the moving train you also get the illusion of movement. The same happens in meditation. If you attend to interference it starts interfering; if you don't, well—you are safe.

The Absolute is motionless, but His ray of Creation is full of motion. Although all motion is His own creation, He never gets involved in it. In meditation the Atman can also be surrounded by moving interference and still He can remain detached and motionless. Absolute recharges the energy of the universe by dissolving it and we get recharged with energy by sleep in the night. This is tamas's way of re-charging the body, but in meditation in deep rest and peace we also recharge the being and not only the body.

* * *

Dr.R. People are happy and unhappy during the day according to the circumstances. When H.H. speaks of being happy, does he mean to make an effort to come out of unhappiness, or be happy in spite of circumstances?

H.H. This creation is a movement, In this movement whatever is favorable to mind is pleasant and unfavorable is pain. The creation of pleasure and pain is of the mind. The Atman feels and feeds on bliss, and is not at all moved by or desirous of pleasure or pain. One has to start with body. When body is still and firm, the prana becomes balanced, the control over Manas is easier. Mind is mobile, but one should just ignore its movements. It will come back if left unattended. Thus Manas and Buddhi could become still. Lessening desires will still the Chitta and make way for deeper stillness. In deep stillness, meditation works.

H.H. It is natural for Manas to become one with the object of the senses. If one hears music, one becomes one with it, and if you look at the musician you feel all his bodily movements in your own body. Now if you look away from the musician, you will—although hearing the music—not be moved by the bodily movements of the musician. So, the key is the attention to movements of mind. Stop attending to the moving mind and you will be attentive. The moment you see that you are not attentive is precisely the moment you have the opportunity to get out of it.

* * *

H.H. Buddhi is a *substance* which gives rise to thought and ideas. It is subject to the three gunas: tamas, rajas and sattva. It is influenced by time and space. The surroundings usually determine in which direction Buddhi is going to produce thoughts and ideas. If people are subjected to good influence the Buddhi will give rise to good and better thoughts. If they are in the company of rajas influence they will have same type of thoughts, and if surrounded by tamas, certainly they will go that way. This is the condition of the common man whose Buddhi is not stilled. On a higher level where Buddhi is stilled, then the outside influences have no effect. He could walk in anywhere and still remain unaffected by the influences of time and space. Regarding the change in Buddhi, one could easily experience many shifts in one single day, as for example the gear of a motor car is changed many times according to the level and traffic on the road. Buddhi likewise changes to good or bad according to the company. This law of course doesn't apply to one whose Buddhi is pure and still. He will not be subject to any influence anywhere.

* * *

H.H. Now the question has arisen: "How to love the Atman, our own Self?" What is the Atman? How is it? As long as we do not know the Atman, we will not understand, so our love for the Atman will not increase. To gain the knowledge of Atman we require a steady state of mind. The more our mind is at peace the more will we know about Atman. Mind can be looked at in different ways.

This time I will take our mind in the sense of Antahkarana and its four functions of Manas, Chitta, Buddhi and Ahankar; in which Buddhi takes decisions about an act, Chitta does its recollection, Manas makes a determination, and Ahankar regards this five-and-a-half to six-foot body to be "I." That is Ahankar.

It is actually the Atman which is the motive force behind the three bodies. I say this in order to throw some light on what Atman is and how it keeps the functions of this body going. This body is like a replica or model of the Atman, and in relation to this, it is Atman which gives power to this body. When we make our mind steady then we come face-to-face with the Atman.

Through some easy method we have to settle down in *meditation* in order to arrive at a steady state. Manas, Chitta, Buddhi and Ahankar, all four are very, very restless, always moving on to this side and that. So meditation is nothing but to bring these four forces to rest. When this has been achieved then we are able to see Atman.

If a mirror is covered with dirt you will not be able to see your face as it actually is. On account of our past—samskaras—the mirror of our mind has become dirty, so we are not able to see the picture of Atman correctly, and as a result the mind becomes bored. This boredom drives you away from meditation. When you begin to clean the mind you start to see Atman, and then you will start to derive pleasure in meditation. In this case the question of boredom or of running away will not arise. This cleaning of Chitta is essential for glimpsing the Atman. It is cleaning the mirror.

This is only achieved by meditation. The steadier the mind the cleaner the mirror, and the clearer will be the image of the Atman. Then you will begin to derive pleasure in meditation. With this pleasure the mind will not get bored.

Q. There is a question here. What do we say to people who say to me "There is too much dirt, I cannot remove it?" What can one say to them to encourage them more?

H.H. The steadiness will remove it—making the mind steady. It takes some time for a piece of cloth to get dirty—it may take several days—but it can take only ten or fifteen minutes to wash it clean. In the same way the dirt, which has accumulated on our mirror for ages and ages needs only a little meditation for its removal. So people must not lose heart.

Take the example of a room, which has been kept shut up for a number of years. In the course of all those years much dirt and dust has accumulated there. When we enter that room and switch on the light, we see that it is dirty, so we start cleaning it. As soon as we press the switch there is light, but we cannot clean it at once; it takes some time.

What is this light? It is the light provided by meditation! Most worldly people with no light in them live without knowing of the existence of dirt and dust. Meditation gives you the light to see the dust, so that you can then take the necessary action to remove it.

Q. In the beginning there are large particles to remove and later there are small particles, finer particles to remove, and when at that stage, that fine particle seems as big as the large particle did before.

H.H. As we continue with the process of cleaning, the magnifying power increases, so that we notice smaller particles more readily than before. But when the dirt is completely removed we don't see any dirt either inside or outside. And so the smaller particles look bigger due to the increase of the magnifying power.

Q. It seems very important not to be discouraged by the magnified particles.

H.H. That's right. It is not a question of becoming discouraged because it is the magnifying power which makes them look bigger. Actually they are not bigger, they only appear bigger, so we need not be discouraged.

* * *

Q. The Shankaracharya has told us that the aim in meditation is to stay in the silence. Some people get to the silence, but do not stay there. What instructions should they receive?

H.H. In the early stage of meditation it is quite possible that one may not enter the silence, and even if one did, one may be out very soon. This stage is creating a level, so every minute of it is of value, although one may not be able to recognize what is happening inside. All that is happening is in the dark. But if one finds that staying in silence is broken, then one can reassure oneself with emotion and Buddhi that this only is the way to bliss and one should attempt again. Even with these gentle efforts if one can't reach silence, one is spared violent vibration and tensions of the day, and secondly the speed of the heartbeat is slowed, which saves energy for the body.

* * *

Q. His Holiness has spoken of meditation itself as yoga, practice of meditation as dharana, and the repetition of mantra as japa. Could he say more about it?

H.H. This is a journey of the individual Consciousness [Vyashti] in to the Universal Consciousness [Samashti, the Absolute].

One starts the mantra, and repeats the mantra, one initiates this at the level of the individual [the Vyashti], and then this repetition of the mantra is leading on to the bare thread of meditation, which is the dharana. This movement is aimed at only one thing, and that is to cut out or diminish the activity—the rajas involved in life. Although it is known as the "practice of meditation," yet this "practice" is leading toward the end of all activity. Slowly and gradually this march toward non-activity takes place and one reaches the realm of union [yoga], which is stillness or unity. This is the experience of Self as universal: Here there is no duality and there remains no place to move on to, and there is no *time* to change to, for He is the place, the time and also the substance. In that profound silence, stillness or yoga all movements stop, and there is only "One without a second" and that is Atman Himself, the Observer.

This does not mean that all relationships and agitations would have disappeared from our inner universe: For it only indicates that there is no initiation of any agitation from the Self. We know that there are five levels of consciousness known as unconscious, sleep, dream, awake and samadhi. This particular state, which we are considering, is unique and does not come under any one of the five "states of consciousness."

When one comes away from that state then one feels joyful. Just as when one goes to see some great man and returns with indescribable joy and enthusiasm, feeling that everything seems good, beautiful and pleasant. That state of yoga is devoid of all vikshepa, agitation, desire, need, ignorance, and is profoundly still, without any hankering, fully satisfied and complete in all respects.

* * *

H.H. The ultimate end of the meditation is to reach this profound stillness and this is very deep. No meter can measure it. It is without end. But what you have to remember is that it is not necessary to have that for long periods at a time. The whole half hour is simply a preparation for two or three moments of this stillness which is enough and will set you up for a long time after; just as if you take a little food and drink, you can go on actively for many hours before the next meal. Longer meditation doesn't guarantee anything further as regards the profound stillness. Most of the time is spent by people churning their mechanical thoughts in mechanical rotation. Those who manage to dive deep; they come out with potentiality emanating from the will of the Absolute.

During the great war of India, described in the *Mahabharata*, one day a man called Karna was appointed Commander-in-Chief of the whole army. On the way to the battlefield, his charioteer said to him: "Although you are a great warrior and an efficient leader, it will not be possible for you to vanquish Arjuna because he is supported by Sri Krishna who has achieved this profound stillness."

Karna was very proud of his descent from the sun god and his own strength and efficiency.

The charioteer then told his story about a flock of crows. One of them was strong, clever and good looking and they made him their leader. This king of the crows felt proud of his exploits and, therefore, looked down on all other creatures. One day a young swan appeared in that vicinity. All the crows assembled round the swan and asked him if he knew about the great deeds of their king. He pleaded ignorance and said he would like to meet their king. The king crow appeared and asked the swan about the different types of flight. The swan in his simplicity said that he knew only one style of flight.

The king crow then embarked on an exhibition of 101 styles of aerobatics. After going through all of them, he asked to see the art of the swan. The young swan took off on a graceful, gentle and natural flight and as usual increased his speed only gradually. Since the crow was small and swift, he flew round and round the swan, far ahead and back again. But the swan gradually increased his speed and it was not very long before the crow became tired, his wings trembled, and he ultimately fell into the waters of the sea. The swan came down and rescued the crow and helped him back to his flock and the crow was ashamed of his pride and thanked the swan for his modesty and magnanimity. "You see," said the charioteer. "The swan lived a natural life while the crow occupied himself in aerobatics and cleverness.

"The ultimate victory goes only to the natural, steady, still and simple man: while the clever, smart and articrafty waste their energy in trifling pursuits only leading to their destruction.

"So, my dear master, you must keep in your mind the steady, still and natural Krishna for no one can ever transcend Him or anyone whom He likes to support."

Dr.R. Now that is a true account of the two sides of our brain—the two hemispheres: The crow, the king crow, and all the flock of crows are like the dominant hemisphere—the personality—but the Essence with which the in-turning hemisphere is connected is like the young swan who knows only one style of flight. This has a good psychological meaning. Meditation should be done by the swan and not by the crow! Perhaps it's all the crows trying to meditate, that is our main trouble.

So, all these efforts that one thinks one ought to make are only dominant hemisphere making the efforts—the crows. One ought really to wriggle out of making any efforts at all.

* * *

H.H. When we go into meditation, we reach a spiritual world where quietness prevails like that of a deep undisturbed ocean. No movement, no waves, no currents—everything absolutely stationary. This is the meditational world. When we look out of such a spiritual world, then we become everything and nothing else remains.

Truth

Q. All questions arising seem to contain their own answers. The mind keeps coming back to the shloka of the first Shankaracharya, "Brahman satyam jaganmithya (Brahman is Truth and world is illusion); Brahma jivaiva naparah (Brahma and Jiva are not different)." How can this be made more full? What will increase the inspiration, deepen the devotion and make the being more useful? What am I? Why am I here? And, what is function? In truth I seem to know nothing and so need to find the proper question.

H.H. We should respect the Truth and try to know the Truth. The more we do this, the further we will progress. The words of this shloka were spoken by the original Shankaracharya. If a piece of rope is lying rolled up on the ground, we sometimes mistake it for a snake—we fear that it is a snake. With more light we see that it is only a piece of rope and not a snake, and so all the fear and mental burden disappears. As soon as we know the Truth, that Truth is Param Atman and Param Atman is Truth, then in that case, *the body*, including our actions, thoughts and so on, no longer appears to be a burden. All burden is removed; we are playing a game and knowing it is a game and nothing else, then it doesn't appear burdensome at all. Similarly, when we know the Truth about the world, then the world does not seem to be a burden to our mind. Our role in the world seems to be quite an easy affair. So this is the attitude we should acquire, and with it we should go on performing our duty.

* * *

H.H. Satsang is good company, but the good company is of three types. The compound word *satsang* consists of *sat* and *sang*. *Sat* means truth. It can be the company of the truth, of the Absolute, or Atman. Or it can be the company of true literature (scriptures) or it can be the company of true men (holy men or teachers—in our own terms, a good group).

* * *

Q. In 1974 His Holiness said, that "wars in the name of religion are due to confusion in Buddhi." This seems very important at this time, both in India and all over the world. There are many many groups working toward unity but no one seems to have or to give practical knowledge of this possibility of discrimination, knowledge of Buddhi and the power of the individual to develop his own freedom, his own Swatantra of which His Holiness spoke last visit. In view of what he answered to a previous question, can he say whether there is a way in which we can help as a society with this knowledge of the way forward through right use of Buddhi?

H.H. Dharma is the order of Natural Law, divine or profane, and according to the way an individual, society, nation, religion or civilization sees it they try to put it into action. But a difference arises between seeing Natural Law and putting it into practice. The use of discrimination would provide a better chance of transformation of the individual, society, nation, religion or civilization if there was a real consistency between what has been seen and what is being practiced or enacted. Every society, nation, religion or civilization proclaims that truth is better for peace and happiness. No one claims that untruth can bring prosperity or transformation. This factor of the Natural Law is common to all religions or nations. The trouble is that although universal Buddhi is there to offer the view from truth, because of the sanskars, the truth is either received imperfectly or enacted very differently, not in a consistent way, but simply to gain certain benefits, in spite of the truth being there within themselves. Every individual or society knows the truth within because it was discovered long ago and has been made available to everyone ever since then. Though the truth has always been proclaimed, it can hardly be said that this known truth has been put into practice properly. The proper way to act is to keep total unity and consistency between thought, word and deed

(Manas, Vani, Karma). Thoughts, concepts, ideas, desires, aims, resolutions and ambitions must be spoken out exactly as they arise without any distortions or concealment. Thus one must speak out one's mind truthfully. If the mind is exposed truthfully, it does not matter what is there—others can take true positions in relation to the Natural Law, i.e. the Truth. It should be understood that sanskars differ and everyone can't always think of truth as it really is. But this is no hindrance. If the truth is spoken then others will either come to help and save the situation, or take a proper stand. If injustice is involved, one will be taken to task and the injustice removed. If the desires and concepts are just, they will be met justly.

There is a further complication. When it comes to action most of what has been said is not what is enacted. The result is total confusion. People say A and do B. In this way there is no proper communication or contact with the individual or even the voice of a society or religion. This is the cause of confusion from all sides. There is no meeting point so there are obviously confrontation points. No one can reason because there is no reasonable man with whom to reason. All religions are victims of their own making. They want one thing, they say another and to get their way they behave entirely against the Natural Law.

Everything about individuals, societies, nations and religions these days is ambiguous; their thoughts are secret, their speech is secret and their deeds are secret or deceptive. How can peace and happiness prevail when everything is deception? It is more so now than ever.

If people take to right thinking, right speaking and right action they will become mahatmas [saints], that is what every soul naturally is. Deception is possible by bypassing the Self and taking to secret ways, ignoring the Self. When the Self within is ignored, the man becomes duratma. ("Mahatma is a great soul, duratma is a wicked creature!") Those who do not listen to the Self—which always knows the truth—create wars in the name of religion, nations, societies, cultures or civilizations. The Self is glorious by itself; it needs no transformation or improvement. All that is needed is to express it truly. If conformity and consistency can be brought between thought, speech and action, then the Self and its glory will be seen and enjoyed.

* * *

Q. Could you say something about keeping the line of honesty within? It seems like walking along a very fine line, and it is so easy to slip into a degree of pretense.

H.H. Somehow the common man has lost the practice of keeping in line with the truth. That is why situations can happen where one would slip into pretense or lying. Those on the Ladder who are keeping the practice alive, it is certainly easy for them.

He gave a simile: A very wide broad road is created for human beings to walk upon, and for cycles and motor cars to use. But railway lines are fixed and straight and only about 4 inches in width. These support many engines and carriages running at great speed. Those who practice truth can "keep to the rails" with great ease and speed. Those who do not let the practice of truth waver and slip, and fall into pretense.

One has to understand the truth firmly in one's mind, which [through the meditation] has formed a firm base or foundation for the building. If the foundation of the building is secure, only then can one establish and make a good house, which will stand for some time. But if the base is not sound then the building will fall.

One should exercise discrimination concerning truth, as there may be cases when pure truth should not be expressed. In that case if one has to resort to a lesser truth, then this would not be taken as bad. But if one tries to use the truth for base motives which rest upon false ideas, then this would be called a crime.

Q. How to establish the truth? Because it has been seen that different people have different conceptions of truth.

H.H. Truth is that which transcends all the three times (past, present and future) and remains the same. That which never changes is the truth.

Truth is the substance of the whole creation. Truth is the Absolute out of which the whole creation has emerged, and into which the whole creation will return.

For an illustration: Suppose clay is truth. Then from clay you can make things of many sorts. These things will have their existence in time and space. In time they will he destroyed. So the forms made out of clay are also truth, but they are only relatively true; relative to time and *space*. Once they are broken, they go back to their origin, namely the clay.

So when we are assessing the truth of anything, we also examine or look toward the cause.

As far as the cause is concerned, there are different degrees of cause. The causes of some objects derive from time and space; but beyond that is the "cause of the cause"; the ultimate cause being the Absolute. So one looks for the "cause of the cause" or the ultimate cause, and that would be the truth. That which would never change and which must always be the *same* whatever one likes to think. But about this cause, if one looks for certain ideas related to space and time, then one will see the variations in the reflections of truth. That attitude one should keep, and go on looking for the ultimate cause. As far as the ultimate cause is concerned, there can be no difference of opinion whatsoever.

H.H. (continues) One of the experiences which is common to everyone and which emanates from the truth is the feeling of pure "I," pure Ahankara. An "I" which is not qualified by anything; that is always the same with all people, in all times, and in all places. There can never be doubt with anyone as far as this pure "I" is concerned.

Of course, there are false I's and other I's related to mind, knowledge, Buddhi, Chitta, senses and body, and this or that in the phenomenal world. All these I's keep on changing from place to place and time to time. Because they are changing, they cannot be called truth. Whilst they are present, they may be true; but after that, since they perish, they do not remain within the fold of truth. So far as the individual is concerned, you can see that there is one truth common to all of us which no one has any doubt about.

Suppose someone has the idea that to follow the line of truth is not profitable. Then suppose one takes two people and asks one of them to follow the line of truth and the other the line of lies for a whole day—and carry out their jobs. By the end of the day, you will find the one who speaks lies cannot communicate and deal with the world at all; while the man who stuck to the truth has been able to sail along well, although he would experience certain drawbacks in the beginning. Once he establishes the truth in his relations with others, and people feel sure that he will stick to it, then all his losses in the early stage will be recovered because of the trust in truth which is common to all people in the world.

To prove that speaking a lie renders one unfit to deal in the world, one can take any lies and exercise them in an extreme form and one will see that one is not suitable for any activity in this world. So it is only "a touch of lie" that appears to work fairly well for people and then only in some cases. In the majority of cases it is the truth, which keeps the wheel of the world turning smoothly.

Those who want to practice truth should have a little more courage and stick to the truth. They will find that some losses may occur at the beginning, but ultimately they will be the winner.

Dr.R. There is on record that an Irish priest recently preached a sermon which he began, "My friends, we ask God to help us to keep along [the] narrow line *between* truth and falsehood." That is the Irish way of putting it!

H.H. If the basis of one's dealings are true—truth itself—then if the place and time cause one to have recourse to a little lie then it is excusable (laughing).

H.H. (continues) This is a very interesting subject for all of us. There are certain latitudes, which are given to people. These have been mentioned in the *Mahabharata*. There are five or six situations in which resorting to untruth is forgiven for the sake of greater truth. But in all cases the aim must be the establishment of truth and secondly, speaking falsehood must be followed by a penance for purification [clarification] of the heart. This means that falsehood should not be used for the sake of personal gains as such. The instances are:

1. When a cow which is supposed to be sacred in India, is being pursued by a butcher, with an axe: At a crossroad, the butcher being unsure which way the cow had gone asks a passerby whether he has seen a cow going past? Then the passerby, in order to save the life of the cow, is permitted to resort to falsehood, and say that he hasn't seen the cow!

Other instances are quoted also from the *Mahabharata* where this ethical point was being discussed.

2. If a robber wants to know where the wealth is in your house: In order to save your lawfully acquired wealth one can resort to lies. (laughter from us all during these examples).

3. In the case of humor, when only fun is the object, one can sometimes speak untruth in order to keep the vein of amusement and joking.

4. If a girl has got to be married and if she is not beautiful, then again one can speak an untruth and say she is at least an average looking girl! Then she will get married. (*Dr.R.* Every gentleman should say so, surely!)

5. With the object of saving lives of human beings (as well as cows) then again untruth can be resorted to.

But in each case it must be followed by a penance, which must be voluntarily undertaken, then the impurity gathered by such deeds will be washed out.

* * *

Dr.R. Is it that in pure Buddhi intellect and emotion are one and one can know the Truth by intuition?

H.H. Buddhi, the pure intellect, is the active principle. It earns for the Self and passes the valuables to heart which holds the treasury. Every one of these valuables come only through Buddhi. It is the only instrument we have through which the values of everything seen or unseen is derived and also given away as well. The heart, which is the seat of emotion, keeps the treasure. At the moments when one finds unity with outer world, Buddhi allows heart to respond directly. When one is saturated with sattva and Buddhi is pure and heart is responding, then Truth is flashed by intuition or one gets inspiration under state of Being. One can't command such situations.

Dr.R. The word discrimination appears intellectual; should it not be understanding, which combines intellect and emotion?

H.H. Truth is only experienced when emotional and intellectual centers join. Alone intellect is dry. Real knowledge comes from unity of intellect and emotion.

* * *

Dr.R. Anyone who knew P. D. Ouspensky well would agree that the real meaning of his life was his courageous search for Truth — Truth at any price; and he showed this chiefly by his example.

* * *

Dr.R. I have mentioned that, by increasing the love of truth in oneself, by endeavoring to reach the source of truth in oneself, and by seeing mirrors of oneself in other people, our weaknesses naturally fall away and dissolve. Paying attention to them — attacking, for instance, these weaknesses — only strengthens them, because it concentrates attention on them. You don't "delve about in the darkness," as the Shankaracharya says. "You go for the light," and then all the dark patches will be enlightened. It is very important for us to get this point of view — not to dwell on difficulties and weaknesses, and so on. What you don't attend to ceases to exist after a certain time. Go for the truth!

Unity

H.H. The essence of all myths centers on the oneness of God. Some prefer the nirguna [abstract]; others prefer form and depict God in the drama of creation. This is saguna—or the realistic approach. They call God by various names and describe Him according to their culture. The wise look for unity and poets give descriptive glory. Ordinary man enjoys whatever he receives through his family tradition. Very few seek the truth of His unity, conscious freedom and blissful detachment. The Absolute must be one—it cannot be two. If there were two absolutes, then there could never be one truth and duality would always prevail. There will be no peace, no reason, no freedom and no permanent bliss. Every vision or myth would be incomplete, blurred and ambiguous. Uncertainty would reign everywhere.

Consider the story of the two artists, previously told. The two promised to produce the same result. The emotional one took to the painting of actual images. The other, the rational one, simply cleaned the wall and polished it like a mirror until all blemishes were removed. When the partition (the cloud) was removed, the actual painting was reflected exactly on the other side. This simply illustrates the unity of the creative force, and all types of myths aim to show the absolute unity of God. In pure Antahkaran simple myths arise but in impure Antahkaran they result in complexity.

Dr.R. At one of His Holiness's discourses to his people here at the ashram he said that "Bhakti purifies one, cleanses one and presents one before the Param Atman at one's best." Cannot this be taken as referring also to the supreme moment of physical death, since it is the last desire of the dying man that determines his next life?

H.H. This question of unity with the Absolute has different facets. It can be said that every individual in the world has some unity with the Absolute every day. If he did not have some unity and communication daily it would be almost impossible to sustain life.

Nothing in this creation can happen without some link with the Absolute. For everyone who sleeps at night, in their deep sleep there is some union with the Absolute which recharges his body and *makes* it fresh and does away with his fatigue for the next day so that he can start another day's work. This is also a union, but this is not a conscious union.

It is just a natural happening; nevertheless the union does take place. Then there is the initiation into meditation and the full meaning of the scriptures. Those who meditate, they consciously go into that unknown every day and establish their relationship —not through deep sleep, not through ignorance but with some consciousness. Because of this a relationship is established with the Absolute, and as days go by, one day one will have to transcend this physical realm and establish the deeper relationship. But if you *think* about these relationships or unities with the Absolute you will see that it is not the body that unites—the mind also remains outside, and everything is left behind except the Self. The union takes place only of the Self with the Param Atman—everything else is left behind.

All one can do is to prepare oneself and do one's duty as best one can. If one has learned to do one's best every day one should not think about the final journey because whatever one has been able to do is enough—nothing more could have been done, and the rest will be added by the Absolute. The Absolute will look after it when nothing more could have been done in these circumstances. Even then, if there was something more yet to be done the Absolute will create the favorable situation for the next life where one would be able to work better for the complete union. We here, in this room, can do whatever we think right—more than that we don't have to do—we cannot claim, we need not be afraid. The dispensation is in the hands of the Absolute and we should trust that He will do good for everyone who has tried to establish the relationship with Him.

* * *

Q. When I start with the idea that I am going to my dearest it is just an idea, I don't feel this great welling-up of love, but maybe this is because I am looking for the end at the beginning?

H.H. The question of starting at the end is very interesting because in Consciousness there is no disunity at all, no separation—there is no beginning and there is no end. The concept of it was given to us as a sort of incentive, such as is given to children to embark on some activity. It is helpful, as far as it can go, because it does lead people to go in a better way. They disconnect themselves from many other things.

When they are going to meet some elderly beloved relative, they pay more attention to this than to other things. But since in Consciousness everything is united, you will see that no one is going to meet anybody anywhere! And yet one has to go through the meditation only to undo the hindrances, undo the layers of ignorance, etc. The concept that it is the same thing means that Consciousness is only one thing outside or inside. The Absolute has manifested himself in the office, in the family, in the close quiet of the bedroom, and even in deep sleep when not even the senses interfere with the individual.

Now, somehow we have forgotten that the Absolute is immanent everywhere and is ready to meet us with its full force—not only that one meets the Absolute in samadhi with full force, but this Absolute is ready to meet you as a table, as a chair, as food and everything. It is the ignorance which has covered our vision, and we have to come out of this ignorance—we cannot do it unless we go into meditation. When we have learned to come very close to this undifferentiated unity of the Self, then we will see that the Absolute, which appears to be outside and seemingly separated, becomes united with yourself and there may be a time when there is no beginning, there is no end, there is no inner, and there is no outer; it is the same Absolute available everywhere, and there is never any separation.

Whenever any unity is experienced it immediately brings bliss into actions, and this can only happen when there is Consciousness active. All unity takes place in consciousness and in every conscious act there is this bliss supporting itself. So, when one takes food, picks up a piece of fruit, which is juicy and one tastes and experiences the freshness of the juice, a little bliss bursts out in the enjoyment of eating and the sweetness of the taste. The Vedas declare the Absolute an "Rasa Vai Sah," "He is the juice or Essence." Now this bursting out of the enjoyment, even if in eating an ordinary thing like fruit, is in essence an experience of the consciousness of the Absolute himself, because the Absolute has manifested himself as the juice, and the fruit and the eater.

Everything is always united but because of ignorance this process has been forgotten and it has to be brought into action once again. In the Vedic text the same thing has been explained by stating that there are two ways of approaching unity - one is the *anvaya* and the other is *vyatireka*. Anvaya is the way of unity by addition; vyatireka is the way by separation or subtraction, in the sense of discrimination. So, by *discarding* things one after the other one reaches the Self because that is at the end of everything. By *addition* one comes to the idea of Samashti where the Param Atman prevails, so whichever way you choose to go, ultimately you will come to the Absolute either as Param Atman or as Atman. Whatever seems useful to one at a particular time one should respond to by either of the two ways, for one can see that if the discrimination, True Knowledge, the viveka, prevails, then there is no separation of any sort. It is the same Absolute available within during the meditation, and also available everywhere in every type of relationship which we find in this external and manifest world. There is none else to meet but the Self.

* * *

Q. Is it helpful to bear the guru in mind as a preparation for meditation, and is it not also helpful to bear the guru in mind when one is faced with decisions in ordinary life?

H.H. The Atman, the Param Atman and the guru are the trinity of the same unity. In fact there is no difference between the Atman in the individual, the Param Atman and the guru. Because of the situation in the universe, because of these three aspects of mala [thick dirt], vikshepa [dispersion] and kashaya [attachment] all due to avarana [ignorance], this unity is not fully materialized. But it can certainly be evoked and brought into action by remembering, as you asked. The moment one remembers the guru or the Param Atman or the Atman, then this unity comes into action, and because of this remembering a force is made available to the individual. The grace becomes immanent, so H.H. certainly agrees that before meditation, or before one takes any decision in daily activities, business or life, it is good that one should remember any of the three, so that the energy is made available. When the action is complete, then also one should remember in a sort of thanksgiving way.

* * *

H.H. In the natural setup of this creation there is this unity, which is logical, which is natural, which is causal. In fact nothing is separated or divided in the causal realm. We can take it on trust that on the causal level there will always be unity. But apart from the causal level, unity can be achieved on the subtle level. Whenever you have a thought it will reflect all the light; and words which you have heard here, will present itself in some form, and the guru will be there. So whatever light, whatever knowledge, whatever promptings come to your heart, even when the guru is not present in physical form, then you should see that the union is taking place in the subtle level. It is the union of the guru or the Param Atman through the knowledge in the individual, which is also immanent and present.

As far as the physical realm is concerned it is also the creation of the Absolute, and the unity is there though it may be difficult to see, and difficult to comprehend, but nevertheless be assured that the unity is always there. Whenever you remember, it becomes immanent. Even if you do not remember, it is still there but not consciously known.

* * *

416   *Teachings of H.H. Shantanand Saraswati*

H.H. There is a Sanskrit poem, which is the uttering of a man who seems to have offered everything to the Absolute. He says:

Oh my Lord my whole being is Yourself,
and Buddhi which has been given to me is Your consort.
The five pranas, which You have offered me are your attendants.
My body is the temple in which I worship You.
Whatever I eat, or wear, or do is part of the worship which
I keep on performing at the temple.
Even when this body goes to sleep I feel I am in Samadhi
    with You.
Whenever I walk, or anything, I feel I am going on pilgrimage
    to You.
Whatever I speak is all in praise of You.
So whatever I do in this world in any way is all aimed at You.
In fact, there is no division in this life of unity with Yourself.

This is the sort of situation, which one has to find in oneself, and this situation is charged with sattva. Unity is not something, which one is aiming at, but unity is something, which one has to experience every moment in every action, so that whatever one does is in praise or worship of the Absolute. When that situation exists in one's mind, in one's being, then one is in constant union with the Absolute.

* * *

Q. H.H. said "unity is not something one is *aiming* at, but to be experienced in each moment, in every action." This and what he said yesterday about the pronoun "this" *makes* me think I have had a dualistic approach to *"unity in action"*—that I will "know" this state. It is like union in deep meditation where there is no experience, no knowledge of it—just the unity in action in the present moment. Is this correct as it may remove misunderstandings and make the possibility seem much nearer and more practical. When a person truly serves others, he does not think at that moment "I am of great service to others"—he just serves.

Unity

H.H. One aspect of the Self, or unity, was described yesterday—whatever cannot be indicated by the pronoun "this." There is another aspect of the Self, which needs to be understood and experienced in action—that whatever we indicate by the pronoun "this" is only a manifestation of the same Self within, which cannot be indicated. So whenever one enters into any action, or any relationship with this world, which is indicated by all sorts of pronouns one should also keep in mind that the same Self has manifested in different physical and non-physical forms. Anyone who wants to serve others is in fact serving the Self, which has manifested.

Q. Was it really that one shouldn't look for experience of unity, but be the unity?

H.H. In our discipline two processes are adopted, as previously described: One is vyatireka and the other is anvaya. Anvaya follows vyatireka, so any person who is being disciplined and put on the Way is first given vyatireka. By this discipline one simply segregates everything, which is non-Self, and this is done only to establish the authority and existence of the Self.

Having established the authority and existence of the Self, which is not seen by any sensory medium, then it is also necessary for this system to go through the anvaya process to establish the unity of the whole creation. Otherwise, having separated the Self from the non-Self it leaves some scope for duality to dwell, and this duality must be annihilated; and this is done through anvaya, which means that everything one comes across in this creation is a manifestation of the same Self whose authority has been established. Neither in knowledge, nor in action, nor in experience should duality come.

Many different objects are made from iron and steel—such as tools, scooters, fans etc. Although the *name* of the metal is one, the manifestations, which come out of it are many. On the metaphysical realm it is very necessary to understand the unity of the metal so that everything about the different objects manufactured are known from the unity of the metal, which means the properties and constituents are the same whatever the objects may be.

In the same way we have to understand that the whole world

of "this" and the Self is nothing but the same thing: Essentially it is the Self manifested in different ways which have to be known, experienced and put into practical action with the same idea of the unity.

* * *

Q. Mr. Ouspensky has written, "Fusion, inner unity, is obtained by means of friction, by the struggle between 'yes' and 'no' in a man." The need for such friction played a definite part in his teaching on self-development, and speaking from experience, I have found great benefit in my life from facing up to difficulties and by trying to find the right way in which to deal with them. Can this be seen as the act of discrimination between conflicting desires, or does such a conflict rob one of the energy to experience Consciousness?

H.H. The conflict can be tackled in two ways. When the application of consciousness is for the resolution of the conflict, then certainly there is discrimination. But conflict multiplies conflict and leads to destruction. Then certainly it is not discrimination; it is something not advisable. There is a Sanskrit saying, "By discussion, the understanding of the wisdom rises." This conflict is very similar to discussion within oneself. If it leads to unity, certainly it is discrimination but if it does not lead to unity, then it is not advisable. It is a waste of energy and consciousness.

* * *

H.H. The final stage of knowledge is where there are no images. It is yourself and the mango—the thing which you want to know—who are you? There is no difference between you and that, therefore there are no two persons, no two identities, only one identity, so that there are no "in between" steps. When you have become the same thing then you do not exist at all. There is only one thing in existence—there can't be any steps in between.

According to our philosophy, this body is made of five ingredients; similarly the cosmos is also built of five elements. Now our original Sankara said that the cosmos and I actually is one, but is one in existence, that is we see from the point of view of existence, the substance is the same but actually the two things are different. So what Lord Shankaracharya said was that this is the same as that in substance only; so as long as you keep I and you different this difference between you and I, the objective of dhyana is not achieved. When knowledge is achieved then this difference between I and you disappears. There is no you there is no I, there are no two things, both are the same. So when you put the question that I have perceived that, then you are keeping your identity separate from that. So that would not arise when you had achieved that knowledge. There is no action; it is purely knowledge.

Glossary

Advaita: Non-dual; without a second. School of Vedantic thought associated with the name of Shankara, based on the truth that there is nothing separate from or other than the divine. The Absolute is One: no particle or aspect of anything (concerning body or mind) can have a separate existence by itself.

Aham and Ahamkar(a) (or Ahankar[a]): *Aham* refers to universal I or ego which is unconditional. *Ahamkar* refers to ego as experienced by an individual—*kar* meaning vehicle—in which the pure Self (Atman) is reflected. Described as "pure" or "impure." "Pure" when unconditional or unattached to anything, at one with universal; "impure" when it becomes the "I-maker" attaching itself to possessions of all kind—me and mine, egoism. One of the four components of soul (Antahkaran).

Ananda: The principle of pure Love, happiness or Bliss. One of the three attributes of the Absolute. (See also: Sat and Chit.)

Antahkaran(a): All that relates to our psyche or mind, as distinct from our physical body. Sometimes called soul or "inner instrument," as distinct from the "outer instrument" of the physical body. All that makes our inner world of experience possible. Has four parts: the thinking mind (Manas), the evaluating mind (Buddhi), the ego-maker (Ahamkar), and the memory store of all previous experience (Chitta).

Atman and Param Atman: *Atman* is usually translated as Self, the embodiment of universal Self or Being which is called *Param Atman*, the Absolute or Supreme Self: Brahman. It shares the same characteristics of full Consciousness, all Knowledge and innate joy, Love or Bliss. The ever-present basis of the consciousness of "I": unmoving, unchanging and eternal, with no gender and favoring everyone impartially. The word "God" is the nearest equivalent for us.

Glossary

Buddhi: That aspect of our minds which appreciates qualities and makes decisions/choices. It evaluates and discriminates.

Chit: Universal Consciousness, True Knowledge or Intelligence that exists whether or not we experience it. One of the three attributes of the Absolute (the other two being Sat and Ananda).

Chitta: All that we hold in memory and which can be recalled. Acts like a filing system. (That which can reflect Universal Consciousness, or Chit.)

Dharma: Natural Law. Recognition that the natural world of physical phenomena, human action and thought are governed by universal law. All things and events are part of an indivisible whole. *Sanatan Dharma* (eternal religion) is behavior that is in harmony with this unity.

Gunas: The three fundamental qualities inherent in everything and every situation. There is no equivalent translation in the English language. *Sattva* is the quality of harmony, balance, goodness, truth, love, happiness; *rajas* is the quality of movement and activity of any kind; and *tamas* is the quality of inertia, sleepiness, depression, ignorance. All are present everywhere in varying amounts.

Manas: Is concerned with gathering all information and presenting it, like files, to memory (Chitta). For much of the time it is preoccupied with circling thoughts and images.

Samskar (or Sanskar): Tendencies, traits or habits, some of which we are born with and some we acquire in this life. They give rise to our mental and moral character. They can vary in quality and be modified.

Sat: Existence, reality, that which is always there, Truth, Knowledge. One of the three characteristics of the Absolute (the others being Chit and Ananda).

Certain English words are also given distinctive meanings.

True Knowledge and knowledge: True Knowledge refers to knowledge of the unseen or inner world which relates to our experience. It is unrelated to time or space and so is true for all time and in all places. All other knowledge relates to the seen or outer physical world, which is relative to time and space, and so impermanent (changeable). At times referred to as the "Real" and "unreal" world.

Consciousness: When used with a capital "C" it refers to universal Consciousness or Chit. Otherwise it refers to the fluctuating individual consciousness of which we are all aware. Much was said in earlier years about "levels of consciousness," but toward the end of his life Dr. Roles strongly affirmed that "There is only one consciousness. All 'levels' are levels of impediment."

Self: A clear distinction between "self" and "Self." With a small "s" it refers to an individual's consciousness of his own personal identity with its bodily make-up and personal characteristics: assumed to be "separate" and distinct from all others. When spelled as "Self" it refers to our true being as one with Universal Being, with all its attributes. Synonymous with Atman—"of one being with the Father." "Self-remembering" means what it says—the practice of mindfulness.